Life On The Back Side Of The Sport Of Kings

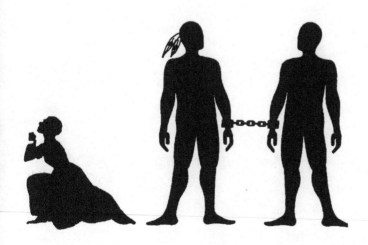

Life On The Back Side Of The Sport Of Kings

AMERICAN APARTHEID, A NEVER ENDING STORY

James S. Wright

ISBN: 1496148746
ISBN 13: 9781496148742

ABOUT THE AUTHOR

In 2014, I was a 66-years old African American male. I was born in Dorsey, Maryland, a small rural community in Anne Arundel County, about 10 miles South of Baltimore City. My grandparents, Wilbur and Louanna Wright, both deceased, instilled in me a strong moral background, the foundation of which was religion and the church; they raised me from the time I was two-years old. My father is the Rev. James S. Wright Sr., who now lives in Alabama, separated from my mother, Estelle Hebron Thomas, now deceased, when I was 10 years old. I have three brother and three sisters. I talk more about my mother and some of my other relatives throughout my book.

I was educated in the local public schools and I attended Maryland State College (University of Maryland Eastern Shore), but I did not graduate. However, in 1975, I did receive an Associate of Arts Degree from the Anne Arundel Community College. I am married to the former Jacqueline Brogdon. I have three daughters; Shawn, Lorraine (Kevin) and MeChelle; a son, Alan; and seven grandchildren; Kiana, Jamar, Marquis, Ramir, Jamira, and Kobe, and two great grandsons, Anthony and Carlos, and one great granddaughter Skyler. My god-daughter, Tiffany Mims, and her daughter Regan Carter, are also part of my family. I mention the names of my wife, children and grandchildren, because they are the most important people in my life. I live with my wife Jackie and my son Alan in Woodlawn, Maryland, a suburb of Baltimore City. In addition, I am an ex-marine and an ex-police officer, who has worked as a public servant for the State of Maryland for over

38 years. I believe in God. I love my Family. I believe the United States of America is by far the best Country in the world.

At different stages in my life, I was told that I have a talent for writing and I was encouraged to pursue a career that would further develop that talent. The recognition of my talent as a writer started with my High School teachers, continued with my college professors and followed me to my professional career as the secretaries, who typed my reports for work, would comment on how much they enjoyed reading, what would normally be boring information on a routine event. I started my professional writing career in 1991 and published my first book, *"American Apartheid"* in 1997. My second book, *"No Land No Mule No Freedom"* was published in 2002, and my third book, *"The Back Side of the Sport of Kings"* was published in 2014.

The first question you might ask as you select one of my three books is how and why did I come up the titles; *"American Apartheid"*, *"No Land No Mule No Freedom, American Apartheid, The Saga continues"*, and *"The Backside Of the Sport of Kings, American Apartheid, A Never ending Saga"?* The truth is that we judge people by our first impressions and books by their covers. A perfect example is the fact that you are about to read my latest book. The explanations for the titles of my books will be made clear as you continue to read them. The next question you might ask is "Why did I write these books?" When asked why the man climbed the mountain, his response was because it was there. My response to why I wrote my books; they needed to be written. I joined the Marine Corps because I thought I could make a difference for my Country. I became a police officer because I thought I could make a difference in my community. I wrote these books because I think they will make a difference in how Americans look at the topic of racism.

I am an avid researcher of both African American and United States history. Yes, these books are about racism in America. I am quite sure you already figured that out when you read the titles. The red, white and black colors on the book covers represent the three races of people that make up the history of this Country. These books do not contain any unknown facts or discoveries about the history of this

Country. Most of the historical references in these books are common knowledge. What make my books unique is they contain are very fresh and very opinionated perspectives on the subject of African American History and the subject of racism and racial equality in the United States.

My purpose in writing these books is to jump-start the stalled vehicles that drove Americans to the battleground where the war for racial equality was fought in this Country. For the past 25 years or so, the Civil Rights Movement, which was very aggressive in the 1960s and 1970s, has slowed to a crawl. The fight for racial equality is far from over. I hope that my writings will inspire a rebirth of the Civil Rights Movement. My Constitutional rights under the First Amendment, which guarantees freedom of speech and freedom of press, support the opinions in these books. What makes them unique is that my opinions are very close to, and may even be, the facts. They also present a different account of American history. My opinions of U.S. history may not be the same as the lessons you learned in grade school, but they will be just as interesting.

Three of the most important points that I want my readers to get are that, (1) knowledge is power and (2) education is the key to knowledge, and (3) history needs to be taught in more than one color and from more than one perspective. Unlike your typical textbooks, my account of what may or may not have happened before and after the recorded events in history is my opinion. If you are looking for the accurate dates and times when these historical events actually occurred, I suggest you check some reference books in your local library. There are no "footnotes" in my books. This is not a term paper or a thesis. These books are a wakeup call for those of us who have gone to sleep on the problem of racism in America. I hope you will enjoy reading my works as much as I have enjoyed writing them.

DEDICATION

I like to think that I have a God given talent for writing, and I hope that I have used this talent to bring attention to certain aspects of black American history that have not been addressed from the perspective of an African American. Unfortunately, no matter how much I write, I cannot capture the entirety of any aspect of black American history in my books. What I have done is just merely scratch the surface and provide a snap shot of what is an enormous amount of information about my ancestors. I strongly hope that the information I have provided will whet your appetite for more information about African Americans. In order to provide an in-depth documented study on African American history, it will require teams consisting of hundreds of black anthropologists to conduct the detailed research needed to accurately recreate the events that comprise our past. I am encouraged by the fact that many colleges and universities are offering courses in African American History. Although most of the information provided in the courses is the result of research conducted by white historians, the fact that the courses are provided increases the interest in the subject matter. One of my many goals in writing black history is to inspire others to continue the research and dig even deeper to uncover facts and information about the history of African American.

Let me make it perfectly clear; I admire the men that work on the "Back Side" of thoroughbred horseracing. I grew up in a working class family; my grandparents raised me, and their own three children on a combined income of less than $20,000. My grandmother was a manual laborer in the quartermaster laundry at Ft. Meade Army Base for 33 years before she retired. My grandfather was a manual laborer for the B&O Railroad for 30 year before he became a crane operator, a job he held for another 17 years before retiring with 47 years of service. My grandparents made sure that I had ever opportunity to get a better education than they did. Their goal for me was to find a career where I could earn a living using my brain rather than my braking my back. My grandparents were my role models. I was proud of them and I never felt any shame that they did not graduate from elementary school or that they were manual laborers. They provided food for me to eat, put clothes on my back and supported me in achieving any goals I set out to accomplish in life. There is no shame in digging ditches, picking cotton, working on the "Back Side" or any other form of manual labor that puts food on the table and supports you and your family. I admire any man that will do an honest day's work to support his family.

When I was growing up every male member of my immediate family, which included my grandfather on my mother and father's side, worked on the Railroad. Naturally, I thought that when I was old enough I would follow in the footsteps of the other males in my family and work on the Railroad. In addition, until I was about ten years old, I enjoyed the luxury and thrill of riding the train with my grandparents for free from Baltimore City to Pittsburgh, to New Jersey, to New York and to Cleveland. I used to dream about being the Engineer on a train. Although the majority of the manual laborers during my grandfather's days on the railroad were black, the more skilled and higher paying jobs like being an engineer or conductor on a train were limited to white men only. Like other manual labor unions, in the early 1960s, the African American members of Brotherhood of Railroad Workers and Pullman Porters became a force to be reckoned with in America. Black men were now performing jobs like engineers and conductors. However, shortly after the black members of the union gained power and respect, the pay increased and with an increase in pay, the complexion of the manual laborers on the railroad in America changed from predominantly black men to mostly white men.

The Men and Women of the Back Side

In order for you to understand the importance of the men and women that work on the "Back Side" of the sport of thoroughbred horseracing, compare it to the sport of auto racing. Whenever I watch National Association for Stock Car Auto Racing (NASCAR), I see a fine tuned automobile. In horseracing, you see a well-conditioned equine athlete. When you watch an auto race on TV, you always see the pit crew at work. You will see the driver of the car pull into the pit, which is located in the middle of the track's oval, to have their car serviced. We watch as the pit crew change tires, fills the tank with fuel, make minor repairs to the body of the car and then send the driver back onto the racetrack. In auto racing, we pay a great deal of attention to the systematic and efficient function of the pit crew. In fact, many a racecar driver has credited the speed and efficiency in which the pit crew serviced the vehicle during a race as the difference in winning or losing. Before and after an auto race, you get too listen to comments from the driver of the car and the mechanics, the pit crew chief and engineers that took part in creating and maintaining this fine-tuned racing machine. Before and after a thoroughbred horse race, you get to know the trainer who conditioned the horse, the owner of the horse and the jockey assigned to ride the horse during the race.

However, when you watch a thoroughbred horse race on TV, you never see the pit crew or team responsible for this well-conditioned equestrian athlete. *"Life on the Back Side of the Sport of Kings"* gives you a look at the team that prepares a thoroughbred horse for a race. I will give you a chance to learn some little known facts about the "pit crew" for thoroughbred horses. This book looks at the history of the black men and women that have earned their living taking care of thorough-bred horses. As with my other books, I have conducted a great deal of research, and just as I have done with my other books, I have also used historical data passed along to me by the people who actually lived through it. One of many men that have provided me with information about the history of the "Back Side" is Howard "Gelo" Hall, retired patrol judge for live races held at Pimilco and Laurel Racetracks in

Maryland. It is nothing short of a miracle that anyone could work in the same profession for over 66 years. Yet, Mr. Hall has stood the test of time and is still making a major contributing to the sport of thoroughbred horseracing in his home State. Howard "Gelo" Hall has dedicated his life to the sport of thoroughbred horseracing. Therefore, I find it only fitting that I dedicate this book about the "Sport of Kings" to a "Crowned Prince" of the "Sport of Kings" and a wonderful human being, Howard "Gelo" Hall.

Howard "Gelo" Hall

There was an old cowboy song that I listened to and often sang as young child called *"Home On The Range"*. The words are; *"Home, home on the range, where the deer and the antelope play. Where seldom is heard a discouraging word, and the skies are not cloudy all day."* The man who wrote the words to this song must have known Howard "Gelo" Hall. I have known "Gelo' for over 35 years. In the time that I have had the privilege of knowing this unique man, I have never heard him say a discouraging word and I have never heard anyone say a discouraging about him. Now, when the moral fiber that once held this Country together is rapidly decaying, it is hard to find a man with the strong moral fiber like that of Howard "Gelo" Hall. If you know him, you will agree that no matter what the weather or the season, "Gelo" carries the sunshine with him. He has a smile on his face and a kind word on his lips no matter what he is doing or no matter where he is going. Howard "Gelo" is a walking encyclopedia of the history of the sport of thoroughbred horsing in Maryland, Delaware, Florida, New York, New Jersey and West Virginia. Mr. Hall is over 85-years old and his mind is as sharp as a tack. I have dedicated this book to Howard "Gelo" Hall, who, I have justifiably proclaimed to be a legend in the sport of thoroughbred horseracing in the State of Maryland. Howard "Gelo" Hall is a living example of why we need to preserve our history in books for future generations.

According to Howard Jr. aka "Gelo", he made his first visit to the racetrack in 1935. Like most six-year-old boys, he thought it was something very special to be able to go to work with his father, Howard Sr., and fell in love with the sport of horseracing. When asked what kind of job his father had, "Gelo" proudly replied that his father was a "Factotum"; and he defined it as being a "trusted individual" in the racing office. Ok, I will be the first to admit that I had never heard the word used before. However, after listening to "Gelo" describe some of the duties and responsibilities assigned to his father, and comparing it to *Webster's Dictionary* definition of factotum; which is an old word meaning a general servant or a person having many diverse activities or responsibilities, I realized that "Gelo's" description of his father position in the racing office was complete and accurate. Although "Gelo" is 85, when he talks about his father, I could clearly hear a loving son, talking about a man, whom he was very proud of and whom he respected. It was so very refreshing to listen to "Gelo" talk about Howard Sr. He was an African American born in the early 1930s, whose role model was his father. It made me feel even better talking to "Gelo", because my role model was my grandfather.

The Goldfield Hotel & Boxing Champion Joe Gans

Prior to becoming a fixture in the Maryland Racing Office, Howard Sr. worked at a hotel owned by Baltimore Legend, Joe Gans, who from 1902-1908 was the World's Lightweight Boxing Champion. In 1906, Joe Gans fought a contender named Oscar Nelson in Goldfield, Nevada. The fight lasted 42 rounds and Mr. Gans was the victor. After that fight, he returned to Baltimore and opened a hotel on East Lexington and Colvin Streets. In honor of his most recent victory in the ring, he named the facility the Goldfield Hotel. In Baltimore, Joe Gans's Goldfield Hotel, known as a "black and tan" club because whites went there to hear another Baltimore Legend, a young black piano player named Eubie Blake. Mr. Blake performed at the hotel from 1907 until 1911 when Joe Gans died. James Hubert "Eubie" Blake, born on February 7, 1887, to former slaves Emma and John Blake at 319 Forrest Street in Baltimore, Maryland. Mr. Blake rose from a Baltimore hotel bar piano player to a National and International star entertainer.

Eubie Blake was a composer, lyricist, and pianist of ragtime, jazz and popular music. With longtime collaborator Noble Sissle, Mr. Blake wrote the Broadway musical "Shuffle Along" in 1921. This was one of the first Broadway musicals written and directed by African Americans. As I listened to "Gelo" telling me about the Goldfield Hotel, which is no longer open. I thought to myself, if I were to ride pass the main branch of the U.S. Post Office in Baltimore City, would I hear the mellow sounds of Eubie Blake echo around the "Baltimore Shot Tower", now an iconic tower located near the main post office. In the 1960s, the Goldfield Hotel was torn down and the main post office built on that site.

If you have not figured this out by reading my other books, I need to explain that from time to time I like to adds historical references that have no connection to the subject matter. I may repeat this message from time to time throughout this book.

"Gelo" made it quite clear that his father was not just a servant. According to "Gelo", his father's duties included handling confidential information that was limited to persons assigned to the racing office. Just as his son is well respected by his peers today, Howard Sr. was also well respected by the white professionals that worked in the racing office during the "JIM CROW ERA". The fact the Howard Sr. was a "Factotum" opened doors on the "Grandstand" side of the sport of thoroughbred horseracing to his son that were normal reserved for "whites only". "Gelo" could not remember exactly how long his father worked in the racing office. However, he did recall that his father was working there at least five years before the big match race in 1938 between *Seabiscuit* and *War Admiral*. "Gelo" was a witness to the famous Seabiscuit verses *War Admiral* "Match Race" in 1938. A "Match Race" is a race between two horses. A 10-year-old standing on his tiptoes in the grandstands with his father, witnessing one of the most historic horse races of all time. "I did not know it would be catapulted into such a historic event," "Gelo" says of the experience. "I knew it was an important race but just how important, being a 10-year-boy at the time, all I could think of was how excited everyone was to be there".

Big Gelo and Little Gelo

Before we go too far, I need to explain to you how Howard Hall, came to be called "Gelo". When I first heard the name, like most of the people that have not known Howard Hall Jr. very long, I associated the name "Gelo", with the popular dessert, J-E-L-L-O. In my years on the racetrack, it is a common practice or a rite of passage, for everyone on the "Back Side" to have a nickname. For most of us, a nickname had something to do with the person's character, habits or physical makeup. "Short Man" was short, "Long John" was tall and "Fat Mike" was fat. It would have been a reasonable assumption that "Gelo" likes to eat JELLO, but that is not how Howard Hall got his nickname. In this case the nickname was passed along from his brother Angelo, who when the two brother were growing up in Baltimore City was "Big Gelo", which in turn made Howard Hall Jr. "Little Gelo". Angelo "Big Gelo" Hall was an accomplished musician, who studied the piano at an early age.

Howard Jr. recalled that his brother could read music, and he could also play by ear; meaning that if he heard a song, he could play that song without needing the sheet music. In the days before television, most black families owned a piano and Angelo displayed his talent as a musician by playing the piano in homes throughout the neighborhood. In addition, "Big Gelo" loved to play basketball in the backyard with the people from the neighborhood. During 1930s, it was commonplace in the black neighbors throughout the city to have a handmade basketball goal in the backyard or alley. "Gelo" recalls that one of the "guys"; his brother's close friend, Robert Watts, played on the neighborhood basketball team. Robert Bernard Watts, in 1960 was the first African American judge appointed to the Municipal Court of Baltimore City by Governor J. Millard Tawes. Another member of the neighborhood basketball team was Walter W. "Yul" Carr, who along with Josiah Diggs, and Dr. James Hilburn, in 1917 opened the Dunbar Theatre, the first theatre for African Americans in Baltimore Maryland. The more I talked with "Gelo" the more I am captivated by his recollection of not only thoroughbred horseracing history, but also the history of Baltimore City. I have lived in and around Baltimore my entire life, yet, I had never heard of Joe Gans, the Goldfield Hotel, the Dunbar Theatre or that Judge Robert Watts was the first African American judge appointed to the Municipal Court of Baltimore City. Again, this supports the fact that we need to teach history in more than one color and from more than one perspective.

Gelo Loves Horses

You would think that "Gelo" developed his love of horses at an early age from accompanying his father to Pimlico. In fact, "Gelo" fell in love with horses long before he made his first trip to the racetrack. Like most young boys, "Gelo's" attraction to horses started by hanging out at the neighborhood stables. You need to understand that in the late 1920s and 30s; horses were still a major part of street traffic in Baltimore City. Most of the neighborhoods in Baltimore City had a stable. "Gelo" recalls that two of the most popular stables in his neighbor were Al White's Riding Academy on Retreat Street and the stable managed by Jimmy Hector on McCullough Street and Cloverdale Road. "Gelo" remembers how some of the most prominent families in Baltimore would come to these two very popular stables to rent horses to ride. Another one of the many fond memories that "Gelo" has of his father and the racetrack was in 1942, Howard Sr. witnessed his 14-year-old son, Howard Jr., gallop a horse at Pimlico for the first time. In chapter two, America First Superstar Athletes, I talk about Jimmy Winkfield, the great African American jockey. After his riding career was over Jimmy Winkfield became a trainer. "Gelo" recalled that on the morning before the race, he "blew out", a term used for a short workout, the last horse Jimmy Winkfield saddled as a trainer in Maryland. As a point of reference, compare "Gelo's" contact with Jimmy Winkfield to being a caddy for Tiger Woods at the Masters.

As you continue to read this book, you will get a better understanding of the athleticism required to be an exercise rider. The mere fact that Gelo was able to earn a living as an exercise "boy" at age 14 speaks volumes as to his athletic ability. Yet, "Gelo' wanted to make it perfectly clear that he learned how to gallop horses from Mose Taylor, the head exercise rider at Foxcatcher Farm for trainer Frank Bonsal Sr. "Gelo" not only galloped horses that were in training for races, he broke yearling or "babies" on the Foxcatcher Farm.

The Foxcatcher Farm was one of the legendary thoroughbred racing operations in the State of Maryland. A list of owners that stabled their horses at Foxcatcher Farms with trainer Frank Bonsal Sr. included Harry L. Straus, who in 1933 invented the first electromechanical totalisator system in the United States. The electronic totalisator, aka "Tote Board", keeps a running account of all the money bet on each horse for a race and automatically calculates the current odds for each horse in that race. Mr. Straus founded the American Totalisator Company, better known as Am Tote. The first Am Tote system, used at Arlington Park in Illinois, began the era of honest, reliable wagering and payoffs for the sports of thoroughbred horseracing. Some of the more notable horses owned by the Foxcatcher Farms were *Pilaster*, a steeplechase champion, *Nahodah* and *Quarter Moon*, champion sprinters and *New Moon*, who ran against *Count Fleet* the 1943 Triple Crown Winner.

Another famous owner at Foxcatcher Farms was Marion DuPont Scott, a member of the family that founded the DuPont Company in Delaware. Not only was Ms. DuPont was famous for the horses she owned, she received National attention for her contributions to equine medical research. She reportedly donated over 4 million dollars to this noble cause. Although most of the owners and trainers that "Gelo" worked for at Foxcatcher Farms are dead, he is still very careful to say Mr. or Mrs. when talking about these rich and powerful white people. At 85 plus, it amazes me that "Gelo" still uses the term Mr. and Mrs. out of respect and out of habit. While working at Foxcatcher, "Gelo" met and became lifelong friends with a young white boy, Rodger Gill, who became a very successful horseman on the Maryland Racing Circuit. "Gelo" made a point of telling me that Rodger treated him like his equal and you could sense by the way that "Gelo" talked about Rodger and the fact that he made reference to him by his first name, that the two men had formed a bond that continued until Rodger Gill died. "Gelo" also made it point to tell me that he attended Rodger's funeral.

Read all about him

In a story that appeared in the Baltimore Sun newspaper on May 18, 2007, the day before the 132nd running of the Preakness, the second jewel of the Triple Crown, Sumathi Reddi wrote, "They just don't make 'em like Gelo anymore." Quotes from that same story are as follows, "Gelo's been here forever," says Lucy Kessler, a horse owner from Mount Airy. "This place [Pimlico] would not be what it is without Gelo." John Burke III, a steward for the Maryland Jockey Club, remembers Hall from his days as a horse trainer a jockey's agent. Mr. Hall represented the top jockeys of his day, such as Mickey Solomone. Mr. Burke recalls going to Florida to race horses in the winter. As soon as Mr. Burke installed his phone at his winter home in Florida, it started to ring. "I didn't even know my own phone number, and here's Gelo calling," says Mr. Burke, age 71, now living in Ellicott City. Gelo said, "Listen, you got those two horses at Calder Race Track. You need a jockey." Burke picked his jockey and they won both races. Mr. Hall shakes his head, laughing at the memory. "Gelo Hall is one of the great people of racing," says Mr. Burke. "If you've been in racing on the East Coast, you know Gelo Hall."

The Sun newspaper article concludes with the fact that "Gelo" would be on duty on Saturday, May 19, 2007 for the Preakness. I was very pleased that this young white reporter chose Howard "Gelo" Hall as the feature for an article. This article would be read by thousands of racing fan around the world, who were hungry for anything written about the upcoming 2nd Jewel of the Triple Crown because "Gelo" is one of the most distinguished African Americans in the history of thoroughbred horseracing in the State of Maryland.

"Gelo" does not think of his personal accomplishments as being those of an African American, he would rather have his achievements in the sport of horseracing recognized as being those of a GOD fearing, all American, from the City of Baltimore, Maryland. However, as a writer of African American history, I would be remiss if I did not point out my disappointment with the lack of local and National media attention to this following fact. For just the second time in the in 116 years of the Triple Crown Racing Series, Shirley Cunningham Jr., an African American Attorney from Kentucky, is part owner of *Curlin*, the horse that finished third in the Kentucky Derby, won the 2007 Preakness and finish 2nd in the Belmont Stakes. Not since 1891, when another African American, also from Kentucky, Dudley Allen of Lexington, co-owned and trained the 1891 Derby winner *Kingman*, who was ridden by the great black jockey Isaac Murphy.

I know what you are thinking. Why should it matter that a black man is part owner of the Preakness winner and a horse that finished on the board in all three Triple Crown Races? The reason it matters is because it is such an infrequent occurrence, and it is such a noteworthy accomplishment for an African American in this sport. The personal triumph of Dudley Allen and Shirley Cunningham can be compared to the Venus Williams winning at Wimbledon years after Althea Gibson, a fact that the media gave special attention too. I will have to admit that one of my favorite cable TV channels ESPN, dropped the ball by not doing an in-depth feature on Shirley Cunningham and comparing his success in the sport of thoroughbred horseracing racing, with his fellow Kentuckian, Dudley Allen, who was also the direct descendant

The 2007 Preakness winner *Curlin* is not only named for Charlie Curlin, a legendary African American slave from the State of Kentucky; Shirley Cunningham is his direct descendant. Shirley Cunningham is Charlie Curlin's great grandson. Charlie Curlin of Trigg County, Kentucky was a slave whose name will live forever now that the horse called *Curlin* has won the Preakness. Reportedly, the story behind this intriguing Preakness winner is much larger than one colt's performance in the 2nd jewel of one of America's greatest horse races. The story goes back to the decade before the inaugural 1875 Kentucky Derby; the story takes us down the road Southwest of Louisville to the border of Tennessee and into rural, secessionist Trigg County. Reportedly, a slave named Charlie Curlin, signed on with the Union Army in the United States Colored Troops. Like many soldiers in Kentucky companies of the U.S. Colored Troops, Charlie Curlin found himself assigned to Camp Nelson in Central Kentucky. According to published quotes from Shirley Cunningham, "Charlie Curlin was truly confused about whom he was fighting and that was very clear from stories he told when he got back home. Although Charlie Curlin's confusion over his wartime identity might seem strange to us, it could have been more the norm in the context of his time and place".

"If only we had an explanation from Charlie Curlin himself, we might understand how it was for a veteran of the Federal Army's U.S. Colored Troops who returned home to live in a county that had wanted to secede from the United States. Kentucky's Civil War history is confusing enough when viewed from the whites-only perspective. Imagine how it must have been for African Americans who could not read and probably did not often hear the truth." The story of Charlie Curlin, and the U.S. Colored Troops, is a familiar one. Unfortunately, the familiarity is limited to students of Black History. For a glimpse at what slaves, former slaves and blacks born as free men, endured as members of the first "Colored" Troops in United States, I recommend the 1989 movie "Glory". It is heart-warming stories like the now famous thoroughbred horse *Curlin* being named after a slave that I hope will encourage those who follow the sport of thoroughbred horseracing to read books about African American history. In all this talk about Shirley Cunningham being part owner of *Curlin*, I failed to mention that along with winning a Pulitzer Prize, it has been a long-term goal, hope and/or dream of mine to own a thoroughbred that wins a Triple Crown Race.

After my second interview with Howard "Gelo" Hall, I concluded that there was no way that I could capture the essence of his life's experiences in the sport of thoroughbred horseracing and the history of Baltimore City in a single chapter of this book. Interviewing "Gelo" was like eating Maryland Crabs. The more you eat the more you want. What usually happens when I am eating crabs is that my fingers get tired or cut from all the crab shells, but I never really get enough of that tasty Maryland Crabmeat. The same thing happens when I am talking to "Gelo", my fingers get sore from all the notes I have taken or we run out time, but I never get tired of listening to the pearls of wisdom and the knowledge that comes from the memory of Howard "Gelo" Hall. *"Life on the Back Side of the Sport of Kings, American Apartheid a Never*

Ending Saga" is the last book in the American Apartheid trilogy. It was also to be my last book, as I had planned to retire from my full time job as an Administrator for the State of Maryland, and my part-time job as a writer to pursue other interest. However, I have decided to either write a book on the life and times of "Gelo" or assist Howard Hall Jr. in writing his life's story.

Gelo" has a tremendous amount of respect for the black pioneers of the sport of thoroughbred horseracing. When he talks about the African American men and women who he admired as owners, jockeys, exercise riders and grooms, you can hear the reverent tone in his voice as if he were speaking about biblical characters. So many names, so many memories, so many contributions made by black men and women that whites historians have failed to include when the chronicle the history of thoroughbred racing in the State of Maryland. These African American men include exercise riders named Isadore "Spike" Counts, the Clay brothers, Raymond "Pee Wee" and George. Grooms named Chester Moore, Rodney Noel and "Whiskers", Carroll Griggs, and the Booker brothers, Fred and Raymond. A top riders on the Maryland Racing Circuit, Basil Hall, and owner/breeder, Beulah and Anthony Allen, who were relatives of the late Isaac Murphy, the greatest black jockey of all times. I need to make it clear that "Gelo" never used the term "black" when referring to African Americans, because growing up during the "JIM CROW ERA" in this Country, when he heard a white person call a "colored" person "black" it was usually followed by the "N" word and it was always an insult.

Over the past 45 years, I have spent a considerable amount of time on the "Back Side" of the racetracks in Maryland. I can remember when they held live racing at Bowie Race Track and Marlborough Race Track in Prince George's County. Bowie Race Track is now a training center for thoroughbreds and Marlborough Race Track is now an Equestrian Center used for horse shows and other related events. Marlborough Race Track is still one of my favorites and, according to his diary; President George Washington was one of the first to wager money at the track. *Miss Casey Jane*, the first thoroughbred that I owned, was stabled and trained at Bowie Race Track. The best she finished in a race was third place in a cheap maiden-claiming race at Marlborough Race Track. *Miss Casey Jane* earned $338 for her third place finish and I keep the check stub for Marlborough Race Track as a souvenir. I have listened as some of the "old timers" on the "Back Side" talked about race meets at other small tracks in Maryland, but I never really got any detailed information about these tracks. Now I know if you need detailed information about the history of Maryland Thoroughbred Horse Racing, all you need to do is ask "Gelo". According to "Gelo", along with the current Maryland racing venues of Pimlico, Laurel and Timonium, the "Old" Maryland Racing Circuit use to include live racing at The Cumberland Race Track in Allegany County, and the Havre de Grace Race Track in Hartford County.

The Havre de Grace Race Track, or "The Graw" as it was called opened in 1912 and closed in 1950. Havre de Grace, French for "Harbor of Grace", got its name during the American Revolution, when the Marquis de Lafayette decided that the setting, at the mouth of the Susquehanna, reminded him of France's Le Havre. "The Graw" considered one of the better known and most frequented racetracks in the Country, featured horses like the great *Man o' War* and *Seabiscuit*. Reportedly, it was at Havre de Grace, the late Sam Riddle used to say, that *Man o' War* ran his greatest race. That was in 1920, when *Riddle's Big Red*, carrying the heaviest weight he had ever been made to carry 138 pounds, ran away with the Potomac Handicap in his usual style and set a new track record for the mile-and-a-sixteenth while he was about it. *Man o' War* was in his heyday that year, and so was Havre de Grace. Halfway between Philadelphia and Washington D.C., "The Graw" drew crowds from 100 miles or more away, North & South. The 1948 Triple Crown Winner *Citation* was beaten here in April 1948 by *Saggy*, who would later go on to sire the great champion *Carry Back*. Reportedly, *Citation's* loss was blamed on three things: *Saggy's* love for the mud; the fact that another horse forced *Citation* very wide, and jockey Eddie Arcaro, who was riding the champion for the first time, was instructed not to abuse the champion so close to the Triple Crown. Citation would never lose another race.

Dedication

Daddy and The B&ORR

Today, the old Cumberland Race Track is being used for auto racing. My grandfather worked for the Baltimore & Ohio Rail Road. I
remember him talking about spending several nights in Cumberland
repairing the rails on the train tracks. My grandfather told me there
were very few black families that lived in Cumberland during the 1920s,
30s and 40s. Black railroad workers could not stay in the "white only"
hotels; they had to find rooms with the local black families. Times
have changed in Cumberland; in the 1920s, 30s and 40s black families
moved to Cumberland to work for the B&ORR and in coalmines. In
the 1980s and 90s many more black families moved to Cumberland
to work in the Federal and State Correctional Facilities in Allegany
County. Here I am, many years later, in the late 1990s; thinking about
my grandfather's experience while I stayed at a Holiday Inn located
next to the B&ORR tracks in Cumberland. I was on a business trip
for the State of Maryland, conducting and inspection of the State
Correctional Facilities; as I sat in the restaurant of the Holiday Inn,
having a quite dinning with my co-worker, a white female; I just imagined the hostility this would have caused among the white citizens of
Cumberland during my grandfather's visits. Yet, as I sat with this white
woman, in what is still a predominately-white community, no one paid
any attention to us. Times are changing!

Stories like the one I just shared with you about my grandfather;
never made it to your history books or even to your local newspapers.
However, after talking with "Gelo", I found that the reason I did not
know about some of the black pioneers of Maryland Horse Racing
was that no one has ever taken the time to record their stories. In
the late 1930s, Laurel, Bowie and Pimlico were the major tracks on
the Maryland Racing Circuit, and the circumference or the distance
around the racing ovals at these tracks was at least one mile. The other
lesser racetracks like Timonium and Cumberland were either ½ or five
eighths of a mile, Havre de Grave was ¾ of a mile and Marlborough
Race Track was the smallest at three eights of a mile. The major tracks
are called "Milers" and the smaller tracks are called "Bull Rings". The

so-called "Bull Ring" race meets were always part of the State or Local County Fair. In Maryland, the smaller the Race Track, the smaller the purses, and the lesser the competition for the owners of the smaller racing stables. As a young exercise rider, "Gelo" traveled the Maryland Racing Circuit from track to track. Just like my grandfather's experience, the African Americans that worked on the racetracks had to travel to Havre de Grace and Cumberland. Black horsemen had to stay on the racetrack in the rooms provided over the stables or if they wanted to stay in town, find rooms with local black families in the area.

The Bull Rings

According to "Gelo", it was at the "Bull Rings" were black jockeys, like Carroll Griggs, "Dusty" Johnson, and Louis Scott got an opportunity to showcase their riding talent on horses owned and trained by the lesser known horsemen in Maryland. According to "Gelo", Carroll Griggs was one of the finest riders, black or white, to throw his legs over a horse. Yet, in conducting my research, I was unable to find any documented information about the riding career of Carroll Griggs. Of course, after advising them that I had talked with "Gelo", all the other "Old Timers" that I talked to afterwards had stories about the "Bull Rings" and the black jockeys like Carroll Griggs, Raymond "Skeets" Holland and Louis "Scotty" Scott, who at close to 77 years old is still training horses at Pimilco. In conducting my research, it was easy to find information about the old racetracks in Cumberland and Havre de Grace. The question is why did not the same white historians that so eloquently captured the colorful memories of these old racetracks, chronicle the contributions of the African American who help make these "Bull Rings" so popular?

As an eight-year-old boy, "Gelo" was fascinated with the array of beautiful bright colors worn by jockeys during a race. "Gelo's" desire to be a jockey's agent was sparked by the attraction to the assortment of colors worn by jockeys. If you are not familiar with the sport of thoroughbred horseracing, 90% of the professional jockeys that ride thoroughbreds use a licensed agent to find them a horse with the best chance of winning each race. A winning jockey receives 10% of the purse and the winning jockey's agent receives 10% of what the winning jockey receives. Depending on the size of the purse, the jockeys that finish second and third may receive 5% of the purse and even the jockeys that finish out of the money receive a minimum of $50 for just riding the horse. An average jockey makes about $60,000 a year for just riding in five races a day, five days a week. The purpose of an agent is to find horse that will earn the jockey 10% of large purses. Winning large purses not only makes money for the jockey, it makes money for the jockey's agent. A journeyman jockey can survive on just the average mount fees. However, the only way an agent can survive is to find his/her jockey horses that win races and large purses. The bottom line is that no jockey's agent could survive on 10% of $60,000 a year.

Jock's Agent

To be successful, a jockey's agent has to be a great salesperson that has the ability to accept constant rejection without holding a grudge. They have to convince trainers and owners that their jockey is the only one that gives the trainer/owner's horse the best possible chance of winning a particular race. Unfortunately, 10-15 other agents are trying to convince that same trainer/owner that their jockey can do the same. To complicate matters, the trainers/owners, no matter how good their horse might be, are always after the number one jockey in that tracks jockey colony. Therefore, the best jockeys usually have their pick of the best horses in a race and the other lesser jockey's agents have to fight for the leftovers. Having given you a glimpse into the jockey–agent relationship, we will add another wrinkle into the mix; a young African American jockey's agent named Howard "Gelo" Hall Jr. As you can well imagine, during the "JIM CROW ERA" in America, the overwhelming majority of trainers, owners and jockeys in the sport of thoroughbred horseracing, were white men. In such a competitive occupation, when your employer's very livelihood depends on your ability to sell his talent, why would a jockey hire a black agent?

The answer to the question is simple, any jockey, trainer or owner that has spent time at the racetrack was familiar with the character of Howard "Gelo" Hall. As a young man, I often heard older men and women give young men a compliment for outstanding behavior by calling them a "gentleman and a scholar", which not only spoke to the person being courteous, but being exceptionally honorable as well. "Gelo's" exemplary character makes him a perfect example of a gentleman, and a scholar that any jockey, regardless of the color of their skin, would be proud to employ him as an agent. "Gelo's" demeanor had been honed by many years of observing his father perform his duties as a "Factotum" in the racing office. Along with his knowledge of horses and the sport of horseracing, provide him with the skills necessary to be an excellent jockey's agent. "Gelo" refused to let the color of his skin be a handicap in acquiring the best mounts possible for his employer. "Gelo" was a jockey's agent for 20 years and over the length of his career, he worked for jockeys named Carlos "Speedy" Gonzales, Bobby Fitzgerald, Luigi Gino, Arnold Illiescu, and Mickey Solomone.

In the world of thoroughbred horseracing, most of the professionals associated with the sport have a role model, or someone that they have used as a guide to a successful career. According to "Gelo", the first and only African American jockey's agent on the Maryland Racing Circuit was Morris "Jake" Smith, the former black owner/trainer, whose employer was jockey Mike Sorentino.

"Gelo" had several successful jockeys and with that success, you would think that it would have opened the door for other African Americans to be hired as agents by jockeys. However, in my 40 plus years at the track, other than "Gelo" the only other black jockey's agent in Maryland is J.D. Brown. "Gelo's" eyes lit up with pride when he talks about "J.D." because he knew his father Hayes Brown, for a long time. Mr. Brown, who died in 2000, was one of the few black trainers in the State from the early 1950s that worked the old circuit. After he retired from being a full time trainer, Hayes Brown went on to become a clocker, patrol judge and then stable manager at Laurel for 20 years. According to published reports, when "J.D.'s" mother died in 1996, he saw his father slide into depression, moping around the house, until one day he looked at his son and said, "We should buy a horse. J.D. and his father had a good run with the horses, including striking gold with a claimer named *Testifly*, who turned into a blazing beast and won a slew of stakes races and more than $500,000. After his father died, JD continued to hang around the track. Reportedly, a popular Maryland trainer, Eddie Gaudet suggested he become a jockey's agent and hooked J.D. up with a young jockey named Richard Monterrey. When his rider moved on the J.D. picked up new jockeys and is currently working for the 21-year-old apprentice Carlos Quinones, and the veteran Nick Santagata.

"Gelo" life as an agent was like a circus entertainer, wherever the racing circuit raised a tent that was where "Gelo" hung his hat. Today, we race in Maryland from January through June; take a break for 6-8 weeks and we start back in August and race through the end of the year. During the late 1940s through the late 80s, the races moved from Maryland to Delaware, to New Jersey, to Florida; and all the people that earned their living working with horses moved from track to track. "Gelo" recalls sleeping on the beaches in Florida and renting rooms from black families in Delaware and New Jersey. The tracks in New Jersey were located near the major nightclubs such as the Cherry Hill Farm and the Latin Casino. Over the years, "Gelo" had established an excellent reputation as an intelligent, well spoken, gentleman. Throughout his career as a jockey's agent, the white racing officials as well as white trainers at tracks up and down the East Coast called upon "Gelo" to escort well-known entertainers that owned thorough-bred horses and frequented the racetracks. These famous entertainers included such stars as singer Eydie Gormé, who "Gelo" described as being a very special lady and the legendary Motown singing group, "The Supremes". "Gelo" recalled being teased by the fellows on the "Back Side" because he was a married man and was hanging out with the "Supremes", three very beautiful young women.

The Love of Jazz

"Gelo" is a jazz enthusiast, and during the time he spent in New Jersey, he was able to enjoy live performances by some of the great jazz bands of this era, such as, Count Basie, Duke Ellington, Harry James and Louie Prima. "Gelo" recalls a day at Garden State Race Track in New Jersey, when he was walking through the grandstand and turned to see the late great Harry James standing no more than an arm's length away from him. As an agent traveling from track to track, "Gelo" met prominent African American trainers such as "Whitey" Nixon, at old Keystone Race Track, which is now Philadelphia Park. Mr. Nixon trained horses for a Hall of Fame NBA Superstar, the late Wilt Chamberlain, while he was playing basketball of the Philadelphia 76 ers. At nearby Charlestown Race Track in West Virginia, "Gelo" met Sylvia Bishop, an African American trainer who owned a nightclub in Charlestown. "Gelo" remember going to Ms. Bishop's club to see another legendary Superstar, Tina Turner, perform live and in person at this little nightclub in West Virginia. What "Gelo" came to find out was that Tina Turner was a horseracing fan, that she had met Ms. Bishop while attending the races at Charlestown Race Track, and they became close friends.

According to published reports, Sylvia Bishop may have been the first African American woman licensed to train thoroughbred horses in the United States. Sylvia Bishop died on December 27, 2005 at Jefferson Memorial Hospital in Ransom, West Virginia. Ms. Bishop was an owner and trainer of thoroughbred racehorses for more than 60 years until she retired in 2000. Ms. Bishop was a member of the West Virginia Horsemen's Association. She said, "When I began training horses back in 1938, men were definitely shocked and surprised to see me, the fact that I was a woman, and on top of that a black woman, was almost too much for some of the fellows. But I loved horses and horseracing far too much to let my dream go". According to Equineline.com, the Jockey Club of America online racing information system, Ms. Bishop's horses won 44 races between 1987 and 2000, earning a total of $166,633. I was familiar with Ms. Bishop's career as a trainer, but in talking with her friends and relatives, they never mentioned her nightclub or her relationship with "Queen" of Rock "N" Roll, Ms. Tina Turner. It is amazing how good it makes me feel when I am able to capture these little tidbits of African American history that should have been part of the mainstream data available to everyone, rather than hidden away in the memories of a few African Americans like Howard "Gelo" Hall.

TABLE OF CONTENTS

About the Author   vii

Dedication   xi

Introduction   xxxv

Chapter 1   The History of "Race" in
Horseracing - Slavery: Y2k2 & Beyond   1

Chapter 2   America's 1St Sports Super Stars   52

Chapter 3   "Jack of All Trades"   115

Chapter 4   My Ole Kentucky Home   156

Chapter 5   The Future   215

Chapter 6   History Does Repeat Its' Self   257

Chapter 7   The End of My Trilogy - A Never
Ending Saga   316

INTRODUCTION

There is very little documented America History on slavery from a black slave's perspective. I have read some of the writings of well-educated slaves that provided a limited black perspective on slavery, such as those done by Frederick Douglas, born into slavery, but was most recognized by Americans for his accomplishments as freed man and as an abolitionist. In addition, I have read documents written by Nat Turner, a black hero, who fought against slavery by leading a rebellion against white plantation owners. However, because it was a crime punishable by death for a black slave to read and write, very few slaves risk dying in order to chronicle their life experiences as slaves. In spite of the risk of death to slaves that could read and write, white and black historians have found original documents that were written by slaves. Some of the original slave documents were handed down from one generation of black families to the next. However, the families of former slave owners passed down most of the original documents that were authenticated as having been written by a slave. The reason these former slave owners maintained these documents was to use them as evidence that a slave could read and write, and the slave was then put to death as punishment and as example to other slave not to learn to read or write.

Whenever I think about the fact that my black slave ancestors were lynched just because they knew how to read or write it makes me sick. Yet, it also inspires me to continue to read and write and encourage other African Americans to do the same. Knowledge is power and education is the key to knowledge. The white plantation owners were afraid that if slaves were educated they would no longer be able to control them. In my opinion that was the main reason, our black ancestors were not allowed to read or write. If the white masters discovered that a black slave could read, they would make an example of that slave by killing them in front of other slaves. The punishment for being able to read and write was so severe, that few slaves had the courage to try to learn. Some white plantation owners did educate some slaves as proof that any animal could be trained the same as they would train a dog or a horse. Groomed and educated black slaves were used to amuse and provide better service to their white masters. A few slaves had the courage to risk death and learned to read and write while they were still on their white owner's plantation. Others managed to learn to read and write when they escaped the chains of slavery. Other runaway slaves were educated in the schools in Northern States and across the border in Canada.

I truly admire other black American writers like Alex Haley, who took the time and energy to recreate a portrait of slavery based on a collection of stories passed down from one generation of African Americans to the next. There are those that claim Mr. Haley's book, "Roots", was fiction and not based on any events that could be authenticated. In my opinion, all the white historian's portrayals of slavery in the U.S. are fictional. It is my strong opinion that the only people that can authentic the horrors experienced by my black slave ancestors are my black slave ancestors and they are all dead. Yet ever public school system in America uses books written by these white historians to teach white and black children about slavery. It is my hope that the American History teachers throughout this Country will allow our children to learn about slavery from Alex Haley's book "Roots" and from my books *"American Apartheid"* and *"No Land No Mule No Freedom"*.

My new book, "The Back Side of the Sport of Kings", is about life on the "Back Side" of the Sport of Thoroughbred Horse Racing in America. The "Back Side" or the barn or stable area, is where the thoroughbred horses, the Stars or Equestrian Athletes of the sport of racing are housed. The "Back Side" is the part of the sport of thoroughbred horseracing that the public rarely gets to see. As with my other books, *"American Apartheid"* and *"No Land No Mule No Freedom, American Apartheid, the Saga Continues"*, I provide the reader with the opinionated perspective of an African American, regarding historical events that make facts and information about the black Americans who make their living working with thoroughbred horses, an interesting subject. This book provides historical data on a lifestyle that started in slavery and has survived and moved on to the next millennium.

We have all heard the social and economic references associated with an individual or group being from "the other side of the tracks". The other side of the tracks is usually the domain of lower income and minorities citizens. In most areas, this social and economic division of citizens is actually marked by railroad tracks that run through the center of a town or community. The railroad tracks separate the rich from the poor or the black from the white. In the sport of racing, the social and economic division is physically separated by the Clubhouse and Grandstand of the racetrack. For over 300 years, from the Grandstand or Clubhouse of the racetrack, racing fans have seen horses being lead to the track from the stable area before each race and returned to the stable area after the race. For the most, that is all the average racing fans knows or cares about what goes on the "Back Side". Racing fans and the general public need to know that on the other side of walls that separate the Grandstand and Clubhouse from the stable area, there is an entirely different world that exists, and that world is the "Back Side" of the Sport of Kings.

Thoroughbred Horseracing is part of professional sports, and like all other sports, it is designed to be entertaining to its patrons. In every entertainment business, be it sports or live theater, there are thousands of men and women that work behind the scenes. The behind the scene staff provides the support services necessary to insure that the show always goes on. Just as with the people who work in the stable area of the racetrack, the public rarely if ever sees the men and women that work behind the scenes of the entertainment business. In the theater, movies and TV, you have specialist who handle the cameras, make-up, wardrobe and set design. In outdoors sports like baseball and football, you have the field maintenance crew, stadium clean-up crew and locker room attendance for the players. Without these hard working people, we would not enjoy the excellent entertainment that is provided in this Country today. Over the years, most of the professional that work behind the scene of the entertainment business have risen from an unorganized work force with low paying jobs with no benefits and no future, to an organized work force with trade unions that feature highly skilled positions with high salaries and benefits.

Unfortunately, better salaries and benefits has not been the case for the people that work behind the scene in the thoroughbred horseracing business. Based on my what I have been told by my ancestors, the world of the "Back Side" mirrors the look of this Country when black men were slaves; and if there has been any improvement over the years, it still reflects the images of the 1920s and 30s when Americans were suffering through the great depression. I grew up in a community that had no electricity or indoor plumbing. I used an outhouse at home, at school and even when I went to church for the first 6 years of my life. Fortunately, as I got older living conditions in my neighborhood got better. However, I have never forgotten what it felt like to go outside to use the toilet or to use a kerosene lamp to find my way around the house at night. My experiences with sub-standard living conditions, gives me some creditability in being able to recognize the same living conditions that are commons place on the "Back Side". I will expound on those sub-standard conditions later.

I am not an expert or an authority on the sport of thoroughbred horseracing. Therefore, throughout this book; I may use the phrases or terms "according to published reports", "reportedly", and "accordingly", to indicate that these facts and/or this information may be from a published source that I discovered during my research for The Back Side of the Sport of Kings". No matter how good and no matter what resources we use, no writer can accurately recreate the specific details of a historical event that occurred over 150 years ago. History is like a bullet fired from a gun. Once you pull the trigger and the shot is fired, you can never change the direction of a bullet. However, you can try to repair the damage and the effect of that bullet. The same can be said about the history of America. My style of writing is to insert points of interest in certain historical events that will not change the events, but might help to repair some of the originally damage or effects of that event due to the different perspective of the writer.

Although this is my third book, I am still a novice when it comes to the business aspects of writing and publishing a book. Before I became a writer, I never fully understood the importance of having an "Introduction" at the front of a book or excerpts from the book on the back cover. I have come to learn, understand and appreciate the fact that avid readers, do in fact judge a book by its front and back covers, and they read the introduction to determine if they want to purchase the book. I have also discovered that no matter what I write in this book, I cannot please everyone. A certain group of readers will reject it simply based on the title and author and others will love it for those same reasons. Regardless of which category you fit into, I make you a promise that if you continue to read this book you will find facts and information that you never heard before; written in a unique style.

The most exciting thing about writing a book and having it published is the fact that your words will live forever. My books, which contain my thoughts, will influence minds for centuries to come. That is why I take writing so very seriously. As you read my books, you will find that they are filled with emotion. The questioned that I am asked most often whenever I encounter my reading public is "What makes your books so special?" The answer to that question is very simple. The fact that I wrote it is what makes it special. The fact that I used my time, which is so very precious to all beings, to sit down a write a book for you to read and enjoy is special. Before this book was written, no other human being had ever put these particular thoughts on paper. A thought, no matter how similar it may seem to be, is as unique as a snowflake or your fingerprints.

As I am writing this book, my son is in college and at least once a week he is given an assignment to do a report on a current event. My son was in the 3rd grade when he read my first book *"American Apartheid"*, and from the 3rd grade through his 3rd year in college whenever he had an assignment to write about a current event, he used an excerpt from one of my book. This is another reason I feel my book is special. Although I fully understand the teacher's concept of a current event, because we had the same assignment when I was in the school, the actual terminology for the assignment should be a recent historical event. After years of using Dad's book to complete current event and other book report assignment, the teacher in my son's school advised him that it was time to use another source as a reference. Now, to complete this assignment, he will cut out an article from the newspaper or a magazine and summarize the subject of that article for his report.

We think of history as events that occurred in the "Olden Days" or hundreds of years ago. When in actually, some of the most significant historical events of all time happened just yesterday. You will have to understand that in the blink of an eye or as soon as an event in time moves from the now to the past, it becomes history.

The fact that my books address the history of blacks in America, from the "Olden Days", to things that happened yesterday, also makes them very special. I have readers frequently approach me to tell me that they actually witnessed an incident that I described in one of my books. Although the person may have read about the event in a newspaper or magazine, they share with me how they enjoyed reading about the event from the perspective of an African American.

Just in case you did not know or you need to be reminded, my books deal with the history of racism and racial discrimination in America. Although I write about historic events, I do not consider myself a historian. My motivation in writing my books is that history needs to be taught in more than one color and from more than one prospective. I write about events from the past from the prospective of an African American. Most accounts of black history do not take the time to personalize the events that shaped who and what we are today. I write about historical events. How they affected my family and me. I tell stories like you may have heard from your grandparents. I talk about my friend, my family and people I have met along the way. Black history is not just about slavery, Frederick Douglas, Benjamin Baneker, George Washington Carver, Martin Luther King or the Civil Rights Movement. Remember, black history actually includes facts and information about the lives and events of real people like you and I.

The themes of my books deal with acts of racism and racial discrimination from the past that still exists today. I choose thoroughbred horseracing as the foundation for my third book. It is a major industry in America and in my opinion; it continues to be a major contributor to racism and racial discrimination in this Country. The sport of thoroughbred horseracing has been dubbed the "Sport of Kings", and based on how my ancestors have been treated by the sport in America; I found this to be a very appropriate name. The reason that I say the Sport of Kings is a fitting name is if you take a good look at the history of the sport of thoroughbred horseracing in America, it is divided into two specific and separate classes of people. On the "Front Side" of horseracing, you have the nobility, upper class or white-collar workers. On the other side, the "Back Side", you have the proletariat or lower class. The blue-collar workers or what used to be black slaves. If you check your local library, you will find hundreds of books that address the glamour or the "Grandstand Side", "Clubhouse Side", "Front Side" and the Aristocrats of the Sport of Thoroughbred Horse Racing and the horse racing industry.

In your public library, you will find books on famous horse races, racehorses, jockeys and trainers. The most famous races are the Kentucky Derby, the Preakness, the Belmont Stakes and the Breeders' Cup Series. The most famous fictional stories on the sport of horseracing are the books and movies, *National Velvet* and *Black Beauty*, and your real life stories include books and movies about horses such as *Man o' War, War Admiral, Pharlap* and *Seabiscuit.* Most of these books were best sellers before they were converted into award winning movies. Yet, what you will not find are any best sellers about the African Americans jockeys of the past; no bestselling books which means there are no movies. In addition, you will not find in your local library any books that provide detailed information and facts about the non-professional black men who work behind the scene in the stable area. From the time thoroughbred horseracing became a sport and major industry in the U.S., African Americans have played a major role in its development.

The contributions of African Americans from the past to the sport of thoroughbred horseracing deserved to be better documented.

Before I talk about life on the "Back Side", I need to give you a little background on my relationship with the sport of horseracing. I use the word relationship because I love thoroughbred horse racing with the same passion and energy that I love writing. I actually love the way the barn smells. I even enjoy the smell of straw after horses have used it to relieve themselves. Sounds a little gross does not it. Yet, the people who work on the "Back Side" say that once those barn smells get into your system, you will be hooked on racehorses and the sport of racing for the rest of your life. Although I am addicted to the sport of thoroughbred horseracing, I am not addicted to the lifestyle and work required for those who make their living on the "Back Side". Can you imagine getting out of bed at 4 am just to go to the racetrack to watch horses being trained and groomed? I love the way they move so gracefully on the track and I love the way the act so majestically going to and from the track to the barn for training or an actual race. Thoroughbred horses are very temperamental and the behavior is unpredictable. One minute they are calm as could be and not even the sound of a noisy crowd bothers them. In the next minute, they could be startled by a whisper or a little bird and erupt in a panic. Yet, being around horses is very calming and for me it relieves the stress I have built up from having to deal with people.

I have been attracted to thoroughbred horseracing for as long as I can remember. In 1978, I became addicted to the Grandstand Side of racing when as an Anne Arundel County Police Officer; I was assigned to Laurel Racetrack as part of a security detail. Although we were not supposed to bet on the races while in uniform, I managed to find a way around that rule and I wagered a few dollars on my first horse race. I do not remember if I won or lost. However, I never forgot the thrill of watching a live thoroughbred horse race after placing a bet on one of the horse in that race. Since 1990, I have been blessed to be the full or part owner of seven thoroughbred racehorses. As a child, I dreamed of becoming a professional baseball or football player. Owning a race-horse is like owning your own professional baseball or football team.

You own the horse; you pay the trainer, the blacksmith, the veterinarian and you call the shots. Watching your horse run in a race provides the opportunity for you to experience the thrill of victory or the agony of defeat. Either of the experiences, winning or losing, is breathe taking and unforgettable.

According to the my aunt "Zeedie", whose real name is Gertrude, the reason I am addicted to the sport of thoroughbred horse racing is because my mother took me to the racetrack when I was still in her womb. My mother, the late Estelle Thomas, whom this book is dedicated, loved thoroughbred horse racing, and frequently talked about how she would "hang on the rail" when she was young. "Hanging on the rail" is a term used for thoroughbred horse racing patrons who stand next to the outside rail at the racetrack and cheer for the horse that they have placed a wager or bet. My mother was and my aunt Zeedie still is a "two-dollar bettor". A two-dollar bettor is a racetrack patron who comes to the track on a regular basis, is a self-proclaimed expert on the sport, but will only bet two dollars per race on the horse with the longest odds. In my mother case, a horse not only had to have long odds, it also had to be gray in color. As she got older, my mother became a devoted Christian and stopped gambling. However, she never lost her love for the sport of horseracing. Even after losing her eyesight, she would sit in front of the TV and listen to the big races like the Kentucky Derby. No matter what the race or the horses that were running in the race, my mother would always shout out "boy, you'd better watch out for that gray hoss". My mother passed away in June 2002; I love my mother and I miss her and awful lot. Sometimes when I am at the track and a gray horse comes out in the post parade, I will think about my mother and tell the people standing around me, "boys, you'd better watch out for that gray hoss".

Different from the main characters in *National Velvet* and *Black Beauty*, the blacks you read about in stories about horseracing; always play the stereotypical happy go lucky farm hands. Today, if you look hard and long in your local library, you may find books about black jockeys and a few African American thoroughbred racehorse owners and trainers. However, you will not find information or fictional stories that feature the black exercise riders, grooms and hotwalkers that give details on how African Americans provide vital support services for the sport of horseracing. "The Back Side of the Sport of Kings" is attempt to revisit yet another of the missing chapters of African American History written from a black perspective. This book will open your eyes to a lifestyle that is not part of American society's mainstream. It is my hope that *"The Back Side of the Sport of Kings"* will continue the traditions that was started with *"American Apartheid"* and *"No Land No Mule No Freedom"*, to inspire Americans to pass on the stories of my African American ancestors. Anyone from the 5th grade and up should be able to read and fully enjoy my books. Remember that American Apartheid is indeed a never-ending saga.

One of the main reasons that African American history written by whites includes documentation about black slaves being married and being part of a family is that for the most part, white Americans want to be recognized for being outstanding humanitarians. Have you noticed that white people love to lead campaigns to save the whales, the bald eagles, and many other endangered species of animals? It is my opinion, based on the ever increasing number of African American males in the correctional system in America, that the black males is fast becoming an endangered species in this Country. Just think about, if the Federal Government declares the African American male to be an endangered species, white America would consider us to be a cause worth saving and finally grant us the freedom, justice, equality and the long awaited reparations we deserve.

As I stated earlier, I love sports. When I was younger, I played baseball, football and basketball on a very competitive level. As I got older, I made the graceful transition from baseball to slo-pitch softball, from full court basketball to half court and from tackle football to flag football. As I got older still, I made the not so graceful transitions to playing no football, to over 60-league basketball and slo-pitch softball. As I am writing this book, I play very little slo-pitch softball and I only play pick up half court games of basketball with friends that I trust not to hurt me. Since I have stopping playing sports, I have started to do a lot more watching games on TV. Now I am an avid sports fan, I even watch tennis, golf and hockey, sports that are considered a non-traditional part of African American culture. My point is that a change in lifestyle does not hurt. If racial harmony and diversity is a change for you, make it gracefully, but by all means make the change.

As you are reading this book, please take into account the book was written in Y2K7 and that the facts that I am writing and the information that I provide may not be published for years after it was written. The good thing about writing books on racism and racial discrimination in America is that the impact of whatever I write will be the same today as it will be tomorrow, ten years from now and possibly forever. Today, white and African Americans tend to take education for granted. The education and training we receive from elementary school through college is an essential part of the preparation for future employment. Whenever I have the opportunity to speak to groups of young students or adults, I try to impress upon them the importance of an education and the importance of studying American History in more than one color and from more than one perspective. The importance of knowing your history is that it will in fact repeat itself. We cannot change the past, but we can have an impact on the future.

Chapter 1

THE HISTORY OF "RACE" IN HORSERACING - SLAVERY: Y2K2 & BEYOND

Due to the fact that we declared our independence from England over 235 years ago after we fought and won the Revolutionary War, you would think that, any reference to a "Sport of Kings" would have long since lost its attraction to Americans. Yet, the sport of thoroughbred horse racing in America is a very lucrative business that has been around for over 400 years. Just think about it. The sport of thoroughbred horseracing and the business of slavery started in the United States around the same time. As we enter the 21st century, both the attitudes that supported the enslavement of my black ancestors and the sport of horseracing have stood the test of time, are alive, and well in America. It is a known fact that thoroughbred horseracing is still a successful entity in this Country and I will explain why I think slavery is still alive and doing well in America a little later in this chapter.

When I studied world history in High School, I was taught that royalty or nobility was a birthright. The offspring of kings and queens automatically become heirs to the throne of their father, the king or their mother, the queen. Consistent with these "Old World" customs, the study of American history for the past 350 years reveals that the social classes in the U.S. were also determined by race, birth and supported by wealth. The same criteria that determined social class in America in the 1600s are still used to determine social class today. Just as it was in the 1600s, if you were born the child of wealthy white parents, you automatically became a member of America's Aristocratic Society. If you were born black in America, in the 1600s or the 21ˢᵗ century, no matter how wealthy your family may be, you became part of a permanent underclass.

Today, many of you think that rich African Americans in the U.S. are part of the upper class. You need really to think again. In order for wealthy black Americans to be treated like upper class white Americans; they have to achieve celebrity status by being a famous entertainer, athlete or politician and even then, they are only treated like a white person if they are easily recognizable in public. Studies have proven that a well-dressed white man will receive better treatment than a well-dressed black under the same circumstances in this Country will; the only exception is if the black man is a recognized celebrity. I make a point to say recognized black celebrity because there are several published incidents were black celebrity that fit a certain criminal profile and were not recognized, have been arrested by the police and treated the same as any other black criminal suspects that fit that same profile.

If you do not believe me, asked the black Hall of Fame baseball player Joe Morgan and recently retired professional baseball player, David Justice. They both were arrested in an airport for no other reason than being black. Remember the way the Philadelphia police treated Allen Iverson, star Basketball player for the Philadelphia 76er's, when he was arrested for allegedly breaking into his cousin's home at 4 am, and threatening him with a gun. Reportedly, Iverson was looking for his wife, who he allegedly put out of the house naked after they had an argument. From all indications by the TV reporters, Iverson was treated like a king. If I remember correctly, during arrest booking process, the police allowed Iverson's uncle to stay in the cell with him. That is what I mean when I talk about being a recognized black celebrity. When you see Pookie or Babie from the "Hood", ask them if any family member was allowed to stay in their cells to protect them when they were arrested. The question; is this the same Philadelphia Police Department that allegedly planted drugs on black suspects to insure a conviction? What a difference being able to score 30 points per game in the NBA and a multi-millionaire means to being a victim of racism in America.

The Sport of Kings

Nowhere in America is class more dominant than the sport of thoroughbred horseracing. In order for you to understand how the class system was developed in thoroughbred horseracing, I need you to know a little about the origin of the sport. According to most white historians, the competitive racing of horses is one of man's most ancient sports, having its origins among the prehistoric nomadic tribesmen of Central Asia who first domesticated the horse about 4500 BC. I used the term white historians because a white person wrote the majority of the historical documentation found in the local library. No matter how black I am or how black I try to make my books; I have to start in the library to find most of the documents needed to conduct the research necessary to complete my books.

For thousands of years in Europe, horseracing flourished as the sport of kings. According to accounts of modern history, the most popular form of the sport is the racing of mounted thoroughbred horses over flat courses at distances from three-quarters of a mile to two miles. Other forms of horseracing are harness racing, steeplechase racing, and quarter horse racing. Today in the United Stated, the sport of thoroughbred horseracing is a major venue for legalized gambling. Second only to baseball, horseracing is the most widely attended spectator sport in America. Over 60 million people attend over 8,000 days of racing, and wagered over 10 billion dollars each year. It may be the Sport of Kings, but the common worker supports it just the way they do baseball, mom and apple pie in America. By the time man began to keep written records, horseracing was an organized sport in Civilizations from Central Asia to the Mediterranean. Chariot and mounted horseracing were events in the ancient Greek Olympics by 638 BC, and the sport became a public obsession in the Roman Empire. History records that in Britain, in 200 AD, racing began using horses from the Roman invaders' stock. These early warhorses were selectively bred for their qualities of strength, power, courage and speed. Most of us have either read the book or saw the movie and remember the thrilling chariot race from *Ben Hur.*

Just a little aside, how did actor Charlton Heston, the man who played Moses and *Ben Hur* in two of the greatest movie ever made, become the President of the National Rifle Association? In my opinion, the NRA ranks alongside the Loyal Order of Moose, the Skin Heads, the Neo Nazi Groups, and the KKK, as racists white organizations in America. I know that some of my readers have already started to wonder, if horseracing was a part of every Civilized Nation, does this reference include the Nations of Africa? I do not have any documented references to support horseracing in Africa. However, I do have documented references to support the fact that there were Kings and Queens in Africa during the same timeframe as other Civilization began in Europe and Asia. Therefore, since horseracing is the "Sport of Kings", I feel it is safe to assume that there was some form of horseracing in Africa and that it was attended by the African nobility of that time. Let me stop here to say, I write about Black American History, and in doing so, I do not try to link every historical reference back to my ancestral roots in Africa.

Reportedly, the origins of modern racing began in the 12th century, when English knights returned from the Crusades with swift Arab horses. Over the next 400 years, Arab stallions were imported and bred to English mares to produce horses that combined speed and endurance. The first horse races were held for nobility and were match races between the fastest horse from each settlement or town with a private wager on the outcome of the race. During the early 1700s, horseracing became a professional sport. Match racing gave way to races involving several horses on which the spectators wagered. Racecourses sprang up all over England, offering increasingly large purses to attract the best horses. The increase in the size of purses made breeding and owning horses for racing very profitable. Accordingly, the rapid expansion of the sport created a need for a central governing authority. In 1750, racing's elite met at Newmarket, England to form the Jockey Club. The rules and regulation established by the Jockey Club for thoroughbred horseracing are stilled use today to the guide for controlling the sport of horse racing around the world. The Jockey Club wrote complete rules of racing and sanctioned racecourses to conduct meetings under a specific set of rules. Standards defining the quality of races soon led to the designation of certain races as the ultimate tests of excellence. In Europe, since 1814, five races for three-year-old horses have been designated as "classics." Three races make up the English Triple Crown: the 2,000 Guineas, the Epsom Derby, and the St. Leger Stakes.

Coming to America

The British settlers brought horses and horse racing with them to the New World, with the first racetrack laid out on Long Island, New York as early as 1665. Reportedly, the first thoroughbred to reach this Country was *Bulle Rock*, imported in 1730. In 1798, the stallion, *Diomed*, was imported to Virginia. Accordingly, *Diomed* was a racing legend in England, having won the first English Derby in 1780. However, the horse proved to be useless in the stud barn. When he was sold to a Virginia breeder in 1798 at age 21, it was assumed that his best days were behind him. Yet, when *Diomed* found himself on American soil, his problems as a stud disappeared, and over the next ten years, he sired enough successful progeny to immortalize him as the father of the American thoroughbred. *Diomed* laid the foundation for a strong line of thoroughbreds in America that would eventually rival the best in the world. At this particular juncture in the history of thoroughbred horseracing, it should be noted that rich white Southerners owned the majority of the African slaves as well as the majority of thoroughbred racehorses. These valuable horses as well as all the other livestock owned by the rich white Southerners were taken care of by my black slave ancestors.

Slavery and Horseracing

During the years prior to the Civil War, a slave taking care of racehorses for their white masters, included grooming, training, being the exercise rider in the morning and the jockey during the afternoon races. I will address each of these professions later in this book. How many of you racing fans think about slavery when you watch the Kentucky Derby or the Breeders' Cup on TV? It should come as no surprise that the study of my African American ancestors will link them to most ever famous event that occurred in this Country. Why is that white plantation owners trusted my black slave ancestors to take care of their children and the valuable thoroughbred horses and today, the ancestors of those slave owner will not trust African America enough to share freedom and equality. It was not until the 1690s that Southern colonies were able to open racetracks. From the years prior to the Revolutionary War through the end of the Civil, every available piece of cleared woodland in the South went to the production of cotton or tobacco. However, as the over-planted land grew fallow and became useless for the cash crops, the flat space was snatched up, and thoroughbred horse racetracks opened throughout the South. Williamsburg, Virginia became the center of Southern racing, attracting the elite colonists from miles around to bring their horses together in match races similar to those famous match races held in New York between Northerners and Southerners as we moved closer to the Civil War.

Reportedly, as settlers moved farther West, they took racing with them, and by 1840, Illinois, Missouri, Texas, and Louisiana all hosted racing events. The bluegrass of Kentucky and Tennessee welcomed horse breeders as they moved West. The "1848 Gold Rush" carried the thoroughbred to the Far West Coast of California. On the East Coast, racetracks were slowly gaining favor and were hosting more and more people from all classes. The first racetracks in America were cleared fields with a course marked for the horses to run around. The new racetracks were built with grandstands and rails were constructed to separate the spectators from the actual racing surface. As part of the migration of thoroughbred horseracing from Southern States to the far Northeastern States and the West Coast, so was the migration of the black slaves that tended these valuable animals. As it was in England, the traditional surface for racetracks in America was grass. According to published reports, in 1821 Union Race Course opened on Long Island, New York with a "skinned" dirt track. The dirt track was fast, and Union Race Course became the model for future American tracks. Reportedly, Union Race Course was influential for another reason as well. In 1823 Union Race Course hosted the first of the great match races between thoroughbred horses that were bred and owed by Northerners against horses that were bred and owned by Southern.

Horse owners, from each of the politically and economically different sections of the Country put up open challenges, offering purses to prove their horse better. Reportedly, while these North versus South horse races were run at least partly in fun, everyone that attended these races was aware of the political implication that were attached to each race. Regardless of the politics involved in the match races, these thoroughbred horse races reportedly attracted larger crowds than any other sporting event in American history to that point. Unfortunately, it was another match-up between Northerners and Southerners, in the Civil War, that brought thoroughbred horse racing to its knees. The traditional breeding centers of Virginia and the Carolinas were devastated. Pastures were torn up, and thoroughbred horses stolen or killed by union soldiers desperate for both mounts and food. In the North, thoroughbred horses were confiscated by the U.S. Government and used by the military, and racetracks were closed or used as army training camps. In my opinion, horseracing in the State of Virginia never recovered from the devastation of the Civil War. After the Civil War, rather than return to breeding champion thoroughbred horses, Virginia turned to tobacco as the crop to return the State to prosperity.

After the Civil War, other areas of the Country that were not deeply marked with battle scars were the first to return to the business of thoroughbred horseracing. California racing flourished toward the end of the nineteenth century, while Kentucky and Tennessee emerged, relatively unscathed, and became the new centers of American thoroughbred horse breeding. The North was able to reopen tracks in New Jersey and Pennsylvania. The center of racing on the East Coast after 1865 rested squarely in New York State. A new racetrack was opened in 1863 in Saratoga Springs, New York. The elegant Saratoga Racetrack is the current home of the Thoroughbred Racing Hall of Fame. Beginning in the late 1880s and for the past 125 years, the State of Kentucky has excelled as the Thoroughbred Horse Breeding Capital of the Entire World. In the late 1990s, Kentucky bred yearling colts routinely sold at auction for 2 million dollars. It should come as no surprise that horses bred in Kentucky have won the Kentucky Derby more than horses bred in all the other States combined. The secret to Kentucky's success must be in their "Blue Grass"!

If you build them, they will come

Reportedly, the development of organized racing did not arrive until after the Civil War. With the rise of an industrial economy, the amount of money being gambled on racehorses caused a rapid increase in the horse racing industry. By 1890 there were over 300 thoroughbred horse race tracks operating across the United States. In the early 1900s, horse racing in the United States was almost wiped out by antigambling sentiment that led almost all States to ban bookmaking. According to published reports, by 1908 the number of racetracks in the U.S. was reduced to just 25. That same year the introduction of pari-mutuel betting for the Kentucky Derby signaled a turnaround for the sport. Many of the old racks reopened and new racetracks were built as State Legislatures agreed to legalize pari-mutuel betting in exchange for a share of the money wagered. The rapid growth of the sport without any central governing authority led to the domination of many tracks by criminal elements. In 1894, the Nation's most prominent track and stable owners met in New York to form an American Jockey Club, modeled on the English Jockey Club, which soon ruled racing with an iron hand and eliminated much of the corruption.

In addition, to the stable influence of the American Jockey Club, the great Equestrian Superstars, *Man o' War* and *Seabiscuit*, the most popular thoroughbred horses of the early era of racing, and the American Triple Crown, a series of three races that consists of the Kentucky Derby, the Preakness, and the Belmont Stakes, brought spectators flocking to racetracks. Today, thoroughbred racetracks exist in about half the States in this Country. Public interest in the sport focuses primarily on major thoroughbred races such as the American Triple Crown and the Breeders' Cup races, which offer purses of over a $1,000,000. The infusion of money from Corporate Sponsors like VISA, Budweiser and liquor companies that make Early Times and Jim Beam have done for thoroughbred horseracing what Corporate Sponsors did for automobile racing. I have talked about racetracks being built and the development of the sport of racing. In the early years black and white racing fans were segregated the same as white and blacks at any other sporting event in America during the "JIM CROW ERA". As I am writing this book in 2007, when I started school in 1954, segregation was the law of the land.

I remember watching movies about baseball and boxing and when the cameras were turned on the crowd, black and white fans were always separated. As a child, when I watched these movies, I never paid any attention to the fact that black and white never sat in the same section of the stadium or arena. Now when I watch these old movies it upsets me that these imaginative filmmakers could not look into the future and show whites and blacks enjoying a sporting event together. I guess the same could be said about writers like Jules Verne, who wrote books about the future. In my opinion, Jules Verne was one of the greatest visionary writers of his time. Yet with all his foresight, Mr. Verne failed to specifically identify any black characters when his imagination took him *20,000 Leagues Under the Sea the Sea*, on *A Journey to the Center of the Earth* or on a trip *Around the World in 80 Days*. The problem I have with the lack of racial diversity in Mr. Verne's books is that our school systems refer to his works as classics; as excellent examples of what the future holds for the human race and make his books required reading for our children. Most readers prefer fiction to non-fiction, the make believe to reality, as evidenced by the success of the Harlequin Novels and the fact that more movie scripts are based on fictional character than real life. I have to admit that one of my favorite pastimes is watching reruns of the Science Fiction TV and movies series *Star Trek*.

The reason I am a big *Star Trek* fan is that Gene Roddenberry, the creator of *Star Trek*, is a true visionary. I admire Mr. Roddenberry's vision because he had the courage to stay committed to his ideas and dreams no matter how they were perceived by his peers and the rest of society. Why is it that some of the other great white American visionaries of the past. The same visionaries responsible for the airplane, automobile, the pony express and railroads that linked the East and West, revolutionary ideas and inventions that changed this Country forever; use those vivid imaginations to include African Americans as partners and allow us to share the "American Dream" of equally regardless of Race, Creed or Nationality. The reason I feel Gene Roddenberry is a true American visionary. When he created the fictional plots and characters for *Star Trek* his imagination took him to worlds far beyond the 21st century. He was able to envision worlds that were diverse. Worlds that allow human beings of all shapes, sizes and colors could exist in harmony. If you compare the fictional creations of Gene Roddenberry with those of Jules Verne, you will find that both men had ideas and visions that were way ahead of their time. Many of the fictional inventions and ideas referred to in the writings of Jules Verne became reality. Based on man's advancements in outer space travel, it is well within the realm of possibility that the fictional inventions of Gene Roddenberry will someday become a real part of our lives.

Just think about it, one day when the real life character of Captain James T. Kirk, from the Star Ship Enterprise, shouts, "beam me up Scottie", he will actually be able to disintegrate, travel through space and time and reappear in another location. However, it is Gene Roddenberry's fictional futuristic ideals of diversity and racial equality that I hope will someday come to fruition and rid America of the hatred and bigotry of racism forever. The reason why I want you think about how a visionary could have an impact on racism in America is because slavery ended in this Country over 140 years and we still feel the aftershock of this tragedy. You never forget a tragic event in history, but you can recover from it. Visions of the future have allowed the Jews to recover from the Holocaust, the Japanese to recover from the Hydrogen Bombings, and the world to recover from generations of war. Yet, the same vision and hopes for a bright future, which was used to recover from the aforementioned tragic events, has not been utilized to assist Americans in their recovery from the aftermath of the racial hatred and bigotry that was born out of the enslavement of my black ancestors in this Country. Why is it that American visionaries of all races, who are responsible for cellular phones, pacemakers, walking on the moon, organ transplants; revolutionary ideas and inventions that changed this Country forever use those vivid imaginations to include people of all races as partners and share the American Dream equally regardless of Race, Creed or Nationality?

Maryland My Maryland

When I first started my quest of writing black American history, I would look at far way States because I did not want to accept the fact that my home State was full of events that were based on racial hatred and discrimination. Prior to writing my first book, I attended races at Pimilco Racetrack in Baltimore, Maryland for years before I found out that the wooden grandstand seats at the far turn were constructed expressly for the use of African American Racing Fans. This is the history lesson that is so valuable to future generations. I remember one of the black "Old Timers" used to watch the races from this section. When I started attending the races at Pimlico, this section was usually empty. I thought the "Old Timer" sat in that section to be away from the noise of the crowd. However, when I asked him why he always sat in this section, he explained that when his family first brought him to the racetrack, the "Colored Section" was the only place they could sit, get something to eat or drink, use the restroom and most importantly, place a bet on their favorite horse. As I am writing this book, Pimlico Racetrack is about to be renovated and these wooden grandstand seats will probably be torn down. I hope that the NAACP will take step to insure that the history of this area will be documented and photographs of the wooden grandstand seats filled with African American racing fans preserved forever.

State racing commissions have sole authority to license participants and grant racing dates, while sharing the appointment of racing officials and the supervision of racing rules with the Jockey Club. Like the Jockey Club in England, in addition to being the governing body for thoroughbred horseracing, the American Jockey Club also took steps to regulate the breeding of racehorses. The Jockey Club traces the pedigree, or complete family history, of every thoroughbred horse racing in America. Although science has not come up with any breeding system that guarantees the birth of a champion, breeders over the centuries have produced an increasingly higher percentage of thoroughbred horses that are successful on the racetrack by following two basic principles. The first is that thoroughbred horses with superior racing ability are more likely to produce offspring with superior racing ability. The second is that thoroughbred horses with proven pedigrees are more likely to pass along its racing ability to their offspring. With all the advances in technology in breeding horses, the men and women that earn their living handicapping horses, have come up with a term called "dosage", which gives an indication of a horse's ability based on their breeding.

Breeding is for the Pure Bloods

According to published reports, champion thoroughbred stallions have the highest breeding value because they can mate with about 40 to 50 mares a year. The worth of champions, especially winners of Triple Crown Races, is so high that groups of investors, called breeding syndicates, may be formed to manager the breeding career of a great stud. In addition to managing the stallions, breeding career, each of the approximately 40 shareholders in the syndicate, entitles the owner to breed one mare to the stallion each year. One share, for a great horse, may result in a foal worth several million dollars. In addition, a shareowner may resell their share at any time. As was the case with most white American culture, the horses we race in this Country have been developed in Europe and are the descendants of the invading Mongol and Aryan masters' warhorses. The breeding of thoroughbred racehorses to improve upon the speed, strength, and stamina of the horses began before the time of Homeric Greece. Today in the U.S., the breeding of thoroughbred racehorses is a multi-billion dollar industry. The bloodline of a thoroughbred horse contains more information than the average human being's family tree. The sport of thoroughbred racing will not allow a horse that does not have documentation of its pedigree to participate in a race.

If you recall from the movie, the horse *Black Beauty* was never allowed to run in an official race because he did not have any papers. Can you image that the aristocratic mindset of the upper class will not allow a horse that does not have proof of his pedigree to compete against a blue-blooded thoroughbred for fear it would lessen the value of that thoroughbred horse. Even though these are animals, this is the root cause of racial discrimination and the irony of this situation is that African American who breed dogs, cats, and thoroughbred horses, support the practice of not allowing their precious thoroughbreds to compete in dog, cat or horse shows against "mutts". Another of the many reason, as African Americans, we need to know our history. In my book *"No Land No Mule No Freedom"*, I compare the breeding of black slaves by their white masters to the breeding of thoroughbred horses. The white plantation masters bred their slaves the same way they bred all the other animals that they owned. The purpose of breeding is to mate a female and male of a species to get the best physical attributes of both the male and female in their offspring. Today, breeding is what keeps the thoroughbred horse racing industry alive in America. The physical appearance or conformation is very important to a breeder of thoroughbred horses. The breeders mate the best male and female thoroughbred horses to achieve an offspring that have speed, stamina, and the physical conformation to that make those offspring attractive on in the horse auction.

The selected breeding of black males and females was done to create the same qualities in slaves as white slave owners admired in their thoroughbred horses. The same purpose was to produce attractive offspring for the auction block. Thoroughbred horse breeders, to protect the quality of the bloodline, would castrate or geld a male horse that showed signs of a physical deficiency. If by accident, a thoroughbred mare mated with a horse that did not have proof of his pedigree, when the foal was born without the distinct markings of the breeders' thoroughbred stallion, the horse breeders would kill the foal and the mare to protect the bloodline. Stallions that mate with a mare other than a thoroughbred are also destroyed to protect the bloodline. Breeders would also geld male horses that were too aggressive and unmanageable as a method to make the horse gentle and easy to control. For the breeders of thoroughbred horses, the mating process is so important, and they get so excited over the prospect of a champion stallion about to mate with a champion mare, they invite prospective owner and friends to watch the animals mate. This may sound a little disgusting to some of you. But to an avid racing fan, watching a great champion stallion like *Mr. Prospector*, mate with an even greater champion mare like *Personal Ensign*, which resulted in an offspring named *Our Emblem*, who was the eventual sire of the 2002 Kentucky Derby winner *War Emblem*, might have been worth the price of admission.

Breeding Horses and Slaves

Believe it or not, everything I said about the breeding of thoroughbred horses can be applied to the breeding of Africans during slavery in America. White plantation owners, just like the thoroughbred horse breeders of today, mated the strongest and most attractive black males and female slaves to achieve those same qualities in the babies of the African slaves. In addition, just as with the thoroughbred horse owners, the white slave breeders derived pleasure from watching black slaves mate. The major different between the breeding of slaves and thoroughbred horses is that my black slave ancestors were not always mated as part of a profit making business; the white slaves masters raped my female African ancestors for their own pleasure, which often resulted in the birth of a mixed race offspring. The other major difference, the mixed race offspring that resulted from the rape would be worthless in the thoroughbred horse business and would be destroyed. Yet regardless of their breeding, a mixed bred African slave was an asset and far too valuable to be destroyed. As part of this lesson, I need to make things clear in order for you to understand what I mean when I talk about the breeding and mating process. Breeding is man's attempt to predetermine how an offspring will turn out by selecting that offspring's parents. Mating is sexual intercourse between a male and female. To make it even clearer, perverted white slave breeders forced their slave to have intercourse while the white slave breeders watched.

Some movie portrayals of slavery in the Deep South show Africans Americans participating in wedding ceremonies while on the white masters' plantation. The stories passed down from one generation of African Americans to the next include tales of slave marriages, momma and poppa, granddad and grandma. In order to make some moral sense out of a very immoral act such as slavery, we need to believe the human concept of family existed during those times. However, based on the fact that slaves were bred, I cannot support the concept of marriage, as we know it today. I do not doubt for a minute, that female and male slaves made every attempt possible to have monogamous relationships. However, in the legal sense, the majority of unions between slaves were not recorded as marriages, and if the slave owner decided to sell either party in this union, my slave ancestors were helpless in stopping the transactions. If the slave owner decided that they would rather mate one of the parties of a "slave marriage" with another slave, again, my ancestors had no way to stop it from happening. Fortunately, many of my slave ancestors escaped and with new their freedom, they were able gain control of their lives; record their marriages, record the birth of their children and record their history.

Unfortunately, just as with horses, to enhance the possibility of reproducing physically attractive black slaves, white slave traders would castrate unattractive African male slaves. The horse breeders gelded unmanageable male horses, and to control aggressive behavior, white slave owners gelded aggressive black male slaves. For those of you who are not farmers or ranchers, and may not be familiar with the terms castrate and geld, I will explain. The terms castrate or geld means to cut off a male's testicles or penis. For you readers, especially you males, imagine having a very sensitive part of your anatomy cut off without the benefit of an anesthetic. My, it hurts me just to think about it. Just as thoroughbred horse breeders treasure a prize stallion, and collect a stud fee from other breeders for allowing the prize stallion to mate with their mares, the white plantation owners collected fees for allowing their prime black male slaves to mate with female slaves from other plantations. I can imagine some of you men smiling and wondering what would be so cruel about being a male stud selected to service hundreds of women. As black male, I find no pleasure in having sex on command and having no freedom in the choice or selection of sexual partners.

Jimmy "the Greek": Fired for telling the truth

A white professional gambler, Jimmy "the Greek" Snyder turned making odds into entertainment as part of the CBS TV network's Sunday afternoon NFL pre-game show. In 1988, his 12-year career with CBS ended abruptly after an interview with WRC-TV in Washington D.C. The TV station's reporter was seeking comment from Jimmy in connection with the birthday of the Rev. Martin Luther King Jr., and was asking him questions about the status of the progress of blacks in sports. Unfortunately for Jimmy, he may have been under the influence of a few too many cocktails, and in my opinion, the TV interviewer took advantage of this to get some deep seeded comments. Jimmy stated that during the Civil War, "the slave owner would breed his big black with his big woman so that he would have a big black kid". "That's where it all started." He said a black athlete was better than a white one because "he's been bred to be that way because of his thigh size and big size." CBS Sports fired Jimmy "the Greek" Snyder the next day after he issued a public apology. After this incident, Jimmy "the Greek" never appeared on TV again and a short time later, he died.

The answer to that question is because racism is ugly and just as it was with the statements made by Jimmy "the Greek"; any reference to racism would be bad for the image of thoroughbred horseracing. In my opinion, the statement made by Jimmy was in direct conflict with white America's "good guy" and humanitarian image and embarrassed the great white TV Executives at CBS. In the business of television, image is everything. Regardless of their personnel feeling, the responsibility of the white TV Executives is to sell commercial time and keep the consumers happy. Therefore, it is my opinion that Jimmy was not fired for his remarks, he was fired because he repeated information that was to remain behind the closed doors of the "For Whites Only Good Ole Boys Clubs", information that when made public; upset the people who pay for the commercials on TV. In my opinion, the reporter who suckered Jimmy into making this statement did it to make headlines and not to bring attention to acts of racial injustice. It is also my opinion that the reporter, who interviewed the Greek, probably knew that after a few drinks Jimmy might give him some very newsworthy quotes. In my opinion, the reporter who conducted the interview took advantage of Jimmy because he was drunk. From a factual historical perspective, Jimmy was telling the truth. Yet, some white Americans were embarrassed because they cannot handle having the truth about the repulsive acts their ancestors committed against black slaves being given public attention. Jimmy "The Greek" Snyder died in April 1996. I have followed his career, and I found him to be an honorable man in a not so honorable profession.

It is my personal opinion that Jimmy "the Greek" Snyder made some inappropriate statements under the influence of alcohol, and that he was not a racist and I miss his commentary. As I continue to explore the subject of racism and racial discrimination in the sport of horseracing, there will be other comparisons to slaves and slavery in America. Some of you may be offended by my comparing the treatment and breeding of horses to that of your African American ancestors. If you are offended, just think about all the money that is spent in the U.S. on the care and treatment of animals, the money that is spent for animal rights, save the whales campaigns, and save all the other endangered species of animals, and what if that same amount of money was contributed to the United Negro College Fund? I think it would be safe to say that if that same amount of money were contributed to the UNCF, every black child in America would be able to attend college free of charge.

Somebody Bet on the Bay

No book about horseracing would be complete unless we talked about gambling and the betting on races. Today, as African Americans, we can take some comfort in knowing that the one place at the racetrack that you will not find any evidence of racial discrimination is at the betting windows. The thoroughbred horse racing industry will bend over backwards to take your money, and regardless of your Race, Color, Creed or National origin, everyone is afforded and equal opportunity to bet the horses. Gambling or wagering on the outcome of horse races has been an integral part of the appeal of the sport since from its' first recorded history and today is the sole reason horseracing has survived as a major professional sport. In some States in this Country, betting on thoroughbred horseracing is the only outlet for legalized gambling.

All betting at American tracks today is done under the pari-mutuel wagering system, developed by a Frenchman Pierre Oller in the late 19th century. Under this system, a fixed percentage, 14 to 25% of the total amount wagered is taken out for track operating expenses, racing purses, and State and Local taxes. To determine the actual payoff for each wager, the number of individual bettors divides the remaining sum of the money wagered. The projected payoff, or "odds," are continuously calculated by the track's computers and posted on the track odds board during the betting period before each race. Odds of "2-1," for example, mean that the bettor will receive $2 profit for every $1 wagered if his or her horse wins. Although I know that the only people to make a real profit from gambling at the racetrack are the owners of the racetrack, I keep trying to win. Yet, I keep losing. If you need to know more about how to gamble at the racetrack, you can find books on handicapping horses at your local library.

Now that you have had your history lesson on the sport of horseracing, let us look at the development of the racist class system in thoroughbred horse racing industry. According to most accounts of American History, the white man left Europe to escape the tyranny of living under the rule of kings and queens and to seek religious freedom.

These same white men hold freedom as being so precious and worth giving up everything for including their lives. Yet, it was the white men who established the same oppressive class system in America based on one's race and economics status. Remember, in order for the nobility to rule they must have subjects to rule. In the sport of kings in the U.S., the subjects that have been lorded over in America are for the most part Black Americans.

Throughout this book, I will be reminding you that most of the information contained within is based on my opinions and my perspectives. However, you will also find references that are based on historical facts. Whether you are white, black or red, there are segments of American History that will remain the same. No matter what color the person is or who tells the story. Most of the dates and statistical data that appear in my book are the same, as you would find in most historical accounts of the same events. For the most part, my opinions and perspectives about thoroughbred horseracing are based on my personal experiences, observations and interviews.

911 - Going to the Races

Beginning in the early 1970s, my interest in thoroughbred horse racing lead me to visit racetracks located in Maryland, West Virginia, Delaware, Pennsylvania, and New Jersey. The configuration of each of these tracks is different, but the attitudes of the people who work the Grandstand and the "Back Side" were always the same. In my travels to tracks that are located in the Mid-Eastern States, I met people who have worked at other tracks from Maryland to California, which includes all the States in between. As a result of my conversations with some very unique characters, I was able to obtain valuable information from horsemen and horsewomen; people that work on the racetrack love to talk and I love to listen to them talk. I been told that I write in a conversational and/or story telling style and this style was perfect for writing about the lifestyle of people who make a living working in the thoroughbred racing business.

This book barely scratches the surface of the racism that exists on the "Back Side" of the sport of Kings. It is my hope that after reading my book you will seek out other books or talk to people who work and live on the "Back Side". Some of you may be asking why after over 140 years of freedom in America, a black man is still talking about slavery. The answer, African Americans are not equal and not all black people are free. Another reason I will continue to talk about slavery and racism in American is that white people still have not paid for the pain and suffering of my black ancestors. If you are old enough to read this book, you are old enough to remember that the tragedy of 9 - 11 left an ugly scar on America that will never be forgotten. It is safe to say that every one of you that reads this book remembers the incidents of terrorism that occurred in this Country on September 11, 2001. Like some of you, I was personally touched because the plane that struck the Pentagon seriously injured my best friend's niece. As a result of this disaster, U.S. citizens of all Races, Colors, Creeds and National Origins, came together as one Nation to let the terrorist that attacked our Country know that they could not dampen the American spirit. Why is it in America that we can fight together in war, but we cannot live together in peace?

Thousands of Americans lost their lives on 911 and this Country united as we have done in the past whenever we are under attack. From Coast to Coast, Americans reaffirmed their patriotism by waving the U.S. Flag, reciting the Pledge of Allegiance, and singing "God Bless America, My home sweet home". Again, I ask the question, why is it that Americans can fight side by side in war, white, black and red soldiers and return to hating each other after the war is over and forgotten? Why is that we never see white supremacist groups like the KKK or Neo-Nazi Party protesting the U.S. Armed Forces use of black soldiers to protect their freedom. Why would a true white racist or bigot want to owe their freedom to African Americans soldiers who fight and die to protect them? Why does the 911 loss of thousands of U.S. citizens as a result of terrorist acts have a greater impact on the social consciousness of white America than the loss of millions of my Africans ancestors as a result of 400 years of slavery.

The More Things Change

I get so emotionally involved in my writing that sometimes I get a little off track. I not apologizing for expressing my feeling, I just want to make sure that my readers do not get lost. There is a saying in America that "the more things change, the more they stay the same". Racial discrimination in America is a perfect example of that statement. The sport of thoroughbred horseracing is by far the first professional sport in the U.S. to employ African Americans and it is the first professional sport that allowed black and white athletes to compete against each other in the same arena at the same time. Over the past 50 years, as the numbers of black professional athletes in the U.S. have increased in the popular sports like baseball, basketball and football, the number of African American jockeys has hit an all-time low. Racial discrimination and disparity in sports is old news in America. The trials and tribulation of the first black athletes to break the color barriers in professional sport has been well documented. It is so well documented that when an African American becomes the first in a professional sport in the U.S., they were dubbed the "Jackie Robinson" of that particular sport or event. Jackie Robinson opened many doors for African Americans and other minorities in sports. Just as it was with Jackie Robinson, my problem with the documentation of the first black athletes to break the color barriers in professional sports is that white men wrote most of it. How can a white man do justice to the pain a suffering of a black man who is being persecuted by the players on the opposing teams as well as his own teammates and fans because of the color of his skin?

Racism in Horseracing

That being the case, why did we not hear about the racism in the sport of thoroughbred horseracing? According to a passage of scripture from the Bible, "the first shall be last and the last shall be first". This is why the first professional sport in America to hire black athletes was thoroughbred horseracing. It is also the last sport in America to get any attention for the horrible working conditions and the racist practices and attitudes of the white people that manage it. Some people on the "Back Side" of racing live and work in conditions that compare to the description of slave quarters. Why is it that no one has ever taken an up close and personal look at the "Back Side" or stable area of the sport of thoroughbred horse racing? Why do the black leaders that champion the fight against racial injustice in America, not direct just a little attention to the plight of the thousands of African Americans who work on the "Back Side" that are being victimized by the racist attitude of the white track owners and white track Executives in the sport of thoroughbred horseracing.

The transition from Black & White to Color

On November 3, 2002, I was watching Monday Night Football, the Green Bay Packers versus the Miami Dolphins. When they introduced the starting defense for the Packers', all eleven players were black. In the late 1960s, when I watched the Packer's win the first Super Bowl, I doubt if they had eleven African Americans on the entire team. In this November 2002 game, the Miami Dolphins had a black quarterback. In the late 1960s, no professional football teams in the U.S. that featured an African American quarterback. In Y2K2, NFL teams in Southern cities like Miami, Nashville New Orleans, and Atlanta, all with African Americans as their starting quarterbacks, 30 years prior, I never thought I would live to see the day. I often ask myself the question, why is that professional athletes and entertainers have learned to work together as a team, regardless of race and the rest of society is still having problems with the same issues surrounding racial equality in America?

Today, black athletes dominate professional basketball and football in America, and yet the overwhelming majority of the owners of professional basketball and football teams in this Country are white. On an average, black professional football and basketball player make more money than their white counterparts do. However, as we enter

2014, the number of professional sports teams has increased, yet there is not one African American majority owner of a major sports team. Yes, two black Hall of Fame NBA players, Michael Jordan, is major shareholder of the Carolina Cougars NBA team and Magic Johnson is a major shareholder of the Los Angeles Dodgers. However, they do not compare to the white men, Jerry Jones, who own the Dallas Cowboys and Robert Kraft who own the New England Patriots. In addition, the number of African American head coaches in professional basketball does reflect the percentage of black players. In 2014, African Americans make up over 70% of the players in professional basketball and football. However, blacks have never made up 70% of the management staff in the NBA or NFL. Although there has been tremendous progress in hiring African Americans for management positions in sports, we still have a long way to go before we achieve that "level playing field".

Just as it is today, black athletes dominate professional basketball and football; African American athletes dominated the sport of thoroughbred horseracing from the 1600s through the early 1900s in America. The same as it is today, the exceptions to that domination was the ownership of horses and the management of racetracks. Unfortunately, in the mid 1900s, the dominance of black jockeys and trainers disappeared from the face of thoroughbred horseracing in America, leaving just a few books and articles written by mostly white writers, to chronicle the careers of these black professional horsemen. The diminishing number of black jockeys and trainers seems to have happened without a hint of a protest from the African American community. There was not one demonstration, not one march or protest to bring attention to this tragedy. Has there ever been one article in a major sports magazine or one segment of a TV sports or news program to discuss the vanishing African American presence in the sport of thoroughbred horseracing? I wonder if Jesse Jackson realizes that the professional sport of thoroughbred horseracing ranks second to professional baseball as a spectator's sport and it has even fewer African American athletes and front office Executives than Major League Baseball.

Small in Stature: Large in Bankroll

Professional jockeys are some of the wealthiest athletes in the world; yet, they receive very little attention from the sports media. An event such as a jockey falling off a horse during a race and being seriously injured will make headlines. Racecars get more attention from the sports media than racehorses. Thoroughbred horseracing is a sport that has no season. Every day in America, at some racetrack, in some State, there is a thoroughbred horse race. There are more thoroughbred racetracks and professional jockeys in this Country than professional arenas and players for baseball, football, and basketball combined. If you check the Daily Racing Form, you would find there are only a handful of States in the U.S. that do not have a racetrack. Yet, on a National level, thoroughbred horseracing only gets the National media spotlight in the spring for the Triple Crown Races that are restricted to three year olds horses, which features the Kentucky Derby, and in the fall for the Breeders' Cup, which features the Classic for horses that three olds and up. The fact that they race 364 of the 365 days a year, with Christmas being the only day off throughout the Country, could be the reason the National sports media gave up on trying to provide daily routine cover of the events involving thoroughbred horseracing.

No Glamor on the Back Side

The sport of thoroughbred horseracing is very popular in America. When the average sports fan sees any media reports or telecasts related to horseracing, it will usually show the glamour and pageantry of the Grandstand Side or the Clubhouse Side of the sport of thoroughbred horseracing. The "Back Side" is far removed from the glamour and pageantry you see on television. Before I go any further, I need to make something very clear to my readers. I used the terms ugly and "slave like" to describe the working conditions on the "Back Side" of racing. I used the word ugly and slave like as descriptive terms, and if you have read my other books, you know that I feel the enslavement of

24

my ancestors in America was the most despicable set of circumstances that any human being ever had to endure. Nothing, and I repeat nothing, can compare to the horrors of slavery. My use of the term "slave like" should be considered in the same vain as the term "hell like", a description of something very bad. Therefore, when I use the term slave like to describe the working conditions on the "Back Side" of horseracing, you can just imagine how horrible those conditions are.

The lack of media cover may be the reason black leaders; Jesse Jackson and the late Johnnie Cochran have never looked at the racism that is running rampant in the sport of thoroughbred horseracing. In Y2K3, Johnnie received a lot of media attention when he threatened to file a lawsuit against the NFL. Mr. Cochran threatened to sue the NFL if they did not hire more African Americans as head coaches. Jesse had the cameras rolling a few years earlier when he lead a group that was protesting that black were not being hired as manager, general managers or as front office Executives in general. In my book, Johnnie will always be a hero for his defense of a black accused of killing a white woman and a Jew and winning the case when 80% of white America thought the man was guilty. For me, Jesse's greatest accomplishment in the battle for equality for African Americans was his run to be nominated as the Democratic Party's Presidential Candidate, which resulted in a record number of blacks registering to vote in this Country. Now, in my opinion, Jesse Jackson and Johnnie Cochran only shows up to support a black cause or event if they think they will get TV coverage.

I applaud both Johnnie and Jesse for their efforts in trying to improve the hiring of minorities in baseball and football. As I stated before there has been a significant improvement in the number of blacks in Executive positions in professional sports over the past few year. However, most people fail to realize that the African American candidates that qualify for jobs, as baseball or football managers, coaches or front office Executives are former black athletes who are already millionaires. All Jesse and Johnnie are doing is helping the rich get richer. What I would like for them to do is focus the power of their celebrity status on the African American that are struggling to make a living working on the "Back Side" of the Sport of Kings. I hope that this book will gain the attention of some of our more prominent black leaders and they will be inspired to look at the racial disparity in the sport of thoroughbred horseracing.

No Career Ladder for African Americans

Many white trainers and jockeys that retire from the racing end of the sport become Racing Stewards, while others retired white jockeys and trainers are hired by the track owners to fill high-level Executive positions in the front office of the racetrack. For those of you that a not familiar with the inner working of the sport of thoroughbred horseracing, a Steward in racing can be compared to a judge in a courtroom. In each State, the Racing Stewards insure that all the rules of the sport are obeyed before, during and after a thoroughbred horserace. If there are any violations of the rules, by a jockey, trainer, owner or any other person licensed to work on the racetrack, the Stewards conduct an inquiry or hearing to resolve the issue. Just as there is a Chief Judge that supervises all the other judges in the court system. A Chief Steward supervises all the other Racing Stewards at the racetrack. The point here is that in my 40 years around Maryland racing, I have never seen an African American appointed to the position of Racing Steward.

The natural progression on most jobs is to start at the bottom and work your way up to the top. I can only speak for what I have witnessed and experienced on the Maryland Racing Circuit. Yet, I would be willing to bet a month's pay that no African American has reached an Executive level position in the sport of thoroughbred horse racing after starting their career on the "Back Side". Most blacks start on the "Back Side" as a hotwalker, move from hotwalker to exercise rider or groom, from exercise rider or groom to stable foreman, from stable foreman to assistant trainer, and on the rare occasion from assistant trainer to trainer. Recently, a few African Americans have been hired to work for racetrack management or the "Association" in the Test Barn, the Starting Gate, cleaning up in the paddock after races, and working for track security and maintenance. Unlike working on the

"Back Side", jobs with the Association come with health benefits and a retirement plan. At the end of their careers to supplement what little money they receive from social security, retired "Back Side" workers usually return as freelance hotwalkers or night watchman in the stable area.

When blacks complain about the lack of African Americans in top-level Executive positions, the standard response from white Corporate America is there are no blacks that qualify for these positions. I will be the first to admit, for a long time in this Country, there were no blacks that had the knowledge, experience and education required to fill Executive positions in Corporate America. The reason for the lack of qualified African Americans for Executive positions is very simple; we were denied access to equal education. It was a crime punishable by death if a slave could read and write. After the Civil War, the white man granted us our freedom. However, for the next 100 years, which included the "JIM CROW ERA", it was illegal in most States for blacks to be educated in the same classroom as whites. Some of you may be thinking that if blacks were being educated, they would have the same opportunity as whites. Remember that I said that blacks were denied access to equal education.

Level Playing Field

The current term for an equal opportunity is a "level playing field". Some white as well as black Americans think that because of the progress that has been made in achieving racial harmony in this Country, that there is a "level playing field". Let me say this for those of you that think that the playing field is level for all Americans regardless of Race, Color, Creed or National Origin; you are probably watching the wrong game. Give a white carpenter and a black carpenter the job of building the same house. Now give the white carpenter brand new building materials, a brand new hammer, saw and nails. Now give the black carpenter building materials from a house that was recently torn down, a hammer with a broken handle, a saw with missing teeth and bent rusty nails. Now guess which carpenter will build the better house. If you think that this story is just make believe, again, you have definitely being watching the wrong game.

The story about the black and white carpenters is a perfect example of the progress of the education system in America. White students attended new schools that had the most up to date equipment and were educated using the latest edition of new textbooks. While black students attended rundown schools that had used broken down equipment and were taught from used books with missing pages that were handed down from the white schools. Like that story about the black and white carpenters, it not hard to guess which student received the better education. In 1865, if the same white men that governed this Country would give us both freedom and equality, 140 years after the Civil War, the playing field would be level for blacks in America. What is freedom without equality? The answer is being a slave without chains. In 1865, if black children would have been able to walk into the same classrooms as white children; if black men would have had the equal opportunity to compete for the same jobs as whites; and earn equal pay for doing the same job as whites, today the playing field would be level.

As of the year 2014, there has never been an African American to hold a top-level position in Racetrack Operations or as a Thoroughbred Racing Official in Maryland. Just think about it, not one black General Manager, Vice President, Racing Secretary, or Steward in over 135 years. Since the racetracks in Maryland are privately owned, the lack of diversity in management can be directly attributed to the narrow mindedness of the racetracks owners. Maryland is the home of the Preakness, the second jewel of the Triple Crown. Maryland is also the home of the National Headquarters for the NAACP. You would think that the NAACP would not allow such a blatant act of discrimination to flourish so close to home. It could be, like most African Americans, the NAACP has never been made aware of the lack of diversity in the horseracing industry in Maryland. Like my other books, I will be sending an autographed copy to the current CEO of the NAACP as soon as it is published.

Blacksmiths are not Black

More astonishing, and in my opinion an even greater act of racial discrimination, than the fact that in my 40 years on the "Back Side of the Sport of Kings" in Maryland, I have never encountered an African American Veterinarian, is the fact that I have never seen an African American Farrier, better known as a blacksmith. How ironic, all the "blacksmiths" used to shoe thoroughbred horses in Maryland are white. Should they be called "whitesmiths"? What makes this a horrendous act of discrimination is that, unlike the lack of an African American presence on the Grandstand Side of the Horse Racing Industry, there have always been masses of black workers on the "Back Side" of the Horse Racing Industry.

Why is it that when a task that was originally performed for white America by black slaves becomes a profession that commands a $60,000 to $100,000 salary, white America can no longer find qualified African Americans to perform that task? Unfortunately, due to a cultural language barrier, if you took a survey in the stable area of the racetracks in Maryland and asked a groom or hotwalker if they knew the name of a good Farrier, you would probably get a blank stare or they would just tell you no. Yet, if you asked the same groom or hotwalker if they knew the name of a good blacksmith, without a moment's hesitation they would give you a name.

Just as it was with jockeys, thoroughbred horse trainers, and health care providers for racehorses, from the early 1600s to the 1800s, African Americans trained, rode, groomed, provided the health care and they took care of all the equipment needed for their white masters' thoroughbred horses to race, which included horseshoes. In 2014, it is an insult to black slaves that put shoes on thoroughbred horses that African American are not hired as blacksmiths on the "Back Side" of racetracks in Maryland. The white masters taught my black slave ancestors the skills required for molding metal into a horseshoe and to nail those shoes to a horse's foot without causing any damage to the foot its' self. After being taught these skills, the old slave "Blacksmith" passed his knowledge on to the next young black slave who would someday take his place.

Over the years, the equipment used in the sport of horseracing has evolved as in all other sports. A perfect example of the evolution of sports equipment is the comparison of a baseball glove and football helmet used in the 1940s to the gloves and helmets used today. Every athlete wants his or her equipment to be lightweight, durable, and better than whatever was used in the past. The same rules apply to the sport of horseracing. In America why are the words "better", "improved", and "high-tech" only associated with white people. Should we change the "Made in America" label to "Made in white America"? I do not have a problem with progress or the fact that over time, technical advances result in better products.

Same Job Same Pay

What I do have a problem with is that African Americans are not given the same opportunities as white Americans to advance with the times. Why is it that progress and technical advances in America has never been a favorable experience for blacks? After being in this Country for over 400 years, why could an African American not have been the first Astronaut? Blacks become the beneficiaries of new technology in America after whites are sure that the technology will not have an impact on the balance of power. Just as the designers of modern basketball, football and baseball shoes, the modern farrier attends school to study the anatomy of the athlete, the thoroughbred horse, to determine how the design of the shoes effects each individual horse's running style. During the transition from slaves to free men, blacks were not provided the training required to operate the equipment required to mold the updated styles horseshoes. Today's white Farriers belong to an exclusive fraternity and that fraternity excludes African Americans.

African American athletes play a prominent role in most of the popular sports in the U.S. In addition, the average black consumer spends millions of dollar on sportswear and equipment. Therefore, it is no surprise that the major sports equipment companies in America employ large numbers of black people throughout their organizations. African Americans serve as President, Vice President, CEO's and board members for sporting good chains such as Converse, Nike and Adidas. In 2014, African Americans have started to invest in professional team sports. As we enter 2014 a group of black men purchased an NBA franchise and have an own a professional racecar team. I believe that in the very near future more African Americans will start to invest in the sport of thoroughbred horseracing and become owners of horses that compete in the Triple Crown and Breeders' Cup races. When more blacks become involved in ownership, the color of the faces that hold front office positions in the sports will change. In addition, there will be substantial increases in the racial diversity of the men and women who work on the "Back Side" as trainer, jockeys, veterinarians and farriers.

Why is it that more African American did not become Veterinarians? The answer is simple. In order to compete as an animal doctor, you needed access to equal higher education, which was denied to black Americans until after the WWII. When equal access to education was granted, you needed a license to practice and that was denied in most States until the mid-1960s. When African American Veterinarians received a license to practice, they very rarely if ever would be called upon to treat expensive thoroughbred horse. Just as the negative media attention given to white owners of professional baseball, basketball and football teams that would not sign a black quarterback, hire an African American coach or manager, or hire a black Executive in the front office, things have changed and racial diversity is the now a growing trend in the major sports. However, racial diversity has not found its way to the "Sport of Kings".

Dr. Roger D. Estep

Please do not let me give you the wrong impression about the lack of black veterinarians in the State of Maryland. On the contrary, one of the most prestigious Doctors of Veterinary Medicine in American history, Roger D. Estep, an African American, was born in Clarksville, Maryland. Dr. Estep received a Bachelor of Science Degree from my alma mater, Maryland State College in 1951 and a Master of Science Degree in 1957 from Pennsylvania State University. He served as an Instructor of Poultry Husbandry at Pennsylvania State College from 1957 to 1958. In 1962, Dr. Estep earned his Doctorate in Veterinary Medicine from Tuskegee Institute.

After receiving his PhD, Roger Estep joined the faculty of the Howard University College of Medicine. He was appointed Research Veterinarian and Instructor of Physiology. In 1965 through 1966, Dr. Estep was President of the National Capital Area Branch of the American Association for Laboratory Animal Science. He has been a member of the Board of Directors of the American Association for Laboratory Animal Science and of its Executive Committee since 1967, serving as President in 1971. In 1970 Dr. Estep became Executive Assistant to the Vice President for Health Affairs at Howard University. In 1971, he was appointed Executive Assistant to the President of Howard University. In 1971, Dr. Estep became the Director for the Division of Research Services for the National Institutes of Health. In 1989, Dr. Estep became Howard University Vice President for Development and Vice President for University Relations. He is also a member of the Council on Accreditation of the American Association for the Accreditation of Laboratory Animal Care and other professional organizations. He serves or has served on several Federal Councils or Committees, including the Intergovernmental Ad Hoc Committee of the National Academy of Sciences.

The amazing thing about the information that I just provided you about Dr. Roger D. Estep is that as a young man in my late teens and early 20s, I hung out with members of Dr. Estep's family. At that the time, I did not know about Dr. Estep or about any of his many accomplishments. The Estep's are a very large family that lived in the Howard County communities of Guilford, Simpsonville, and Clarksville. What used to be rural black communities have now become the suburbs of the large metropolitan area of Columbia, Maryland. The fact that I never really knew any of the important facts about Dr. Estep life until

I conducted the research for this book is another example of why we need African American history written from the perspective of someone like me. Dr. Estep grew up in Clarksville, which is about 10 miles North of Laurel Race Course. With this famous doctor, and native son of Maryland living so close to the racetrack, you would think that the track owners or top-level Executives would have invited him to be a consultant for their track veterinarians. In all my years at the racetrack, I have never seen a black veterinarian. I have seen a number of female veterinarians at racetracks in Maryland. A female veterinarian was actually the Chief State Veterinarian for years at Maryland racetracks.

Old Remedies

My slave ancestors treated sick horses by using remedies that were passed down from one generation of slaves to the next. I am very familiar with remedies passed down from one generation to the next. My grandparents, who raised me, treated me with all sorts of homemade medicine when I was sick. Today, the black grooms on the "Back Side" use remedies that have been passed along to them from the "Old Timers", to cure horses of everything from ulcers to muscle soreness. I watched my uncle, Charlie Hall treat a horse with over the counter medications used for people. When it worked, the white veterinarians started prescribing the same mediation and billing the trainer for treatments and medication that could have been purchased at the local drug store. It should come as to no surprise to African Americans that the same home remedies used by black slaves to cure sick horses, has now become the sophisticated treatments used by expensive white veterinarians who have patented these home remedies and now sell them and make millions of dollars. If you are a student of American history, you are already aware of the many inventions, i.e., medicines, herbs, and other remedies that were discovered by African and Native Americans that have been stolen by the white man. It was easy to steal an invention from a Native or African American because the U.S. Patent Office would only take applications for patents from white people.

Earlier, I talked about betting on horses. According to published reports, did you know that over 10 billion dollar is wagered on horseracing; that over 60 million patrons attend thoroughbred racetracks in the U.S; and that the 10 billion dollar wagered on horseracing does not include the annual revenue that thoroughbred racetracks receive for parking, admissions, and concessions? A trip to the racetrack may not be as expensive as going to a baseball game, but it is very close. Reportedly, the thoroughbred racing industry, and the State and Federal Government each make at least 14 to 25% of the revenues, approximately 15 billion dollars a year, generated from thoroughbred horseracing. With all the money generated in the U.S. by the racing industry, you would think everyone associated with the sport would be making a decent salary. Yet the black and minority workers on the "Back Side" of the Sport of Kings are barely surviving.

Back to the Plantation

After the Civil War many freed slaves returned to the plantation. There is very little documentation to support the actual transition of black slaves to paid employees in the South after the Civil War. The main reasons black slaves returned to the plantation was fear of the unknown, they were not readily accepted by white America and in most cases, and they had no other place to go. Black slaves were denied the right to an education. Their skills limited by the fact that their white masters only taught them how to operate equipment necessary to maintain the plantation. Therefore, farming and taking care of livestock were the only opportunities available to former black slaves. Also, let us not forget that thousands of freed black slaves were taken captive by white bounty hunters and forced to return to the plantation. If they refused to cooperate with these bounty hunters or if they tried to escape, these free African Americans were killed. After the Civil War, black slaves were given their freedom, but were they free?

Throughout America, wherever there was a need for cheap labor to harvest crops, you would find thousands of migrant workers. I watched documentaries on TV about lifestyle of migrant workers,

34

living in trailers and tent cities as they move from place to place to find work. The reporters that have done stories on the plight of the migrant worker have also used the term "slave like" to describe the working conditions for migrant workers. The reason U.S. Labor Department and the U.S. Immigration Department have not conducted investigations into the sub-standard working conditions of migrant workers in America is the same reason the Government choose not to investigate the working conditions that former slaves were subjected to after the Civil War. That was because at one point the majority of the migrant workers were either African American or illegal immigrants and neither group had a strong base of voter participation in this Country.

Before I upset the other minority races such as the Hispanic and Native Americans that work the "Back Side" of thoroughbred horseracing, I have not forgotten you and I know that you face many of the same problems as African Americans. I also realize that Hispanic, Black and Native Americans need to come together to end racial discrimination in the U.S. As a black American, I can only feel your pain from a black perspective. I am a firm believer in allowing all races and colors of Americans to tell their own stories from their own perspectives. For me to try to write about the plight of Hispanic and Native Americans in the Country would be the same as the white man writing about how African American survived slavery. I encourage other minorities to write their own American History.

Minimum Wage

Today the term "Minimum Wage" is a very recognizable phrase in America. Do you think the freed black slaves that returned to the plantation were ever considered eligible for a minimum wage? After the Civil War, there was a slow gradual change in the way African Americans were treated in U.S. Make sure you put heavy emphasis on the slow and gradual when it comes to the way change occurred. For the former slaves that returned to the plantation, the only difference was that their white masters no longer legally owned them and they could not be legally bought and sold on the open market. Note I said legally, because the illegal trading of black workers for profit continued long after the 14th Amendment to the U.S. Constitution became the law of the land. In 1938, the Fair Labor Standards Act or Wages and Hour Act was passed by the U.S. Congress to establish minimum living standards for workers engaged directly or indirectly in Interstate Commerce. A major provision of the act was establishment of a minimum wage. The initial minimum wage was 25 cent an hour with a maximum workweek of 44 hours. The maximum workweek was later changed to 40 hours. The Fair Labor Standards Act has been amended repeatedly, with changes expanding the classes of workers covered; raising the minimum wage; redefining regular-time and overtime, and equalizing pay scales for men and women. Unfortunately, like most of the laws passed in the U.S., they are delayed and modified when it comes to having a positive impact and improving the quality of life in the African American community.

Remembering Curt Flood

The former professional baseball player, the late Curt Flood, who played centerfield for St Louis Cardinals, used the comparison to being slaves when he sued Major League Baseball over Free Agency in 1970. Much like the black slaves, prior to free agency, professional athletes that played for teams in America, were the property of the team owner, and could be bought and sold at any time. However, unlike my black slave ancestors, prior to free agency professional athletes were paid a very good salary to play a game, and they were treated like royalty. Prior to free agency, the average salary for a professional athlete was around $30, 000 higher than the average salary for most Americans. The lawsuit filed by Curt Flood against Major League Baseball was not about the money. It was about freedom and the right to choose. The same applied to my African American ancestors. It was not about working for the white man for no wages. It was about not having the right to choose and the loss of freedom that made the enslavement of blacks such a horrific event in American History.

Mr. Flood sacrificed his career as a Major League Baseball player to fight for freedom and choice for all professional athletes. In his lawsuit, Curt Flood said that he felt like a slave. At the time, he filed a lawsuit, Curt was making close to $100,000 a year. I support, applaud and admire what Curt Flood did for professional athletes in America. What I cannot support is Curt Flood comparing his right to choose where he plays a game with the freedom taking from my ancestors when they were sold into slavery. Just imagine Curt Flood felt like a slave making $100,000 a year. If my African American ancestors had received ½ the average income of white America during the time they were slaves; most black people would be rich today and the need for reparation would be nonexistent.

In his lifetime, Mr. Flood may have witnessed many acts of injustice against African Americans, which included being beaten, lynched and denied equal rights. As African Americans, whenever we witness a horrible act by a white man committed against a black person or feel that the white man has treated us less that than a human being, we compare it to the most awful experience in the history of black Americans, and that is being a slave. However, no matter how horrendous these acts of injustice were, they were done to black people who were free men and women and not slaves. The word "slave" is something horrible. Based on the stories passed down from my family, the only slave like conditions that still exist in America is the migrant worker and the black people who work on the "Back Side of the Sport of Kings".

The low salaries earned by the men and women that work on the "Back Side" of horse racing is a very serious issue and I will address later in this book. However, first I need to look at the slave like conditions that these men and women work. I often speak of slavery in America in the year 2014. However, it is not the same as the slavery of the pre-Civil War Era. Before the end of the Civil War, slavery kept my black ancestors in iron chains and put scars on their backs from the whips of their white masters. Yet, the modern era of slavery in America is still restricted to black people. The chains that bind blacks in America are no longer on our legs; but they are on our mind and spirit. The leather whips used by the white masters to put lashes on our backs has been replaced with the white man's total lack of respect and their demeaning attitudes, which leaves scars on our minds. Black slaves that returned to plantation after the Civil War and worked with the white plantation owner's thoroughbred racehorses were given little more than room and board in exchange for their services. Today, on the "Back Side" of the sport thoroughbred horse racing, black exercise riders, grooms and hot-walkers are allowed to supplement their incomes by living in the stable area. Like their slave ancestors, the rooms used by the modern black racetrack worker are over the barn. At some of the racetracks, rooms are actually on the same level as the horses. I love the smell of the stable area, but I would not want to go to bed each night and wake up to that smell every morning. Having black stable employees live in the stable area is an example of another tradition carried over from slavery.

Racism is still alive and well

Racism still exists in professional sports, including the National Football League. For over 35 years, black players have filled the majority of the rooster spots on professional football teams in the U.S. and they deserve respect from the white owners. If the old Southern plantation mentality in this Country did not exist, white team owners would routinely hire black men to manager teams that are made up of approximately 65% to 75% African Americans. As it does in all other aspects of American society, racism still exist in professional sports, including the National Football League, where for over 25 years, black players have filled the majority of the roster spots on professional football teams in the U.S. and they demand respect from the white owners. As an example of the influence of black professional football players, it was rumored that the NFL failed to award the State of Arizona the opportunity to host another Super Bowl based on the fact that the State did not honor Martin Luther King's birthday as a State or National Holiday.

However, shortly after the State changed its' stance on MLK and decided to celebrate his birthday as a holiday, the Super Bowl was once again played in Sun Devil Stadium in Arizona. As was the case with the bus boycott by African Americans in Mississippi, the potential loss of millions of dollars changed the minds of the white voters in the State of Arizona. These boycotts, by the black players in the NFL and the black citizens of Mississippi, accomplished their intended goals of MLK's birthday being declared a holiday, in a State that, in my opinion did not feel a black man deserved to have a State or National Holiday in his honor. Black citizens of Mississippi gained the right to sit in bus seats that had traditionally been reserved for white passengers only.

These boycotts, by the black players in the NFL and the black citizens of Mississippi, accomplished their intended goals of MLK's birthday being declared a holiday in Arizona and Mississippi. In my opinion, white people in these States did not feel a black man deserved to have a State or National Holiday in his honor. A boycott by the black citizens of Mississippi earned them the right to sit in bus seats that had traditionally been reserve for white passengers only. The other and just as important result of these boycotts was the respect black people gained from white America. The use of a boycott by a small group of African Americans sent a message to White America that was very loud and very clear. Black people can band together as a group to defeat the oppression, bigotry and injustice of the racially motivation actions of white America. White America can forget their racial prejudice to cheer for black American athletes, entertainers, war heroes, and other blacks that have achieved some form of celebrity. They can also forget their racial prejudice if it means losing money.

Boycott the Derby

It is advertised as the greatest two minutes in sports because more people watch the Kentucky Derby than any other sporting event in the world. Celebrities from around the globe, Kings, Queens, Presidents, movie stars, etc., have made personal appearances at the Kentucky Derby. People pay more attention to this thoroughbred horse race than Major League Baseball's World Series and the NFL's Super Bowl. Yet, over the past 40 year this major sporting event that was once the showcase for black jockeys, has shown very limited participation by African Americans. Between 1875 –1902, African American jockeys won 15 of 28 Kentucky Derbies. I In 1989, Hank Allen, former professional baseball player, became the first African American trainer in 78 years to saddle a horse in the Kentucky Derby when Northern Wolf ran sixth to winner Sunday Silence. The lack of a visible African American presence on the at the Kentucky Derby is probably why the white management and owners of Churchill Downs Racetrack can get away with waving the Confederate Flag and playing "My Ole Kentucky Home" during the post parade which are both insults to the black ancestors of African slaves.

Do you really think that the white managers and owners of Churchill Downs Racetrack or any other white official in the State of Kentucky care if African Americans are offended by the playing of "My Ole Kentucky Home" at the Kentucky Derby? I will explain why the song is an insult to African Americans later in this chapter. I would love to see the expression on the faces of these same white managers and owners of Churchill Downs if Jesse Jackson or the late Johnnie Cochran decided to look into whether the playing of the song "My Ole Kentucky Home" was appropriate for a public sporting event. What do you think would happen, if Jesse showed up at the Kentucky Derby, leading a group of protesters and got National media coverage to address this racially sensitive of the song "My Ole Kentucky Home" being as an insult to African Americans? Can you imagine the look on a white judge's face in Louisville, Kentucky if the late Johnnie Cochran had walked into his court to file an injunction to stop the playing of "My Ole Kentucky Home" at the Kentucky Derby?

An Insult to the 1st Jockeys to Win the Derby

Let me explain why the song, "My Ole Kentucky Home" is offensive and insulting to African Americans." In 1929, "My Kentucky Home" written by Stephen Foster in 1853, was adopted as the State song of Kentucky. The lyrics, *"Oh, the sun shines bright in the old Kentucky home, 'tis summer, the darkies are gay."* These lyrics suggest that the "darkies" a derogatory term used for black slaves, were actually happy working in the field in the hot sun. Regardless of what race you are, you would have to be crazy to be happy working outside for no pay in the heat of the summer. I wonder if they took away Stephen Foster's freedom, forced him to work in the hot sun, and raped his wife and daughters, would he be gay. Americans fight and die for freedom. How could anyone think a man could be happy without it?

In America, white people pay an abhorrent amount of money for tickets and they pack the stands and stadiums to see talented black athletes play a game. These talented black athletes are paid a lot of money, but they make even more money for the white team owners of sports teams and for the white Corporate Executives of companies who use these same black athletes to endorse their products. Ride through the parking lot of professional sporting events in Atlanta, Georgia, New Orleans, Louisiana or Charlotte, North Carolina and you will see as many Confederate Flag bumper stickers on car and trucks as you would at the Kentucky Derby. The reason you will not see them inside the arena for these sporting events is the impact African American athletes have on that sports revenues. The dollar sign gives black professional athletes the power to command the respect of white team owners. The leading source of revenue in the State of Kentucky is the thoroughbred racing industry. White people control the majority of that revenue. The fact that the African Americans in Kentucky that work in that industry are manual laborers, who earn less than $30,000, equates to black not having any power or respect in the racing industry in Kentucky.

Why not play the song?

The playing of "My Ole Kentucky Home" is an established tradition at the Kentucky Derby. I guess some of you might be asking the question; why should they not play Kentucky's State Song at the most prestigious event held in that State? The answer is that before, after or during the event/game, no other major professional sport in the U.S. honors the memory of the Civil War and slavery. What do you think would happen if the Seattle Seahawks and the Denver Broncos met in the 2014 Super Bowl in New York and as part of the pre-game ceremony they played "Dixie" over the loud speakers and the players from each team had to run on to the field carrying a Confederate Flag? Just imagine, football players waving little Confederate Flags as they run on to the field. What makes this even more amazing and even harder to imagine is that at least 80 of the 106 players are African American. I do not want you to spend a lot of time thinking about this scenario because it will never happen. Even if all the games were played in the Deep South, if the white owners of NFL teams attempted to force black football players to march around carrying a Confederate Flag, the Super Bowl would never be played in the U.S.

Today, most of the African Americans that work on the "Back Side of the Sport of Kings" earn approximately $9.00 an hour and they work from 6 am until 1 pm, 365 days a year with no days off and no holidays. If not for my inability to describe the horrors endured by my slave ancestors, and it would be disrespectful to their memory, you might say that the only difference between being a slave and working on the "Back Side" are that slaves had longer hours. Slaves were paid less and did not have the right to choice their profession. Like former black slaves, "Back Side" workers are required to report for duty in the blazing heat or freezing cold. Like the U.S. Postman, nothing is to keep the "Back Side" workers from their appointed rounds. However, unlike the Postman, the "Back Side" workers or the black slaves did not have a Labor Union to protect them and if they miss one day of work a year, they could be fired and sometimes are fired for missing one day's work.

In 1986, Japanese students visiting the Kentucky General Assembly sang the song as a gesture of respect, but Carl Hines, a Democrat, and the only black State Representative at the time, was quoted as saying that the lyrics "convey connotations of racial discrimination that are not acceptable". Within days, Hines sponsored House Resolution 159, which revised the lyrics to "My Kentucky Home" and changed the word "darkies" to "people" at all official State functions involving the performance of the song. Am I missing something here? Is the word

42

"darkies" the only thing that makes this song offensive to the black people of Kentucky? In my opinion, the black citizens of Kentucky should conduct a boycott of the businesses, which include the race-tracks, until the State Song is changed and the racist "My Kentucky Home" would be gone forever. This action would be similar to the boycott conducted by the black citizens of South Carolina to have the Confederate Flag removed from atop the State Capital Building. The State of South Carolina lost millions of dollars when many of their black citizens refused to shop in the State during the 2007 Christmas holiday season. It is my hope that if enough blacks from Kentucky read my book, they will conduct a boycott to have the State Song changed.

"The young folks roll on the little cabin floor, all merry, all happy and bright." The reference to the "young folks" is young black slaves. Young African American slaves, who were old enough, worked in the fields alongside their parents. Black slave children that were too young to work in the field stayed behind with a nanny, who nursed and took care of the masters' white children as well as their own. Based on my own experience of working in the fields all day during the summer, when I got home, I took off my clothes, took a bath a laid down under the shade tree. In my opinion, the only logical things that my black slave ancestors did at night was eat and sleep; the young slaves, when they were done working, would have been too tired to roll on the floor. In addition, the slave cabins were shabby wooden shacks with dirt floors. If for some unimaginable reason, young slaves wanted to roll in the dirt, they could have stayed outside and rolled in the dirt.

"*They hunt no more for the possum and the coon, On the meadow, the hill and the shore, they sing no more by the glimmer of the moon, on the bench by the old cabin door.*" After working in the field all day, slaves would go out at night to trap possums and raccoons to add to their stew pots because they rarely got meat from their white masters. Notice that Foster made a point of mentioning that only black slaves ate opossum and raccoons, which was meat that no self-respecting white Southern would ever think about putting on their table. Foster's reference to my black slave ancestors singing outside their cabins at night was not for the entertainment of their white masters. The only singing done by slaves was spirituals, sung as prayers to God to end their suffering and to give direction to runaway slaves. If runaway slaves were close enough to a plantation to hear singing, they knew they had to go in the opposite direction to avoid being captured and to escape to the North to freedom. I cannot get over the fact that white people actual believed African slaves were singing because they were happy. I am glad the white slave masters never figured out that the songs being song by slaves were both prayers to God, and signals to help runaway slaves find their way North.

"The head must bow and the back will have to bend, wherever the darkey may go." The fact that blacks had to keep their heads bowed and their backs bent should have made it clear that my ancestors were not happy. Even more offensive than the use of the word "darkey" is the fact that whenever black people were in the company of, or about to approach a white person, slaves had to bow their heads. Something that should be added to your history lessons; slaves could actually be lynched or shot on sight for merely looking into the eyes of a white person. Can you imagine being punished just for making eye contact with someone of a different race? This song was written in 1853, and yet in the year 2014 there are still areas in the Deep South in America where black men are still afraid to look a white person in the eyes for fear they might be lynched or shot. Why a State would select and continue to support a song that has lyrics that preserve racist customs is unbelievable. To have African Americans bow their heads to show respect and fear for the white people. This is an indication that the State of Kentucky has no respect for African Americans and has no fear of what actions the black community might take to remove the song.

1998: James Byrd lynched in Jasper Texas

By the way, for those of you who think that white men are not still lynching African Americans and that lynching is a thing of the past in the U.S.; just remember that in 1998, a black man was lynched in Jasper, Texas. For a white Southerner like Stephen Foster, that fact the he pictured black slaves bowing their heads, and shuffling along and grinning for the white man was natural. As slaves, my African American ancestors bowed their heads, and did whatever else they needed to do to survive. Maybe if James Byrd, bowed his head, grinned, shuffled along as he walked and spoke in a "yassa boss" tone to the white men who stopped him on the road, he would still be alive in Jasper Texas. How could anyone in the State, white or black, think that Stephen Foster wrote this song to be equally complementary to both the white and black citizens of Kentucky? Stephen Foster never thought a "darkey" as ever being his equal; never thought of a black man as ever sharing the same rights, voting, owning property, or being educated. In 1853 when he wrote this song, Stephen Foster had no idea that someday the African Americans that he looked down on all his life as slaves would be free men.

"*A few more days, and the trouble all will end, in the field where the sugarcanes grow. A few more days for to tote the weary load, no matter, 'twill never be light, a few more days till we totter on the road, then my old Kentucky home good night.*" In his song, Foster was talking about eventually growing old and dying, which would cause him to leave his Old Kentucky Home. These lyrics clearly indicate that Stephen Foster thought, even in death, that blacks would always carry the burden of being slaves. However, rather than look at these ending lyrics as a negative, in my mind this became the only bright spot, in what were extremely narrow-minded lyrics. For me, the only enjoyable moment garnered from this song is that as early as 1853, the sad heartedness in the final lyrics of Stephen Foster's "My Ole Kentucky Home", may have been the result of him envisioning the beginning of the Civil War and the end of slavery in America.

Unfortunately, there are still blacks that feel they need to continue in the traditional behavior of slaves on the old plantation in order to survive life in America. These African American feel they have to shuffle along and grin whenever they encounter the white man or they will suffer the same consequences as the black slaves of the past. It does not help the plight of African Americans that there are just as many whites today that practice the same racist traditions that were the described in the lyric written by Stephen Foster in 1853. To add insult to injury to the African Americans that live in Kentucky, the white managers and owners of Churchill Downs Racetrack are so proud of Stephen Foster that they named a graded stakes race in his honor. I wonder if they considered having an African American present the trophy to the winner.

For us in the black community, racists are a dying breed in America, which realize that the days of the white racist dominance will soon be over; most of white America that still practice racism are as sad Stephen Foster was when he realized his days on the Old Kentucky Home were slowly dwindling. I hope that they are just as sad and one day and like Stephen Foster, these white racists will be just as dead. What upsets me most, about the flying of the Confederate Flag and songs like "Dixie" and "My Ole Kentucky Home", is that they keep this slave owner mentality alive. As long as there are a few racists with violent tempers that still support the old Southern traditions, black people will continue to be the victims of random acts of racially motivated violence and discrimination.

I have made this point in each of my other books; I cannot and do not place all the blame on the white man for the racism and racial discrimination in America. There are facts that are not part of your mainstream history lesson and are not a frequent or popular topic of conversation in the black community that must be considered when we discuss who was responsible for the spread of racism in America. Facts, those included, but were not limited to, such actions as, Africans selling other Africans to white slave traders. Black slaves that worked in the white masters' mansion feeling they were superior to the black slaves that worked in the fields. Black slaves taking pride in the fact that they were being used by their white masters to catch and return other runaway slaves to the plantation. Black slaves fought with the Confederate Army against the Union soldiers that were fighting and dying to win black slaves their freedom. These facts need to be included in Black History classes. Like most other aspect of history, these negative actions by African Americans, which helped to support racism and racial discrimination in this Country in the past, are being repeated by blacks today.

As I have stated before, when my ancestors were first brought to this Country as slaves they did whatever they had to in order to survive in white America. After the Civil War, my freed black ancestors had to do whatever they could in order to survive the "JIM CROW" laws that governed white America. As African Americans entering 2014, we should rejoice in the fact that "JIM CROW" is dead and we no longer have to do whatever it takes just to survive in America. When it comes to race, there may not be a totally level playing field in the U.S., but we now all get to play in the same game. We have the white supporters of Apartheid on the run. However, as African Americans we still have to face the question, when will the last generation of blacks, who continue to exhibit this slave like behavior in America, cease to exist? For some black people who suffer from the disease of low self-esteem, continuing to live the life of servants of white masters may never end. In my book, *"No Land No Mule No Freedom"*, I made the point that racism is a disease, and that this disease affects blacks and whites equally, and this disease can and will be cured. As a proud African American male, I fully support the need to pass on the history of slavery in America to our children so that they may in time, pass it on to theirs. However, the demeaning behavior that comes along with having a slave's mentality must die.

Born In the USA

If I were born in America prior to 1865, I would have been a slave. If I were born during the early 1900s, the "JIM CROW ERA", I would have made the same adjustments that ever African American in this Country made or I would have been lynched or murdered the same way that millions of blacks were killed in the past. However, in the year 2014, there is no excuse for any black man or women to allow the white man to physically and mentally treat them like slaves. The reason I can say this is that Federal and State laws have been changed to make overt acts of obvious racism in the work environment a crime. In addition, the Civil Rights Movement united blacks in America for the cause of fighting for racial equality and freedom. Before the days of the National Association for the Advancement of Colored People (NAACP), Martin Luther King and Medgar Evers, blacks in America were unable to form an army to help fight the battle for freedom and racial equality. The NAACP, along with the media and strong black political leaders, will not allow the blatant acts of racism from our past to be part of the future of African Americans in the U.S. During the "JIM CROW ERA", an angry mob of white men would have stormed the courtroom and with very little resistance from law, enforcement and they would have lynched O.J. Simpson, the accused murderer of a white woman and a white man.

"Boy" was better than the "N" word

If the practice of racism in the work place is a crime, why does it still exist in some place and not others; like on the "Back Side" of the sport of thoroughbred horses racing? Have you ever seen the movies that feature Dinosaurs and have a theme such as the "Land that time forgot"? Well the Back Side of the racetrack, as well as a few other isolated areas in America, is a part of the Sport of Kings that time forgot. When it comes to how white people are allowed to treat African Americans on the "Back Side", most of the old rules of the "JIM CROW ERA" still apply. The white thoroughbred horse owners and trainers still refer to grown black men as "boys". It is commonplace for a white owner/trainer to approach a group of black men on the "Back Side" and shout, "One of you boys come take this horse." It is just as commonplace for a white trainer/owner to use the "N" word when they get angry with an African American worker on the "Back Side". Just to make it clear, the "N" word stands for "nigger", in case you have been living in a cave for the past 20 years.

The sport of thoroughbred horseracing and the enslavement of my African ancestors started in America around the same time. The Civil War ended the physical and legal act of the enslavement of blacks in America. However, as I write this book, I am 65 years old. Over the past 40 years, I have met black men that are old enough to be my father, who work on the "Back Side of the Sport of Kings" and shuffle, grin and yassa boss, whenever they come in contact with a white man. I am not talking about black men who live and work in the Deep South. These African Americans work and live in the Mid-Atlantic State of Maryland. They live in the Baltimore and Washington D.C. Metropolitan Area. The population in these cities is predominately African American. In this region, we have the added protection against racial violence of having the Chief of Police for Baltimore City and Washington D.C. both being African Americans. In this area, we have large numbers of black representatives in State and Local Government, as well as one of the largest alliances of black clergy in America. This being the case, why do some African Americans continue to exhibit the mentality of a black slave?

At Pimilco Racetrack, a white female trainer who actually bragged to anyone would listen about how she used a buggy whip to discipline a black male worker who was guilty of abusing a horse. This trainer would have used her buggy whip if the perpetrator of the crime were white, black, red or green. Unfortunately, the issue is that the whipping of a black man by a white woman with a buggy whip brings back the haunting images of slavery and the "JIM CROW ERA". This incident involving the white female trainer should have been reported to track management and there should have been an investigation. Yet, all that happened is what usually happens on the "Back Side" or in the slave quarters. That is talk, more talk and some posturing and speculation by the white bosses that they would have done the same thing if they caught a man abusing a horse, and the African American workers on the "Back Side" making threats of doing physical harm to any white person that would try to hit them with a whip. Although there was no racial motive on the part of the white female trainer, the posturing from both groups is based on the white man's slave ownership mentality and the black man's mentality of being the white man's slave. Unlike the early day of slavery in America, the white man's threatening words usually resulted in harsher physical punishment and even death for some blacks. Today, the threats of the white man result in the firing of blacks or more work and less pay.

Today in the Deep South, like their African American ancestors did for over 300 years, blacks continue in the jobs that were at one time performed strictly by slaves. They still work in the fields, picking cotton, chopping tobacco and sugar cane. As it was during the days of slavery in the Deep South, African Americans are doing most of the manual-labor that involved working outside and enduring the elements in the South. There was a time in America when manual laborers, such as carpenters, bricklayers, auto mechanics and assembly line workers did not make a lot of money. The forming of a strong organized labor force or unions changed the wages and working conditions for most of the manual labor workforce. Unions made Corporate Executives respect the demands of the manual labor force. Unfortunately, the black manual labor force in the Deep South and on the "Back Side" of horseracing has failed to organize. Due to their lack of organization, African Americans have failed to gain the respect of white Corporate Executives in the Agriculture and Horse Racing Industries.

When I was growing up every male member of my immediate family, which included both grandfathers worked on the railroad. Naturally, I thought that when I was old enough I would follow in the footsteps of the other males in my family and work on the railroad. Until I was about ten years old, I enjoyed the luxury and thrill of riding the train with my grandparent for free from Baltimore City to Pittsburgh, to New Jersey, to New York and to Cleveland. I used to dream about being the engineer on a train. Although the majority of the manual labor-ers during my grandfather's days on the railroad were black, jobs like being an engineer or conductor on a train were limited to white men only. Like other manual laborer unions, in the early 1960s, the African American members of Brotherhood of Railroad Worker and Pullman Porters became a force to be reckoned with in America. Jobs like train engineers and conductors were now being filled by African Americans. However, shortly after the black members of the union gained power and respect, the complexion of railroad workers in America changed from predominantly black to mostly white.

Fortunately, for me, it was about the same time that I realized that African Americans could not get jobs like Engineers or Conductors on trains. I realized that I did not have a work ethic that was conducive to working on the railroad or at any form of manual labor. Many young people follow in the footsteps of their parents when it comes to choosing an occupation. Like their fathers and mothers before them, these young people become doctors, lawyers, police officers and fire fighters. Based on my experience, most of the African Americans that work on the "Back Side" have followed in the footsteps of members of their family. African Americans have worked on the "Back Side" of thoroughbred racing for over 400 years. The fact that black workers choose to continue the tradition of working on the "Back Side" is acceptable. What is not acceptable is that any group of African Americans chooses to continue the tradition of allowing the white people in the sport of thoroughbred horseracing to treat them like their slave ancestors.

Chapter 2

AMERICA'S 1ˢᵀ SPORTS SUPER STARS

The best all-around athletes in the sport of thoroughbred horseracing and a critical partner in the success of all racehorses are jockeys and exercise riders. During the same time in history of thoroughbred horseracing when slaves were jockeys, they also performed the duties of exercise rider. Being an exercise rider is a highly specialized position that requires a ton of experience and athletic ability. It is the exercise riders, who works with horses on a daily basis and provides critical insight and feedback to trainers and owners on the attitude, feel, and quirks of each horse. Most thoroughbred horse trainers require that an exercise rider weigh between 120 to 135 pounds. Most trainers will also tell you that a good exercise rider is worth their weight in gold. The trainer may give specific instructions to an exercise rider as to what to do with each horse when their sent out to the track to train. However, it is very difficult for 120 - 135 lb. exercise riders to control the behavior of a 1,800 – 2,000 lb. animal that has a brain the size of a walnut, the temperament of a 2-year-old child and the explosive power of a racecar.

Exercise Rider

An exercise rider must be experienced at riding horses at extremely high speeds under potentially dangerous conditions. The remarkable talent and athleticism of jockeys and exercise riders is in the strength and agility they possess in their hands, arms, and legs, which allows them to control horses during the 20 to 25 minutes they spend on the training track. Jockeys and exercise riders use their hands and legs to control a horse's speed and direction and all professional riders have the physical ability to handle a horse as they go through their basic daily workout on the racetrack. The special talent or gift is the exercise rider that gets on the same horse every day and can develop a relationship with that horse that allows that exercise rider to communicate just how the horse is feeling to the trainer. The key to success is for the exercise rider to follow the trainer's instructions and make the horse do what the trainer feels is necessary to condition the horse. However, an experienced exercise rider, based on their knowledge of each horse, will make a determination on the racetrack and make adjustments based on what they needs to be done with each horse to achieve the goals of the trainer.

It is an exercise rider's ability to communicate with both the horse and trainer that provides the extra edge that means the difference between making it to the winner's circle for a picture after a race or returning to the barn hot and dusty as just an "also ran". For you non-racing fans, an "also ran" is the comment they use in the racing results column in the newspaper for horses that ran in a race but failed to finish first, second or third. Exercise riders are like stunt men in the movies. They take the risk, the spills and sustain the injuries while training horses to prevent jockeys from having to face some of the same risks and possible injuries during actual races. Exercise rider works with "green" or inexperienced horses in order to teach them how to behave under racing conditions. Exercise riders teach horses how to break from the starting gate, control their speed during a race and to change leads during a race to preserve their energy, which will allow them to finish stronger.

Free Lance

There are very few jobs on the "Back Side" that come with benefits, i.e., health insurance, paid vacations, or sick leave. Therefore, like jockeys, exercise riders are independent contractors who work 7 days a week. Also like professional jockeys, if an exercise rider does not work they are not paid. Further, like jockeys, some exercise riders enter agreements to work strictly for one trainer or one stable. However, most of the exercise riders that I have met over the years worked "Free Lance"; which means they worked for the trainer and stable that paid them the most money per horse and they went from barn to barn getting on as many horses as possible during training hours. On the Maryland Thoroughbred Racing Circuit, the cost a "Free Lance" exercise rider is $10 – $15 per horse. In Maryland a "Freelance" exercise rider, on a day when everything is clicking, and they do not have to wait on trainers or grooms to get horses ready to go to the track, can make $100 to $150, starting when the track opens for training at 6 AM until the track closes for training at 10 AM.

I am not an expert on any profession associated with thoroughbred horseracing. Yet, it is my very strong opinion, that exercise riders and grooms are the hardest workers in the sport. The exception to that opinion would be the few jockeys that double as full time exercise riders. In Maryland, we feature live racing 5 days a week with an average of nine races a day. However, on off days for live racing in Maryland, some of the jockeys that are based here in Maryland travel to nearby tracks in Delaware and Pennsylvania to ride. Yet, in all my years of attending the races, I have never witnessed a week of racing where the same jockey rode in every race for 7 days. In comparison, an exercise rider gets on 10 horses a day 7 days a week while most jockeys only ride in 6 to 7 races of a 9 race card. In addition, for each race a jockey will spend about 12 to 13 minutes on the horse while an exercise rider spends for 25 to 30 minutes on each of the horses they take to the track.

One of the luxuries that separate a race rider and an exercise rider is that jockeys have the option of deciding whether they want to ride a particular horse in a race, while a "Free Lance" exercise rider has to ride the tough one as well as the sore ones in order to make a living. Most jockeys have an agent that will make every effort to find the best horse in a race for their client to ride. If a jockey happens to get on a horse that he or she feels is unsafe to ride, they can bring it to the attention of the track veterinarian and have the horse scratched from the race before the start. If an exercise rider decides to become as selective as jockey in determining which horses they choose to ride, that exercise rider will soon be looking for a new career somewhere outside of thoroughbred horseracing. Finally, most jockeys ride professional until their late 40s or early 50s. I personally know of at least six exercise riders whose careers have extended well into their 60s. It takes a long time for jockeys and exercise riders to recover from their injuries after being thrown from a horse or taking a spill on the racetrack. You can just imagine that at age 60, it becomes even more difficult to recover from the injuries sustained from being thrown or a horse falling on the track.

Unlike black jockey, hundreds of African Americans in this Country that still make a good living as exercise riders. Although there is a greater number of African American exercise riders than black jockeys, the number of young African Americans in Maryland that are starting their careers as exercise riders are few and far between. One of the reason there are fewer young black exercise riders it that as I am writing this book, the growing trend on the "Back Side" for exercise riders is rapidly moving toward young white women, who very good with horses and rarely have a weight, are replacing both white and black men in this profession. Another major factor that dissuades young black men from seeking a career as an exercise rider is the disparate treatment that is based solely on race. In Maryland, the black exercise rider faces the same roadblock as the black grooms and other African American that works on the "Back Side of the Sport of Kings", the inability to move to the next level or climb the Corporate Ladder. For example, on the Maryland Thoroughbred Horseracing Circuit, I have seen white exercise rider's move up to become jockey agents or trainers. Other white exercise riders get part-time jobs working for the Maryland Racing Association as outriders, or assistant starters; many of these jobs come with benefits and paid vacations.

Second Jobs

For those of you that are not familiar with the term outrider and assistant starter, an outrider is similar to a traffic cop on the racetrack.

In the morning when the racetrack opens of the workout period, there are times when 40 to 50 horses could be on the track at the same time. It is the outrider's job to make sure all the exercise riders follow the safety rules for galloping horses and to help out with unruly horses and "pickup" or catch any "loose" or runaway horses. In the afternoon, the outrider is responsible for ensuring jockeys on horse and riders on ponies obey the rules for safety before and after each race. The outrider must make sure that there are no obstructions on the racetrack prior to or during a race. During a race, if an object that would impede the safe completion of a race makes its way onto the track, it is the outrider's job to warn the jockeys to prevent injuries to riders and horses. An assistant starter loads horses in the starting gate before a race. The starter is the person that actual pushes the button to open the starting gate to begin each race. If they are lucky, a few black exercise riders get to "pony" horses to the races in the afternoon, which means they have to escort horses to the track between races for a fee of $25 per race.

I know that a few white exercise riders work part-time as valets for jockeys. A jockey's valet is responsible for maintaining a jockey's equipment, which includes their uniforms, boots and saddles. The valet is responsible for placing the handicap weight assigned to each jockey before each race in the jockey's saddle. The valet carries the saddle and the jockey's whip to the paddock and assists the trainer in saddling the horse his jockey has been hired to ride. After the race, the valet helps to unsaddle the horse and carries their jockey's saddle and whip back to the jockey's room. On average, the jockey's valet makes one percent of whatever purse money their jockey makes during a race. During the era when slavery was legal in this Country, my black slave ancestors were maids, butlers and valets. You would think that in the profession of being a servant to white people, that we once dominated, African Americans would not have a problem being hired as a valet. Yet, in the 40 years that I have been coming to the races, I have only seen two black valets, and they only worked the Maryland State Fair races at Timonium. One of those black valets was the late "Cocky" Johnson, a former trainer and Stable Manager at Pimlico Racetrack. The average journeyman jockey earns at least a million dollars a year in purse money, which means the jockey's valet earns $10,000 a year.

Based on my observation and experience as a horseman, being a valet does not require any obvious skills or talent that could not be learned in a short amount of time. For the life of me, I cannot understand why more jockeys do not hire black valets. Many white exercise riders work part-time as parking lot attendants in the afternoon on race days. I have been coming to the racetracks in Maryland for over 40 years, I have only seen one African American working as a parking lot attendant, and that was my uncle Charlie Hall. Now you might be asking yourself, what is the big deal about being a parking lot attendant and not having any African Americans employed to do what would be consider such a low-level job? Well, if you have ever been to either of the two major racetracks in Maryland, you would see that the parking lot attendants make anywhere from $100 to $150 a day in tips. On weekends, holidays and major racing event, i.e., Preakness and Maryland Million, they can make 3 times that amount. It would take the average exercise rider or groom a month to make what some parking lot attendants make in a week. Why is it that I see these blatant acts of racial discrimination but they go undetected by the white Executives that manage the racetracks in Maryland? It is easy to notice that there are no African Americans working on the parking lots where they would have the opportunity to make extra money. Yet, when the Grandstand and Clubhouse at the racetrack close for business, you will find plenty of black people cleaning up the trash left by racing fans.

The Deacon

Let us get back to the exercise riders. The first exercise rider that I had the opportunity to get to know was the late Thomas "Mouse" Snell, aka "Deacon" Snell. When I first met Mouse in the early 1980s, he was working galloping horses at Laurel Racetrack for King T. Leatherbury, the trainer that has saddled the most winners in the history of Maryland Thoroughbred Racing. When I met Mouse, he was close to 60 years old and his career as an exercise rider was nearly over. However, like most of the other "Old Timers", after he retired from being an exercise rider, Mouse became a hotwalker for Leatherbury. As an exercise rider, Mouse had a reputation of being particularly good with young green horse horses that were hard to handle on the racetrack during training. Mouse was tall for an exercise rider, but he was lean and very strong. He had big hands, so big in fact that when he shook my hand it got lost in his firm grip. His strong hands and gentle disposition made him an exceptional exercise rider. I have no idea why they called him "Mouse". It could have been because he was as quiet as a mouse or with his narrow face and baldhead; he looked like a mouse. It is funny that in all the years I saw him on the racetrack, I never heard anyone call him by his given name.

I knew Mouse for close to 30 years and his physical appearance had barely changed. Although he was over 75 years old when he died, his weight was just a few pounds more than when he galloped horses, he never had facial hair and he shaved his head. If you did not know him, you would think he was closer to being in his early 60s than being close to eighty. Away from the racetrack, I would later find out that Mouse and my Stepfather, Francis Thomas, who we affectionately called "Uncle Wye", had been close friends for years. They even attended the same little community church in Pumpkin Hill. After a time, Mouse joined my mother church in Laurel and became a Deacon, losing the nickname Mouse and now choosing to be called "Deacon" Snell. After my stepfather's death, Deacon Snell became a close companion to my mother. He would accompany her to church functions and after my mother eyesight started to fail, Deacon Snell would assist my mother with her Bible studies by sitting and reading to her from the Bible. Over the years since becoming a Deacon, I noticed that he felt uncomfortable talking about his days on the racetrack.

I will always remember Deacon Snell as a great exercise rider, a family friend who sang at my mother's funeral. If you are asking why I included all the personal information about Thomas "Deacon" Snell, well it was to makes the point that any book written about historical events should have a touch of personal flavor because history is about life and life is about your personal feeling and experiences. I want my readers to become emotionally involved when reading my books. I also want my readers to realize that the people that we meet in life are all part of our personal history. Although each of your encounters in life may not be documented in a book, they are still just as important as any event that is documented as a historical event. In 1995 at Laurel Racetrack, I met Johnny Bradford, who most people on the "Back Side" called Johnny "B". He was an experienced exercise rider, who had his own pony business on the side. Like Deacon Snell, Johnny was at least 60 years old when I met him and he was still going strong.

Johnny B

When I owned a horse named *Kegler*, Johnny B stabled one of his ponies in the same barn. After galloping horses in the morning, Johnny would return to the stable area to take care of about five ponies. Johnny used a pony to escort horses to the races in the afternoon. He also least or rented ponies to other riders to escort horses to the racetrack in the afternoon. I talked to Johnny frequently about thoroughbred horses, the different trainers that he had worked for, his ponies, and life on the "Back Side" and life in general. Just like me, Johnny loved to talk. He loved to talk about his farm and his favorite subject was his young daughter. When I met him, Johnny's daughter was just two years old. In 2003, I did not spend as much time around the "Back Side" as I usually do, and one night as I was having dinner out with my family, I saw Johnny B. his significant other and his daughter. To my surprise, the normally talkative Johnny B could barely open his mouth. I would later find out that he had a stroke. He had retired from galloping horses. On some rare occasions, Johnny would show up on the "Back Side" to work as a hotwalker in the morning or after races in the afternoon.

Donald Gardner

One of the most amazing characters I have ever met on the "Back Side" is Donald Gardner. In the world of sports, stories about athletes that are able to perform well past their prime make sporting news on a regular basis. In the case of Donald Gardner, the ability to perform well past his prime is an understatement. When I started writing this book, Donald was over 70 years old and was galloping at least 10 horses every morning. After working on the "Back Side" in the morning, Donald "pony" horses to the track for races in the afternoon. In 1948 at age 16, Donald started galloping horses. He received one dollar for each horse he galloped. You would think with the rising rate of inflation over the past 65 years, Donald would make more than the 10 to 12 dollars per horse. I was born in 1948, which means that as I started writing this book in the year 2003, I was 55 years old, and Donald has worked 55 years as an exercise rider. My grandfather worked on the railroad for 47 years before he retired and I thought that was a very long time to work on the same job. In 2003, I had worked on the same job for 25 years. Most of the time that I am working I was bored. After 25 year on the same job, I actually hated to get up to go to work and face another day of the same boring routine.

Just imagine Donald Gardner getting out of bed at 4 am nearly every day for 55 years and going to work at the same occupation. I would best describe Donald's ability as an exercise rider as being very steady and very patient with horses, but also he could be very demanding if he thought a horse was not giving him his best. One day I asked Donald how he managed to do the same job for 55 years. In his raspy voice, Donald told me that he started working at the racetrack because that is what the men in his family did to earn a living. Once he started riding horses, he loved it and he has been riding horses and loving it ever since. When I met Donald, he was one of the regular exercise riders for horses stabled at Pimlico for the leading training in Maryland, King T. Leatherbury. Donald continued the tradition of men in the Gardner family working on the "Back Side". I wrote about Donald's brother Morris in chapter three, "Jack of all Trades". Donald did not talk much because he had his larynx, better known as the voice box, removed many years before I met him. Donald' brother "Frog" had the same operation. In fact, so did my grandfather. The common factor in the lives of these three men is that they were all heavy cigarette smokers. In 2014, there are still members of the Gardner family working on the "Back Side".

The Best of The Best

In 1995, I was fortunate enough to meet and get to know one of the best exercise riders ever to mount a horse in the State of Maryland, Jesse Jones. How did Jesse Jones come to be rated as the best exercise rider in the business? Jesse received his rating from his fellow exercise riders, and the grooms and trainers who actually witnessed his talent with horses on a racetrack for years.

"But he that filches from me my good name robs me of that which not enriches him and makes me poor indeed". It is extremely rare that I would use a quote from the great William Shakespeare, and if I were to use this quote in a conversation on the "Back Side", I seriously doubt if anyone would recognize it as having come from the famous play "Othello". Yet, the quote is the foundation of what makes the black men and women the work on the "Back Side" special. "Back Side" workers do not make a lot of money; therefore, they attach a great deal of importance to their good name and reputation. The good name and reputation of Jesse Jones was passed along to me the same was that most of the information that I have written about was obtained; I listened while the worker talked and told stories.

I heard about Jesse Jones from my uncle Charlie Hall, from two grooms, Willie Kee and Stymie, and from two exercise riders Donnie Krone and Mouse. They all told stories about the amazing things that they had witnessed Jesse do on the back of a horse. Many of the trainers that I have gotten to know over years consider Donnie Krone to be one of the best exercise riders in Maryland. Yet, when I met Donnie, he was quick to admit that he was one of the best, but that he would always be second to Jesse Jones. I had the privilege of closely studying Jesse as he galloped a horse trained by Anthony "Tony" Dutrow. I was at Laurel Racetrack early one morning to watch my horse, *Legendinthemakin* train. As the *Legend* was finishing his training, the *Legend* and I were headed back to the barn. Rather than leave the track and go to the barn area, I stayed because I had noticed Jesse on the track galloping a horse. Trainers usually send young horses out in pairs, and this morning Tony had sent out a pair of horses with Jesse on one and a young white male exercise rider on the other. On any given morning that I have been at Laurel, I have seen riders gallop or jog a horse around the mile and an eighth track one time, 1 ½ times and even as many as twice around. On this particular morning that I was watching Jesse, I watched him as he jogged this horse around the track three times and each time he passed me I could see that he was verbally giving instructions to the young white exercise rider that was next to him. What amazed me was that the two horses and riders moved in tandem as if they had choreographed this workout before they left the barn area. After the third time around, I just knew Jesse was finished and would be headed back to the barn to get on another horse. However, when they reached the gap in the track were they would normally exit, Jesse and the other rider let these two horses speed up and again in tandem, the two horse ran full speed from the turn down the stretch and past the finish line. For those of you that might not be familiar with the training regiment for thoroughbred horses, this was an awesome workout. It just happened that Tony was standing near me as I was watching his horses train. I commented that I thought it was an awesome performance for such young horses.

To my surprise, Tony gave all the credit for the workout that I had just witnessed to Jesse. Tony shared with me that he frequently allows Jesse to use his own judgment in determining how much a horse needs to do once they get on the track in the morning. Of course, I could not wait until the next time I saw Jesse to talk to him about what I had witnessed on the track. I saw Jesse later that same day at the races at Pimlico. When I asked him about the workout that I had witnessed early that morning, Jesse was more than glad to tell me about it. He explained that he was given instructions to the other exercise rider as they went around the track. As it related to Tony's comments, Jesse stated that he had worked for Hall of Fame trainer Richard "Dickie" Dutrow, and that he had known his son Tony since he was a young boy. Jesse told me that just as he had established an understanding of trust in his ability as an exercise rider with the father, he had developed the same type of relationship with the son. Jesse stated that Tony trusted him to make the right decision when it comes to how to manage the training of a horse once that horse reaches the racetrack in the morning. Jesse was the best and that was why Tony Dutrow hired him.

To say you are the best is one thing, but the proof is in the pudding. In the case of being the best exercise rider, the proof is in winning races in the afternoon. Jesse loved to bet on horses and when I would see him at the races, he would always have some first-rate inside information. Along with my love of horse and horseracing, the other reason I enjoyed hanging out on the "Back Side" was that I had access to a lot of information. I have already established that the people that work on the "Back Side" love to talk, and sometimes if you just listen, you can find out some very valuable information about a horse that is about to run in a race. Aside for the information about other horses, whenever one of the horses from the Dutrow barn was running in a race, Jesse would tell me whether it was wise to place a bet. On occasions when I would asked Jesse about one of Tony's horses that he galloped in the mornings, he would say, "he is as good as hands can make him", or "you don't have to worry, cause this horse will finish." When an exercise rider tell you that a horse will finish, he means that the horse will be running strong at the end of the race and will not get tired down the home stretch. As I am writing this book in 2014, Jesse's has retired from the racetrack.

George "Spider" Anderson

Baltimore, Maryland is the home of the Preakness Stakes; the second jewel in sport of thoroughbred racing's Triple Crown. Baltimore, Maryland is also the home of George "Spider" Anderson, a black jockey, who rode the winner of the 1889 Preakness. Yet, as I conduct my research for this book, the accomplishments of this African American jockey are conspicuously absent from Pimlico Racetrack's Hall of Fame. Accordingly, there is no mention of Mr. Anderson in the 1889 Preakness guide, and reportedly when he arrived at the track on May 10, 1889, his horse, "Buddhist", was the only one entered in the race. Former Maryland Governor Oden Bowie, who created the Preakness in 1873, decided to enter *Japhet* to avoid *Buddhist* from winning in a walkover. Reportedly, Governor Bowie's attempt to make the race competitive was in vain. The black jockey, George Anderson, brought his horse *Buddhist* home in a gallop and won a $1,000 for S.S. Brown, the horse's owner. In a city that has a population that is 75% African American, why have we forgotten Spider Anderson? Why the schools in Baltimore City and throughout the Maryland do not honor this great African American athlete during Black History Month?

The State of Maryland named a city, a racetrack and a college, all of which are in Prince George's County, in honor of the white Governor Oden Bowie, who created the Preakness. I even went to Arundel Junior High School in "Odenton", Maryland, which was also named for Governor, Oden Bowie. Yet, in Baltimore, I cannot remember if they named any area in the city where Spider grew up after Mr. Anderson. Both Baltimore City and the State of Maryland have promotions that insure tourist visit sites dedicated to famous white Maryland athletes such as the Babe Ruth Museum located in Baltimore's Inner Harbor and the Cal Ripken Museum located in Aberdeen. The city has a memorial for Johnny Unitas, the Hall of Fame quarterback of the Baltimore Colts, who passed away on September 11, 2002. There is a statue of Johnny Unitas at the Baltimore Ravens Football Stadium and the new football field at Towson University in Maryland, is named Johnny Unitas Stadium. These athletes are indeed legends in their respective sports and they deserve to be recognized for their accomplishments.

When I am not writing, I spend a lot of time on both the "Back Side", a.k.a. the stable area, and in the grandstands of Maryland's thoroughbred racetracks. I have been hanging out at racetracks for over 30 years, and I have never heard any of the "Old Timers" around the track tell stories about the black jockey, George "Spider" Anderson, who was born and raised in Baltimore. The black men on the "Back Side" love to tell tales and swap stories. In fact, some of the information in my book is based on the tales that I have heard at the racetrack. Over

the years, I have heard stories about "the good old days" of horseracing in Maryland that involved black trainers, exercise riders, grooms,
and hotwalkers. Yet, none of the African Americans that either work
at the track or are frequent visitors like myself, rarely if ever talk about
famous black jockeys from the past. The reason for the lack of interest
on the "Back Side" and in the African American community in general
for Spider Anderson is the lack of documentation about his life and
his career.

As a baseball fan, I have heard "Old Timers" tell stories about
the great black stars of the Old Negro Leagues, such as Cool Papa
Bell, Satchel Paige and the legendary Josh Gibson, who played for a
short time in Baltimore with the Elite Giants. The City of Baltimore
recently dedicated an athletic field to honor the memory of Leon Day,
a hometown hero who was inducted in baseball's Hall of Fame for
his accomplishment in the Negro Leagues. The 50th anniversary of
Jackie Robinson becoming the first black baseball player to play in the
white professional league, combined with the Veteran's Committee
of Major League Baseball's Hall of Fame inducting players from the
Negro Leagues into the Hall of Fame, made the history of the Negro
Leagues a popular subject. Negro League Baseball and former Negro
League Baseball player become so popular in America that they have
their own clothing line featuring old Negro League Uniforms, and
former Negro League players have their own lecture and autograph
tour. In fact, memorabilia from the Negro Leagues has become valuable collector items. Why we do not have any memorabilia or at least
a memorial in Baltimore to honor the accomplishment of the great
black athlete George "Spider" Anderson? In Maryland, if you look
at the daily racing program, you will see that they name horse races
in honor of every Tom, Dick and Harry that you can think of, yet, I
cannot remember a race being named in honor of George "Spider"
Anderson.

Although I am not really a Babe Ruth fan, I am fully aware of his
much-publicized professional baseball career. The reason that I know
so much about the accomplishments of Babe Ruth is because Major
League Baseball made his name synonymous with the game its' self.

On the other hand, I am a big fan of both Cal Ripken Jr. and Johnny Unitas. As a young sports fan, I watched "Quarterback Johnny U" lead the Baltimore Colts Football to two NFL championships. I am not a shame of the fact that as a young boy, whenever I played quarterback in our neighborhood pickup football games, I wanted to be Johnny U. As I got older, I could not help but admire the work ethic of Cal Ripken Jr. with the Baltimore Orioles Baseball Team as he broke Lou Gehrig's record for the most consecutive games played. From time to time, the local media will run a story on Cal, Johnny or Babe to honor the memory of their careers in sports. Why has the local media in the Baltimore area not run stories about George "Spider"? As an African American who resides in the Baltimore area and as an avid thoroughbred horseracing fan, I am offended by the lack of recognition that Marylanders have given to the legendary black jockey, George "Spider" Anderson.

I fully realized that in the "JIM CROW ERA" of the early 1900s, it would not have been a sound marketing strategy for the white promoters of the Preakness to feature a black jockey to encourage white racing fan to attend the big race. Yet, the white promoters of the second jewel of horse racing's "Triple Crown", fail to mention the fact that a black jockey, Spider Anderson, not only won the race in 1899, he was born in Baltimore, the "Home of the Preakness". In my opinion, the reason the promoters of the Preakness are not trying to enlighten the racing public about the accomplishment of a local African American jockey is because they have no interest in encouraging or attracting black racing fan for the Preakness. In all the years that I have watched the local media coverage of the Preakness, they make a special effort to interview groups of white people that travel come from out of town to attend the big race. I hope someday the residents of Baltimore will correct this error and build a memorial to honor George "Spider" Anderson. It is also my hope that this book will help to raise the consciousness of the citizens of Baltimore and make them aware of the fact that during Preakness Week, a great African American sports legend, George "Spider" Anderson, is not receiving the accolade that his accomplishments so rightfully deserve.

Black Jockeys

Why am I making all these fuss about black jockeys? The reason African American jockeys are very important for me, is there needs to be some attention given to the lives of these famous black Americans jockeys to provide examples of successful role models for young black athletes that are diminutive in stature and feel that a career as a professional athlete may be out of the realm of possibility. Did you know that at the turn of the century, most of the jockeys in thoroughbred horseracing were African Americans? In the first Kentucky Derby, in 1875, 13 of the 15 riders were African Americans, which included the winning rider, Oliver Lewis. Just imagine African American jockeys once dominated the Kentucky Derby, the single most popular sporting event in the world, an event that is watched on TV by more viewers worldwide than any other sporting event in history. Yet, your white American History books fail to make a significant point of this fact for our children.

As I stated earlier, as we enter the next millennium, Major League Baseball, in conjunction with the Major League Baseball Hall of Fame in Cooperstown, New York, has finally started to recognize and appreciate the accomplishments of the African American athletes that played in the Negro Leagues. Annually, more and more players from the old Negro Leagues are being nominated for induction into the Baseball Hall of Fame. It took the sport of professional baseball about 50 years after Jackie Robinson broke color barrier for white owners of MLB teams to do the right thing in remembering the Negro Leagues. Teams of today, in cities that supported Negro League Baseball, honor those teams by dressing in the old Negro League uniforms from time to time while playing in an actual MLB games. When will the white authorities in the sport of thoroughbred horseracing make the effort to honor the African American jockeys who were the grandfathers of modern jockeys of today?

There are a few black jockeys in the Thoroughbred Horse Racing Hall Fame. Based on their accomplishments in the sport, the few black jockeys in the Thoroughbred Horse Racing Hall Fame is an insult to the memory of those great athletes and to the African American community in general. White historians fail to put the accomplishments of black jockeys in the proper perspective. African American jockeys winning 15 of the first 28 Kentucky Derbies, should have been compared in history to two black teams, the Kansas City Monarchs and Homestead Grays winning 15 out of 28 World Series in the 1900s. It would be the same as the Harlem Globetrotter, world famous black basketball team, winning 15 National Basketball Association (NBA) championships while competing against white teams in the 1940s.

Again, this supports my premise of why history needs to be taught in more than one color and from more than one perspective. Although the Kentucky Derby is a major sporting event in America, most young people in this Country are more familiar with Major League Baseball's World Series, the National Football League's Super Bowl and the National Basketball Association's Championship. If today, history teachers compared the accomplishments of the African American jockeys of the past with the modern day accomplishments of black athletes, it would be easy for students to understand the magnitude of the accomplishments of the African American jockeys. Compare the black jockeys to black athletes like the Los Angeles Lakers' star Kobe Bryant, the Philadelphia Eagle's star Michael Vick and the New York Yankees' star Derrick Jeter. If the accomplishments of the black jockeys were put in the proper perspective, the title of the First Superstar Athletes in America would need no further explanation. In addition, if they were put in the proper perspective, the accomplishments of black jockeys would be the main attraction in the Thoroughbred Horse Racing Hall Fame and there would be more African American inductees.

Every African American athlete I mention in this chapter deserves to have a book written about him, and a few of them already have biographies and other documentation on their accomplishments in a library near you. This is my third book and the increasing number of black historians that I have discovered while conducting my research encourages me. This is why I always remind my reader to visit the local library or visit the Internet to find interesting facts and information about African American history.

Early, I talked about George "Spider" Anderson not being recognized for his accomplishments as a jockey by the State of Maryland. What I hope to accomplish with my book is for the readers to not only recognize the name George "Spider" Anderson, but to conduct their own research in order to learn more about this famous athlete. Knowledge is power and the more we know about men like Mr. Anderson, the more we want to know and eventually we can persuade the powers to be to include information on this great athlete a place like the Thoroughbred Horse Racing Hall Fame.

They Rode for Free to Earn Their Freedom

It probably comes as a surprise to you to find out that in all likelihood, the tradition of the great American professional athletes in the U.S. actually began with black jockeys. More than likely, jockeys were the first professional athletes in any organized sport in America, white or black. History is very clear on the point that black slaves were the first jockeys for thoroughbred racehorses in America. In addition, history is very clear that the sport of racing thoroughbred horse came to America with the first settlers. What history is not clear on is that before we had professional baseball and football players, we had professional jockeys. How could black men be the first professional athlete in America when they came here as slaves? Although, most of the black slaves that rode horses for their white masters, rode for free because they had no choice, other black slave jockeys rode thoroughbred horse to victory in exchange for their freedom. There may not have been an actual exchange of money between the horse owners and the black jockeys for their services rendered, but there was a barter system. In the early 1900s, the black superstar Jockeys made more money and had a better lifestyle than their white jockeys.

White slave masters created a barter system to improve the performance of the black slaves that had a special skill. Black slaves that could pick the most cotton, chop the most wood or clear the most land, would receive extra portions of food or were first in line to receive the white masters' "hand me down" clothes and shoes. It was a common practice for black slaves to use a special talent or skill to barter with their white masters. The slaves would exchange the performance of that skill or talent for something that was more precious than silver or gold; and that thing was freedom. A black slave bartered with the white man for freedom for himself and sometimes for his mate and their children. Remember the scene from the TV series "Roots" where the black slave "Chicken George" won his freedom for his ability to handle the fighting roosters. The white slave masters wagered a lot of money on the outcome of this "Cock Fight" and therefore, it was in his best interest to win this particular fight. The talented "Chicken George" used this to his advantage and won his freedom.

For the benefit of Marlon St. Julien and all the other black jockeys and future black jockeys, the history of the African American Jockeys begins with slavery. White plantation owners left the care, training and racing of thoroughbred horses to their black slaves. For the record, and some added material for your American history lesson, there is a point that needs to be made clear about my African American ancestors who were called "free men" and not slaves. In studying American history, prior to 1865, you often find references to free black men and women that lived in the U.S before Congress passed the 13th Amendment to the Constitution. Prior to 1865, in order for a black man to be truly free in America, they would have to escape to Canada or Mexico. Therefore, the correct term for African Americans that were not legally owned by white man should have been black slaves that purchased the right to own themselves from their white masters. These "so called" free black people had to carry proof wherever they traveled in the U.S., that they did in fact purchase their freedom form their original owner. Without that bill of sale or their "papers", a black person could be legally returned to their original owner and be forced back into slavery.

In reading most books and most other documented accounts of American history authored by white people, they rarely mention, address or provide details about the brutal and inhuman realities of slavery in this Country. Why is that? The answer is simple; the same reason they used the term free men to describe some African Americans living in this Country prior to 1865. Any reference to the cruel and inhuman treatment of black slaves would make the Founding Fathers of this Country responsible for these acts seem like cold-blooded cowards. The old rule in recording history is that whoever writes the story gets to make the heroes. Throughout my early school years, any lessons taught in history or sociology classes left me with the impression that all white American men in my textbooks were all heroes. From Presidents George Washington, Ulysses S. Grant and Dwight D. Eisenhower, to General George Armstrong Custer, all white heroes fought to defend freedom, democracy, truth, justice and the American way; just like another white hero named Superman.

For white historians, labeling blacks as free men prior to 1865, allowed them to soften some of the horrible images and scars left from the reality of slavery by showing the more human side of white America that not all Africans in this Country were slaves. White Americans were heroes. Yet, whites from other parts of the world that fought against the American way of life were always portrayed as villains. Some of these same white historians have no problems using every despicable term in the dictionary to describe white Europeans like Hitler and using those same despicable phrase to describe the treatment of the Jews during the Holocaust. Famous white American war heroes and politicians are prominent in the recording of American history. Yet, the names of thousands of black slave jockeys were not recorded. White historians recorded the names of the famous horses and their white owners, but failed to include the names of the slaves that trained and rode these horses. The fact that the names of these great black athletes are missing from American history is another example of the tragedy of not allowing our slave ancestors to record their own account of the famous events involving African Americans.

The 1st Triple Crown Winners

In 1875, black jockey Oliver Lewis rode *Aristides* to a two-length upset victory in the first running of the Kentucky Derby. The time of the race, 2:37 3/4, established an American record for a thoroughbred horserace run at the distance of 1 1/2 miles. Reportedly, Mr. Lewis was instructed by the owner/trainer to send *Aristides* to the lead to ensure a fast pace and set up the race for stable mate *Chesapeake*. As instructed, Mr. Lewis sent Aristides to the front and as the field rounded the far turn and headed for home, Chesapeake was far behind. Reportedly, the owner of the two horses, H. Price McGrath, told Mr. Lewis "Go on!" when he looked over at McGrath for a sign. Later that year Oliver Lewis guided *Aristides* to a second place finish in the Belmont Stakes. Along with winning the first running of the Kentucky Derby, Mr. Lewis won three races during Churchill Down's inaugural meet to take the honor as the leading rider.

Reportedly, Oliver Lewis never rode in another Kentucky Derby. However, according to published reports, he was on hand to watch the 33rd running in 1907. Today, when a famous athlete returns to the scene of one of their greatest accomplishments in that sport, the owners and managers of that sporting venue, plan a big celebration to honor the return of the conquering hero. At a baseball game, they would throw out the first pitch. At a football game, they would participate in the coin toss to begin the game. In the sport of thoroughbred horserac-ing they name a race after the famous person and have that person present a trophy named for that individual, to the winning owner or trainer of the winning horse. I was unable to find any information as to whether the owners and management of Churchill Downs honored Mr. Lewis in 1907 when he returned to Kentucky for the Derby. Due to the fact that "JIM CROW" was still the law of the land in 1907, I doubt very seriously if the white Executives in charge of Churchill Downs and the Kentucky Derby wanted to the celebrate the return of a black man in front of a crowd filled with thousands of white Southerners.

The more I research the events that have occurred in African American history, the more I see how they continue to repeat them-selves. A black jockey, who wins the most prestigious race in the history of the sport of thoroughbred horseracing, is never hired to ride in the race again during his career as a jockey. In 1992, Clarence Edwin "Cito" Gaston was the first African American Manager of a Major League Baseball team, Canada's Toronto Blue Jays, to win a World Series.

Cito Gaston, being the first black manager to win the World Series was a noteworthy accomplishment in African history and the history of MLB. In 1992, the Toronto Blue Jays became the first team from outside the boundaries of the U.S. to a World Series. Not only did Cito manage the Blue Jays to victory in the 1992 World Series, he lead them again as they repeated as World Champions in 1993. Cito Gaston was the manager of the Toronto Blue Jays from 1989 – 1997 when he was fired. He was rehired by the Toronto Blue Jays in 2008 and fired again in 2010. After winning the Kentucky Derby, Oliver Lewis never rode in the race again. In 2014, a manager that won back-to-back World Series, Cito cannot find a job as a manager of a major league baseball team.

If you check the history of MLB, you would find a regular pattern. White managers that have been fired by one team are hired by another team; especially white managers that have won a World Series. There was a point in time when the white owners of MLB teams used the lack of experience managing at the Major League level as the reason for not hiring an African American to fill vacant manager or general manager positions. This situation is referred to as a "Catch 22" or vicious cycle; you cannot qualify for a job unless you have experience and in order to get experience you need to be hired for the job. Every MLB team that has a vacancy covets baseball managers that have taken a team to the World Series. The only managers they covet more are the ones that have taken a team to the World Series and won. In over 100 years, only eight men have won more World Series than Cito Gaston.

The first African American to integrate an area or event that was formerly for whites only is called "The Jackie Robinson" of that particular occurrence. For the black baseball manager Cito Gaston, he now has the unfortunate distinction of being the "Oliver Lewis" of baseball. Although very little information is available, it was reported that Oliver Lewis worked for a bookmaker after his career as a jockey was over. During the early 1900s, bookmaking was legal and most of the wagering on thoroughbred horseracing was done through a bookmaker. Accordingly, after watching a race, Mr. Lewis provided the bookmakers with detailed information on how the horses ran. The bookmaker used the information from Oliver Lewis to set the odds the next time some of the same horses from this race ran again. Reportedly, this method of race result notes was later developed into charts that served as a forerunner to the Daily Racing Form and Equibase Systems. The Daily Racing Form (DRF) and the Equibase Systems are the Wall Street Journal of thoroughbred horseracing. Professional Thoroughbred Racing Handicapper's would be lost without the past performance charts in the DRF. The next time you read a past performance chart to handicap a horse race, think about the fact that an African American jockey, named Oliver Lewis, helped to develop this process.

On the 1st Saturday in May 2000, Marlon St. Julien became the first African American jockey to ride in the Kentucky Derby in 79 years. In 126th running of the first jewel of thoroughbred horseracing Triple Crown, Marlon rode Curule, owned by the Godolphin Racing Inc.'s Stables, to a 7th place finish. St. Julien is a native of Lafayette, Louisiana, where he worked on his uncle's farm as a youngster, and was more interested in playing football than riding horses. He turned his attention to becoming a jockey following his junior year in high school and began riding at Evangeline Downs in 1989, winning his first race aboard Sadie's Sensation two weeks into his career. Shortly after his career as a jockey began, St. Julien was involved in a five-horse spill, suffering multiple injuries, including a broken sternum. He almost gave up riding at that point, but instead of giving up, following two months of recovery; he was back in the saddle. Following his gradua-tion from high school, St. Julien continued riding in Louisiana before temporarily moving "his tack", a term used for a jockey's equipment, to racetracks in California. St. Julien returned to Louisiana before ven-turing to Lone Star Park for their inaugural season in 1997, where he won the first race at the Texas track, with "I Are Sharp" in the Premier Stakes.

According to other published reports, on May 6, 2000, Marlon St. Julien became the first black jockey in 79 years to ride in the Kentucky Derby. As I have stated before, without the ability to record our own history, from time to time we get different and conflicting accounts of the same event. For my readers, while conducting my research for my book, "No Land No Mule No Freedom, my references indicated that prior to 2000, the last black jockey to ride in the Kentucky was Jess Conley in 1911. I found it very disturbing that, according to a published statement, St. Julien does not want to be known as a black or white jockey, but just a jockey. I am sorry Mr. St. Julien, just as the black community needs Tiger Woods to identify himself as an African American Golfer to preserve the accounts of his exploits; we need Julien to identify himself as an African American Jockey for those same reasons. Another reason we need Julien to stand up and be counted as an African American, is the report of the event that created the confusion between 1911 or 1921, failed to name the black jockey that rode in the 1921 Kentucky Derby. We do not want historians to forget your name and that you were an African American when they write about this event a 100 years from now. In 2013, a black jockey, Kevin Krigger rode in the Kentucky Derby and the Preakness.

Famous Horse and Famous Rider

In this chapter, I will highlight the lives of a few of the most famous African American Jockeys in the history of the "Sport of Kings". Throughout this book, I associate the names of African Americans in the sport of thoroughbred horseracing with the names of great horses that these black men were associated with during their careers. Most of these great thoroughbred champions became the sires of other champions. Although the names of famous African American jockeys, grooms, exercise riders and trainers may not be mentioned in reports that document the history of the sport of thoroughbred horseracing in America, the names of these great horses will always be listed in the records of the bloodline or family tree of their offspring. Why associate the name of the famous horse with the name of a famous black jockey? It is my hope that my readers will remember the name of the famous African American when they hear or see the name of these great thoroughbred champions.

In 1806 "Monkey" Simon was the first African American jockey, whose name appeared in the record of a horse race in the U.S. "Monkey" Simon was a regular rider at the Clover Bottom Race Track in Nashville, Tennessee. Regrettably, the first recorded name of an African American jockey would have the demeaning characterization of being called "Monkey"! The sad truth is that the early documentation about the jockeys used in thoroughbred horseracing just referred to the rider as the "boy" who was up on the horse. Therefore, rather than list the black slaves name for the record, they just simply referred to the jockey as the "boy". The sad part about it is that white men had a habit of calling all black men boys, a habit that continues today. The term "boy" is the officially used today when trainers and owners are asked to name a jockey for a particular race. The racing office will request that a trainer name a "boy" to ride. Apprentice riders are traditionally known as "bug boys" because they receive a 5-10 pound weight allowance, depending on the number of races won and the length of time they have been riding.

A black jockey, William Walker won the 1877 Derby aboard *Baden Baden* for African American trainer Ed Brown. A native of Woodford County, Kentucky, Mr. Walker was born into slavery in 1860 at General Abe Buford's Bosque Bonita Farm near Versailles, Kentucky. In 1871, as an 11-year-old, he began his riding career at Jerome Park and rode his first winner later that year in Lexington. By age 13, Mr. Walker had secured his first stakes victory. One of his greatest victories was aboard "Ten Broeck" in a famed four-mile match race at Churchill Downs, on July 4, 1878, with the California-based mare "Molly McCarthy". Mr. Walker was Churchill's leading rider on five occasions. He won the fall meet of 1875-76 and the spring meets for 1876-77-78. After retiring, Mr. Walker became a trainer and was considered an expert in thoroughbred breeding and bloodlines and served in an advisory capacity to John E. Madden, breeder of five Kentucky Derby winners. Reportedly, Mr. Walker attended 59 consecutive Kentucky Derbies, not attending a single race until his death on September 20, 1933.

William Walker is buried in Louisville Cemetery and during Derby Week 1996, Churchill Downs placed a headstone, detailing Mr. Walker's career, at what was previously an unmarked grave. This is another example of the lack of respect for African American athletes of the past. Historians document the fact that Mr. Walker attended

59 straight Kentucky Derbies, yet, they fail to document if he was ever honored for his riding accomplishments at any of those Derbies. These same historians documented the fact that the white Executives of Churchill Downs Racetrack, as a tribute to this great black jockey, put a marker on his grave 63 year after his death. The question is how was a native son of the State of Kentucky, who rode a horse to victory in the Derby, the most popular sporting event held in that State, who won five riding titles at Churchill Downs, buried in an unmarked grave? Do you think that a famous white athlete like Mickey Mantle would have been buried in an unmarked grave in his home State of Oklahoma?

The reason this bit of information about William Walker is important for students of black history is that white historians have record the fact that Churchill Downs placed a marker on Mr. Walker's grave as an amiable act. Placing the marker on William Walker's grave, with his friends and family in attendance when he died in 1933 would indeed have been admirable. However, waiting 63 years was an act of cowardice caused by the fear of how a "JIM CROW" society would react to a group of white Southerners honoring an African American. Prior to this hollow tribute by officials from Churchill Downs, it should come as no surprise that Mr. Walker was buried in an unmarked grave. For years, in parts of this Country, the families of African American war veterans were denied the right to be buried in cemeteries that were reserved for white war veterans only. I talked about this injustice in my other books. It is a shame even in death, some people feel obligated to hold on to the racial prejudices.

According to published reports, at age 15 in 1892 Alonzo "Lonnie" Clayton rallied "Azra" to an impressive nose victory in a three-horse field to become the youngest jockey to win the Kentucky Derby. Born in Kansas City, Missouri in 1876, Mr. Clayton followed his brother into the riding profession. During the summer of 1888, Mr. Clayton launched his career as an exercise rider for E.J. "Lucky" Baldwin in Chicago. Mr. Clayton stayed with Baldwin for about a year before moving on to work for D.A. Honig, who had a string of horses in Clifton, New Jersey. Mr. Clayton rode a horse named "Redstone" in his first race in 1890 at the Clifton track, and earned his first career victory later that year. Mr. Clayton had four Derby mounts in his career with a victory, two seconds and a third. He also guided the Kentucky Derby winner "Azra" to victories in the Champagne Stakes, Clark Handicap and Travers. Mr. Clayton also won the Kentucky Oaks twice as he rode "Selika" in 1894 and "Voladora" in 1895. He distinguished himself by capturing the 1893 Churchill Downs jockey crown during the fall meet. Mr. Clayton is only one of four African American jockeys to compete in the Preakness as he finished third in 1896.

Young and Old

African American jockey James "Soup" Perkins nicknamed for his love of soup; began riding in 1891 at the tender age of 11 years old and won his first race at Kentucky's Latonia racetrack that same year. I remember that at age 11, most of the young boys from my neighborhood felt lucky if they had a chance to ride a little pony at the Maryland State Fair. For me, to ride an 18 hundred pound spirited thoroughbred racehorse at 11 years old would be like a voyage on the Star ship Enterprise from Star Trek. At age 15, "Soup" Perkins won the 1895 Kentucky Derby aboard "Halma" to join fellow African American jockey Alonzo Clayton as the youngest winning riders of the event. According to published reports, James "Soup" Perkins died in August 1911 while attending the races in Hamilton, Ontario. The mention of these young black jockeys bring back the memories of two white jockeys; "Cowboy" Jack Kaenal, who won the 1982 Preakness Stakes at age 16 on "Aloma's Ruler"; at 18 years of age jockey Stevie Cauthen won the 1978 Triple Crown aboard the great "Affirmed". I remember both events very well because I was able to watch these young white jockeys on live TV.

In professional sports there is always talk about the youngest or oldest person to hold a record in that sport. Whenever they play the World Series, they mention the youngest pitcher ever to win a World Series game. In baseball, just over 50 years after breaking the color barrier, African American superstars like the Hall of Fame's Hank Aaron and Willie Mays, and stars like Ken Griffey Jr. and Barry Bonds are mentioned in the same discussion as the legendary Babe Ruth. When the black golfer, Tiger Woods, first came on the scene, they made constant references to him being the youngest golfer ever to win this major golf event or that major golf event. Before Tiger Wood, no African American golfer had ever won the Masters, the most prestigious event in the sport of golf. Whenever they talk about Tiger, they compare him to the greatest white golfers of all time. Yet, when they talk about the accomplishments of Jack Kaenal and Stevie Cauthen in thoroughbred horseracing, I never remember any reference to the young black jockeys of the past, Alonzo "Lonnie" Clayton or James "Soup" Perkins.

In addition, whenever there are family members in the same sport or there is more than one professional athlete in the same family, the sports media always brings it to your attention. Soup" Perkins' brothers, William and Frank Perkins, were prominent thoroughbred horse trainers during this same time that he was a jockey. Although he never saddled a winner, William Perkins started six horses in the Kentucky Derby during his career. As a sports fan, I remember that if one brother in the sport was famous, they would always mention the lesser-known brother to add a little color to any story about their accomplishments. Whenever Paul "Daffy" Dean pitched a game, he was always referred to as the brother of Jay Hanna "Dizzy" Dean. The same applied to Dom DiMaggio when he got a hit in a game; he was referred to as the brother of the great Yankee Center Fielder Joe DiMaggio. The most recognized African American brothers in baseball are the Aarons and the Allens.

In 2014, the most famous set of siblings on the plant are the African American professional tennis players Venus and Serena Williams. Their accomplishments in the world of professional tennis have revolutionized the game. Discussions regarding modern day women's professional tennis usually start and end with discussions about the Williams sisters. Unlike most sports, thoroughbred horseracing industry is traditionally a family oriented business. Families breed, own and train thoroughbred horses and as the ownership and responsibility of other business are passed along to the next generation, it is very much the case in the sport of horseracing. It would be an injustice to the sport for me to single out just one combination of brothers, sisters, fathers, that have been highly successful in the thoroughbred horseracing business. There are literally tons of books and other documents to support the accomplishment of these famous horseracing families' accomplishments as well as the exploits of other famous sports families. Yet, I wonder how many people that have read about or witnessed the accomplishment by these famous families, ever stopped to think about James "Soup" Perkins and his brothers and what when they accomplished in the sport of thoroughbred horseracing.

African American, Willie Simms, was one of the few jockeys, white or black, to have a perfect Kentucky Derby record. He rode in two Derbies, on "Ben Brush" in 1896 and in 1898 on "Plaudit", and won on both occasions. In addition, Willie Simms won the 1898 Preakness Stakes on Sly Fox, and he won two Belmont Stakes, 1893 on Commanche and in 1894 on Henry of Navarre. This made Willie Simms the only black jockey to win all three races of the Triple Crown classics. Today, there are jockeys that have won over 3,500 races and over 20 million dollars in purse money that have never come close to having the kind of success in the Triple Crown Races as Willie Simms. During the 1890s, the Hall of Fame Jockey Willie Simms became the first American jockey to ride a winning horse in a race in England. While he was there, Willie introduced the "short-stirrup" riding style and was hugely successful against "long-stirrup" riding style of the English jockeys.

Unfortunately, along with Willie's new short-stirrups came the unflattering description by white jockeys as looking like "a monkey on a stick" when he rode. Here we go again with the monkey reference. As you may recall from early in the chapter, "Monkey" Simon was the first African American jockey whose name appeared in the records of a horse race in the U.S. After checking several sources, I was unable to locate first name for Mr. Simon other than "Monkey". Why is it that when we become better at doing something than white people we are ridiculed for our accomplishments? It was bad enough that after achieving success in this sport, we had to endure being treated as second-class citizens. Why can we not just be referred to as good athletes rather than being insulted? Until recently, it was an acceptable practice in America for white people to make those kinds of demeaning remarks about black people like calling us monkeys in public. The change in what was politically correct came when the famous ABC TV Sportscaster, the late Howard Cosell, referred to a black running for the Philadelphia Eagles Football Team "as that little monkey" on a National broadcast.

As a result of his "tell it like it is" commentary on Monday Night Football, Howard Cosell had a love him or hate him relationship with America. This relationship made him one of the most popular TV Broadcasters of all times and a target for criticism from the news media. After his "little monkey" comment on National TV, the media severely ridiculed him for what they described as a racially insensitive statement. Since the Cosell incident, we may experience some covert racist comments, but very few white sports commentators or white TV personalities in general, make racially offensive comments when addressing the public regarding an African American. Like the racially sensitive comments made by the late Jimmy "the Greek" Snyder, the racially sensitive comments by Howard Cosell marked the end of his career as a commentator on Monday Night Football. Ironically, my personal opinion about the late Howard Cosell is much the same as my opinion about Jimmy "the Greek"; neither man was a racist.

In the world of sports, being recognized only by a nickname is usually an indication that you are a very popular athlete. Babe, Tiger, Dizzy, Hit Man, Rocky, Deacon, Big Daddy and Sugar, just to name a few of the nicknames associated with the some of the greatest athletes of all time. Can you imagine all the accomplishments of black athletes of the modern era like Tiger, Sugar Ray, Hit Man and Deacon being recorded under a nickname only? In the 1800s, as a common practice, whites called their black slaves names that suited the occasion. From the book and made for TV movie "Roots", I cannot remember if the black character "Fiddler" was ever referred to by any other name. He was given the named "Fiddler" because he entertained white folks on the plantation by playing the fiddle. My problem with the nickname "Monkey" for Mr. Simons is that all the other famous athletes with nicknames have a recorded legal name. "Monkey" Simons is the first black jockey in the history of the sport, without knowing his first name, it will be very difficult to trace his roots. I hope that someone somewhere has some documentation that provides evidence of "Monkey" Simons' family and that they provide that information to the Thoroughbred Horseracing Hall of Fame.

Jimmy Winkfield

A black jockey, Jimmy Winkfield was born near Lexington at the small crossroads of Chilesburg, Kentucky, went from being the young-est of 17 children in a family of sharecroppers, to riding in races for $8 a month to eventually riding for $1,000 a race. He won back-to-back Kentucky Derbies in 1901 on "His Eminence", and 1902 on "Alan-A-Dale". Mr. Winkfield was the last black jockey to win a Kentucky Derby. Like most of the black jockeys of his era, was under tremendous racial pressure from white jockeys who were upset that the African American jockeys were being selected by white owners and trainers to ride the best horse, which resulted in the black jockeys being more successful and earning more money than their white counterparts. Eventually, the conflict between white and black jockeys spilled over to the racetrack and resulted in rough riding tactics during actual races. Reportedly, at a track in Chicago there was even a riot between black and white jockeys.

Reportedly, Jimmy Winkfield's riding career took a turn for the worse when he was blacklisted after breaking a contract with one horse owner and riding for another. In addition, in support the "JIM CROW" laws, most white owners and trainers were switching to white jockeys as the sport was becoming more noticed by the public. As a result, Mr. Winkfield got fewer good mounts and in 1904, he left America to ride for in Europe for a Polish Prince and a German Baron. Jimmy Winkfield was very a popular rider in Russia where he stayed on to ride regularly. During the early 1900s, Jimmy was earning upwards of $100,000 a year. Mr. Winkfield making $100,000 in the 1900s would translate to about 10 million dollars today. It is hard to imagine an African American Athlete making that kind of money during the "JIM

CROW ERA". We are talking Michael Jordan and Tiger Wood kind of money. In 2014, all the multimillionaire jockeys in this Country are white or Hispanic.

In 1919, the Russian Revolution swept through Odessa. Jimmy Winkfield, who was riding in Odessa, organized a group of his racetrack associates, mostly jockeys, trainers and their families, and together they took some 200 racehorses a distance of about 1,000 miles to escape the war. Mr. Winkfield settled in France and married a Russian baroness. In France, Jimmy returned to horse racing as a jockey, trainer and owner. He was very successful in the racing industry in France until the Nazis invaded, and commandeered his horses and stables. Jimmy Winkfield continued to ride for another decade, and eventually his wins tallied over 2,600. In 1930, he retired from riding, and became a trainer. During World War II, he returned to South Carolina and worked at an Aiken horse farm, but went back to France in 1953 and lived there to the age of 91.

According to published reports, in 1961, 60 years after he first rode to victory in the Kentucky Derby, Mr. Winkfield returned to Louisville for the race. Rather than being acknowledged as a Derby Legend, Jimmy Winkfield found the same lack of recognition and respect from whites that he experienced in the early 1900s when he was a rider. In spite of the fact that he was invited to a pre-Derby dinner at Louisville's luxurious Brown Hotel, according to Jimmy Winkfield's daughter Liliane Casey, the hotel was still segregated and so the doorman would not let them in. Mr. Winkfield eventually was admitted, yet according to Ms. Casey, they were snubbed and ignored by the other dinner guests. Another case of that "Old Kentucky Home" mentality exhibited by whites that is still alive at the Kentucky Derby today. At the 2002 Kentucky Derby, with his daughter, Liliane Casey and one of Jimmy Winkfield's grandchildren, who just happens to be a veterinarian that specializes in horses, in the stands at Churchill Downs, the late Jimmy Winkfield and his family was formally recognized at a post-race reception for the Derby winner.

Mr. Winkfield's story is featured in the Kentucky Derby museum and Mr. Winkfield's supporters are pushing his admission to the Thoroughbred Hall of Fame, where he would join two other African

American jockeys already honored there. Again, I ask the question as to why the citizens of Maryland are not pushing to have George "Spider" Anderson inducted into the Thoroughbred Racing Hall of Fame. The fact that these two great black jockeys have not received the recognition they deserve is another example of the lack of knowledge in the African American community of the accomplishments of these great athletes. There is an old saying that the squeaky wheel gets the grease and it is my hope that enough voices from the black community will demand that historians add more than a brief comment about Mr. Winkfield and Mr. Anderson in the record book and they will demand that these men be enshrined in the Thoroughbred Horseracing Hall of Fame.

The Great Issac Murphy

I have already talked about Willie Simms, one of the African Jockeys inducted in the Thoroughbred Hall of Fame in Saratoga, New York; one of the other black jockeys in the Hall of Fame is Isaac Murphy. He is most often referred to as the best black jockey ever. However, according to many published reports, Isaac Murphy is the greatest jockey the sport of thoroughbred horseracing has ever known black or white. During his career, Mr. Murphy won on 44.5% of all of his mounts, and usually found the winners circle without use of whip or spur. According to published reports, when the shorter race distances replaced the four-mile heat races, the jockey's ability to take immediate and complete command of his mount was essential. One of the first individuals to gain a reputation as a brilliant jockey with a perfect sense of timing and pace was Isaac Murphy. The late Marjorie Rieser Weber, a principal researcher of Isaac Murphy and other black jockeys, concluded that "he was considered the greatest judge of pace the Country had ever seen, the near-perfect jockey who rode with his hands and heels and only drew his whip to satisfy the crowd. His integrity and honor were the pride of the turf."

Isaac Murphy was born "Isaac Burns" in Lexington, Kentucky in 1861. The exact date of his birth is unknown. Out of respect for his contribution to the sport, racing historian used January 1, the date designated as the birthday of all thoroughbred horses, as Mr. Murphy's birthday. Personally, I think this was a proper tribute to a great man. However, this is another case of the need to research and develop information to provide an accurate account of one of the greatest athletes of all time. What is the importance of a first name or the exact date of birth? For African Americans, it holds the same importance as knowing the first names and exact date of birth for George Washington and Abraham Lincoln. Some of my readers might think it blasphemous for me to compare the names of Washington and Lincoln with those of former black slaves. Yet, it is just as importance when our children study black history and read about "Monkey" Simons and Isaac Murphy, that they know the reason why we do not know Mr. Murphy's exact date of birth or Mr. Simons' first name and we celebrate the birthdays of two white who were born years earlier.

In all likelihood, when Mr. Murphy was born, his black slave parents could not read or write and lacked the ability to document the date of his birth. Remember, in 1861 it was against the law for black people to know how to read or write. In addition, Mr. Murphy was born during the Civil War and white plantation owners in the South were more concerned with protecting their property than recording the birth of a newborn black slave. Mr. Murphy was known as Isaac Burns when he began his riding career and rode his first race in Louisville on May 22, 1875. In 1876, at his mother's request, he took on the last name of his grandfather, Green Murphy. As was the case with many of my slave ancestors, Mr. Murphy did not get the opportunity to know his father well. James Burns was a freed slave who enlisted in the Union Army during the Civil War and died in a Confederate Army prison camp.

Isaac Murphy was not only a "gentle man", but a gentleman as well. He won praise from everyone who knew him, even trainers and jockey he rode against. Mr. Murphy never lodged a claim of foul against any other rider, nor were the stewards ever required to call on him regarding a foul he committed during a race. Due to the fact that he was a black jockey riding against many white jockeys, white trainers and white owners, for Mr. Murphy not to claim a foul or to have one claimed against him was an amazing accomplishment for a black man during the "JIM CROW" ERA". Mr. Murphy, by far the most famous and most successful black jockey in the history of the sport, was the first jockey to win three Kentucky Derbies and in 1955, he was the first jockey to be inducted into the Hall of Fame in Saratoga, New York. According to the records of the era, which may have been incomplete, at one point, Mr. Murphy won on 628 of 1,412 mounts. In comparison, the best jockeys of today only win on 340 of 1400 mounts.

Published records indicate Mr. Murphy's first winning mount was Glentina, at the Crab Orchard Park in Lexington on September 15, 1876. He was the only jockey to have won the Kentucky Derby, the Kentucky Oaks, and the Clark Stakes, all three at one meeting in 1884. Mr. Murphy was the first rider to have back-to-back Derbies in 1890 on Riley and in 1891 on Kingman. Mr. Murphy's three Kentucky Derby wins were unequaled for 39 years, until Earl Sande won his third in 1930, and not exceeded for 57 years when Eddie Arcaro won his fourth Derby in 1948 and his fifth in 1952. Mr. Murphy won three Hindoo Stakes in 1883, 1885, and 1886; the Latonia Derby in Kentucky on May 23, 1887; and four of the first five American Derbies at Washington Park, Chicago, Illinois, in 1884, 1885, 1886, and 1888. At Saratoga, New York, in 1882 he won an incredible 49 victories in 51 starts. I included these statistics in order for you to grasp the magnitude of Mr. Murphy's accomplishments. He was the Babe Ruth, Ty Cobb, Willie May, Hank Aaron, Michael Jordan and Tiger Woods of the sport of thoroughbred horseracing.

By the way, I love to compare the notorious racist and bigot Ty Cobb to a black athlete whenever I get the chance. I truly hope that it causes him to roll over in his grave and that it provides a little discomfort for the Ty Cobb fans and white racists of the world. In 1994 the movie "Cobb" starring "Tommy Lee Jones" about the life of Ty Cobb, made it very clear that he was a bigot and racist that hated African Americans. Ty Cobb was born in rural Narrow, Georgia. He was nicknamed "The Georgia Peach". Some of the best athletes that ever lived are not in the Hall of Fame because they are black and yet a white racist like Ty Cobb sits front row center in the MLB Hall of Fall in Cooperstown, New York. They will not let Pete Rose into the

Baseball Hall of Fame because he bet on baseball and because he will not admit he bet or apologize. Pete Rose broke Ty Cobb's MLB record for the most hits in a career. They are both white and they were both fierce competitors on the field. What makes a racist any better than a gambler?

In my opinion, Pete Rose did bet on baseball because he had a gambling problem. He has an addiction to gambling, which would probably lead him to make a bet on whether or not the sun would shine tomorrow. However, because I have followed his career from day one, Pete Rose was a winner and he would never bet on his own team to lose a baseball game. When I was playing baseball, Pete Rose, whose nickname was "Charlie Hustle" was a role model for black and white kids. I would like to have my son show the desire and love for the game that Pete Rose exemplified. Yet, there is no way I would want anyone to use Ty Cobb as a role model. I know I have gotten off the subject. However, it is important for my readers to understand. It is more acceptable in white America for an athlete, worthy of admission to his or her sport's Hall of Fame, to be a racist rather than a gambler or a black man whose accomplishments occurred during the "JIM CROW" ERA". If Pete Rose and George "Spider "Anderson are not allowed in their respective sport's Hall of Fame, it is my opinion that the racist Ty Cobb should be kicked out.

I will get back to talking about Isaac Murphy. It was reported that a few weeks before Murphy's 1884 Kentucky Derby victory on *Buchanan,* the horse had nearly unseated Murphy at the post in Nashville, Tennessee, and then bolted over the track. Only the owners' threat of suspension induced Murphy to ride *Buchanan* at the Derby. He won his second Kentucky Derby in 1890 on Riley and his third on *Kingman* in 1891. At the Coney Island Jockey Club, Sheepshead Bay, New York City, on June 25, 1890, Mr. Murphy won by a head in one of his most memorable races. It was a match with *Snapper Garrison,* whose final surges gave birth to the phrase "Garrison finish", used not only in horseracing but also in other sports. Lucky Baldwin, the famous California horseman, at one time paid Mr. Murphy $10,000 a year on retainer. During his peak, Murphy was earning about $15,000 annually, and his services were in great demand. When asked by a younger jockey what the key to his success was, Murphy replied, "Just be honest".

To be given a retainer of $10,000 to ride is a lot of money even by today's standard. In Mr. Murphy's day, the retainer and his annual salary would equate to $1,000, 000. For those of you that do not understand what a retainer means for a jockey; the jockey receives a fee to ride an owner's horse before the race. In addition to his or her percentage of any purse money won as a result of the race. Today, there are about 30 - 40 jockeys that earn a million dollars a year. Only the best of the best receive a retainer. Mr. Murphy retired from the saddle in 1895, after a 20-year career. He had a serious weight problem, and during the off-season winter months, his weight would reach 140 pounds. Mr. Murphy dieted strenuously prior to the spring race meetings, and his body was weakened and subject to infection, which led to pneumonia and his death on February 12, 1896. Just as it is today, being overweight was a curse for jockeys during Mr. Murphy's day. In a 2002 episode of the HBO series "Real Sports", they interviewed several jockeys about the problem of being over-weight.

Did you know that the average weight of a professional thorough-bred horseracing jockey is between 110 and 114 pounds? If a jockey weighs over 114 lbs., he or she is considered overweight. During this, Real Sports episode, one of the jockeys confessed that he was hooked on diet pills and other illegal drugs to control his weight. As a result of his addiction, he was often suspended from racing and eventually lost his jockey license. The jockey also explained how they would force themselves to throw-up after meals and between races to maintain the 114-pound weight limit. The continued practice of throwing-up food to lose weight is what caused the death of Isaac Murphy. If not for his weight problem, Mr. Murphy may have lived to ride another 20 years and win 800 additional races. I do not remember if the Real Sports Reporter included the fact that the great black jockey Isaac Murphy died of a weight problem.

Isaac Murphy died in Lexington, leaving an estate of $30,000 to his only heir, his wife Lucy. To illustrate the level of respect this man had earned, more than 500 of racing's most distinguished members attended the funeral. The cemetery in which Murphy was originally buried was abandoned, the wooden marker decayed away, and there was a very real threat that thoroughbred horse racing's greatest jockey might be forever lost. Fortunately, some people remembered the precise location he was buried and found the grave of Isaac Murphy. His remains were relocated to the "Man o' War" Memorial Park, Fayette County, Kentucky, and a more permanent marker records his deeds. Mr. Murphy lies only a few feet away from the great thoroughbred racehorse, Man o' War and thousands of racing fans every year visit them both. For those of you that might not understand the significance and the impact of the fact that and African American, Isaac Murphy, is buried next to a racing legend "Man o' War", should compare this to Jackie Robinson being buried next to Babe Ruth.

Isaac Murphy's career inspired other black men in the late 1800s and early 1900s to become jockeys and follow in his footsteps. Unfortunately, African Americans from the 1950s never heard about the exploits of Isaac Murphy. Instead of Mr. Murphy, black kids from the 1950s choose to follow in the footsteps of black athletes named Jackie Robinson and, Jim Brown. I will be the first to admit; there are hundreds of books about the late Isaac Murphy. I will also be the first to admit that in my 40 plus years around the sport of horseracing, I never really knew that much about this great African American athlete. The problem is that of the hundreds of books written about Isaac Murphy, the black jockey, 99% were written by white authors. The reason that is a problem is that most of the readers of these books are also white and the chances of white readers spreading the word about the accomplishments of a black man so that the message will reach the black community is "slim and none". The only other way the exploits of Isaac Murphy would be communicated to African Americans is through the school system or the media.

19th Century Black Jockeys Vs. Y2K NFL and NBA

Just imagine, for over 300 years the locker rooms for jockeys at thoroughbred racetracks in the U.S., from the 1600s through the early

1900s, looked like the locker rooms today in the NBA and NFL, full of African American males. The only problem with this thought is that today, a black jockey in the locker room reserved for professional jockeys at thoroughbred racetracks, stands out like a fly in butter milk. After the end of the Negro Baseball League in the late 1950s, the number of professional black baseball players in America has diminished. Young African American athletes seem to gravitate toward basketball and football. In my opinion, black kids do not want to take the time to develop the skills necessary to play baseball. This could be the same reason we do not have many African American jockeys. Young blacks do not want to take the time to develop the skills necessary to be good jockeys.

Another reason African Americans need to study and understand the plight of black jockeys is that history does repeats its' self. For over 50 years, from the late 1860s through the early 1920s, over 300 hundred professional black jockeys had ridden horses at racetracks across this Country. During the late 1880s and early 1900s, the ratio of black to white jockeys was 5 to 1 in favor of black jockeys. African American jockeys dominated the sport of horseracing; they made more money than their white counterparts. Today, black professional football and basketball player dominate their sport and make more money than their white counterparts. Today the ratio of black to white jockeys in the U.S. is more than 50 to 1 in favor of the white jockeys. As the popularity of the sport of thoroughbred horseracing increased, the number of racing fans increased. Just as it is today, the majority of racing fans are white. In the late 1920s, the white racing fans made it clear to racetrack owners, who in turn made it clear to the thoroughbred horse owners and trainers that they wanted to see jockeys that looked more like them.

The black jockey became the victim of the laws of supply and demand. The increasing supply of white racing fans in America demanded to see white jockeys, and that resulted in the majority of black jockeys being put out of business. Today the same trend is developing in the National Basketball Association. During the late 1990s and into Y2K, with the exception of the Boston Celtics and the Utah

Jazz, it was rare for a NBA team to have more than one white player in their starting five. In 2014, black players made up close to 85% of the NBA. The last time I attended a NBA game the white fans out numbered the black fans 10 to 1. Most of those white fans sat in the expensive seats down near the floor. Most of the black fans sat in the cheap seats that where located a few feet away from the rafters. The white kids at these games dressed in Michael Jordan, Allen Iverson and Dennis Rodman jerseys.

It was obvious that most white parents did not mind their children wanting to be like Mike, because he has wholesome all-American image. However, it was just as obvious that white parents; do not want their kids idolizing other black players like Dennis Rodman or Allen Iverson because they have been labeled as troublemakers. Dennis and Allen wear gaudy tattoos; have been arrested for allegedly being involved in illegal drug or violence related circumstances and are associated with the gangster rap segment of society. For years, the white NBA team owners satisfied the white majority fan base with American born white superstars like Larry Bird, Jon Stockton and Bill Walton who are great white role models. Although there have been many attempts to find replacements for these American born white superstars, the white NBA owners have started a trend of featuring wholesome white foreign-born players as the team's superstar. As African Americans, the laws of supply and demand could result in the faces of the NBA changing from black to white.

Movies Vs. Real Life

In July 2003, a movie about" Seabiscuit", one of the most popular thoroughbred horses in the history of sports, was released. In 1949, the first movie about "Seabiscuit" was filmed. The movie featured the late Barry Fitzgerald and the late Shirley Temple in the starring roles. Just as it was in 1949, the remake of the movie features the 1938 match race between "Seabiscuit" and the famed "War Admiral". Long before I ever saw my first thoroughbred horse race or made my first visit to the "Back Side", I had heard about "Seabiscuit" and "War Admiral". Just as the men in the African American community talked about Babe Ruth and Jack Dempsey, they talked about the great Seabiscuit and War Admiral. In 1938, all professional sports venues in America were segregated. Yet in spite of the white racist attitudes that would not allow African Americans to compete in the same arenas with whites, black people loved sports and they attended sporting events and cheered for white athletes from the "colored section" of the sporting venues.

Since the early 1960s, I have seen the 1949 version of the movie about Seabiscuit at least 10 times and after watching it repeatedly, I learned more and more about this famous horse. I was at Pimlico when they filmed the match race scenes for the 2003 "Seabiscuit" movie. During the filming of this scene, Gary Stevens and Chris McCarron, both members of the jockey's Hall of Fame, rode the horses that portrayed Seabiscuit and War Admiral. For me the remake was just as exciting as watching the real thing. One day, I was talking about the Seabiscuit movie when a co-worker, everyone called him "Mr. Bill", told me that he actually saw the 1938 match race between "Seabiscuit" and "War Admiral". Mr. Bill, who was 11 years old at the time, shared his 65-year-old recollection of the big race that he viewed through a fence on Northern Parkway just outside of Pimilco Racetrack. Mr. Bill told me how he stood next to his father and his six-year-old brother while his two-year-old brother sat on his father's shoulders.

Mr. Bill and his father and brother had to watch the race threw the fence because there were only a limited number of seats and space in the colored section inside Pimilco Racetrack. This match race was one of greatest sporting events of all time and everyone, black or white, within a hundred miles of the Baltimore area, wanted to see the big race in person. I listened as Mr. Bill talked about his view of the race from the top of the stretch as these two great thoroughbreds thundered past him. He described the race as if it happened just yesterday. With the excitement of a young boy, Mr. Bill told me that Seabiscuit had the lead down the stretch and that no matter how hard he tried; War Admiral could not catch him. It was a moving experience for me to hear an eyewitness account of this great sporting event. Stories like the one shared by Mr. Bill are my inspiration for writing history in more than one color and from more than on perspective.

While America applauds the second coming of a movie about a horse, we have not had the first movie about the most famous black jockey in sport of thoroughbred horseracing. Issue like this also inspired me to write history from a black perspective. In my opinion, the only reason we do not have a movie about the life of Isaac Murphy is that he is not a household name. There is movie about the life of Jackie Robinson, the first black to play Major League Baseball. There have been several movies made about African Americans boxers. The movie "The Great White Hope" is based on the life of the first African American Heavyweight Boxing Champion, Jack Johnson. "The Brown Bomber" is based on the life Joe Louis, who in my opinion was the best professional fighter of all time. Heavyweight Champion Muhammad Ali, the most recognized name in the world of boxing, has two movies that were made about his life and Light Heavyweight Champion Ruben "Hurricane" Carter, who was falsely accused and sent to prison, has a movie about his life.

If you are a household name with lots of media attention, they even make movies about your life story when you are still in your 20s. They made a TV movie about the life of the black professional golfer, Tiger Woods, shortly after he became the first African American to win the Masters Golf Tournament. Michael Jordan has a made for TV movie about his life and career that include the tragic loss of his father. The accomplishments of Isaac Murphy as a jockey are of an equal or greater magnitude as the accomplishments of the black athletes I have just mentioned. Yet, they all have movies about their lives and Isaac Murphy does not. Maybe, if someone like Spike Lee does not beat me too it, I will make enough money to produce a feature film about the life of Isaac Murphy that will include the history of the other African American jockey of the last 200 years. Just think about it, every year around the 1st Saturday in May, the date for the Kentucky Derby, to be able to watch a movie about the life of the greatest jockey of all times, Isaac Murphy.

The 1ˢᵗ Black Professional Athlete?

Whenever I make a statement, i.e., black jockeys were the first professional athletes in the U.S., it may encourage a debate that Marshall "Major" Taylor, "the fastest bicycle rider in the world" during the late 1890s and early 1900s, was the first African American professional athlete in this Country. Major Taylor was a "superlative athlete with a graceful style and amazing suppleness and speed". Born in 1878 near Indianapolis, Indiana, he worked in bicycle shops as a youth. The shop owner provided Marshall with a military style uniform that he wore when he performed bicycle tricks to amuse the customer. People began to call him "Major". After meeting an ex-champion Professional Bicycling Champion, "Birdie" Munger, who recognized and encouraged his natural talent as a rider. Birdie became his coach and Major Taylor turned professional in 1896. Major Taylor began his racing career in Indianapolis, but racism was intense in America and especially in the Midwest, so Mr. Taylor moved to Massachusetts where he was able to race in a less hostile environment. In the late 1890s and early 1900s, Massachusetts may have been less hostile racial environment for Mr. Taylor. However, from 1974 through 1988there was a series of protests and riots that occurred in Boston, Massachusetts in response to the passing of the 1965 "Racial Imbalance Act", which ordered public schools in the State to desegregate.

Reportedly, in spite of it all the racism during the "JIM CROW" ERA", in 1894 at age 16, Mr. Taylor was a world-class sprinter, at 18, world champion at 20, and U.S. professional bike rider by age 21. In 1898 and 1899, Taylor's record setting speeds attracted the attention of the European promoters who offered him contracts to ride for pay. By the end of the 1901 season, Mr. Taylor, who was still only 22 years old, had competed at every important European track, meet and had defeated the champions of every major European cycling nation. He established numerous world records over short distances, and in 1899, he won the World Spring Championship in Montreal, Canada, becoming the second black athlete to win a world title. Major won the American sprint championship in 1900

and in 1901; he defeated every European champion during a phe-
nomenally successful European tour. Major returned to Paris for
five more seasons of racing, spent two winters in Australia, and
retired from racing in 1910. A devout Baptist, Taylor refused to
race on Sundays, sacrificing potential awards and prize money for
his religious beliefs.

Major Taylor became very well known and quite wealthy racing his
bicycle all over the world. He won in the presence of dangers associated with racial hatred because he was an excellent athlete and relied
on his knowledge and confidence in his ability. Mr. Taylor was a true
honest sportsman who was passionate about his sport but never a participant in unfair racing tactics, making him an excellent role model
for today's athletes. I shared this information about Major Taylor for
a number of reasons. To assist those of you that plan to research and
develop your own opinions about the first African American athletes
in the U.S. In addition, I wanted to bring to your attention how the historian described Major Taylor, "superlative athlete with a graceful style
and amazing suppleness and speed", the same stereotypical depictions
of an African American athlete that are still used by the white media
today. White writers will describe a black athlete physical attributes;
yet, fail to mention how intelligent that black athlete has to be in order
to be successful in his or her sport.

Another reason that I wanted to include facts about Marshall
"Major" Taylor is that at the time I am writing this book, a white professional bicycle rider, Lance Armstrong has won his 7th consecutive
Tour de France Bicycle Race. The Tour de France is the most prestigious bicycle race in the world and ESPN Sports has deemed Lance
Armstrong's feat of winning the race 7 times to be one of the greatest
accomplishments ever by any athlete. It should be noted that in 2012
Lance Armstrong was stripped of his Tour de France victories for using
performance-enhancing drugs. Just as it was hard for black jockeys to
get white owners and trainers to give them mounts, it is equally hard
for black professional bike riders to get white sponsors and bicycle
makers to give them the money necessary to defray the cost of training
for an event like the Tour de France.

In order to survive and be successful as a professional bike rider, you need a sponsor who is willing to pay for your training, equipment, travel and lodging. Just as it was with African American professional Isaac Murphy, no black person has chosen to carry on the tradition established by the great black professional bicycle rider, Major Taylor. Again, it is my hope that my mentioning of Major Taylor in my book will inspire young African Americans to pursue careers as professional jockey and bicycle riders. By the way, they did make a movie about the accomplishments of Marshall "Major" Taylor and the title is "Ride to Glory". When people in the media start singing the praises of Lance Armstrong, in the black community we can remember the accomplishment of the famous African Americans that rode horses and bicycles.

The Colored Hockey League

The fact that we as African Americans forget some of the major historical events that have an impact on our future is evidenced in the world of sports. The same fate that eliminated the dominance of black jockeys in the sport of Thoroughbred Horseracing; is the same destiny that awaits African American athletes that plays professional baseball, basketball and football. Major professional sports and the major colleges in America are slowly reducing the dominance of black players on their football and basketball teams. It has been over 70 years since Jackie Robinson broke the color barrier in professional baseball. After the Brooklyn Dodgers opened their door to black players, other teams in the National League quickly followed, by signing black players from the Negro Leagues. When baseball, America's favorite pastime and most popular professional sporting event, opened its doors to hire black players, it was just a matter of time before professional football, basketball and even professional hockey, with its predominately white fan base, hired their 1st black players

Did you know that for 30 years from 1895 through 1925, there was a professional hockey league exclusively for black players? The Colored Hockey League (CHL) was comprised of the sons and grand-sons of runaway African American slaves that had escaped to States along the Canadian border, to Canada and Nova Scotia. Reportedly, in 1851, Harriet Tubman, "Black Moses", began relocating members of her family and other slaves that she had helped to escape to St. Catharines, Canada West, which is now part of Ontario. North Street in St. Catharines remained Ms. Tubman base of operations until 1857. Reportedly, while in Canada she worked at various activities to save money to finance her activities as a Conductor on the "Underground Railroad". She also attended the Salem Chapel BME Church on Geneva Street. Sometimes I think we forget that black slaves that escaped from the oppression of slavery in the "DEEP SOUTH" could only find true freedom and safety across the border in Canada. We need to be reminded that the next to his "Gettysburg Address", the other renowned document associated with President Abraham Lincoln is the "Emancipation Proclamation". A masterful document made slavery illegal in Confederate States only. Therefore, it should come as no surprise that African slaves that escaped from the United States, found freedom in Canada started families and communities that have remained intact as we enter the next millennium.

The CHL helped pioneer the sport of ice hockey by changing this winter sport from the primitively played game for "white gentleman" of the nineteenth century to the modern fast moving game of today. In an era when many white men believed blacks could not endure cold, that their ankles were too weak to effectively skate, and that blacks lacked the intelligence for organized sport, the black men of the CHL defied these defined myths. Like the Negro League Baseball teams, the CHL was a black community institution. The administrators of the CHL were well-educated men such as Baptist ministers. The CHL produced, among other star quality athletes, an innovative goal tender for the Dartmouth Jubilees, named Henry Franklyn. Reportedly, Mr. Franklyn was the first recorded goalie to throw his body down on to the ice and stop a shot. Today, no one can conceive of a goalie that would not throw his body down in front of the net to block a pluck. During the period between 1895 and 1925, the white print media refused to acknowledge the accomplishments of either Henry Franklyn or the rest of the CHL. The fact that the white media refuse to acknowledge their existence did not stop the Colored Hockey League. However, the systematic undermining of their performance caused the merchants at the Halifax Green Market, a key component of black commerce, to withdraw their financial support and the league folded. After 1925, white Canadians were free to claim hockey as their sport.

It should be noted that in 1950, the first person of African descent signed a professional hockey contract. He was Arthur Dorrington a Canadian. After serving in the U. S. Army, Mr. Dorrington signed with New York Rangers and played with one of team's farm clubs. However, instead of moving up to the NHL in 1950, Mr. Dorrington chose to play for Atlantic City Seagulls of Eastern League, who he led to a league championship in 1951. Almost 10 years after Jackie Robinson broke the color line in professional baseball, in 1958, Willie O'Ree became the first black man to play in the National Hockey League (NHL). Mr. O'Ree played for the Boston Bruins during the 1957-58 seasons and retired from professional hockey in 1980. In honor of his pioneering spirit, the NHL created the Willie O'Ree All-Star Game that is held every year at the Junior World Championships.

I will be the first to admit that I very seldom watch professional hockey. However, I did not watch professional golf until Tiger Woods started playing. On the rare occasion that I have watched a hockey game, I could count the number of black hockey players on one hand. Much like football, the game of hockey requires a player to have speed, agility and physical toughness. Although the game is played on ice, the players are padded and they wear what appear to be very warm uniforms. NHL players make a very good salary. Therefore, I asked myself, why more African Americans do not play professional hockey? The answer to the question became clear when my 12-year old son asked me to sign him up for Little League Ice Hockey.

At my son request, I looked into what it would take to participate in a hockey league for kids his age. First, there were no ice rinks in our neighborhood. To participate in a hockey league it would require him to be at the nearest ice rink, a 25-minute drive from our house, at 4:30 am M-F for practice and games. Saturdays or Sundays were game days, which meant I would have to be committed to hockey 7 days a week.

All of these factors were a deterrent, but if my son wanted to play ice hockey, I would make the sacrifice. Unfortunately, I just could not get over another major hurdle. In order for my son to qualify to play in this ice hockey league, he would have to take a series of skating lessons and pass several hockey skill tests. After completing the lessons and passing the test, he would qualify to be assigned to a team. What knocked me and my son out of the ice hockey business, was the total cost for skating lessons, equipment and league fees was just under $1,000 for an eight-week season. The cost for ice hockey was more than the fees for five year of Little League Baseball, Football and Basketball combined.

Now I know why there were so few black hockey players. How many African American families can afford to invest that kind of time and money in a sport for a child that would probably be just as happy playing basketball, baseball or football? When I was growing up in rural Anne Arundel County, Maryland, there were certain sports that were too expensive for blacks to play. The other reason that there are so few blacks in the NHL is because of the majority of hockey fan are white. Can you imagine the potential for riots in the stands with all the fighting in the NHL if black and white hockey players were fighting on a regular basis? African Americans have made major strides in professional tennis and golf. Social and economic segregation that has kept African Americans from being more visible in professional golf and tennis is the same reason blacks are not adding ice hockey to their professional sports resumes. As African Americans continue to level the social and economic playing fields, we will become dominant figures in any game that requires speed, agility and physical toughness and pays a lot of money to its stars.

Blacks In Harness Racing

The initial information about the CHL came from watching ESPN, the cable sports news network. ESPN put together a series of sports related history and general historical trivia stories from 50 different States in 50 days. As a loyal viewer of ESPN, I found it a unique programming initiative for the network to provide some interesting information. In addition to the CHL, I saw a story about Standardbreds or Harness Racing in the State of Mississippi. During an ESPN segment, I learned that African Americans in the State of Mississippi were continuing a tradition that was passed down from their slave ancestors. That tradition was training standardbred horses for harness racing and participating in actual harness races as sulky drivers. A sulky or race bike is a lightweight, two-wheeled cart that is attached to either side of the harness, and the driver sits close behind the horse. Standardbreds move in a lateral gait, which means they move both legs on the same side forward in unison; for example, it is left front and left rear legs; then follows suit with both legs on the other side; right front and rear legs. The difference between Standardbreds and Thoroughbreds is the amount of equipment pacers and trotters wear on the racetrack. All Standardbreds wear the basic equipment of a harness and a bridle, along with a Buxton martingale, which keeps the harness from slipping. Standardbreds race in sulkies, also known as race bikes.

According to published reports, Standardbred Horseracing has long been known, as the sport of the people. Both the sport and the breed are as much a part of our American landscape as cowboys and apple pie. Harness Racing takes place at numerous tracks and fairs across North America, and is most popular in the Midwest and the East. Just as I have done with Thoroughbred Horseracing, I have watched Harness Racing on TV for years. Back in the 1970s, I used to go to Freestate Racetrack, the harness track in Laurel, Maryland and watch live harness races. Before they started to simulcast live harness races at the thoroughbred tracks or "flats", the only way to follow harness racing was to go see it live at a Harness Track. I can remember on Fridays, I would leave the Thoroughbred Track in Laurel after the last race and travel about three miles or so up the road to bet on the trotters. As much as I loved the sport, I had no idea that there were black Harness Race Drivers.

In conducting my research about African Americans in Standardbred horseracing, I found that George Teague Jr. is the Tiger Woods of Harness Racing. The problem with not knowing your history, until I discovered facts about blacks in Harness Racing, I associated the name

George Teague with the NFL All Pro Defensive Back for the Dallas Cowboys. Harness Racing's George Teague, Jr. practically grew up next door in Melfa, Delaware. His father, George Teague, Sr. was a Standardbred trainer, who had his own training track in Keller, Delaware. After graduating from high school, George Jr. went to work for his father full-time in the racing business. George Jr. started training Standardbreds on his own in 1991 and since that time has won over 600 races and won over nine million dollars in purse money. George Jr. is a standout in Harness Racing because unlike the trainers of thoroughbred horses on the flat tracks that earn 10% of the purse money, he is the owner, trainer and driver for most of his horses. This has earned him nearly 100% of those nine million dollars. Although he has conditioned many talented horses over the years, George was fortunate enough to train the 2004 Standardbred Horse of the Year, Rainbow Blue.

Black Jockey: Up Close and Personal

During my years spent hanging around the racetrack, I have had the privilege of meeting a few of the African American jockeys that rode in Maryland and West Virginia. The first black jockey I met was James "Jimmy" Thornton. Like Isaac Murphy, Jimmy Thornton was a gentleman. He was very courteous and always had a smile on his face. Jimmy was best known for being the exercise rider and for riding races for the local African American trainers who conditioned horses that ran on the Maryland Circuit and at Charlestown and Shenandoah Downs Racetracks, the two half mile tracks located in Charlestown, West Virginia. According to some of the Old Timers, Jimmy was most successful when he teamed with a Maryland based black trainer, the late Hayes Brown, whose son is currently a thoroughbred racehorse owner and a boxing manager/promoter in the Washington D.C. area. Most of Jimmy mounts and wins and most of his career accomplishments were the result of riding at Charlestown and Shenandoah Downs. Ironically, Jimmy was killed when his horse fell while riding in a race at Charlestown Racetrack.

The first thoroughbred horse that I personally owned was a three-year-old filly named *Miss Casey Jane*. With my uncle Charlie as my consultant, I purchased *Miss Casey Jane* in 1989 for $5,000 from a trainer named John Salzman, who had a stable full of horse at Laurel Racetrack. Although I was introduced to the sport of horseracing as a bettor in the late 1960s, I became a fixture on the "Back Side" after I purchased *Miss Casey Jane* in 1989. The racetrack opens every morning promptly at 6 am for training. In order to get to track on time, I would get up mornings at 4:30 am and drive 40 miles from my home in Baltimore to the racetrack in Bowie, Maryland just to spend three hours watching my trainer work with my horse. After the trainer finished with my horse, I would hang around and watch the other trainers and grooms take care of their horses. I just loved being at the racetrack. I would usually hang around until about 8 am and then I would drive back to my home in Baltimore to get ready to go to work. Of course, I would always be late for work on the days I went to the racetrack, but during that time in my life, my job away from the racetrack did not really matter. I was so obsessed with the sport of horseracing that I would call in sick because I would be too tired to go to work after driving back and forth from Bowie. On Saturdays and Sundays when I did not have to rush home to go to work, I would stay at the racetrack until noon and sometimes even later.

I hired an African American trainer at Bowie Racetrack, Oscar "Biscuit" Williams, and for her first few races, I employed a black jockey named Wayne Barnett. I remember Wayne telling me that he had a good feeling about riding *Miss Casey Jane* because he had a daughter named Kassie. In spite of all his good will, Wayne never got *Miss Casey Jane* to the Winner Circle, as a matter fact, *Miss Jane Casey Jane* died a maiden. A horse is considered a maiden until it wins a race. After more than six starts at tracks in Maryland, I realized that the horses running here were too tough for *Miss Casey Jane*. In 1989, after managing just a third place finish at Marlboro Racetrack, the lowest level of racing in Maryland, I sent *Miss Casey Jane* to William "Wash" Berry, a black trainer at Charlestown Racetrack, and before she had the opportunity to run her a race, *Miss Casey Jane* broke her ankle in a training accident and had to be euthanized.

Before each race, Wayne and I had a chance to get to know each other on a personal basis. Wayne rode *Miss Casey Jane* at least four times before he told me that his agent refused to allow him to ride her again. For those of you that are not familiar with the jockey and jockey agent relationship, I will briefly explain. Most professional jockeys hire an agent to solicit trainers for horses for their jockey to ride. A good agent has the skills necessary to determine which horse in a field of horses entered for a particular race has the best chance of winning. After making the determination as to which horse has the best chance of winning a particular race, the agent will contact the trainer or owner of that horse in an attempt to convince the owner/trainer to use his/her jockey. The agent salary is 10% to 25% of what the jockey earns from the purse money for finishing first, second or 3rd in a race. Wayne's agent did not want him to ride my horse because she never finished in the money and therefore, his agent never earned a dime from the four times he rode *Miss Casey Jane*.

Wayne is a real down to earth young man who I later found was a very good all-around athlete. I played basketball and softball with Wayne and although he was only 5'3" or 5'4" tall and 114 lbs., he displayed a great deal strength and talent in both sports. Wayne was only moderately successful as an exercise rider and jockey on the Maryland circuit. Wayne replaced Jimmy Thornton as the black jockey of choice for the African American trainers that had horses stabled in Maryland. However, with the exception of Hank Allen, there were not enough black trainers to keep Wayne busy. The truth be told, with the majority of the trainers in Maryland being white, it was very difficult for Wayne to get mounts. Yet, when he moved his tack to West Virginia, Wayne became a racing Super Star at Charlestown Racetrack where he won several riding titles. Like Isaac Murphy, Wayne's career as a jockey was cut short due to a weight problem. Over the years, he made several attempts at comebacks, but Wayne, who had a very muscular frame, could not maintain his weight at 114 lbs. for more than a few months at a time.

Wayne Barnett finally quit riding and the last time I had a chance to talk to him was in the fall of 2000. Although, I followed his career in the Racing Form, I had not talked to Wayne since 1995. In the fall of 2000, Wayne was working at Laurel Racetrack as an exercise rider and on this particular morning, he was coming off the track on a horse I was interested in buying. A black trainer, who shall remain nameless, was trying to convince me that the horse Wayne was riding was sound and well worth the $6,000 asking price. As he was slowly riding this horse from the track back to the stable area, Wayne spoke to me, he said it had been a long since he last saw me, and he asked how I was doing. I replied that it had been a long time and we engage in some general conversation about the past and he told me that he was trying to get in shape for yet another comeback. I wished him luck, but all the time I knew that his career as a jockey was over.

Wayne told me that he heard me talking about buying the horse he was on. He said the horse was sore, could not breath and that I would be making a mistake if I bought this horse. This black trainer, who lived in my mother's neighborhood and my brother use to work for, was trying to take advantage of me. Wayne saved me from making a big mistake. Again, I have not seen or talked to Wayne since that day. Years later, I am still thankful for the advice he provided. The fact that Wayne looked out for my best interest is a perfect example of being kind to the people that you meet in life because you never know when you might need a helping hand. The big horses in Wayne's career were "Tong Po", a Derby contender trained by Leon Bluezwich and "Northern Wolf" a record-setting sprinter trained by Hank Allen. Wayne Barnett's name may not appear in any other books about the sport of thoroughbred horseracing and yet, I am honored to have his name in my book.

The Hardest Working Jockey I know

In 1997, one of my best friends, Willie Kee, who trained two of my four winning horses, *Snipes Tornado* and *Irish Crossing*, left Laurel Racetrack, where he was a groom and moved to Pimilco Racetrack to

104

become the Assistant Trainer for the King T. Leatherbury, the leading thoroughbred racehorse trainer in Maryland history. Until Willie
moved to Pimilco, I had spent most of my time experiencing the "Back
Side" of racing at Bowie Racetrack, which is now a Training Center,
and at Laurel. Willie introduced me to the "Back Side" at Pimilco and
he introduced me to the African American jockey Charles W. "Charlie"
Forrest, who in my opinion is the hardest working person in the sport
of horseracing. *"The Back Side of the Sport of Kings"* is my third book. If
I had the work ethic of Charlie Forrest, by this time in my life, I would
have written and published at least 20 books.

When I first saw Charlie Forrest, he was a 10 lb. "Bug" or apprentice
rider on the Maryland Racing Circuit. Weight concession given to an
apprentice rider are usually 10 pounds until they ride their fifth winner, seven pounds until the 35th winner and five pounds for one calen-
dar year from the date of that 35th winner. The apprentice jockey rules
vary from State to State, but the basic weight allowances are consistent.
Apprentices do not receive an allowance when riding in a stakes race.
All jockeys going from track to track must have a receipt from the clerk
of scales from their track verifying the jockeys' most recent total number of wins. They are known as a "Bug" riders from the asterisk used to
denote the weight allowance on the racing program. Three asterisks
for a 10 lb. weight allowance two asterisks for a 7 lb. allowance and one
asterisk for a 5 lb. allowance. For whatever reason; his lack of experience as a rider or not being assigned to ride good horses or the fact
that he just might not have been that good of a jockey, it appeared to
me that it took Charlie almost two years to win the 35 races that would
qualify him to lose his 7 lb. apprentice allowance.

For the past 40 years or more, thoroughbred horsing in Maryland
has been a hotbed for apprentice riders. Young jockeys have come here
to begin their apprenticeships year in and year out, and have gone
on to be very successful as journeyman. Yet, Charlie Forrest seemed
to keep his "Bug" for years. When I first noticed Charlie, he never
seemed to ride in many races and he definitely did not win many races.
However, on the rare occasion when he did ride a winner everybody
seemed to be rooting for him. The workers on the "Back Side" and

the racing fans in the grandstands all seemed to love Charlie Forrest. The reason I think everyone roots for Charlie is his outstanding work ethic. I mentioned Charlie's work ethic because for seven days a week, he worked as an exercise rider and for 5 days a week, he worked as a jockey riding at Maryland tracks during the day and traveling to West Virginia to ride at Charleston Racetrack at night.

This daily routine requires Charlie to be in the jockey's room two hours before post time, which is either 12:35 or 1:05 pm in Maryland and remain until post time of the last race, which is usually around 4:30 or 5 pm. After the last race in Maryland, Charlie makes the hour and a half drive to West Virginia to ride at Charleston where the 1st race begins at 7:15 pm and the last race may not end until 11:30 pm. Other jockeys from the Maryland Racing Circuit ride at Charleston or in New Jersey at night. What makes Charlie Forrest special? After driving home to Baltimore, Maryland from Charleston, West Virginia, which means Charlie gets to bed at night around 1:30 am, he is up at 4:30 am to work his second job; exercising horses for trainers at Pimlico, Laurel and sometimes he drives for an hour to exercise or "work" horses for trainers at the Bowie Training Center. On occasions, Charlie leaves the main tracks in Maryland when they close for training at 10 am and goes to one of the local thoroughbred horse farms to work a horse. I do not know another jockey in Maryland or anywhere that works as hard as Charlie Forrest.

During the early days of his riding career, it was said that the only way Charlie Forrest could get a trainer to give him a mount in the afternoon was in exchange for his services as an exercise rider in the morning. When he first started riding, Charlie did not have an agent to solicit mounts from trainers and when you come right down to it, how Charlie was able to get trainers to let him ride their horse does not matter. What does matter is that Charlie is successful African American jockey. As a black man, he has succeeded in a profession that is now dominated by white men in this Country. Charlie is a perfect example of what can be accomplished by hard work and the willingness to stick through the tough times. He always greets you with a smile, a firm handshake, and a kind word of encouragement. With his hectic schedule, he rarely has the time to stop and talk. Charlie is one of the nicest people I have ever met. Charles W. "Charlie" Forrest is the perfect role model.

A Dying Breed!

As we entered the early 1900s, there was a sudden drop off in the number of African American jockeys riding at racetracks in the U.S. Just as it was with all other professional sports and every other aspect of society in America during this time, the "JIM CROW" laws of the land did not allow blacks to ride on the same racetrack as whites. During the height of the "JIM CROW ERA" in America, blacks could not work or live in the same area, go to school or even play on the same fields as white people. Before Jackie Robinson was born, black jockeys and black boxers were the first African Americans athletes that were paid to compete in the same event as white athletes. Although black jockeys were the first, the most famous African American to break the color barrier was Jack Johnson, the first black World Heavyweight Champion.

African American athletes have come a long way in this Country. From the day Jackie Robinson broke the color barrier in Major League Baseball, a sport that cheered admitted racist like the "Georgia Peach" Ty Cobb and Enos "Country Boy" Slaughter, white America finally cheered for Jackie. White America cheered as Joe Louis beat a white German to become the World Heavyweight Champion and Jesse Owens won four Gold Medals at 1932 Olympics that was attended by a famous bigot, Adolph Hitler. A NFL team located in the Nation's Capital, with the name a nickname "Redskins", which I find to offensive to Native Americans, was lead to victory by Doug Williams, the first black quarterback to win a Super Bowl. Tiger Woods became the first African American to win the Masters in professional golf at a private club in Augusta, Georgia that just a few years ago, would only allow blacks to come in to clean, cook or caddy.

Just think about it, 250 years ago in America white people paid as little as $100 or as much as $5,000 dollars to purchase my black ancestors as slaves. Today, the white ancestors of those former slave

owners pay as much as $10,000 to sit at courtside to watch the ances-
tors of slaves play a game. To paraphrase a saying made popular by
the famous black promoter Don King, "this could only happen in
America". As we entered the new millennium, the most popular athletes in the world are black men and women that are easily recognized
by their first names, i.e., Michael; Shaq; Tiger; Kobe Lebron; Venus
and Serena; and they are all multi-millionaires, who make just as much
money from commercial endorsements as they do playing their particular sport. The commercial endorsements for Michael Jordan, Tiger
Woods and Lebron James, are estimated at over 400 million dollars.

Wanting to "be like Mike" and play basketball replaced boxing and
baseball as the sport to play to get out of the poverty and despair of the
black ghetto. Tigers Woods, golf, and Venus and Serena Williams, tennis, made sports that had been traditional reserved for wealthy white
people, popular in the African American community. I applaud these
positive changes in American society. Jackie Robinson played baseball
and was the first black person to become a professional in one of the
three major sports in America; yet, in 2014 the number of professional
African American baseball players has diminished. Today Latinos,
Hispanics and Asians are replacing African Americans as the minority
race with the most players in MLB. My concern is that I would hate to
see the end of players like Willie Mays, Hank Aaron and Barry Bonds
in MLB. It is up to the African American community to replenish the
number of black baseball players in this Country. We need to teach our
kids about the black baseball players of the past in order to preserve
these legends for the future.

The number of blacks in professional baseball is a sharp contrast to
professional football where 35 of every 55 players on a team are black
and an even sharper contrast to professional basketball where every 8
out of 12 players are African Americans. As we enter 2014, the number
of African Americans in NFL remains stable. However, in the NBA,
white owners have gone to Europe in an attempt to recruit athletes for
the game played on the court that will look more like the fans in the
seats. This same trend happened in professional baseball, thoroughbred horseracing and professional bike riding. African Americans do

not fill the stands for professional sporting events and therefore, team owners and sponsor want a product on the field that their customers can associate with, and that product in professional sports is becoming more and whiter. The history was barely documented and we have all but forgotten the America's first superstar athletes, the African American Jockeys, it is my hope that we will not forget the African American athletes of this generation.

Today, black athletes dominate professional basketball and football in America, and yet the overwhelming majority of the owners of professional basketball and all the owners of professional football teams in this Country are white. In 2010, although blacks dominate the roosters of professional football and basketball, we still are far behind as team front office Executives. There are more black coaches in professional basketball than any other professional sport in America. On average, black professional football and basketball player make more money than their white counterparts. However, in 2014, the number of professional sports teams has increased, yet we still only have one African American, Michael Jordan, owner of a major sports team. In addition, the number of African American head coaches in professional basketball does not reflect the percentage of black players. For example, African Americans make up over 70% of the players in professional basketball, and blacks only make up 30% of the coaches. In professional football, African Americans make up over 70% of the players and although there has been tremendous progress in hiring African Americans for management positions in sports, we still have a long way to go before we achieve that level playing field that we have heard so much about.

In the 1960s, I can remember a MLB All Star game where six of the nine starting players selected to the National League team were African Americans. During the late 1960s, it would have been very difficult to pick and All Star team in the National League that did not include Hall of Fame inductees; Pitcher Bob Gibson, 1st Basemen Willie McCovey, Shortstop Ernie Banks, and Outfielders Willie Mays, Hank Aaron, Lou Brock and Frank Robinson. Baseball statistics date back to the early 1900s. Prior to 1948 white players held all the records.

During the early years of professional baseball, names like Babe Ruth, Ty Cobb, Dizzy Dean, Mickey Mantle, and Ted Williams that were synonymous with Major League Baseball. However, after 1948 and through the remainder of the century, African American baseball players dominated the game and took control of most of the hitting and base stealing categories in Major League Baseball. For example, from the 1900s through the 1960s, 100 of the top 100 home run hitters in MLB were white. In only 50 years, half the time that it took their white counterparts, as we entered the new millennium, African Americans baseball player had taken over 33 of the top 100 leading home run hitters in MLB, occupying five of the top 10 spots.

Baseball historians had thought that no one would ever surpass the 714 home run hit by the great Babe Ruth. In 2014, both Hank Aaron with 755 and Barry Bonds with 762, have far exceeded the 714 home run mark of Babe Ruth. For the perfect example of the diminishing number of African Americans athletes participating in a sport, all you need to do is take a close look at college and professional baseball today. In 1948, when Jackie Robinson signed a contract with the Dodgers, it became the dream come true for young black men. African American boys could now turn their God given talents as baseball players into a high paying profession. In the 1950s, baseball was now an alternative road out of the poverty-stricken black communities of the South, with their run down shacks and the only job opportunities available for blacks was working in the cotton fields or on the railroad. There was also a similar alternative road out of the black Northern urban neighbors and the ghettoes that featured rat and roach infected high-rise apartments, where the only job opportunities were the minimum wage jobs working in as a janitor or housekeeper.

The famous black singer, composer and pianist, Ray Charles asked the question as he listened to a popular white singer perform a revised version of one of his old songs, "What have they done to my songs? They picked my brain like a chicken bone. What have they done to my songs?" If Jackie Robinson were alive today, he would probably look at baseball and say, "What have they done to my game"? Branch Rickey, the owner of the Brooklyn Dodgers, the first Major League

Team to hire an African American to play professional baseball, was an economic visionary. Branch signed Jackie Robinson away from the Negro Leagues because he saw the potential in the increased revenue from African Americans attending MLB games. White Historians has credited Branch Rickey's as being a great humanitarian for signing Jackie Robinson. White Historians made the same mistake when they anointed President Lincoln the Great Emancipator. A thorough study of the signing of the Emancipation Proclamation and the signing of Jackie Robinson will reveal that both were done for strictly economic reasons. In the late 1960s through the 1990s, many African Americans viewed the fact that NCAA Division One schools had finally opened its doors to talented black athletes as a positive change. What we as African Americans failed to realize was with this acceptance of blacks in Division I schools, we were about to lose these talented athletes at our traditional black colleges and universities. The same destiny that awaited Negro League Baseball after the signing of Jackie Robinson is the same fate that awaits the athletic programs at major Black Colleges and Universities.

The migration of the most talented African American athletes to predominately white Division One Colleges and Universities started in1966 when Texas Western used an all-black starting five and played only its African American players to defeat the legendary coach Adolph Rupp and the all-white team from the University of Kentucky to win the NCAA Basketball Tournament. For close to 30 years the white media had anointed the University of Kentucky, under Coach Rupp, a powerhouse in college basketball. However, rather than admit he was defeated by a better team "Adolph" Rupp, a typical white Southerner, made statements that cast doubt on both the talent and intelligence of the African American that played for Texas Western. If I had been a writer for a black newspaper in 1966, I would have attributed coach Rupp's racist remarks to another notorious racist named "Adolph". Again, this is a perfect example of how our history continues to repeat its' self. White men have always questioned the integrity and intelligence of black athletes. As early as 1948, Jackie Robinson was described as being gifted, talented and a natural athlete. Very rarely was it mentioned in the media how intelligent Mr. Robinson was as a ball player. Jackie was an outstanding scholar who he attended college at UCLA and was an officer in the U.S. Army.

The white media cannot accept the fact that African American athletes are just as intelligent as white athletes. Six years after Texas Western defeated Kentucky, in 1973 it was Johnny Rogers who became the straw that finally broke the camel's back to break the "color line" in Division I sports. When Johnny helped the University of Nebraska defeat another legendary coach Paul "Bear" Bryant and the University of Alabama football team in the 1972 Orange Bowl; shortly after they were defeated by teams featuring black athletes, both Kentucky and Alabama, formerly all-white athletic programs, recruited and signed their first African American athletes. The impact on predominately-black school athletic programs, such as Grambling, Southern, North Carolina A & T, Morgan and Maryland State College, was the same as the impact on Negro League Baseball. The revenue from football and basketball suffered a steady decline. The greatest negative impact from the loss of talented African American athletes at black colleges was on the sport of baseball. Although baseball is not the major sport at most black colleges, many MLB teams used black colleges to develop African American baseball players. If Jackie Robinson were alive today, he would probably look at baseball and say, "What have they done to the college baseball game"?

The African American male in baseball in college, in high school and in little leagues has become an endangered species. Blacks would rather play basketball year round than to participate in baseball during the spring and summer. To their credit, MLB has tried to develop inner city baseball programs to attract minorities to the game. Unfortunately, it takes less space to put up a basketball court than a baseball diamond. Economically, it takes more money to run a baseball league than it does for basketball. With the attraction of young superstars living high school and making millions in the NBA, baseball is finding it harder and harder to compete with basketball. The black baseball player is going the way of the black jockey; history does repeat its' self. I am tired of listening to the all the old baseball players that are badmouthing the modern day players for using steroids or performance enhancing drugs. In a TV interview, Hall of Fame baseball player and the first African American manager in Major League Baseball, Frank Robinson was very critical of any of the "new age" players that might have use performance enhancers to improve their ability to play the game of baseball. In fact, Frank was so judgmental in his comments that he proposed a lifetime ban for any player that was found guilty of using steroids and Frank Robinson felt that the player's accomplishments in baseball should be removed from the record books.

It is a proven fact that one of the most difficult things to in sport is to hit a round ball with a round bat. It is my opinion and the opinion of most that have played the game, there is not a pill, cream or potion you can take to help to improve your ability to hit a baseball. It is a God given talent and the way to improve is with practice and more practice and even then the best players in the world are only successful a third of the time. Frank Robinson was a great baseball player, but just as I have talked about the "Crab Syndrome" having a negative effect on politics, it can have a negative effect on sports. It is up to legendary Hall of Fame baseball players like Frank Robinson, Hank Aaron, and Bob Gibson to join with other African American Hall of Fame baseball players and spread the word about the love of baseball. The great Willie Mays has come to the forefront as the leading ambassador for African Americans in baseball. In 2014, whenever he does an interview, Willie Mays has nothing but positive things to say about the game, and always tells how much he loved to play baseball.

In 2007, Carsten Charles "CC" Sabathia, a young African American pitcher for the Cleveland Indians, made a public statement that MLB needs to do something to encourage more young black kids to play baseball. At the time, that he made this statement CC was the only African American player on the previous year's roster. The problem with CC's statement is that it may be too little and much too late. If young black player like CC had studied their black American history, they would have known that the same way that African American jockey relinquished their domination of the sport of thoroughbred horsing, the same thing could happen to black baseball players in America.

History does and will repeat its' self. The NBA is rapidly changing from a league dominated by African Americans to a league that has seen a steady increase of white players from Europe, Canada and South America. Why would the NBA make the switch back to being a league dominated by white player? The answers are very simple. The quality and skill level of the white foreign player has vastly improved over the past 20 years; the majority of the owners of NBA teams are white; and the majority of the fans that buy the high price tickets to attend NBA games are white.

Wake up black basketball players that aspire to one day reach the NBA. Protect your positions in the game before you lose them. Your demands for high salaries and your unprofessional behavior could someday leave you on the outside looking for somewhere to play. The problem with us is that we cannot see the handwriting on the wall. Just think, in a league that featured black superstar players like Lebron James, Kobe Bryant, Allen Iverson, Dwayne Wade Shaquille O'Neal and Carmelo Anthony; yet, in back to back years 2005 and 2006, the media voted a white player, Steven Nash as the MVP in the NBA. The NFL is predominately-black player, but the star position, quarterback is still dominated by high paid white quarterbacks. However, in 2014, there are an increased number of teams in the NFL that feature an African American at the quarterback position. The teams that start a black quarterback are quick to highlight their attributes as being agile, elusive, fast, and strong-armed. The media has never placed a strong emphasis on the intelligent of a black quarterback. Prior to the 2014 Super Bowl, sport analyst continued to describe the white quarterback for the Denver Broncos, Peyton Manning, as intelligent and the black quarterback for the Seattle Seahawks, Russell Wilson, as athletic. In the over 40-year history of the Super Bowl, there has only been two black quarterbacks and two African American head coaches to win a Super Bowl. On November 22, 2002, Ozzie Newsome was named general manager of the Baltimore Ravens, making him the first African American to occupy that position in the NFL. In 2013, Ozzie became the first African American General Manager win a Super Bowl ring when the Ravens defeated the San Francisco 49ers in Super Bowl XLVII.

Chapter 3

"JACK OF ALL TRADES"

I open this chapter with a poem titled "Being Black in the Workplace". The reason I opened with this poem is that it describes the plight of the average African Americans who strive to succeed at his or her particular craft in this Country. For most African Americans, it has been and continues to be a struggle to coexist in the workplace in this Country. As black people, we face the same social, economic and cultural stereotypes in the workplace that our ancestors faced over 100 years ago. The changes in technology have not eliminated the racist attitudes and bigotry of the past. I wish I knew who the author was for the following poem because I would have loved to be able to give him/her credit for these words. The words in this poem describing the problems are so very true and they express exactly how I felt on a daily basis on my job. I received it via email at work and I immediately copied it and posted it on my bulletin board for all to read.

"They take my kindness for weakness. They take my silence for speechless. They consider my uniqueness strange. They call my language slang. They see my confidence as conceit. They see my mistakes as defeat. They consider my success accidental. They minimize my intelligence to "potential". My questions mean I am unaware. My advancement is somehow unfair. Any praise is preferential treatment. To voice concern is discontentment. If I stand up for myself, I am too defensive. If I do not trust them, I am too apprehensive.

I am defiant if I separate. I am fake if I assimilate. Yet, constantly I am faced with work place hate. My character is constantly under attack. Pride for my race makes me, "TOO BLACK". Yet, I can only be Me!, And, who am I you might ask? I am that Strong Black Person who stands on the backs of my ances-tors achievements, with an erect spine pointing to the stars with pride, dignity, and respect, which lets the work place in America know that I not only possess the ability to play by the rules, but I can make them as well!! Author Unknown "

The Jacks of All Trades

This chapter is dedicated to the African American horsemen who for lack of a level playing field became grooms, the men I consider the "Jacks Of All Trades" on the "Back Side". In introduction, I talked about the professionals that provide the support services that ensure the show goes on as scheduled. Remember, as you read this chapter, I am writing about black American History. Although there are no statistic to supports this statement, based on information provided by the "Old Timers" that work in the stable area, over 50 years prior to the time this book was published, the late 1940s and early 50s, 85% of the grooms working in the Sport of Thoroughbred Horseracing in America were black men. Over 50 years before that, the late 1890s and early 1900s, nearly 100% of the grooms working on the "Back Side" of thoroughbred racetracks were African Americans. If you go back another 50 years, the late 1850s to the 1865, not only were 100% of the men who worked with thoroughbred racehorses in the stable area black, they were all slaves.

American horseracing has its deep roots in Virginia, where the tal-ents of African American horsemen made them among the most highly valued slaves in colonial times. In writing about African American his-tory, I try to stay away from returning to the "Mother Land". My books are about my African ancestors after they arrived in this Country. This is why my books are considered Black American or African American history. In my other books, I do refer to the fact that my black African ancestors participated with white Europeans in establishing an eco-nomic partnership that involved the selling of black slaves. I also wrote about the transporting by ship of black slaves from Africa to America. I try not to write about the "Africa to America" episode of black American history. However, I do need to provide some background as to how my ancestors gained their knowledge and experience with horses. When I think about Africa, I think about lions, tigers, poisonous snakes, giraffes and elephants. The closest thing in Africa to looking like a horse would be a zebra.

Knowledge is indeed power, and education is the key to knowledge. I have said that so often and yet it still amazes me when I find new facts about my ancestors while conducting my research. I knew my ancestors in Africa raised cattle, I wrote about that in "No Land No Mule No Freedom". The fact that native Africans raised cattle in the "Mother Land" made it a very easy transition for former black slaves who left the Southern plantation as freed men to work on cattle ranches as cowboys in the West. The Oyo Empire, established in West Africa in the 1400s, was known for its use of horses. The Oyo may have adopted the use of the cavalry during the sixteenth century. The United States Army's 10th Cavalry were known as "Buffalo Soldiers". After the Civil War, the black soldiers that fought in the Union Army, along with other recently freed black slaves, migrated to the West and joined the U.S. Army to fight the Native Americans. Although the Civil War was over and slavery had ended, white and black soldiers were not allowed to serve together. Just as in the Civil War, black soldiers, led by white officers formed the 10th Cavalry.

Black Cavalry

Just in case you are not familiar with the 10th Cavalry, the Native Americans gave the African Americans the name "Buffalo Soldiers", because their coarse hair and dark skin resembled the buffalo. For the Native Americans that settled in Western Plains of America, the buffalo was their main source of food and clothing. Knowing how highly the buffalo was regarded in the Native American culture, I consider it an honor that the Native Americans called my ancestors that proudly served in the U.S. Army's 10th Cavalry, "Buffalo Soldiers". Today, throughout the United States, African Americans have established chapters of a social organization named the "Buffalo Soldiers" that was formed to carry on the memory and to honor the African Americans that served in the U.S. Army's 10th Cavalry. Now that I know how proficient my African ancestors from the Oyo Empire in West Africa were as horsemen and in the use of cavalry, it should come as no surprise that the former black slaves, some of whom had probably never ridden a horse, became very capable horse soldiers. For you current "Buffalo Soldiers", I hope your organization will continue to research the use of the cavalry in Africa.

The climate in the Southern section of West Africa were the Oyo lived was not conducive to raising horses. Therefore, the Oyo imported their horses from the Central Sudan. The African tribes from the Central Sudan were breeders and traders. Next to the salt and gold trade, trade for horses was one of the most important exchanges between Sub-Saharan Africans and North Africans. The Oyo traded black slaves for European and American horses and equipment such as saddles and carriages as well as the traditional commodities such as cloth, guns, and beverages. Just as the owners of thoroughbred horses were in Colonial America, horses were so highly prized in the Oyo Empire and Central Sudan in Africa that only the wealthy and powerful could own them. There is another fact that made the ownership of horses in the Oyo Empire in West Africa similar to the ownership of horses in Colonial America. The Oyo used black slaves to care of their horses the same as white thoroughbred horse owners use African American slaves to care for their horses in this Country. This information about the Oyo Empire supports the well-known theory that the earliest Civilizations were in fact established in Africa.

Black Trainers

On racetracks, African American trainers were figures of authority because of their character, dignity and expertise. Many black trainers started out as jockeys, gaining the feel for a horse that comes only from time spent in the saddle. As a result of their experience, black trainers knew horses "inside out" and instructed their jockeys in the art of race riding. The white writers of thoroughbred horse racing history relate that the best African American trainers were given their freedom and paid handsomely for their services. Reportedly, because Kentucky's antebellum, pre-Civil War slave laws required freed black men to leave the State, some African American trainers were supposedly slaves, although their status and earning power made them well-respected members of the racing community. In spite of discrimination, many African American horsemen were successful trainers. Raymond White had horses in the 1932 and 1944 Kentucky Derbies and Edison "Ned" Gaines trained King Clover for the 1951 Derby. After 1951, there would not be another black trainer in the Derby until 1989, when I, along with every other Maryland horsemen, cheered for Marylander Hank Allen's *Northern Wolf.*

Other stakes-winning African American trainers that won the Kentucky Derby include Joe Willis, Carl Sitgraves, Arthur Perossier, Jake Bachelor and Oscar Dishman Jr. William "Uncle Billy" Walker, one of the black men who personifies "the best" of American racing was an outstanding jockey. According to published records, Walker won the 1878 "match of the century" at Churchill Downs aboard *Ten Broeck* over *Molly McCarthy,* and he rode in four Derbies, winning on *Baden-Baden* in 1877. When Mr. Walker became too heavy to ride, he turned to training. At the time of his death in 1933, he was the acknowledged American authority on thoroughbred pedigree and consultant to prominent Kentucky breeder John E. Madden on matters of conformation and breeding. Although crippled by arthritis, Walker was a fixture at all the prominent sales, both in Kentucky and New York, a wealthy and elegant gentleman who left no heir to his encyclopedic knowledge. Mr. Walker is buried at the Louisville Cemetery at the corner of Eastern Parkway and Poplar Level Road in Kentucky.

Ansel Anderson, a black slave, trained the great Southern racehorse *Brown Dick.* In 1856, Mr. Anderson was sold to a white man named Keene Richards from Kentucky. When Richards fell on hard times, another white man R.A. Alexander, Richards' friend and neighbor, bought Mr. Anderson, freed him and paid him handsomely for his services. Guided by Mr. Ansel, Alexander's Woodburn Stud became one of the foremost racing and breeding farms of the South. After R.A. Alexander's death, Ansel Anderson, the former black slave, trained the first Kentucky Derby winner in 1875, *Aristides*, for H. Price McGrath.

An African American, Dudley Allen co-owned and trained the 1891 Derby winner "Kingman". Isaac Murphy rode "Kingman". It was probably the first time that a Kentucky Derby winner was owned, trained and ridden by African Americans. Mr. Allen retired from the training horse after having accumulated a good-sized fortune, and lived in Lexington, Kentucky until his death.

Raleigh "Rolla" Colston was associated with horses all his life. In 1875, as a teenager, he rode in the first Derby, but finished out of the money. His success as a trainer came at the turn of the 20th century, when he entered the Derby with a horse he owned and trained, named Colston, finishing third. After Mr. Colston died in 1928, the Thoroughbred Record remembered him as a man "respected by all who knew him; an ornament to his profession and [his] race." The Louisville Herald-Post's reporter, Robert Dundon wrote of him, "He had the real Kentucky background, and was a horseman of the old school."

Ed Brown began his career as a jockey, with Ansel Anderson as his mentor. He went on to be one of the best-known trainers and turf authorities of the late 19th century. Mr. Brown was the winning trainer of the Kentucky Derby in 1877 with *Baden-Baden*, an African American jockey; William Walker rode the horse to victory. This was probably the second black trainer and jockey combination to win the Kentucky Derby. Mr. Brown trained three other Derby winners: *Hindoo, Ben Brush*, and *Plaudit*; and the won the 1893 Kentucky Oaks with *Monrovia*, a filly that he owned, entered in the race under the ownership of "E. Brown & Co." Mr. Brown died in Louisville in 1906. Reportedly, he was one of the wealthiest African Americans in Kentucky.

The trainer is responsible for orchestrating and monitoring the recovery of injured athletes. On most professional sport teams, the trainer is either a medical doctor or a health care professional with a degree in sports medicine. Based on their experience, most professional sport team trainers earn a high six-figure income and have become such an integral part of the team that they are introduced along with the players at games. In today's society, physical fitness is a trend that has become just as addictive as any narcotic. Men, women and children of all ages are involved in physical fitness programs.

Americans, regardless of race, color or creed, spend billions of dollars on merchandise to facilitate their pursuit of physical fitness. We join expensive fitness clubs and buy expensive fitness attire and equipment. Those of us that can afford it, hire a personal trainer to develop and supervise our daily fitness regiment. The most important reason to be physically fit is that it normally helps you to maintain good health. Yet, some of us use physical fitness to enhance our grooming process. We not only want to feel good, we want to look good as well. Today, in most sports, the term used for the person who helps to condition an athlete to perform at their best during a contest and helps the athlete to recover after the physical strain of an event is called a trainer. A professional trainer develops physical fitness programs, which include exercise and diet. Whenever a player is injured while competing, the first person to come to their aid is the team trainer.

Can you imagine going from being the "King of Hill", and then as time passes you now find yourself at the "Bottom of the Barrel"? In a nutshell, that is the story of the transition of the African American thoroughbred horse trainers in America. During slavery, the white masters placed selected black slaves in positions of authority over other black slaves. History records the fact that white plantation owners placed black slaves in charge of other slaves that worked in the field also known as "field hands". Another slave was in charge of the slaves that worked in the masters' house as servants. In addition, there was a black slave who was put in charge of the masters' finest thoroughbred horses and all the other slaves that worked in the stables.

Charles "Charlie Boy" Hall

Just as black jockeys no longer dominate the sport of thoroughbred horseracing, today black trainers in America are few and far between. However, as black jockeys became Exercise Riders, black trainers also took on a new role. How many times have you heard someone called a "Jack of All Trades", which is usually followed by "The Master of None"? After white trainers replaced the black trainers, the former slaves, who became trainers, became grooms because they still had the knowledge and the skill needed to make a horse perform at its best. I give the credit to my mother, who carried me to the racetrack while I was still in the womb, for my love of horseracing. However, the person that introduced me to the "Back Side" of Thoroughbred Horseracing was my uncle, Charles "Charlie" Hall, who worked in the Stable Area in a position called "groom" for close to 30 years. Following in his father's footsteps, Charlie started at the bottom level position on the "Back Side" as a "Hotwalker", and eventually became a groom. After 30 years of working as a groom, Charlie finally became Stable Foremen, an Assistant Trainer and today is a successful owner and trainer of a few horses. When it comes to the sport of horseracing, Charlie Hall is a "Jack of All Trades" and in my opinion a "Master" of the Sport of Thoroughbred Horse Racing.

Charlie has worked closely with every professional responsible for preparing a horse for a race. He has worked for or with some of the best trainers, veterinarians, farriers (aka blacksmith), and exercise riders that ever set foot on the racetrack. If there were a Hall of Fame for Grooms, Charlie Hall would be selected on the first ballot. In 2014, my uncle, Charlie Hall is the Stable Manager for the Laurel Race Course and the Pimlico Racetrack in Maryland. Charlie Hall is old enough to have actually experienced many of the socially, economic and cultural changes that have taken place on the "Back Side" over the last 60 years. One of the things that I have witnessed about the sport of thoroughbred racing is that the people that love it stay in the game forever. Like my uncle Charlie, it is not unusual to find horsemen with 60, 70 or 75 years of experience. Although, I still have a lot to learn about the sport of horseracing, Charlie has taught me many valuable lessons about the "game within the game" of thoroughbred horseracing. I will talk more about the game within the game later on in this chapter.

Charlie's father, Mr. "Buddy" Hall was a groom and although I have known Charlie for over 50 years, I never met his father. Whenever I went to the Hall residence, "Mama" Sarah, Charlie's mother, who was as kind and loving to me, as she was to everyone who ever came to her door, would greet me. Yet, whenever I visited, Mr. Buddy was on the road with the horses. That was life in the Hall's home for as long as I can remember. Mama Sarah stayed home with their 6 children and Mr. Buddy followed the horses from track to track, which meant traveling from Maryland, to Delaware, to New Jersey and as far away as Florida and Arkansas. Charlie Hall's father, affectionately known as "Mr. Buddy" passed the torch of longevity to his son by working on the "Back Side" for close to 50 years. Although I knew his wife and I know all of his children, I never met Mr. Buddy. You see I was very close to the Hall family because Charlie Hall married my Aunt Dorothy and his brother Arthur married her sister and my Aunt Laura. I would have thought that as many times as I have visited the Hall residence during my childhood, my teenage years and even as a young adult, I would have met Mr. Buddy, but during his career as a horsemen, he was rarely home. In the winter, he was in Florida, and in the summer, he was in either Delaware or New Jersey. During Mr. Buddy days on the "Back Side", in order for a groom to keep his job, he had to pack up a travel with the trainer and horses. It would not have been cost effective to make frequent trips home to visit the family.

Fortunately, for me, I got to know and come to love the fine lady who was wife to Mr. Buddy and mother to Charlie. Ms. Sarah Hall, who everyone that ever knew her called Mama Sarah, was a beautiful person. She was the perfect example of the strong black women who are the backbone of their family. Unfortunately, when my uncle Charlie tried to follow in his father's footsteps, my aunt Dorothy could not fill the same role as Mama Sarah. Eventually the strain of Charlie's being on the road, while my aunt Dorothy stayed at home, destroyed their marriage. I believe that true love is hard to find. For my aunt Dorothy, whom we affectionately call "Tootsie", from the time she was a young teenager, Charlie Hall was her one true love. She tried traveling from track to track and even tried staying at home to raise two children while their father traveled with the horses. To her credit, she tried to adjust her lifestyle to that of a horseman's wife, but for her the transition was just too difficult. To his credit, Charlie tried working at jobs other than on the racetrack. He worked on the B&O railroad where he repaired old track and laid new track. He tried being a live in caretaker on the estate of a rich white family in Sandy Springs, which is located in Montgomery County, Maryland. Ironically, one of his duties as caretaker on this estate was cleaning the stable and grooming the riding horses that belonged to this this rich white family. It was not long before the call of the racetrack lured Charlie back to his first and only true love, the "Back Side of the Sport of Kings"

The Grooms Life

In the sport of thoroughbred horseracing, trainers are the professionals that are directly responsible for care and conditioning of the expensive equestrian athletes housed on the "Back Side", as well as the supervision of the support staff the assist with the care and conditioning process. Trainers that only have one or two racehorses, usually handle all of the tasks necessary to properly care and condition their horses without any support staff. Trainers responsible for a stable of four to as many as 100 or more horses will hire support staff, including grooms, to help take of the animals. With the exception of the training schedule, necessary to condition a horse for a race, all the other tasks of for a professional thoroughbred trainer is delegated to an Assistant Trainer or stable foreman and the horse's groom. These tasks include the diet, health and safety, boarding and the administering of any prescribed medication, or chemical supplements. The average racehorse trainer makes about $80,000 a year, the average veterinarian makes about $120,000 a year and in stark contrast, the average groom makes $30,000 a year.

The word and the profession called "Groom" originated in the Royal Households of Europe. A groom could be a helper in the royal kitchen or bedroom, an assistant to the royal valet for a king or prince, and an assistant to the royal butler. Being a groom was the apprenticeship for becoming a valet and from valet one progressed to butler. In some European Countries, a Royal Groom was placed in charge of the stables and horses. In other European Countries, during a war the Royal Groom was called the Marshall and was in charge of all the horses used by the military forces. In 1600s, white American Aristocrats tried to mimic the lifestyle of European Royalty. However, rather than continuing the tradition of using white European servants, with the start of slavery, white American Aristocrats switched to black slaves as household servants. To be European Royalty was a birthright. To be the servants of European Royalty was also a vocation that was traditionally passed down from one generation to the next. Today, in England, to be a servant of the Royal Family is considered a very prestigious position. In fact, in England the Royal Butler is treated like the Chief Executive of a major corporation. Unfortunately, in this day and time in America, most domestic servants are not held in such high regard.

My African ancestors dominated many professions in America during slavery that are still very much part of the black community today. Years ago, maids, butlers, valets, coachmen or chauffeurs, and the stable grooms, all had a historical background of being part of the staff assigned to care for the white slave masters' family in this Country. Unfortunately, when these positions are referred to in American history or sociology classes, they are put in the category of domestic servants, and considered to be a lower class, unskilled positions, that required very little training or education. This stereotype needs to be corrected. The white historians and white school administrators in America fail to provide information that would erase the stereotypes that are associated with domestic servants. White America would rather have blacks reflect the uneducated images of the TV maid "Beulah" and the chauffer "Hoak" and the housekeeper "Idella" from the movie "Driving Miss Daisy" than the sophisticated image of the black TV butler "Benson" who ran a Governor's Mansion. I want to challenge educators to research and develop the more positive aspect of being a domestic servant. Aside from the fact that a more in-depth study of domestic servants would remove certain stereotypes, it could make a career as a domestic servant more inviting to persons who may have at one point felt it was an undignified occupation.

The Royal Servants were and still are very well trained and educated. Royal Servants in Europe and their black slave counterparts in America had to be well trained in the social graces in order to function as household servants in very diverse surroundings. Servants in the royal place and black slaves in the white masters' mansion had to be able to speak more than one language in order accommodate the guest that visited the palace or mansion. Some of my black slave ancestors that could not read or write, yet, they could speak French and Spanish in order to accommodate their masters' houseguest. In comparison with the Royal Servants, on the "Back Side" of the sport of horseracing, a hotwalker would equate to an apprentice valet, a groom would be equal to a King's Personal Valet and assistant to the butler, and the trainer would be the butler. The path to becoming a Royal Butler or a Thoroughbred Horse Trainer requires a combination of years of training and experience. To be a groom in the Royal Household and on the "Back Side" requires an equal amount of training and experience.

Over the last 45 years, I have watched every movie I could find about the sport of thoroughbred horseracing. Before I became acquainted with the professions and characters on the "Back Side", I did not know who the black men were in the movies that always walked horses into the winner's circle after the race. I did not know who and why these black male characters in the horseracing movies always spent time around the barn area with the thoroughbred horses that were the featured stars of the movies. I now know that that these black male characters in the movies were grooms and hotwalkers. Yet, in all the thoroughbred horseracing movies, we have never seen a black character play a featured role. The reason for information about the "Back Side of the Sport of Kings" to be part of your history lesson is to make sure the next time you watch a movie like *Seabiscuit* you will remember the impact that blacks had on the early development of the sport of horseracing.

Why is there such a difference in the salaries of grooms and trainers? The answer is simple. There is only a hand full of black trainers who work at the racetracks in Maryland. A good groom is paramount to the performance of a thoroughbred racehorse and just as important to the success of a thoroughbred winning a race as trainers and veterinarians. The majority of grooms are black, this is still America, and in this Country, a black man will never be equal. The racist mentality of white owners and trainers will not allow them to give credit to an African American groom when a horse performs well; nor will they give fair compensation to a black groom for their contribution to a thoroughbred's performance in winning a race. Earlier in the chapter two, America's First Super Star Athletes, I talk about the lack of professional black jockeys in this Country. We pay little or no attention to the fact that there are very few African American jockeys because blacks in general are not that visible on the Grandstand Side of the Sport of Kings. From the perspective of a racing fan or spectator, it is a rarity to see a black jockey, owner or trainer in the Winner's Circle after a race. The reason for that is that there are very few black jockeys, trainers and thoroughbred racehorse owners.

When Charlie Hall first started working on the "Back Side", for a black man, being a groom was a very prestigious position. In the old days on the "Back Side", being a groom was an honorable profession that was steeped in tradition. In most cases, a groom's experience and knowledge of thoroughbred horses had no equal on the "Back Side". The only people on the "Back Side" that even came close to knowing as much about a thoroughbred as grooms are trainers and veterinarians. Whenever you have horses of equal talent and ability, the well-groomed horse will always perform better than the horse whose care, and grooming has been lacking. When a horse wins a race, the owner receives 60% of the purse for that race. The winning jockey and trainer each receive 10%. The trainer usually gives the groom 1% of the purse if the horse wins. The Racing Commission mandates that jockeys receive a fee for riding and bonuses for finishing first (10%), second (5%), or third (2%) in the races valued at $30,000 or more. Most trainers' get a percentage of whatever the horse makes no matter where the horse finishes in the race. Although it is a standard practice for the trainer to receive a percentage of the owner's purse money, receiving that bonus is strictly between the owner and trainer. Again, in contrast to the bonuses received by the jockey and trainer for their horse winning money in a race, the groom only receives 1% and only receives that if the horse wins. Just think about, in a race valued at $10,000, the owner gets $6,000, the jockey and trainer get $600 each, and the groom gets $60 extra in his pay. Is this fair compensation?

Let us breakdown a groom's $30,000 a year salary and the duties and responsibilities associated with earning that salary. In Maryland, a groom is usually paid $75 to $100 for each of the horses they take care of or "rub". The more horses a groom rubs, the more money they make. The average groom's day starts at 5:30 am and ends around 11:30 am. When the grooms arrive in the morning, they clean the water buckets and give fresh water to their horses. Next, the grooms "pick the feet" or clean the bottoms of the horse's feet of any debris and brushes their coats in preparation for their morning exercise. A horse's appearance outside the barn area is a direct reflection on the trainer and more importantly for the grooms; it is a direct reflection on them. Therefore, a good groom will never let one of their horses leave the barn for morning exercise covered in the straw and/or feces, better known as "muck" that they laid down in the night before. Morning exercise for a thoroughbred horse could be just a walk around the inside of the stable or barn, which is better known as the "shed row", or going to the track for a jog, a more vigorous gallop, or an even more strenuous breeze.

Coming off the racetrack after morning exercise or an actual race, a thoroughbred horse will be covered with dirt and sweat. In warm weather, in order to allow the horse to return to its normal body temperature or "cool out", grooms use a garden hose to give their horses a bath. After the bath the groom or a hot walker will walk the horse around the shed row for 20 to 30 minutes to complete the cooling out process before returning the horse to his/her stall. In cold weather, rather than giving the horse a bath with a garden hose, the grooms will use a hot bucket of water and towels to clean the dirt and sweat off the horse. After the horse is clean, the grooms cover them in a blanket and cool them out. With the exception of race day, a thoroughbred racehorse in training spends 22 ½ of hours each day in a stall. Some horses adjust very well to this schedule and others rebel by constantly running around inside the stall or kicking the walls. If a horse cannot adjust to being in a stall, the extra energy used to show displeasure results in a lack of sleep, weight loss and a failure to respond to training. Part of the groom's responsibility is to come up with a way to get a horse to adjust to being in a stall. Some grooms tie plastic toys or bottles in the stall to give the horse something to play with. They may find them a pet goat or cat. Grooms use just about anything to keep a horse calm; while at the same time keeping them from hurting themselves in the stall and/or being bored.

A Fine Tuned Machine

Certain animals are born with the natural ability to accomplish a specific task. The bloodhound is born to search for man. The beaver is a natural born construction engineer. The thoroughbred racehorse is born to run. Being a groom for a thoroughbred racehorse is best compared to the precision tuning necessary for a high-speed racecar and the patience and understanding necessary to care for an infant child. I compare a thoroughbred racehorse to an infant child because both can do very little for themselves, and both are very unpredictable. I compare the care of a thoroughbred racehorse to a professional racecar because of the precision maintenance required to achieve peak performance from a racecar is also needed to get the maximum performance from a racehorse. Like the parents of an infant child, a groom must feed, water, and change the bedding of thoroughbred racehorses. In addition, like infant children, thoroughbred racehorses have the ability to be calm and then suddenly, for no apparent reason, burst out into temper tantrums. Neither have the ability to communicate. Therefore, it is up to the parents of the child and the horse's groom to determine the source of the problem and restore order before the situation escalates into a catastrophe.

A thoroughbred racehorse weighs 1,500 to 2,000 pounds and stands 15 to 18 hands tall. A hand is a unit of measure used for a horse. A hand equals four inches. Horses are measured from the ground to the tip of their withers. The withers are the large muscles that connect the neck to the shoulders. It is easy to estimate the height of a horse by standing next to their shoulder. Judging from your own height, determine the difference in inches as you look across the horse's withers. For example, I am 5'9" tall. If I am standing next to a horse and the top of my head is even with the horse's withers, I know that horse stands at least 16 hands. If I can look over the horses withers, that horse stands at least 15 hands. I have stood next to some thoroughbred racehorse that it would take a man the size of Shaquille O'Neal to look over their withers and they stand 17 to 18 hands. Unlike a baby child, if a 2,000 lb. thoroughbred horse has a temper tantrum, somebody could be hurt or even killed. Just like a baby's crib, a horse's stall is their living room, dining room and bathroom. A thoroughbred racehorse spends most of his racing career in a stall. Just like a baby's crib, a thoroughbred racehorse's stall must be kept clean to protect the horse from diseases.

Every day, with the possible exception of one Sunday a month and a major holiday each year, the same groom will clean or "muck out" the stall of each of the horses in his or her care. This process includes removing the straw under piles of feces and removing straw from the wet spots where the horse has urinated. The groom separates the straw that can be reused by pushing it against the wall of the stall. The straw that cannot be reused and the other muck is thrown into a wheelbarrow or muck tub and taken to the muck pit located outside the barn. The more recognizable name for the "muck pit" is the "sh_t pit". While the groom is making trips to the muck pit, the straw remains pushed against the wall of the stall, which exposes the dirt floor. Exposing the dirt flooring allows the groom to check the stall for any foreign objects, ruts or holes that could be harmful to the horse. It gives the groom the opportunity to determine if the dirt cushion is thick enough to protect the horse from the concrete underneath his stall. In addition, it allows fresh air to get to the bottom of stall and dirt floor, which helps keep down the barn smells. After all the stalls are mucked out, the groom beds down each stall with fresh bails of straw. After the stalls are cleaned and bedded down, you would think the groom's work would be done or at least be close to finished. However, that is not the case.

Once the stalls are cleaned and bedded, the precision care of a thoroughbred by a groom or the part of the job known as "rubbing" begins. Grooming a horse starts and ends with the feet and legs. As the groom enters the stall, they will get the horse to move around to see if it is favoring any particular part of the body. The groom gets down their knees and starts checking the horse from the ground up for any signs of anything abnormal. Like human athletes, a thoroughbred horse is only as good as their legs. Therefore, during the rubbing process a groom pays special attention to the horse's feet, ankles and knees. Any little knick, bump, scratch or bruise found while the groom is checking the horse is noted and reported to the trainer or veterinarian. If a groom finds a scratch, no matter how small, they will immediately treat it with a local antiseptic to prevent an infection. Earlier, I compared the grooming of a horse to the fine turning of a racecar. "Rubbing" is the main part of the fine-tuning process. There are several stages of rubbing a horse. A "Curry Comb" is a palm-sized brush that has short hard rubber bristles. Using a circular motion, grooms use a Curry Comb to loosen the dirt that is embedded in a horse's coat. No matter how often you hose down a horse, you never remove all the dried up sweat and muck that clings to a horse's body. After the groom uses the Curry Comb to loosen the dirt, they switch to a "Body Brush" to sweep the dried skin and dirt off the horse. Grooms use a "Rub Rag" or an old towel to wipe the horse down.

The wiping process makes the horse's coat shine. The groom also combs the horse's mane and their tails to make sure it is not tangled and is neat and even. The daily removal of dried skin, dried perspiration, and dirt from a horse's coat allow it to breathe and it relaxes the horse's major muscle groups. After the groom has finished with the horse's coat, they use the hoof pick to remove any debris that has been collected during the course of the day from the horse's feet. Then they pack each foot with a mud like substance that acts as a moisturizer and keeps the horse from collecting any debris in their feet while standing in the stall for the rest of the day and night. Finally, the grooms paint the outside of each foot with a liquid that oils the feet to keep the hoof soft and makes them shine. A horse's hoof is like a fingernail. If you do not take care of a horse's hooves, they will dry up and crack or split. If the horse's hooves crack or split, they can be infected and be too painful for the horse to run.

Included in the duties of grooming is to bandaging the horse's front and sometime back legs. A groom will rub a horse's legs in ointments such as alcohol, winter green liniment or "Ben Gay" that will cause surface heat and increased circulation. After applying a heating substance, the groom wraps each leg using thick cotton. Then they secure the cotton by wrapping a cloth bandage around each leg and secure the bandage with large safety pins. Standing in a stall for 22 hours causes a lot of pressure on a horse's legs. The bandages help to support the horse's weight while they stand in the stall. If the horse is larger than normal, or has some hind end problems, the groom will bandage both front and back legs. A horse with a bright shiny coat and well keep mane, tail and feet, is healthy and happy. A horse with a dull looking unkempt coat, mane, tail and feet, may not be healthy or happy. Part of the game within the game of thoroughbred horseracing is to be able to recognize when a horse is healthy and happy. The average patron that comes to a racetrack has no idea what to look for when a horse comes on the track for the post parade. When you are selecting a horse to bet on, the horse with a bright shiny coat and well keep mane, tail and feet, is healthy and happy, and is ready to perform at his or her best and will be a winner. For the most part a horse that looks dull will probably not perform at his or her best and will not beat a horse that looks and feels much better.

Will Harbut & *Man o' War*

As I was conducting my research for this book, I found information on the some of the most famous thoroughbreds in racing history. Just as I love to watch movies and documentaries about the sport of horseracing, I love to read books about the famous thoroughbred racehorses of the past. As of this date and time, I have been fortunate enough to witness three Triple Crown Winners, *Secretariat, Affirmed* and *Seattle Slew*. In my opinion, the best horse I have ever seen was *Secretariat*, who was often referred to as *"Big Red"*. The best race I have ever seen was the 1977 Preakness, which featured a neck and neck stretch battle between *Affirmed* and *Alydar. Secretariat* was indeed a great horse, and he will always be remembered for his 31-length victory in the 1973 Belmont Stakes. *Secretariat* was named as one of the top 100 athletes of the 20th Century. Yet, in the world of thoroughbred horseracing, the stuff that legends are made of starts and ends with a horse named *Man o' War*. According to the "Old Timers" and all other published reports, *Man o' War* was the best of the best. History records that *Man o' War's* day-to-day care was entrusted to his groom Will Harbut, an African American, whose famous saying about *Man o' War* was that "he is de mostest hoss".

Man o' War was not just famous for his racing career. He won 20 out of 21 starts, which includes the 1920 Preakness and the 1920 Belmont Stakes, which he won by more than 20 lengths. *Man o' War* was also the father of the great *War Admiral* and the grandfather of the great *Seabiscuit*. *Man o' War* stood his first stud season in Kentucky at Hinata Farm, and then the following year moved to Faraway Farm, which is also in Kentucky. His groom at Faraway was Will Harbut who at this point had become somewhat of a celebrity himself. Mr. Harbut gladly showed the stallion to farm visitors and spoke at length of *Man O'War's* victories. Before long, Mr. Harbut's words were picked up through National magazines, and the whole Country was quoting his now famous phrase "He wuz de mostest hoss".

Every year, thousands of visitors flocked to Faraway Farm in Kentucky to see the legendary horse and hear his famous stud groom, Will Harbut, tell stories about the champion. Mr. Harbut always introduced his charge as "the mostest horse that ever was" and insisted that *Man o' War* had never been beaten. According to published reports, when a guest asked about the race with *Upset*, the only horse to beat *Man O' War*, Will Harbut always replied that since he had not seen it, the story of the 1919 Sanford Memorial "must have been a lie." Will Harbut, kept ledgers for visitors to sign. When *Man o' War* died in 1947, there were 63 ledgers containing over 1.3 million names.

Man o' War was still loved even after he stopped racing. Many of people came every day to see him. There was no doubt that *Man o' War* and his black groom, Will Harbut was very close. They were always found near each other with Mr. Harbut usually seen wrapping his arms around *Man o' War's* head. *Man o' War* died November 1, 1947 at Faraway Farms in Kentucky. Less than one month before, his beloved groom, Will Harbut had passed away. *Man o' War* had been experiencing heart trouble, and he died of a heart attack. Some say he missed his friend and groom, Will Harbut, so much, that he died of a broken heart. *Man o' War* died at the age of 30 and for 28 of those 30 years, Will Harbut was his groom. What makes this a memorable accomplishment is that the longest most grooms spend with the same thoroughbred horse is about five years. Thoroughbred horses that are retired to stud are taken care of by grooms that work on the farm, but very rarely is it the same groom that took care of them during their racing career. Just imagine spending 7 days a week for 28 years taking care of the same horse. As far as the sport of thoroughbred horseracing is concerned if that is not a record, it has to be close.

The name Will Harbut will always be linked to *Man o' War,* therefore, it will never be forgotten. A reproduction of a painting of *Man o' War* with his owner Sam Riddle and Will Harbut sells for $150 a copy. Will Harbut was famous because of his association with the great "Man o' War". In fact, Harbut was so famous that folk songs were written about him. Yet, in all my years around the "Back Side", I have never heard any of the black "Old Timers" who were grooms themselves, talk about Will Harbut. If you ever see a picture of a black groom in the Thoroughbred Horseracing Hall of Fame in Saratoga, New York, he will probably be holding the shank of a famous racehorse. Please take the time to inquire as to the name of that black man and try to remember for the future. I have no doubt that someone has probably written newspaper and magazine articles and books about the life of Will Harbut. Unfortunately, in the area that I live, the libraries do not feature enough information on famous African Americans in the sport of thoroughbred horseracing to make it easy to conduct research on people like Will Harbut. Unless we make access to information about famous African American readily available, student of today are not going take the time to hunt for the material.

Like Father Like Son

The accomplishments of Will Harbut as a groom are well documented because of *Man o' War*. However, Will Harbut's son, Tom, followed in his father's footstep, but there is very little mention of that fact in the history of Thoroughbred Horseracing. Tom Harbut was the groom for *Nashua*, the 1957 Kentucky Derby winner. The odds of a father and son being the groom for a horse that won a Triple Crown race is a rare as father and son hitting a homerun in the same MLB game. In 1990, Ken Griffey Jr and Ken Griffey Sr, while playing for the Seattle Mariners, became the first father and son to hit back-to-back homeruns in a game. This is the reason why books like mine are so very important. Although I do not write biographies, I do mention the names of African Americans that black as well as white Americans should know and always remember. It is my hope that by mentioning these individuals in my books, my readers might be inspired to write biographies featuring these famous black Americans.

Today, in the world of professional sports, we make a big deal of family traditions, when the sons of famous African American athletes follow in the footsteps of their fathers. In Major League Baseball, Barry Bonds is one of the best players of all time. In my opinion, Barry Bonds is second only to his Godfather Willie Mays. Barry Bonds followed in the footsteps of his father Bobby. In the NBA, Kobe Bryant followed in the footsteps of his father Joe "Jellybean" Bryant. In the NFL, Kellen Winslow, a Hall of Fame Tight End for the San Diego Chargers, had his son become the first round draft choice of the Cleveland Browns.

There are more than a hundred other father and son names that I could mention and still not exhaust the list. In 2014, the most popular father and sons in sports are white. That father and son is Archie Manning and his sons Peyton, starting Quarterback for the Denver Broncos and Eli, starting Quarterback for the New York Giants. Will Harbut's son Tom went on to a very successful career as a groom. According to published reports, Tom Harbut owned half of a horse, Touch Bar that ran in the 1962 Kentucky Derby. Although, the horseracing bug was not passed on to any of Tom's children, reportedly, his grandson Gregory Harbut Jr. is studying to be a horseman. Charlie Hall followed in his father's footsteps. In 2014, he continues to work on the racetrack as the Stable Manager. In his spare time, Charlie is owner/trainer of a few racehorses. As a black trainer for over 20 years, Charlie has probably visited the winner circle about a dozen times. However, as a groom for close to 20 years, he visited the winner circle close to 200 times. In my lifetime, I might not see a biography of the life of Charles Hall. However, for those of you racing fans that collect Preakness memorabilia, Charles Hall's name has been in the official Preakness program for the past 25 years. Copies of these same programs are sent to the Thoroughbred Horseracing Hall of Fame and therefore, like the name of Will Harbut, the name Charles "Charlie" Hall will forever be linked to the second jewel of the Triple Crown; the Preakness Stakes.

Charlie's Big *Hoss*

Like the black trainers before them, African American grooms are some of the hardest workers in the sport of racing. They are also some of the most colorful characters in the sport. Some of the names I am about to mention have never appeared in an official racing program or on any other document that will be preserved or treasured as part of the history of the sport of thoroughbred horseracing. Yet, their contributions to the sport are invaluable and they should be recognized along with the accomplishment of the horses that were entrusted to their care. Not to be recognized for their accomplishments in a sport that they have contributed so much is an injustice. I hope my book will inspire someone with a more in-depth knowledge of the "Back Side" to write a book about black grooms, hotwalkers and Exercise Riders. I start with Charlie Hall, who as a groom was charged with the care of a horse named *Pro Bidder*. Every groom I know or have ever known personally has had one or two horses that were their claim to fame. In Charlie's case, that horse was *Pro Bidder*.

Trained by the late Grover "Bud" Delp, a member of the Hall of Fame, *Pro Bidder* set a record by winning five consecutive stakes races in the State of Maryland. According to Charlie, *Pro Bidder* has such a bad temper that he was the only person that could go in stall without being attacked. No one else could feed *Pro Bidder*, or get him out of the stall in the morning to go to the track. In addition, of course, no one could attend to *Pro Bidder's* daily grooming. Therefore, as a result of this winning streak, trainer Bud Delp told Charlie that he had to work 7 days a week and that he could not take a day off as long as *Pro Bidder* was in training. According to Charlie, he worked 7 days a week for almost 6 months before he got some time off. Can you imagine working 7 days a week from 5 am until noon and returning to work at 4 pm just to feed one horse? I remember *Pro Bidder* and I remember how my uncle Charlie never got to enjoy weekends and holidays with his family because he had to take care of *Pro Bidder*. When you check the record books, you will find information on the accomplishments of *Pro Bidder*, but you will not see a line about the sacrifices that Charlie Hall made to make *Pro Bidder* a champion. Charlie Hall is a perfect example of how the sport of horseracing gets in your blood. You become addicted and just like any other addict; you will make whatever sacrifice necessary to get your high from being a part of the sport of horseracing.

You would think that after all these years, Charlie would be bitter about the sacrifice he made for *Pro Bidder* to be successful. However, it is just the opposite. Today, if you mention *Pro Bidder* to Charlie Hall, his eyes light up like a Christmas tree and his chest will stick out like a proud father after his child is born. In my association with the men and women who have dedicated their lives to working on the "Back Side", personal sacrifices, similar to those suffered by Charlie Hall, are commonplace. To find an African American groom that leads a "normal" lifestyle away from the track, i.e., home, wife and children, is the exception and not rule. You would think that because of the hard work, the low wagers, the strain on family life and the lack of any upward mobility as a career, there would be very few "Old Timers" on the "Back Side". Yet, over the years, I have met several 75-year-old men who are still working on the "Back Side".

An Exclusive Club

My grandfather, Wilbur Wright, worked 47 years for the Baltimore & Ohio Railroad. When he retired, he never had the desire to go to the job site, sit around with his old crew, and socialize. I will have to admit, my grandfather did visit from his old job site. The visits were never for any long periods and only when he was in the area on other business. Since many of the men from my old neighborhood worked on the railroad, when they met at church or other social events in the community, my grandfather and his railroad cronies would talk a little shop. Yet, "Old Timers" that retire from the racetrack come to the stable area on a daily basis to eat breakfast and talk about horses. They set up shop in the track kitchen or in the tack room in one of the barns. They would play cards, have few drinks, beer; wine or whiskey; and the "Old Timers" always talk about the "good ole days" of horseracing. These "Old Timers", most of them are former grooms or Exercise Riders, have dedicated their lives to the care of thoroughbred horses. I talk more about the Exercise Riders in another chapter of this book. Most of the "Old Timers" on the "Back Side" are only known by their first names or a nickname, such as, "Lightning", "Tiny", "Windy", "Long John", "Sleepy", "Stumpy", "Fluffy", "Rip" and "Stymie". I could probably name another dozen or so grooms that I only know by their nicknames.

If you did not know any better, you would think this was an exclusive social club. However, if it were a club, the membership fees are far too expensive. The fees are paid in blood sweat and tears and the insignia to identify its members is a broken-down body. The failing health of these "Old Timers" is the result of working day after day in frigid cold of winter and the blistering heat of summer. There have been extensive studies on the impact to the health and safety of men and women who work in coalmines, steel mills, and other buildings or industries that place workers in constant contact with hazardous materials such as asbestos. The results of these studies have shown that due to the nature job, the people who work in these occupations are at an extremely high risk of being killed or injured. Due to their exposure to the dust and other chemicals in the air that they are forced to breath while on the job, they are put at an extremely high risk of developing lung cancer, heart and other respiratory diseases.

Stress Takes its Toll

In addition, there have been studies on the stress related occupations that include doctors, lawyers, police and firemen and how these occupations affect mental health. The stress of being a police and fireman results in higher rates of domestic violence, divorce and suicide. There have been extensive studies on the impact to the health and safety of men and women who work in coalmines, steel mills, and other buildings or industries that place workers in constant contact with hazardous materials such as asbestos. The results of these studies have shown that due to the nature job, the people who work in these occupations are at an extremely high risk of being killed or injured. Due to their exposure to the dust and other chemicals in the air that they are forced to breath while on the job, they are put at an extremely high risk of developing lung cancer, heart and other respiratory diseases. Further, there have been studies on the stress related occupations that include doctors, lawyers, police and firemen, and how these types of jobs affect mental health. The stress of being a police and fireman results in higher rates of domestic violence, divorce and suicide.

Yet with all these work related studies, to the best of my knowledge, I have never seen or heard of any studies being conducted on the adverse effect of working on the "Back Side". Have you ever noticed that most of the published research conducted on subjects associated with African Americans is usually associated with the impact of drug and alcohol abuse as it relates to criminal behavior, welfare, or birth control? For as long as I can remember, white researchers determined that the health related problems in the black community were attributed to drug and alcohol abuse. These same white researchers reported that alcohol abuse was the number one contributing factor for health related problems for Native Americans who lived on "Indian" reservations. What white researchers fail to report is that the mental and physical health issues in the Native and African communities can be directly attributed to hard working red and black men working themselves to death at whatever jobs were available to improve living conditions for their families and having the white man deny them their equal rights under the law.

Every parent wants his or her child to have better and do better. The added burden of being denied equal rights or an equal opportunity based on the color of your skins does create stress and in turn results in mental and physical health problems. Medical doctors have determined that stress is a silent killer. In this Country, when we teach our children about the history of Native and African Americans, we fail to mention the hopeless of black slaves who were born and died without ever gaining their freedom from the white man. We fail to teach our children about the hopeless of the proud Native Americans who lost their homeland and were force by the white man to live on land the no one else wanted. American history needs to be taught in more than one color and from more than one perspective. It needs to be taught in the colors of red and black and from the perspective of the hopeless black slave and Native Americans.

The black groom is the perfect example of how the same hopeless, suffered by the black slave who was born and died without ever gaining freedom from the white man, is still alive and well today. African American grooms, like their slave ancestors, can literally work their butts off in a profession and never will get promoted to the next level. How frustrating is it for a proud black man to work hard all his life, follow all the rules and face the realization that no matter what he has done, at the end of his career he will be in the same position, doing the same things as when he started. You can read the biographies of successful white men who have risen from the ranks of hotwalker, groom or Exercise Rider to become millionaires as thoroughbred horse trainers. Yet, for a black man this is the rare exception. As African Americans, we have come a long way from the days of slavery. Yet, we still have a long way to go before we achieve total equality in this Country.

I have talked about how being around thoroughbred horses can be an addiction. Although I am not addicted to the hard work, I love everything else about the lifestyle of the "Back Side" with the obvious exception of the practice of racism. I have been a frequent visitor to the "Back Side" for over 40 years; yet, I am still considered an outsider. I have fed and watered, and walked horses. I have given horses bathes, mucked their stalls and brushed their coats, but I have never done any of these things to put bread on the table. That is why people, who make their living working with horses, will always consider me an outsider. I understand a groom's love for the sport. Yet, one of the questions that I have asked myself, from the first day I stepped on the "Back Side" and observed the daily routine of a groom, is why do they continue work as hard as they do knowing that there is no future in it? What is the motivation for a groom?

Professionalism

The motivation for black grooms is the same motivation that my grandfather had when he worked on the B&O Railroad for 47 years. The same motivation for my African American ancestors who worked in the cotton fields in the "DEEP SOUTH", for less than minimum wages. Believe it or not, is was the same motivation that kept my black slave ancestors for going out of the minds working for their white masters for no wages at all. These proud black men and women were all motivated by the fact that they took ownership of their jobs. Pride in your own performance, something that is fast becoming a lost art for those who work in low-income profession, is what motivated my ancestors and is what motivates the black grooms of today. I have heard statements like these all my life. If you have got to do a job, you might as well do it right. A job worth doing is worth doing well. Be all that you can be and be the best at what you do. My grandfather lived by those statements and I am more than sure that his work ethic was passed down from one generation to the next. Regardless of pay, my ancestors used pride and self-motivation to make it through tough situations. How much tougher could it be than being a black slave, working for no wages for a white master; yet, taking pride in your job as the trainer of the masters' thoroughbred horses. These slaves took ownership of their jobs and being proud of their accomplishment provided a feeling of being a man rather than being the white man's property, and for the short time spent training horses, they experienced a sense of freedom.

In a job that will never lead to a promotion. In a job that will never allow you to afford some of the finer things in life. In a job that will result in your failing health and provide you will little or no security for you golden years. Grooms carry on the pride and self-motivation that was passed down from their slave ancestors. A black groom's motivation is to be the best at his profession. Each time one of the thoroughbred horses in his charge takes the track for a morning workout or a race, a part of that groom goes with that horse. Grooms beam with pride whenever a compliment is given for the sharp demeanor of their horse. The groom knows that he is responsible for the horse's shinny coat and the bounce in his stride. More than anyone, including the owner and trainer, because of their blood, sweat and pain grooms experience with each horse; they get a greater thrill after a victory, and suffer a deeper sense of agony after each defeat. Like their ancestors before them, grooms are not in the business just for the money. They take pride in what they do and their satisfaction is from a job well done. The next time you have your shoes shined by an elderly black man on a street corner. The next time you encounter a black restroom attendant when you are at the opera. When you see a black maid, butler or chauffeur; remember, they are not just in it for the money; they take pride in a job well done. This is the kind of information that should be part of our sociology and economic develop course in High School and College. Although we suffer from the white racist attitudes in America that will not give us the equal rights that we deserve, African Americans have a long and storied history of overcoming obstacles and taking pride in our accomplishments. Did you know that some of these "Old Timers" on the "Back Side" are so dedicated to this lifestyle that they rarely ever leave the shed row?

As you are reading this chapter, you might ask the question, is a groom that important to the successful career of a thoroughbred racehorse? I have listened to world famous Trainers, such as D. Wayne Lukas and Bob Baffert, and some prominent Maryland Trainers, like Grover Delp and King T. Leatherbury, attribute their success to the owners for spending their money and the horses for having the talent to win races. With the rare exception of giving credit to the Jockey or an Assistant Trainer, I have never heard these trainers give any credit to the grooms who provide the day-to-day care for these valuable animals. On the other hand, I have heard successful trainers like Ron McAnally and Nick Zito give praises to all the barn help, i.e., Grooms, Hotwalkers, Exercise Riders and Assistant Trainers after a victory by one of their horses. Mr. McAnally made a point to mention that, "I am only as good as my help."

Herman "Bunk" AKA "Moe" Hall & *The Bid*

Let us talk about some other groom's that I have met. Not only did Charlie Hall learn his craft as a groom from working alongside his father, he also learned about the art of being a groom by working with his cousin, Herman Hall, who we called "Moe" or "Bunk", when they both rubbed horses for trainer Bud Delp. Just as the legendary groom, Will Harbut was famous for telling stories about *Man o' War*, all the grooms that I know can talk up a storm about the best horses they have rubbed. I grew up listening to Charlie tell stories about *Pro Bidder*. However, when I met Moe Hall, he took the art of storytelling to a level comparable to that of the tall tales of Steven Kellogg about the giant lumberman Paul Bunyan and Babe the Blue Ox, the railroad worker and steel driven man, John Henry, and the toughest cowboy ever, Pecos Bill, and his horse Widow Maker.

When I was a child, I sat spellbound as I listened to how Paul Bunyan used his big axe to cut down giant redwood trees with one swing, and how Babe the giant Blue Ox could haul away a mountain sized stack of those fallen redwoods. I listened to tales of how a black man named John Henry drove more steel than a machine, and how Pecos Bill and Widow Maker tamed a tornado. As a young man, I was just as captivated as sat and listened to stories about racehorses as told by Moe Hall. He had a little rhythm to his voice as he cranked out what we all knew were exaggerated tales about his "Big Hoss". The "Big Hoss" for Moe Hall was a gray or roan colt called *The Bid*, which was the nickname for *Spectacular Bid*, winner of the 1979 Kentucky Derby and Preakness. According to Bud Delp, *The Bid* was the best horse ever to stick his head through a bridle. Although *Secretariat* was the best horse I have ever seen run, *Spectacular Bid* was by far the second best.

If you asked Moe if *The Bid* could run, he would turn and look at you as if you had insulted his mother and then turn and angrily walk away. However, before he would go too far Moe would stop and say, "boy dis big gray hoss can catch a pigeon". Some of the other sayings if you asked a groom if their horse could run were; "is pig meat pork", is the Pope Catholic, or "is fatback greasy", all of which meant an emphatic yes to the question regarding of whether or not a groom's horse is an outstanding runner. Moe would talk about his "Big Hoss" like a minister preaching a sermon. I remember Moe talking about another horse that he rubbed called *Dancing Champ*. Always eager to have him tell one of his tales, I asked Moe why they named this horse *Dancing Champ*. Now if you know anything about the naming of thoroughbred racehorses, the process takes place long before their first race. The name of a thoroughbred horse is usually a derivative of the horse's stallion (father) or dam (mother). However, in some cases the horse could be named for one of its outstanding characteristics. In this case of this particular horse and in answer to my question, Moe told me that I had find out why they named this horse *Dancing Champ*, the next time he brought the horse to the track for a race.

Well, I could not wait until the next time *Dancing Champ* was entered in a race. When the day came, I stood glued to the Grandstand rail as Moe walked *Dancing Champ* down the track from the barn area toward the paddock to prepare for the race. Moe was dragging his feet as he slowly made his way down the track and *Dancing Champ* seemed to be dragging his feet even slower than Moe's. Both groom and horse gave the appearance that they could care less about being in a race this day. As slow as they were moving, I thought they would never make to the paddock in time for the race. Although he did not look to be that sharp, he was physically a big good-looking colt and when he came to the Grandstand after the post parade, Moe swore to us that this "Big Hoss" could really run.

The good thing about Moe Hall is that he would never short-change you on one of his horses. If he said the horse could run, you had better believe him. The day he told me that *The Bid* could run; all he did that day was set a track record. After making a small wager, I rushed back to the rail to watch *Dancing Champ* run. When the bell sounded and the starting gate sprung opened, *Dancing Champ*, who looked dull and uninterested during the post parade, bolted to the front and with long powerful strides, took the lead and never looked back. He won the race wire to wire going literally running away from the rest of the field. "I told ya the Big Hoss could run, I told ya," Moe shouted out as he hustled off to pose with *Dancing Champ* as they took a picture in the Winner's Circle. After leaving the Winner's Circle on their way back down the track to the barn area, Dancing Champ starting to prance from side to side and bounce along as if he was marching to the beat of his favorite tune. It was then that Moe yelled to me in the Grandstand, and with a big smile on his face he said, "That is why they call him Dancing Champ. Every time he wins a race, he dances all the way back to the barn".

Grooms like Moe Hall felt that the success of their "Big Hoss" was due to the fact that he had laid hands on the horse. I remember Moe telling about all his special homemade remedies that he used to help keep *The Bid* sharp. According to Moe Hall, if a horse was sore, he could reach into his bag of tricks and cure whatever ailment the horse might have. According to Moe, he had the magic touch. The perfect example of Moe Hall's magic was the day *The Bid* ran in the Belmont Stakes. According to published reports, in the early morning of or the night before the Belmont Stakes, *The Bid* stepped on an opened safety pin. After learning of the incident on the morning of the Belmont, trainer Buddy Delp considered scratching *The Bid,* but as far as Bud could determine the horse was not lame. According to published reports, Bud Delp felt that denying *The Bid* a chance at the Triple Crown, and the status that went with it, seemed a drastic measure.

What reporters never mentioned in this story about *The Bid* was that when Moe Hall looked in on his "Big Hoss" that morning before Bud arrived in the stable area, *The Bid* was lame. According to Moe Hall's version of the story, *The Bid* could not put any weight on his injured front foot. The reason Bud Delp did not think *The Bid* was lame is because Moe Hall had used one of his old fashion remedies to help the "Big Hoss" feel like running. For years, Bud Delp had depended on Moe's judgment when it came to taking care of his horses. It was this same judgment that Bud turned to cure whatever ailed the barn's "Big Hoss". Unfortunately, for this particular ailment, Moe's magic did not work. *Spectacular Bid's* foot was sore enough that he favored it, running the entire distance on one lead.

To preserve energy, a thoroughbred will change leads or change which of their front feet hit the ground first when they are running. Running on the same lead for an entire race would tire a horse a lot quicker than if that horse would change leads. After dominating the Kentucky Derby and the Preakness, *The Bid* was unable to withstand the closing drive of *Coastal*. He faded to third, a neck behind Preakness runner-up *Golden Act*, losing the Belmont Stakes and being denied the elusive Triple Crown. What reporters failed to mention is that running a mile and a half against some of the best three-year-old horses in the world, to finish third was a major accomplishment. Only a horse with the superior talent and courage of *Spectacular Bid* could have pulled it off. If "The Bid" had won, there would have been a Triple Crown winner in three consecutive years from 1977 through 1979.

Some reporters blamed the loss of the Belmont stakes and the Triple Crown on *The Bid's* groom, without actually mentioning Herman "Moe" Hall's name, for dropping a safety pin in the horse's stall. Although Bud Delp never pointed the finger at Moe for what happened to *The Bid*, Moe Hall was never the same after the safety pin incident and his "Big Hoss" not being able to fulfill the dream of a lifetime, winning the Triple Crown. However, in my opinion the real reasons *The Bid* lost the Belmont was Bud Delp's ego, which caused him to boast that *The Bid* would break "Secretariat's" 31-length margin of victory in the race, and the inexperience of *The Bid's* jockey Ronnie

Franklin. Trying to win the Triple Crown and break *Secretariat's* record after being told that the horse's foot might be injured, was far too much pressure for the 19-year-old jockey Ronnie Franklin.

The events surrounding *The Bid*, the Belmont Stakes and the Triple Crown would not have bothered old veteran riders like Bill Shoemaker, William Passmore or Eddie Maple, but it in all honesty; it should have rattled the teenager Ron Franklin. According to published reports, before the race, Franklin punched Angel Cordero in the jockey's room. The punch was probable a carryover from the Preakness, when Cordero seemed to intentionally force Ron Franklin and *The Bid* wide as they left the gate at the start of the Preakness. Reportedly, there was some bad blood between Franklin and Cordero and the Belmont Stakes was the first time the two had seen each other since the Preakness. With the altercation with Cordero added to Bud's wanting to break a record and *The Bid's* sore foot, in my opinion, Franklin made the mistake of sending his mount after the lead far too early and at far too fast a pace for a mile and a half race.

In the past, if young Franklin made a mistake during a race, *The Bid's* superior talent would overcome any errors in judgment by his young jockey. *The Bid* was far from being 100% sound and his competition was far too strong and had far too much class for *Spectacular Bid* to run anything other than his best. After the Belmont Stakes, Ron Franklin was fired and for the most part, his career as a jockey was over. In my opinion, for his egotistical faux pas, *The Bid's* owner should have also fired the trainer, Grover "Bud" Delp. Although Ron Franklin was fired for his ride in the Belmont Stakes, he and Bud Delp will always be mentioned whenever most white historians write about the great racehorse, *Spectacular Bid.*

Yet, just as the African American groom, Will Harbut will always be linked to the great thoroughbred horse *Man o' War*, Herman "Moe" Hall's name should always be linked to "*Spectacular Bid*". It took years for writers to understand the relationship between the horse *Man o' War* and his groom Will Harbut. After the first story about Will Harbut appeared in the media, he became a part of the legend of *Man o' War*. As part of his comments to the media, Bud Delp should have acknowledged Moe for his work with *The Bid* but, in my opinion, his ego would not allow him to give credit to a black man when credit was due. Unfortunately, without books like mine, white and African Americans would never know about the black man, Herman "Moe" Hall and his integral part in the success of *Spectacular Bid*, a great champion and a thoroughbred horseracing legend.

Benjamin "Stumpy" Stubbs.

One of the most devoted grooms I have ever met was Benjamin "Stumpy" Stubbs. I remember running a horse out of town and leaving the track early in the morning and returning at midnight. When we left, Stumpy was hanging laundry, saddle towels, rub rages, and bandages, on a clothesline in front of his barn. When we returned at midnight, Stumpy was still in the shed row hanging up laundry. In 2008, Stumpy is one of the last of a dying breed of grooms who are masters of their craft. I use the word craft because grooms like Stumpy and Edward "Stymie" Banks use their knowledge and skill to enhance the performance of the horses in their care by using techniques that have been passed down from grooms for centuries dating back to days when my ancestors were slaves in America.

When I first met Stumpy, he was working for trainer Roger Gill and he was rubbing a horse named *Chas Whim*, who could run equally as well on the dirt as he could on grass. Roger and Stumpy would have *Chas Whim* so sharp before each of his races that they had to put beer in his feed to calm him down and keep him from hurting himself in his stall. Once before one of *Chas Whim's* big races, I asked Stumpy how the horse was doing. Stumpy responded by saying, "he has as good as hands can make him", which means that he had done everything he could for the horse and *Chas Whim* was in the best condition possible. It was the first time I had ever heard a groom make that statement, but I would hear it repeated many times over the next 20 years and just as when I heard it first from Stumpy, the groom's horse would win the upcoming race.

"Stumpy" was either one of the most dedicated grooms I have ever known or he was just crazy. There was this one night, in the early 1990s, when Charlie Hall and I left the racetrack at around 5 pm and rode to Charles Town to bet on a horse. Charlie left his truck in the Stable Area at Laurel and when we returned at 11 pm, we saw "Stumpy" hanging up laundry in the front of Simpson's barn. It was a warm summer evening and Stumpy, who would be the first person in the barn every morning at about 4:30 am, should have been sleep or least relaxing, had decided to wash some saddle towels and bandages. Most of us believed that "Stumpy" spent every waking hour working in the shed row. The truth was that "Stumpy" lived on the grounds of the racetrack and usually had a room no more than 50 feet from the barn. "Stumpy" had a reputation as a groom who paid close attention to every little thing involved in caring for a horse. When he finished grooming a horse, they would shine like new money and like "Short Man"; he rarely led a horse to the paddock that did not win.

"Stumpy" rubbed a horse, for trainer Roger Gill, named *Chas Whin*. This was one of the best all-around horses I ever watched run. *Chas*, his nickname, ran just as well on the grass as he did on the dirt. Unlike some of the other horses I have talked about in my book, because I knew "Stumpy", I got to visit with *Chas Whin* up close and personal while he was in his stall at Laurel. *Chas* was the first horse that I saw get a can of beer in his feed every day. The beer was used to make sure *Chas* went to sleep rather than roam around in his stall all night. *Chas* was a "stall walker". A "stall walker' is a term used for a nervous or restless horse that will walk or run in circles in his or her stall at night. This causes the horse to use a lot of unnecessary energy and lose weight. The beer helps the horse to relax and rather than burning up energy before the race in the stall, the horse saves all the energy for the competition on the track. Roger Gill would send one of the grooms to the liquor store to buy a six-pack of beer for *Chas*. After Roger left the barn around noon each day, only one or two cans of beer from that six-pack made it to *Chas'* feed tub because "Big Mike", a groom that work with "Stumpy" would always drink all the beer that was left.

Chas Whin had a little quirk in his running style. *Chas* used to take the lead coming off the far turn into the stretch, drop down on the rail and allow a horse to pass him on the outside and then regain the

149

lead to draw off and win. I won a lot of money betting on *Chas*. The first time I saw him take the lead and then get passed as he entered the stretch, I almost threw my tickets away, but just as fast as the horse passed him, he retook the lead and won easily. From then on whenever I saw him make his move, losing the lead in the lane, I would boast to whoever was standing near me that there was nothing to fear, because I knew that *Chas* would regain the lead and win the race. In his career, I can only remember one race that *Chas* disappointed me. It was in the "Early Times", a mile and an eighth stake race run on the grass the Friday before the Preakness at Pimlico. *Chas* lost the race by less than a ½ length to *Double Booked*. This horserace was one of the best I ever witnessed and wagered on. Both horses broke the track record that day, but because *Chas* finished second, the record book would only show the name of *Double Booked*.

No matter how good a horse is, in a race, the horse is only as good as the jockey that rides the horse that particular day. Just as the jockey Ronnie Franklin's inexperience had cost the great *Spectacular Bid* a Triple Crown, the inexperience of Allen Stacy, a young journeyman rider on the Maryland circuit, cost *Chas Whin* a victory in the "Early Times" Handicap. In the "Early Times" Hall of Fame jockey Pat Day rode *Double Booked* and what Allen Stacy had not counted on was that Pat Day had done his homework on *Chas Whin* and he knew about his running style. *Double Booked* loved to be in front and when they broke on this day, he went right to the lead with *Chas Whin* running second about 3 to 4 lengths behind. *Double Booked* was extremely fast on the grass. In a shorter race, a mile and a 1/16 at Pimlico earlier in the meet, he had set a track record on the grass course going wire to wire for the victory. As the horses ran down the backside, which is the long stretch after the first turn in a two-turn race, the Hall of Fame Jockey, Pat Day, let Allen Stacy get close with *Chas Whin*. Then Pat Day suddenly urged *Double Book* to use a quick burst of speed that caught Allen Stacy and *Chas* by surprise, as *Doubled Booked* quickly pulled away. *Chas Whin* tried hard to catch him, but *Double Booked* held on to win.

When Charlie Hall first introduced me to the "Back Side" in the late 1960s, most of the grooms that I met were older black men. When

I was reintroduced to the "Back Side" in the late 1980s, I met a much younger group of black men who were now grooms. When I say young, I mean the men were between 19 to 35 years of age. After the Civil War and the end of slavery, African Americans, former slaves, stayed on the plantation and worked in the stable area. In the late 1860s through the early 1900s, there were few employment opportunities for unskilled black people. It was easy and comfortable African Americans to remain in familiar occupations. However, why would young black men of today, who have the opportunity for better education, better job training and the possibility of employment in lucrative positions, choose the back breaking and thankless profession of being a groom?

My Friend Willie

The answer to that question is simple. Life on the racetrack gets into your blood and once it does, you become addicted. There is no better life than horseracing and the "Back Side of the Sport of Kings" for true horsemen. One of my best friends, Willie Kee, is a former groom, who became a trainer. Willie's big horses when he was a groom were *Learned Jake* and *Wait for the Lady*. Like Charlie Hall, Willie followed in the footsteps of his Stepfather, Marshall Turner, who started on the Back Side as a groom and became a Trainer on the Maryland Racing Circuit. Marshall Turner was a well-respected black trainer who died a few years before I met Willie. When I met Willie, he was working at Laurel Racetrack as a groom for King T. Leatherbury. In 1996, while working as an Assistant Trainer for Leatherbury, Willie was responsible for the horses Leatherbury stabled at Pimlico. One of those horses was a filly named *Twofox;* she would later become the dam of *Ben's Cat*, a Maryland Bred gelding who won over 2 million dollars.

After experiencing a financially difficult year working on the racetrack, I offered my assistance in finding Willie a job outside of horseracing. He told me point blank and without any hesitation, that he was not interested. Willie told me that no matter what he had to do, from mucking stalls to being a Hotwalker, he would not be happy working anywhere other than on the "Back Side of the Sport of Kings".

Yes, I do love the sport, but not to that extent. I find it amazing, over 50 years after first meeting Charlie Hall; that I would meet another young black man that would dedicate his life to horseracing.

I have written a little about Charles & Herman Hall and Willie Kee, and this will preserve their names in history for all times. I end this chapter with some highlights about a few other grooms and their special or "Big Hoss". What makes the stories about these men so important to a writer of books on African American history is that they are a dying breed. In 2014, I will have been around the "Back Side" for close to 45 years. Yet, in that short time, I have witnessed a dramatic change in the tradition and profession of being a groom of thoroughbred horses. A profession that was once dominated by black men has been taken over by young white women and Mexican immigrants of all ages. After the men that I have written about are gone, there will never be any more like them. Of course there will be grooms as long as there are horses that need to be cared for, but the new age groom will not have the character, the professionalism or the dedication that was passed down from one generation of African American groom to the next.

Famous Nicknames

I had the distinct privilege and the pleasure of enjoying the company of these grooms for many years on the "Back Side". I will start with Edward "Stymie" Banks who got his nickname from the famous horse and not the character on the Little Rascals. Stymie rubbed or groomed *Private Terms* for Hall of Fame trainer Charles H. Hadry. The reason I started with "Stymie" is because Mr. Hadry's son Charles J. Hadry, who we called "Junior" or "Charlie J", trained *Kegler*, who was my "Big Horse" and my first winner. *Private Terms*, who "Stymie" called *Private*, like *Spectacular Bid*, he was a horse that made a name for himself on the National scene by winning several graded stakes races including the Wood Memorial, on route to the Kentucky Derby. Many of *Private Term's* offspring are still running today in races around the world. There were three things that "Stymie" loved; horses, money and women. He had a hardy appetite for all three. I have known "Stymie" for over 35 years and I have heard him boast about the ability of all the horses he has rubbed. Banks would tout me to bet on his horses because he did not think they could lose. However, it was not the always the case and over the years we both lost a lot of money on horses groomed by Edward Banks.

There was "Short Man", when I met him he was working for J.P. Simpson, he died without me ever finding out his real name, but I suspect he got his nickname because he was in fact a short tubby fat old man. I used to watch "Short Man" in the barn area in the morning. He would never rush to get his work done and, yet, he would finish up the same time as everyone else. It was like the story of the Tortoise and the Hare. The race does not always go to the swift. After 40 years of being a groom "Short Man" had developed a system and that system called for him to take his time; do it right and that way he did not make mistakes or miss anything. Most of the younger inexperienced grooms rush to get finished their work and wind up having to go back and do something over because they did not do it right the first time. I remember whenever "Short Man" decided to take the long walk with a horse from the barn to the paddock; you could count on him coming back with a winner. You see, "Short Man" was one of the "Ole Timers" would not bother to walk to the paddock with one of the horse he groomed unless he thought the horse could win. J.P. Simpson named one of the thoroughbreds that he owned and trained after "Short Man" to honor the beloved groom.

Sherman worked for "Bud" Delp and Morgan work for another Hall of Fame Trainer King T. Leatherbury. Sherman rubbed *Sunny Sunrise* and Morgan rubbed *Ameri Valay*. In distance races of a mile and 1/16 to a mile and 3/16's these were two of the fastest horses on the Maryland circuit in the early 1990s and they were frequently entered in the same races. Both horses were fast and they both did their best running from the front. It was not unusual for *Sunny Sunrise* and *Ameri Valay* to start a race at, what seemed to be, a suicide pace and continue to run together stride for stride throughout the entire race. It was like poetry in motion, neither given the other a break. It was shame that only one of them could win and I remember they took turns defeating each other over the course of about two years. These were not just races between two very talented horses, this a competition for bragging rights between two Hall of Fame trainers and two of the best grooms on the "Back Side". I was not privileged to hear the conversation that took place between the trainers, but I loved to listen to banter between Sherman and Morgan as they both boasted about their laying claim to have the best horse on the grounds.

I could mention many other black horsemen in this chapter. There is my friend and softball teammate Kevin "Motor" Hutton, who followed in the footsteps of his cousins, the Gardner family, to become a groom. Not only was Kevin a good groom, he had an arm like a rocket. He could throw a softball over 100 miles per hour. There was "Ike" and "Windy"; I never knew their real names, and finally there was the late Morris Gardner, who was a gentleman who was highly respected by all who had the privilege to know him. Most grooms loved to brag about their horses and loudly boast about their favorite horse and about their ability to make a difference in how that horse performs. Morris was just the opposite; he was quiet and very confident in his ability to groom a horse and to past his knowledge on to those with less experience. I remember coming to trainer Mary Eppler's barn to visit with the grooms. I stopped to talk to Stymie and Ike. However, when I got to Morris, who was the foremen, he was always very polite to me, but he made it very clear that neither he nor any of his men really had time to talk. However, if I needed to know something about a horse that he was rubbing, he would talk to me while he was working and never miss a beat. You see, even though he was all business, Morris loved to talk about his horses. He knew everything about the horses breeding and what he expected the next time the horse would run. As it was his normal routine, Morris went to his room above the barn after finishing his work in the stable area to take a nap before taking an early morning van ride to New York to run one of his horses. Morris never woke up from that nap. He was good a man and he will truly be missed.

In these few pages, I have barely scratched the surface of what it takes to be a groom. It is my hope that this book will inspire other writer to explore and closely examine the lifestyle of the African American groom and their work on the "Back Side" of the Sport of Kings.

Chapter 4

MY OLE KENTUCKY HOME

Stephen Collins Foster wrote *"My Ole Kentucky Home, Good night"*, *the words and music in 1853. The words to the song are as follows:*
The sun shines bright in the old Kentucky home, 'Tis summer, the darkies are gay, the corn top's ripe and the meadows in the bloom, while the birds make music all the day. The young folks roll on the little cabin floor, All merry, all happy and bright: By'n by hard times comes a knocking at the door, then my old Kentucky Home, good night!
The Chorus: Weep no more, my lady, oh! Weep no more to day! We will sing one song for the old Kentucky Home, for the old Kentucky Home far away.
They hunt no more for possum and the coon on the meadow, the hill, and the shore, they sing no more by the glimmer of the moon, on the bench by the old cabin door. The day goes by like a shadow o're the heart, With sorrow where all was delight: The time has come when the darkies have to part, Then my old Kentucky Home, good-night!
The head must bow and the back will have to bend, wherever the darkey may go: A few more days, and the trouble all will end in the field where the sugar canes grow. A few more days for to tote the weary load, No matter, 'twill never be light, A few more days till we totter on the road, Then my old Kentucky Home, good-night!

Adding Insult to Injury

The Kentucky Derby is advertised as the greatest two minutes in sports because each year more people watch that horse than any other sporting event in the world. Celebrities from around the globe, Kings,

Queens, Presidents, movie stars, etc., have made personal appearances at the Kentucky Derby. People pay more attention to this thoroughbred horse race than Major League Baseball's World Series and the NFL's Super Bowl. Yet, over the past 45 years, a major sporting event that was once dominated by black super star athletes, the jockey who rode in this race, has shown very limited participation by African Americans. I have been following this event for over 45 years, and although there may have been others, I can only remember two black owners that entered a horse in the Kentucky Derby; they were Berry Gordie, founder and CEO of Motown Records, and the entertainer MC Hammer. In the last 45 years, I can only remember there being one African American trainer to enter a horse in the Derby. That was a Maryland based trainer named Hank Allen, who in 1989 saddled a speedy gray colt named Northern Wolf. Some of you baseball fans might remember that Hank Allen once played for the Washington Senators, his brother Richie "don't call me Dick" Allen was a baseball legend that played for the Philadelphia Phillies and the Chicago White Sox.

In addition, during this same span of time, there have only been two black jockeys to ride in the Kentucky Derby. The two jockeys were Marlon St. Julien, who rode "Curule" in the 2000 Derby and Kevin Krigger, who rode "Goldencents" in the 2013 Derby. I will talk more about Marlon St. Julien and the other African American trainers in more detail in other chapters. The lack of a visible African American presence at the Kentucky Derby is probably why the white management and owners of Churchill Downs Racetrack can get away with playing "My Ole Kentucky Home" during the post parade. This song is an insult to my black American ancestors who were slaves. On the other hand, do you really think that the white managers and owners of Churchill Downs Racetrack or any other white officials in the State of Kentucky care if African Americans are offended by the playing of "My Ole Kentucky Home" at the Kentucky Derby? I would love to see the expression on the faces of these same white managers and owners of Churchill Downs if an Attorney, with the National recognition and influence of the late Johnnie Cochran, filed an injunction against the racetrack on behalf of the African Americans citizens of the State of Kentucky for Civil Rights Violation.

Imagine a demonstration at the front gate of Churchill Downs lead by Jesse Jackson after he decided to look into whether the playing of the song "My Ole Kentucky Home" was appropriate for a public sporting event held in America. What do you think would happen if the Rev. Jesse Jackson showed up at the Kentucky Derby leading a group of protesters? Do you think Jesse would get National media coverage to address the political incorrectness of this racially insensitive song "My Ole Kentucky Home" being an insult to African Americans? Can you imagine the look on a white judge's face in Louisville, Kentucky if a lawyer walked into his court to file an injunction to stop the playing of "My Ole Kentucky Home" at the Kentucky Derby? The playing of "My Ole Kentucky Home" is an established tradition at the Kentucky Derby. I guess some of you might be asking the question; why should they not play Kentucky's State Song at the most prestigious event held in that State? The answer is that before, after or during the event/game, no other major professional sport in the U.S. honors the memory of the Civil War and slavery.

Darkies or the "N" Word or "Redskins"

What do you think would happen if the St. Louis Rams and the Pittsburgh Steelers met in the Super Bowl in Atlanta, Georgia and as part of the pre-game ceremony, they played "Dixie" over the loud speakers and the players from each team had to run on to the field carrying a Confederate Flag ? Just imagine, football players waving little Confederate Flags as they run on to the field. Now look at the fact that at least 80 of these 106 players waving Confederate Flags are African American. I do not want you to spend a lot of time thinking or writing about this scenario because it will never happen. Even if all the games were played in the "DEEP SOUTH", the white owners of NFL teams would never attempt to force black football players to march around carrying Confederate Flags at a Super Bowl game played in the U.S. I have addressed this issue in my other books, and just in case you have not read them, let me explain my philosophy as to why, in my opinion, the song, "My Ole Kentucky Home", is offensive and insulting to African Americans.

In 1929, "My Kentucky Home" was adopted as the State Song of Kentucky. Let us examine a few of the lyrics from the song written by Stephen Foster in 1853,"My Ole Kentucky Home". The lyrics, *"Oh, the sun shines bright in the old Kentucky home, 'tis summer, the darkies are gay."* These lyrics suggest that the "darkey" or "darkies" the term used for black slaves were actually happy working in the field in the hot sun. I wonder if they took away Stephen Foster's freedom, kept him in chains so he could not runaway, forced him to work in the hot sun, cut his back open with a bull whip whenever he challenged the white overseer's authority, raped his wife and daughters; would Stephen be "gay". Of course, the word gay in this song means content or happy. American soldiers are still fighting and dying for freedom in countries around the world, how could anyone think a man could be happy without freedom?

In 1986, Carl Hines, the only black State Representative at the time, was quoted as saying that the lyrics "convey connotations of racial discrimination that are not acceptable". Within days, Hines sponsored House Resolution 159, which revised the lyrics to emend the word "darkies" to "people". The word "darkies" was removed so that Stephen Foster's "My Kentucky Home" would not offend the black citizens of Kentucky, and could remain the State's Song.

In 1851, Stephen Foster wrote "Swanee River", the State Song of Florida, adopted in1935, also refers to blacks as "darkeys". The lyrics are as follows: *All de world am sad and dreary, Eb-rywhere I roam; Oh, darkeys, how my heart grows weary, Far from de old folks at home!* Until 2007, it was tradition to perform the official State Song "Swanee River" as part of the inauguration ceremony for incoming Florida governors. The song was not included in the 2007 inauguration ceremony. Some citizens of Florida viewed the song as showing racism toward black Americans. The original lyrics refer to "darkeys" and "a-longin' for the old plantation." In 2007, the Florida Music Educators Association worked in partnership with Senator Tony Hill and Representative Ed

Homan to invite Florida's citizens to submit their entries for a new State Song.

If the practice of racism in the work place is a crime, why does it still exist in some places and not others; like on the "Back Side" of the sport of thoroughbred horseracing. Have you ever seen the movies that feature Dinosaurs and have a theme such as the "Land that time forgot"? Well the "Back Side" of the racetrack, as well as a few other isolated areas in America, is a part of the Sport of Kings that time forgot. When it comes to how white people are allowed to treat African Americans on the "Back Side", most of the old rules of the "JIM CROW ERA" still apply. The white thoroughbred horse owners and trainers still refer to grown black men as "boys". It is commonplace for a white owner/trainer to approach a group of black men on the "Back Side" and shout, "One of you boys come take this horse." It is just as commonplace for a white trainer/owner to use the "N" word when they get angry with an African American worker on the "Back Side". Just in case you have lived in a cave for the past 100 years, the "N" stands for nigger. That is right the same word, "Nigger", that has become a common greeting among young black Americans and is so popular frequently used in Rap music by black performers, is still very offense and distasteful when used by white people.

Let us continue to talk to about the ethnic slurs used for Native Americans and African Americans in the early history of this Country. The reason we need to expound on this subject is another reason why we need to bury the Confederate Flag, Dixie and "My Ole Kentucky Home". Columbus first used the term "Indians" in 1492, yet 128 years later, in 1620 when the pilgrims landed at Plymouth Rock; history recorded the local inhabitants as being "Indians". According to historical records, Amerigo Vespucci landed in South America in 1499 and made a return voyage in 1501. While on his voyage, Vespucci wrote two letters to a friend in Europe. He described his travels and was the first to identify the New World of North and South America as separate from Asia. Remember, Columbus thought he had reached Asia. Amerigo Vespucci described the culture of the indigenous people, and focusing on their diet, religion, their sexual habits, marriage, and childbirth practices. The letters were published in many languages and were distributed across Europe. According to historical records, North and South America were named for "Amerigo" Vespucci. If Amerigo Vespucci returned to Europe after Columbus and before the pilgrims left on their voyage to the "New World", why were not the names of the people that were "indigenous" to this New World called "Americans" rather than "Indians"?

If the name American was not changed from "Indian" when the pilgrims landed, historians should have noted the change as soon as the name America was affixed to this Country. Some might say that the word "Indian" is not offensive. The problem with the word "Indian" is that it takes away from the proud tribal names that Natives Americans should be called. Although I feel a deep kindred spirit to the Native Americans, I must make it perfectly clear that I address this issue strictly as an outsider, as I compare racially insulting names. I will never attempt to give the Native America perspective of the insulting word "Indian". Just as the word "darkey" was used in old Southern plantation song, so was the word "Injun" used in "Dixie Land" the Confederate Army theme song. For example, *"There's buckwheat cakes and Injun batter, Makes you fat or a little fatter. Look away! Look away! Look away! Dixie Land."* Try as I did, I was unable to find any source reference for the term "Injun batter", not that I was interested in finding an actual reference. My point with use of the word "Injun" is the same as the formation of the word "Nigger".

In April 2007, as an Internal Audit for the Maryland Department of Public, I had an occasion to attend a training session on fraud that was conducted by the Association of Government Accountants (AGA). The last speaker for the day was a white woman, who was the Chief Counsel to the Inspector General for the Social Security Administration. As part of her lecture, she referenced a case of fraud that involved Native Americans. However, rather than refer to them as Native Americans, the speaker called them "Indians". During her presentation, the speaker used the word "Indian" a few more times before her portion of this fraud training session ended. After this last presentation was over, I approached the black female and the white male, who were the facilitators of this training session. I suggested that they should advise the last speaker that her use of the word "Indian" was offensive and that she should either drop this case scenario from her lecture or change her "Indian" references to Native American. To my surprise, both the white and black facilitators responded by saying that they supported the use of the word "Indian". I was really caught off guard by the fact that the black woman did not seem to understand my concern over the use of the word "Indian". The black woman and her white counterpart advised me that the legal term used by the Federal Government when referring to Native Americans is "Indian".

Although I was fully aware of the fact that when the welfare and preservation of Native Americans in this Country was assigned to the Department of the Interior, the word that was used in all Official Government Documents was "Indians". There was close to 200 people in this AGA training session, most of who worked for State, Local or the Federal Government; and based on the criteria for being invited to attend this training, one would have to think that the group consisted of some very intelligent people. Yet, I wonder if of the other attendees were offended by the white female speaker's use of the word "Indian".

My mistake was that I thought the United States Government; in its' attempt to be politically correct had dropped the use of the word "Indian" and starting using the word Native American. Just as the laws in this Country starting as far back as the 1800, used the word Negro or colored when referring to my black ancestors in legal documents, although many of these laws are still on the book, today the United States Government uses the term African American whenever these old laws are discussed. In 2007, the University of Illinois lost its appeal to the National Collegiate Athletic Association (NCAA) to retain an offensive "Indian" name for the college mascot. It is about time that a group of Americans finally gets the message that the word "Indian" is as offensive to Native Americans as all the other ethnic slurs used in this Country. My question is why the insulting, distasteful and both historical and politically incorrect word "Indian", is still used by our predominately-white elected Government Officials when referring to Native Americans.

The word "Injun" is an intentionally used disrespectful way for white people to pronounce the word "Indian"; the same as "Nigger" is an intentionally used disrespectful way for white people to pronounce the word Negro. The white man to dehumanize the red and black man used the word "Nigger" and "Injun". Although the Native American should have never been named "Indians", it would have meant holding them in high regard and respect if ignorant white racists correctly pronounced the name. These same ignorant white racists would have given the same respect to my black ancestors if they pronounced the word Negro correctly. The use of the words "Injun" and "Nigger" became even more demeaning when the user combined them with other insults such as "dirty", "dumb", "no account", "ignorant", "black" or "red". The reason I feel so strongly about eliminating the public display of the Confederate Flag, changes the words to the State Song of Kentucky, and "Dixie Land", is that the use of the word "Nigger" and "Injun" are empowered by the Confederate Flag, and the songs "Dixie Land" and "My Ole Kentucky Home". Several States, including Maryland and Virginia, have passed legislation that supported a formal apology to the African American community for slavery. My immediate reaction to that legislation was that it was far too little and far too late.

During slavery and continuing through the "JIM CROW ERA" and during the time when the United States Army was at war with the Native Americans in this Country, it was commonplace and part of the everyday conversation in white society for African Americans to be referred to as "Niggers" and Native Americans to be referred to as "Injuns". It was so commonplace that my black American ancestors answered when they were called "Nigger" and Native Americans answered when they were referred to as "Injuns". It upsets me that over the years my black slave ancestors followed the lead of these ignorant white racists by referring to Native Americans as "Injuns". This was just another case of my black ancestors copying the disgusting behavior of the white man. On the other hand, the Native Americans, who held my black ancestors in high regard, called them "Buffalo Soldiers". The Native Americans had a custom of giving people, even their enemies, honorable names based on their appearance or ability. Many of these names were associated with animals that the Native Americans held in the highest esteem, such as the eagle, wolf, bear, elk and buffalo. I talk about the origin of the name "Buffalo Soldier" in chapter three.

Another point about the use of the word "Nigger" and "Injun" that turns my stomach is the fact that both African and Native Americans use these words when referring to their own people or themselves. Although there is no documented evidence to support it, I believe that the lack of self-esteem was the reason that black and Native Americans used these disgusting words. By enslaving my African American ancestors and by restricting Native Americans to reservations, the white man took away their freedom and their self-esteem. The physical abuse endured by African and Native Americans at the hands of the white man in the early history of this Country has finally been documented. For years, white historians failed to include the inhuman treatment of black slaves and Native Americans as part of development of this "New World". For nearly 100 years, the white males who dominated school boards across this nation, refused to allow a curriculum that would vilify the white male. That is why in any course in school that dealt with the enslavement of African Americans and the wars with the Native American to force them off land that was rightfully theirs, was justified as being necessary evil for the progress of this Country. The white male school boards never mention the cruel and inhuman treatment of African Americans during slavery or the internment of Native Americans on the baring lands of the Midwest or the swamps of Florida.

The Unseen Scars

The scars from the physical abuse endured by my ancestors and the Native American were obvious because they were outwardly visible. However, the scars from the mental abuse of constantly being told that you are less than a human being could not be seen by the naked eye. It is has been verified by soldiers that were captured by the enemy and tortured for information, mental torture is more devastating and has greater long-term effect than physical torture. I cannot speak for the Native Americans, but the African Americans that refer to each other as "Nigger", use the word out of a lack of self-respect. With white slave owners and their white overseers, persistence in calling their black slaves "Niggers", my slave ancestors, out of lack of knowledge that they were being insulted, used the term "Niggers". When slavery was legal in America, slaves that were away from the plantation, when confronted by white people, would identify themselves as being one of "Massar Leroy's Niggers". To my African American ancestors, the word "Nigger" meant that you were the property of a white slave owner. The word "Nigger" became an insult to black people that had gained their freedom.

After the Civil War, white people used the word "Nigger" to remind African Americans that even though they were free, they would never be equal. As we moved through the years after the Civil War, after the 13th and 14th amendments to the Constitution ended slavery, the frustration over not being able to achieve racial equality, may have lead many African Americans to refer to each other as "Niggers". However, after the Civil War and continuing through today, in the majority of African American society, if a white person calls a black person a "Nigger", it is definitely considered an insult. When my grandmother was living, she made it clear that the "N" word was nasty and it was never to be used in her presence. In some States in this Country, if a white person calls a black person a "Nigger", the white person could be criminally charged with verbal assault. In other States, the use of the word "Nigger" in public could be considered disorderly conduct. My African American brothers and sisters, how can we continue to view the word "Nigger" as a racial insult, when black and white Rap Groups are using it in their lyrics like a badge of honor?

"Injun" "Injin" "Nigger" "Nigga" All Offensive

The casual use of the word "Nigger" by young black and by young white men and women literally makes me crazy. I will be the first to admit that I have used the word. I used the word when I was a young boy, even into my teens and early twenties. I stopped the casual use of the word in my twenties when my grandfather gave me a personal history lesson on the definition of "Nigger". After my grandfather's lesson, I only use the word in my books to make a point. I may use the N word when I am angry with someone or something involving a black person. However, I never allow a white person to use the word for any reason in my presence. Matter of fact, I do not allow the use of any racial slurs in my presence from anyone. The modern dilemma with the use of the word "Nigger" is that the rules for how and when it is used have changed. For me, the use of the word "Nigger" by a white person always has been and always will be a racial insult. Yet, today young black and white people use the phrase "that's my Nigga" as a common greeting. They use it when black kids meet other black kids, when black kids meet white kids or when white kids meet other white kids. The word "Nigga" has become a fixture in the Rap Music culture. If the younger generations of white and black kids are casually using the word, when is the use of the word "Nigger" inappropriate?

In November of 2006, Michael Richards, a popular white comedian and the actor who portrayed the character "Kramer" on the long running TV comedy "Seinfeld", gained National attention when he used the word "Nigger" in an angry response to African Americans that were heckling him during his performance at a local nightclub. In this age of modern technology, every movement seemed to be videotaped, as was the episode that featured Michael Richards using the word "Nigger". Within 24 hours, the story, including the video, appeared on every TV news station in America. Michael Richards, who most Americans associated with the wacky character "Kramer", was now a racist. Another black man who was in the audience that night stated that, "He just took all of the air out of the room," "He needs to make a public apology to everyone." Richards was back on stage 24 hours later. He told reporters off the record that he felt sorry for what happened and he made amends; to whom or how, Richards did not say. I watched the video; in my opinion, Richards fit what I have always pictured as a typical white racist using the word "Nigger" to insult an African American that did something to upset him.

According to published reports, a Hispanic comedian, Paul Rodriguez, was at the club when Michael Richards started trading insult with these African American patrons. Mr. Rodriguez stated that he thought Richards' comments crossed the line. "Once the word comes out of your mouth and you do not happen to be African American, then you have a whole lot of explaining," said Mr. Rodriguez. "Freedom of speech has its limitations and I think Michael Richards found those limitations." If I had not seen the video of Richards' racist tirade, I would have found it had to believe. Based on years of watching Richards as "Kramer", I could not envision him as a racist. In an attempt to make amends for his disgusting behavior, Richards met with black leaders, Jesse Jackson and Al Sharpton. Richards apologized to the black community and he reportedly enrolled in a treatment program that specializes in racial sensitivity and diversity training. Richards even appeared on National radio and TV programs. He made no excuse for his actions, and issued a personal apology. Richards' apology for his actions after the fact is just as pointless as the states that issued public apologies for slavery, too little and too late.

Michael Richards's racially insulting outburst at this nightclub surprised his friend and fellow comedian, Jerry Seinfeld. Most of the other white entertainers that were interviewed in reference to this incident were just as surprised as Seinfeld, and they all concurred that Michael Richards was not a racist. What seemed to be lost in this incident was that the use of the word "Nigger" was not the only indictment of Richards as a racist. Richards told his black hecklers that 50 years ago they would have taken them out and hung them by the neck. Richards was 57 years old at the time of this incident. He was born during the "JIM CROW ERA" when it was commonplace for a white man to call a black man a "Nigger" without suffering any consequences. Racism is a disease, and a learned behavior. Michael Richards had controlled this racist disease and behavior in public for years until he lost his temper when he felt these African Americans personally attacked him. Michael Richards retaliated by using the same racial insults that he had used before when he had a confrontation with an African American. In my opinion, Richards is a typical white racist.

Anyone who believes that this was the first time Richards used to word "Nigger" must also believe the moon is made of cream cheese. Just a few months after Michael Richards made National headlines by using the word "Nigger" in public, another white celebrity, Paris Hilton was caught on tape at an exclusive New Year's party using the same word. In the video, Paris appeared to be having a good time when she asked a "camera guy" to come film her dancing to Biggie's [the black Rapper Biggie Smalls] "Hypnotize" with her sister Nicky Hilton. While the two sisters are dancing, Paris goes up to the camera and announces, "We're like two niggers!" when we dance. Reportedly, on this same video tape Paris talked about a "run-in" she had with some woman, presumably a black woman, earlier in the evening and refers to the woman as a "f__kin hoodlum, broke, poor b_cth from like, Compton." First, you need to understand that during this period, everything that Paris and Nicky Hilton did made news. Just like Princess Diana, the paparazzi were always chasing the Hilton sisters because they are the heirs to the Hilton Hotel fortune. According to reports in a popular white owned entertainment magazine, the reason Paris' use of the word "Nigger" on this occasion made the news was because she said "Nigger" with emphasis on the "er", rather than the socially acceptable "Nigga", that is readily used by blacks and white in the Rap culture.

Paris and Nicky Hilton have been in the company of some of the wealthiest African American professional entertainers and athletes in America. It is a proven fact that the doors to white society that had been closed to the average black person are now opened to rich and famous African Americans. This was not the first time that Paris Hilton has used the word "Nigger" in public. Unfortunately, for Paris, her use of the word on this particular occasion came not long after the racist outburst by a white entertainer. Just as it was with Michael Richards, Paris Hilton's use of the word "Nigger" did not disturb me. It was her reported description of the black woman that she allegedly had a "run-in" with, and according to the published remarks about this woman, Paris obviously felt she was far below her social and economic status. The remarks about the black woman were the stereotypical comments of a white racist, that all the people that live in a low-income black

168

community are poor, broke or hoodlums. In my opinion, if Paris Hilton made those comments about a black woman, she is a bigot. In my opinion, if the statement is correct, what Paris Hilton was saying is that the only black people that matter to her are the rich and famous. Unlike Michael Richards, I never read that Paris Hilton issued a public apology for her use of the word "Nigger".

Paris Hilton felt that because she had so many black friends, she was entitled to use the word. In April 2007, yet another white celebrity, Don Imus, WFAN-AM New York syndicated talk radio personality, whose radio show is broadcast live on MSNBC TV, made racist comments similar to those reportedly made by Paris Hilton. In my opinion, Imus felt it was ok for him to make these racist remarks because he was just joking. The day after the women's basketball team from the University of Tennessee defeated Rutgers University for the NCAA Championship, Imus and the white producer of his radio, Bernard McGuirk, made several racist comments about the women that played for Rutgers. "That's some rough girls from Rutgers," Imus said. "Man, they got tattoos"; "Some hardcore hos," said McGuirk. "That's some nappy headed hos there, I'm going to tell you that," Imus fired back. Imus took the verbal assault a step further with the Spike Lee analogy, which McGuirk incorrectly credited to "Do the Right Thing". "The girls from Tennessee, they all look cute," said Imus. "Kinda like a Spike Lee thing – the jigaboos vs. the wannabes." The line was actually used in the Spike Lee movie "School Daze". White people that use words like sambo, coon, jigaboo and wannabe, need to understand that those words are not funny to African Americans.

Nappy Head

The reason I compared the racist comments made by Imus with the racist comments allegedly made by Paris Hilton, is that they share the same the reason for the making the racist comments. The comments attributed to Hilton and by Imus were made based on the perceived class of the black women that play for Tennessee verses the perceived lack of class of the black women that play for Rutgers. Both Rutgers and Tennessee are fine schools, and since both teams featured African American players, why would Imus and McGuirk make these disparaging racist comments about the black players from Rutgers and not Tennessee.

The obvious difference in determining the level of class between these two teams was that Rutgers was coached by an up and coming black female named Vivian Stringer and the legendary white female, Pat Summit, coached Tennessee. Of course, after his comments were criticized as being racist, sexist and insensitive, Imus issued an apology. The problem with the apology from Imus is that he had a reputation of making racially insensitive comments in the past on his radio program to get a laugh. The black community, led by the Reverends Sharpton and Jackson, were upset at Imus. However, rather than the black community being upset with Imus, they should be upset with the radio and TV networks that promote people like Imus.

Imus works for CBS, and appears on NBC, two of the four major networks in America. We as African American need to direct our anger at the real source of the racism; yet, we continue to buy the products that are advertised by Imus' network. Networks the size of CBS and NBC have conducted enough research to know that Imus has a large enough following of white bigots and racists that totally support the disgusting comment made on his radio and TV shows. The use of a boycott by a small group of African Americans can send a message to white America that is very clear; black people will band together as a group to defeat the oppression, bigotry and injustice of the racially motivation actions of white Corporate America. The majority of white America can forget their racial prejudice to cheer for black American athletes, entertainers, war heroes, and other blacks that have achieved some form of celebrity and they can forget their racial prejudice if it means losing money. If we want to change the perception that the word "Nigger" or "Nigga" is not sociably acceptable for use by white people and if we want to make it perfectly clear that, we do not find racial insult amusing, let us keep using the boycott.

The good news is that there was some significant fallout from the comments about the Rutgers women's basketball team by radio talk show host Don Imus. Office supply chain Staples Inc., the world's largest office supplies retailer and Procter & Gamble Co., one of the world's biggest makers of consumer products, pulled their advertising from Imus' show, and another major sponsor, Bigelow Tea said the remarks have "put our future sponsorship in jeopardy." The Imus Radio Show originates with New York radio station WFAN-AM, and is syndicated to other radio stations by CBS Radio; like CBSNews.com, is part of CBS Corporation and the program is also simulcast on the cable channel MSNBC TV.

According to the Wall Street Journal, advertisers do not buy time on specific programs on MSNBC, but instead time on the channel's overall daytime schedule, which meant that Procter & Gamble pulled all its ads off MSNBC. A spokesperson from P& G stated, "Any venue in which our ads appear that is offensive to our target audience is not acceptable to us". In addition, Imus received a two-week suspension from CBS radio and MSNBC canceled his television show. Many Civil Rights Organizations and the National Organization for Women have demanded that Don Imus be fired. However, just as I stated before, a major part of white America supports Imus as evidenced by the fact that General Motors and American Express, two of Imus' biggest sponsors that advertise their products on his radio show, stuck with him.

There is a Market for Racism

Just as with "My Ole Kentucky Home", Dixie Land, and the Confederate Flag, if there were not markets for the racist State Songs, the racist historical flags and the popular white racist radio personalities, the American public would not support them. How can the white people that control the media in this Country make a determination that the word "Nigga" is a socially acceptable reference for African Americans? Let me make it perfectly clear. No matter how you pronounce the words; "Negra" as used by the white plantation owner in the heat of the night, or "Nigger" as used by Michael Richards and Paris Hilton, or "Nigga" as used by the new "Hip Hop" and Rap cultures, they are insults to the majority of African Americans in this Country.

171

Stars & Stripes Vs. Stars & Bars

The white songwriter, Stephen Foster was born, raised and spent most of his life in Pittsburgh, Pennsylvania, and in all likelihood never saw the "Swanee River"; a plantation in Kentucky; or for that matter a black slave. In my opinion, the black citizens of Kentucky should conduct a boycott of the businesses, which include the racetracks, until the State Song is changed and the racist "My Ole Kentucky Home" is gone forever. This action would be similar to the boycott conducted by the black citizens of South Carolina to have the Confederate Flag removed from atop the State Capital Building. The state of South Carolina lost millions of dollars when their black citizens refused to shop in the State during Y2K Christmas holiday season. It is my hope that if enough blacks from Kentucky read my book, they will conduct a boycott to have the State Song changed.

In the "DEEP SOUTH", like their African American ancestors did for over 300 years, blacks continue in the jobs that were at one time performed strictly by slaves. They still work in the fields, picking cotton, chopping tobacco and sugar cane. As it was during the days of slavery in the "DEEP SOUTH", African Americans are doing most of the manual-labor that involved working with your hands, working outside and enduring the elements in the South. By comparison, other than in the "DEEP SOUTH", the rest of America's manual laborers, such as carpenters, bricklayers, auto mechanics and assembly line workers make a good salary. The forming of strong organized labor unions changed the wages and working conditions for most of the manual labor workforce. Unions made Corporate Executives respect the demands of the manual labor force. Unfortunately, the black manual labor force in the "DEEP SOUTH" and the black labor force on the "Back Side" of horseracing have failed to organize. Due to their lack of organization, African Americans have failed to gain the respect of the white Corporate Executives in the Agriculture business in the "DEEP SOUTH" and the white people who run the Horseracing Industry.

Slaves Vs. Back Side Workers

I spoke earlier about the white female trainer who bragged about how she used a buggy whip to discipline a black male worker she witnessed abusing one of her horses. The irony here is that I know this white female trainer. Before this incident, did I think that she was a bigot or racist? In fact, during her younger years she spent most of her leisure time in the company of the black people who worked on the "Back Side". In addition, because of her love of horse, anyone that knows this white female trainer realized that for her, to abuse a horse is a crime, and the punishment for that crime would have been the same regardless of the color of the person responsible for abusing a horse. Unfortunately, the issue is that the whipping of a black man by a white woman with a buggy whip, just as the use of the word "Nigger", brings back the haunting images of slavery and the "JIM CROW ERA".

Although there may have been no racial motive on the part of the white female trainer, the posturing from both groups is based on the white man's slave ownership mentality and the black man's mentality of being the white man's slave. Fortunately, things are not like they were during the early day of slavery in America, the white man's threatening words usually resulted in harsher physical punishment and even death for some blacks. Today, the threats of the white man result in the firing of blacks or more work and less pay. However, the threats of the black workers on the "Back Side" and the mumblings of the African slaves of the past had much the same results, which were no action and more of the same humiliation and frustration to follow.

The sport of thoroughbred horseracing and the enslavement of my African ancestors started in America around the same time. The Civil War ended the physical and legal act of the enslavement of blacks in America. However, in 2014, I am 65 years old; over the past 34 years, I have met black men that are old enough to be my father, who work on the "Back Side of the Sport of Kings" and still shuffle, grin and "yassa boss", whenever they come in contact with a white man. I am not talking about black men who live and work in the "DEEP SOUTH". These

African Americans live in the Mid-Atlantic States of Maryland, Delaware and Virginia. In the Baltimore and Washington D.C. Metropolitan Areas that have a population, that is predominately African American. In this region, we have the added protection against racial violence of having the Chief of Police for Baltimore City and Washington D.C. both being African Americans. In this area, we have large numbers of black Representatives in State and Local Government, as well as one of the largest alliances of black clergy in America. This being the case, why do some African Americans continue to exhibit the mentality of a black slave?

Today, most of the African Americans that work on the "Back Side of the Sport of Kings" earn approximately $9.00 an hour and they work from 5 am until 1 pm or until their work in done, 365 days a year with no days off and no holidays. If not for the indescribable and horrific acts associated with slavery and if not for the fact that it would be an insult and disrespectful to the memory of my African American ancestors, you might say that the only difference between being a slave and working on the "Back Side" are slaves had longer hours. Of course, my slave ancestors were paid less; were not free citizens and did not have a choice of professions. Slaves were not allowed the leave the job site and to go to their own home after work. Like former black slaves, "Back Side" workers are required to report for duty in the blazing heat or freezing cold. Like the U.S. Postman, nothing is to keep the "Back Side" workers from their appointed duties at the racetrack. However, unlike the Postman, the "Back Side" workers and my black slaves ancestors did not have a Labor Union to protect them. In the year 2014, if a "Back Side" worker misses one day of work a year, they face the threat of being fired.

Wake Up Kentucky

Am I missing something here? Did I fall asleep and wake up in 1850 on a plantation in Kentucky? Is the word "darkies" the only thing that makes this song offensive to the black people of Kentucky? "The young folks roll on the little cabin floor, all merry, all happy and bright." The reference to the "young folks" is young black slaves. In some versions of the song, it does say "young darkies" roll on the little cabin floor. Young African American slaves, who were old enough, worked in the fields alongside their parents. Black slave children that were too young to work in the field stayed behind with a nanny, who nursed and took care of the masters' white children as well as their own. Based on my own experience of working in the fields all day during the summer, when I got home, I took off my clothes, took a bath and lay down under the shade tree. The logical things that my black slave ancestors did at night was eat and sleep. The young slaves, when they were done working, would have been too tired to roll on the floor. In addition, the slave cabins were shabby wooden shacks with dirt floors. If for some unimaginable reason, young slaves wanted to roll in the dirt, they could have stayed outside and rolled in the dirt.

When I was about 12, for two long hot summers, I worked on a farm that was owned by a white family. I worked on this farm along with most of the other young black children that were my age and out of school for the summer and a few older black women that lived in the communities near the farm and did not have regular jobs. While we were working, we could see that the farmer's children were also hard at work on the farm. I remember seeing these young white kids driving the farm truck or operating the tractor as their father supervised the workers in the field. They would also help their father load the produce that had been picked by the black workers. I never remember seeing the white farmer's children working side by side with us in the field. Although the farmer's kids were the same age as most of the black children working in the field, they never talk to us about stuff that kids our age talk about. The only time the white kids ever spoke to us was to pass on orders from their father and the tone of their voice made it clear that they were not speaking to us as a peer, but as an authority figure.

Sometimes during our lunch break or at the end of the day before we left to go home, the black kids would play games in the space at the end of the field. The farmer's kids might watch us play, but they never joined in on any of the games. It became clear that they were not watching because they were interested in the games we played, but to report any wrongdoing to their father. Occasionally, as they watched us playing, the white kids would get upset and yell at us to stop before we hurt each other or destroyed something that belonged to their father. Although they sounded serious when they were yelling at us, we never paid any attention to the farmer's children because they were just kids like us. However, if the older black women heard the farmer's kids yelling at us, they would echo whatever the white children were saying to us and tell would enforce the order to stop whatever we were doing that upset the farmer's kids. As I remember, the only workers that the white farmer's children held any long conversations with were the older black women who they called "Aunt" before using their first name.

At the time, I never questioned why these white kids were calling these black women their aunt. Actually, two of the black women working in the field were my great-aunts; Ernestine "Aunt Ninnie" Gatewood and Augustus "Aunt Gus" Hebron, who I knew, could not have been related to these white children. Yet, it never crossed my mind that I should have said or done something to stop these white children from referring to my aunts as if they were their relatives too. The older black women, including my aunts, did not mind being called "auntie" by the farmer's children. As a matter of fact, the black women seemed to have established a bond with the white children, similar to the bond the slaves that I had seen in the movies had for the white children on the Southern plantations. It is too farfetched to believe that my ancestors, who endured such horrific treatment at the hands of the white slave masters, could develop an affectionate bond with the children of the same brutal slave masters.

In my research and studies of American History, I have not found any documentation that breaks down the relationship between the white children of slave owners and the black slaves. Of course I am familiar with "Uncle Tom's Cabin" and "Gone with the Wind", books written by white people that became plays and/or movies, that featured a relationship between slaves and the white children that they helped raise. In the eyes of black moviegoers, Thelma "Butterfly" McQueen and Hattie McDaniel's became Hollywood Superstars after appearing in the movie "Gone with the Wind". In fact, Ms. McDaniel was the first African American to win an Academy Award for Best Supporting Actress for her role in "Gone with the Wind". Just as memorable and popular was the team of Shirley Temple and Bill "Bojangles" Robinson who made several movies in which Mr. Robinson's character played the part of an old black slave that befriended a little white girl, Shirley Temple's character, and they always found a way to dance together. The black characters in these movies were usually called "Mammy, Pappy, Uncle or Aunt" as a title before their first name.

On the big Southern plantations, white slave owners tried to mirror the Aristocratic lifestyle that was part of their European heritage. In an effort to replicate this Aristocratic lifestyle, the white plantation owners trained black slaves to be servants and run the mansion as butlers and maids. There was another servant that was a traditional part of the Aristocratic household and that was the "nanny". According to the encyclopedia, a nanny is defined as "a child's nurse". The traditional nanny was a servant in a large household and reported directly to the lady of the house. Nannies were always female and this remained the case through the 20th Century. The nanny's role currently stands firmly as an important segment of early childhood development and education. The nanny in an Aristocratic household ran her own tiny domain, supported by at least one nursery maid. Because of their role in childcare, they were somewhat more indulged than other servants. Nannies may have remained in the employ of the same Aristocratic family for years, looking after successive generations of children.

If you have read my books, you know that it is my opinion that the most horrendous acts of vile behavior by one human being against another is that of the white slave masters that raped and sodomized my female ancestors who had no choice by to endure these horrific treatment. To further humiliate and shame these beautiful black women, the white slave masters forced them to breast-feed his children. The research of this period has verified the fact that white slave owners raped their female slaves. It has also been made very clear that one of the tasks the black female slaves were forced to do was to be surrogate mothers to their masters' white children or the "nanny". The role of the black nanny ranged from changing dirty diapers, to day and night care, to breast-feeding. I have no idea if the nanny's that were employed by the Aristocratic families in Europe, actually breast-feed the babies placed in their care. During the period of time when the enslavement of black people was legal in this Country, it was a common practice for black female slaves that had recently experienced the birth of their own child, to be taken to their white masters' house to have his new born white children suckle at the breasts of a black slave. I would even go so far as to say that it was the black slave nanny's that put the "nurse" in the word "nursery" when it comes to childcare.

It should come as no shock that the white slave masters used black slaves to nurse their children. For centuries in this Country, white slaves owners treated black slaves like thoroughbred horses. The white slave owners bred and sold their black slaves the same way they bred and sold their prized thoroughbred horses. In the business of breeding thoroughbred horses, when a mare dies during the delivery of a foal, or if the mare cannot produce any milk, or if the mare rejects the foal and will not allow it to nurse, the breeder will find use another mare that has recently had a foal to nurse the orphaned foal. The surrogate mare is sometimes called a "wet nurse" because she has the ability to continue to produce milk long after the foal she delivered stops nursing. A "wet nurse" could also be a mare whose foal died at birth. Unfortunately, the white slave owners used the same methodology as the horse breeders did for their foals; they used female slaves to "wet nurse" his children.

In my opinion, Aristocratic Southern white women were like some of the mares that I just described. After having a baby, the mother either could not produce milk, or she would reject her own child and would not nurse the baby. In some cases, the "lady" of the Southern mansion had far too many social functions to plan for and attend and her schedule did not include any time for childcare. Why should she have to take care of her children when there were plenty of healthy black slave females to do her job? Regardless of the reason, the black nanny was taken from her own children to care for the masters'

178

children. Ironically, because the breeding of slaves was so very profitable, it provided a system of surrogate mothers for the black female slaves that were forced to leave their own children unattended. As a result of the white owners breeding their slaves like cattle there were always other black women around the plantation who had recently had babies and were still producing enough milk to take care of the white owner's children. In some rare cases the nanny was allowed to care of her children whiles she attended to the masters' children. However, when they were all together, the black nanny had to be very careful to make sure that her children remember their places as slaves and treated the masters' children with the proper respect.

By using black nannies to raise his children, the white slave unknowingly owners created a lasting bond of affection between his white children and their black caregivers. Although the female black slaves may have been forced to be a nanny to the masters' children, because of the fact that a child, regardless of race, is so innocent and helpless, it is would be very difficult for a loving caring mother not to develop an attachment, and care for these white children as if they were her own. Children, regardless of race, give unconditional love to their caregiver. They will become attached to their surrogate mother, and the longer they are together the stronger the bond. Remember that children, again regardless of race, become bigots and racists only by emulating the behavior of an adult. The relationship between the black nanny and the white child had a great positive impact on the future of racial harmony in America.

Back to the reason that it did not dawn on me to say anything when the white farmer's kids bonded with the older black women that worked for their father. It did not dawn on me that these older black women that worked in the field alongside me, had the same mentality as the slave nanny and that they wanted to make sure we showed the proper respect for the farmer's children. The main reason I did not speak up was at the age of 12, I was not the student of black American history that I am today. Therefore, I was not familiar with the "ole" white slave owner tradition of affectionately adding a title to the first name of older slaves by calling the older black females "auntie" or "mammy" and the older males "uncle" or "pappy". Again, this is why history needs to be taught in more than one color and from more than one perspective. On the plantation, the white slave owners called the males slaves "boy" and the female slaves "gal" rather than try to remember their names. The longevity of being a good slave is what earned the older men and women the titles of "auntie", mammy, uncle and pappy. During slavery and continued through the "JIM CROW ERA" in America, very few self-respecting white men applied the word Mr. or Mrs. before addressing a black person in this Country. In fact, it would have been considered an act of blasphemy for the white slave masters to use the words Mr. or Mrs. before calling the name of one of their slaves.

Unfortunately, when I was in school we were taught the history of this Country in one color and from one perspective. However, it was just as unfortunate that white children were taught the same way. The primary color and perspective for the education of blacks in America from 1865 through 1954 was white. What happened in 1954; Brown vs. The Board of Education. The white children who attended school during this time were also deprived of the different colors and perspective of the history of America. The inspiration for all my books is that history needs to be taught in more than one color and from more than one perspective and my books are for all Americans regardless of race, color or creed. This incident took place in the early 1960s and by calling older black women "Aunt"; these white children were continuing a racist mentality that started in America nearly 400 years ago. It was my studies and research of African American History that made me realize that the white farmer's children were affectionately calling these older black women "Aunt" because they thought it was a sign of respect given to "colored people" after they reached a certain age.

The problem is that they should have used Mr. and Mrs. before calling the names of these black women. However, based on the fact the white farmer also called these black women "Aunt"; it was obvious that this bad habit was passed down from one generation of white farmers to the next that in their family did not have enough respect for "colored" women or men to call them Mr. or Mrs.. Remember the scene from the movie "In the Heat of the Night", when the "Ole Redneck Southern Sheriff" asked Sidney Poitier's character for his name and he told him his name was Virgil. The Sheriff responded, "What kind of name is Virgil for a colored boy like you". The Sheriff then asked, "What do they call you boy?", and Sidney's character replied, "They call me Mr. Tibbs". You see, Virgil was originally from Sparta, South Carolina and he relocated to Philadelphia, Pennsylvania where he became a Police Detective Lieutenant in the Homicide Division. What the Sheriff really wanted to know when he asked Virgil, "What do they call you boy", is what do the white people up North call you? Sidney's character's response was to let the Sheriff know that in the City of Philadelphia, everyone respected him, regardless of race and they all called him "Mr. Tibbs". The scene I just described as well as another the scene from the movie when Sidney's character, after being slapped in the face by a white plantation owner, immediately slapped him in his face. The reaction of Sidney's character in both scenes sent a message to white America that we as black Americans now demand respect.

The song also contains the following verse. "They hunt no more for the possum and the coon, on the meadow, the hill and the shore, they sing no more by the glimmer of the moon, on the bench by the old cabin door." After working in the field all day, slaves would go out at night to trap possums and raccoon to add to their stew pots because they rarely got meat from their white masters. Notice that Foster made a point of mentioning that only black slaves ate opossum and raccoon, which was meat that no self-respecting white Southern would ever think about putting on their table. Foster's reference to my black slave ancestors singing outside their cabins at night was not for the entertainment of their white masters. The only singing done by slaves was spirituals, sung as prayers to God to end their suffering and to give direction to runaway slaves. If runaway slaves were close enough to a plantation to hear signing, they knew they had to go in the opposite direction to avoid being captured and to escape to the North to freedom. I cannot get over the fact that white people actual believed African slaves were singing because they were happy. I am glad the white slave masters never figured out that the songs being song by slaves were both prayers to God, and signals to help runaway slaves find their way North.

In the DEEP SOUTH, black People still bow their heads

Unfortunately, in 2014 there are still black people in America that feel they need to continue the traditional behavior of slaves on the old plantation in order to survive life in the "DEEP SOUTH". These African American feel they have to shuffle along and grin whenever they encounter white people or they will suffer the same consequences as the black slaves of the past. It does not help the plight of these African Americans that there are just as many whites today in the "DEEP SOUTH" that practice the same racist traditions that were described in the lyrics written by Stephen Foster in 1853 in the song "My Ole Kentucky Home". The white man's use of the word "darkie" is just as offensive as the use of the word "boy", "gal", "buck", "Sambo", and the list could go on and on. To add insult to the injury to the African Americans who live in Kentucky, the white managers and owners of Churchill Downs Racetrack are so proud of Stephen Foster that they named a graded stakes race in his honor. I wonder if they considered having an African American at the Derby bow their heads during the presentation of the trophy to the winner.

"The head must bow and the back will have to bend, wherever the darkie may go." The fact that they had to keep their heads bowed and their backs bent should have made it clear that my ancestors were not happy. Even more offensive than the use of the word "darkie" is the fact that whenever black people were in the company of, or about to approach a white person, slaves had to bow their heads. Here is a fact that should be added to history lessons. Slaves could actually be lynched or shot on sight for merely looking into the eyes of a white person. Can you imagine being punished just for making eye contact with someone of a different race? This song was written in 1853, and yet today there were still areas in the "DEEP SOUTH" in America where black men are still afraid to look a white person in the eyes for fear they might be lynched or shot. The fact that a State would select and continue to support a song that has lyrics that preserve the racist custom of African American bowing their heads to show respect and fear for the white race, is an indication that the State of Kentucky has no respect for African Americans. In addition, the State of Kentucky has no fear of what actions the black community might take to remove the song.

Modern Day Slaves

Whenever I think about the words to my "Ole Kentucky Home", *"the head must bow and the back will have to bend, wherever the darkey may go: A few more days for to tote the weary load"*, it reminds me of the days when slavery was the law the land. It reminds me of the lifestyle of the big Southern plantations and its' slave quarters. It reminds me that the plantation lifestyle supported the fact that black slaves could never be equal in stature to white people. It reminds me that on the Southern plantations, my black ancestors were stripped of their pride and dignity and they could never raise their heads to look a white person in the eyes. It reminded me that blacks slaves were forced to do all the work while white plantation owners reaped all the benefits. Today, over 155 years after this song was written and the end of slavery in America, the words of *"My Ole Kentucky Home"* remind me of the conditions in the NBA and NFL. In this Country, African Americans dominate these two professional sports. Yet, just as they owned the plantation in the South, the majority of team owners in both the NBA and NFL are white and just as the plantation overseers that kept control over the slaves in the field, the white commissioners preside over both sports.

The question you may be asking is how can I compare African American athletes in the NBA and NFL that earn tens of millions of dollars a year, to black slaves that had their freedom stolen away and were forced to work for no pay? Although the black NBA and NFL players of today are not forced to work without pay, the rest of their existence once they sign a contract can be easily compared to that of their slave ancestors. When they sign a contract to play for the NBA or NFL they become part of the team, just as their slave ancestors became part of the plantation. As I stated before, white men own both the teams and the plantations. Again, I know all of you sports fans are finding it hard to follow my logic in comparing millionaire black athletes to slaves. Just turn on the internet, open up your newspaper or turn on your TV and follow the news stories that involve black professional football and basketball players and you will have a better understanding and possibly see where I am going with this comparison. Black players are told how to dress, who they can and cannot associate with and if they do not follow the rules, they are suspended. The personal lives of African American professionals in the NBA and NFL are so closely scrutinized that they literally cannot spit on the sidewalk in public without making headlines.

Lynching by any other name is still Murder

By the way, for those of you who think that white men are not still lynching African Americans and that lynching is a thing of the past in the U.S.; just remember as I discussed earlier that in 1998, a black man named James Bryd was lynched in Jasper, Texas. For a white man like Stephen Foster, the fact that he pictured black slaves bowing their heads, shuffling along, and grinning for the white man was natural. As slaves, my African American ancestors bowed their heads, and did whatever else they needed to do to survive. Maybe if James Byrd, bowed his head, grinned, shuffled along as he walked and spoke in a "yassa boss" tone to the white men who stopped him on the road, he would still be alive. How could anyone today, white or black, think that Stephen Foster wrote this song to be equally complementary to both the white and black citizens of Kentucky? Stephen Foster never thought of a "darkie" as ever being his equal. Foster never thought of a black man as ever sharing the same rights, voting, owning property, or being educated. In 1853 when he wrote this song, Stephen Foster had no idea that someday the African Americans that he looked down on all his life as slaves would be free men.

Will Racism Ever End?

"A few more days, and the trouble all will end, in the field where the sugarcanes grow. A few more days for to tote the weary load, no matter, 'twill never be light, a few more days till we totter on the road, then my old Kentucky home good night." In his song, Foster was talking about eventually growing old and dying, which would cause him to leave his Ole Kentucky Home. Fortunately, for us in the black community, racists are a dying breed in America. I revel at the fact that the days of the white racists dominance will soon be over. Most of the white racists in America, that still practice racism, are just as sad Stephen Foster because the lyrics he wrote indicate that the days of the Old Kentucky Home mentality are slowly dwindling. I hope that just like Stephen Foster, the white racists of the world will be just as dead. These lyrics clearly indicate that Stephen Foster thought, even in death, that blacks would always carry the burden of being slaves. However, rather than look at these ending lyrics as a negative, in my mind this became the only bright spot, in what were extremely narrow-minded lyrics. The reason this made these lyrics enjoyable is that as early as 1853, the sad heartedness in the final lyrics of Stephen Foster's song, may have been the result of him envisioning the beginning of the Civil War and the end of slavery in America.

Columbus Discovered Brown People and Not Red

According to the Washington post, Christopher Columbus left the port of Cadiz, Spain in 1493, with a fleet of 17 ships carrying 1,200 men and the supplies to establish permanent colonies in the New World. The passengers included priests, farmers, and soldiers, who would be the new colonists. Reportedly, "crew members may have included free black Africans who arrived in the New World about a decade before the slave trade began." If this information published by the Washington post were correct, it would verify that the first Africans to arrive in the United States of America were free men. If you look back in history, you see that white or European Americans had a habit of using derogatory terms when referring to people of color. They also had a bad habit of enslaving people of color, a practice that started in 1619 in Jamestown, Virginia.

I have talked about the age-old lie regarding Columbus discovering what we in this Country consider America. It never happened, yet we continue to support this as fact. We even have a "Columbus Day" in honor of the discovery of America. Columbus really did not have a clue where he was when he landed in North American. He called the inhabitants of North America, who lived on the continent for thousands of years before Columbus arrived, "Indians." He branded these so-called "Indians", heathens because they did not speak or understand the language of the Queen of Spain and according to Columbus did not worship the same GOD as these European invaders. According to some reports, Columbus landed in the West Indies and/or the Bahamas. You probably know that the natives of the West Indies were not "Red Men"; they were dark brown or black men.

As an African American, I really do not feel like I am qualified to address the issues that need to be addressed about Native American History. However, as it relates to Columbus and Native Americans, he never actual had an encounter with the true Native Americans of this Country. According to published reports, the name of the people that Columbus first met was the Tainos. Reportedly, they built hammocks to sleep in and the men smoked tobacco while women told stories. In the Taino culture, old people cared for the children and prepared meals. The young women cultivated the fields, while the young men hunted for snakes, turtles, and iguanas. The Tainos worshipped a supreme god but also believed in lesser spirits. Reportedly, when Columbus arrived, the Tainos believed Columbus and his men to be gods. According to Columbus' reports, the Tainos hid in the bushes when they arrived, the Tainos came out to meet Columbus and his crew. I wonder if the Tainos knew, how this encounter with these white people, would change their lives? Reportedly, in the beginning, the Tainos were amazed at the European's ships and their beautiful colors and they welcomed Columbus and his crew into their homes. As it was with most Europeans, Columbus wanted to convert the Tainos to Christianity. Columbus forced some of the Tainos to be his guides as he toured the other islands.

On his return voyage, Columbus took some Tainos captives back to Spain. Based on the stories of the "Middle Passage" from Africa to America, we can imagine what happened to the Tainos captives. If they were treated like my slaves ancestors when they were captives on European ships, we know they were raped, beaten and nearly starved to death. Reportedly, the friendly relations between the Tainos and the Europeans did not last long. During another Spanish voyage, many Tainos were beaten and murdered. When the Spanish became hungry, they ransacked villages, leaving the Taino people helpless. Along with their weapons, the Europeans also brought diseases with them that spread through the Tainos villages like wild fire. The crude weapons used by the Tainos were no match for those used by the European, and an estimated fifty thousand Tainos perished in the year 1494. As a result of the battles, there were many "Indian" captives. The Europeans decided to ship the Taino prisoners in bondage to Spain and 550 captives were jammed onto a boat. The rest were left behind to be slaves to the Spanish that stayed behind. The Tainos that were not slaves were forced to pay taxes and if they refused to pay the tax, they faced death and or starvation. The Tainos were actually homeless in their own land. Life was never the same for the "Indians" after that day in 1492.

Adapt or Die

If I were born in America prior to 1865, I would have been a slave. If I were born during the early 1900s, the "JIM CROW ERA", I would have made the same adjustments that every African American in this Country made or I would have been lynched or murdered the same way that millions of blacks were killed in the past. However, today there is no excuse for any black men and women to allow the white man too physically and mentally treat them like slaves. Federal and State Laws have been changed to make overt acts of obvious racism in the work environment a crime. In addition, the Civil Rights Movement united blacks in America for the cause of fighting for racial equality and freedom. Before the days of the NAACP, Martin Luther King and Medgar Evers, blacks in America were unable to form an army to help fight the battle for freedom and racial equality. The NAACP, along with the media and strong black political leaders, will not allow the blatant acts of racism from our past to be part of the future of African Americans in the U.S. As evidence of a change is the fact that during the "JIM CROW ERA" an angry mob of white men would have stormed the courtroom and with little very resistance from law enforcement, they would have lynched O.J. Simpson, the accused murderer of a white woman and a white man.

To be truthful, what upsets me most is that it actually makes me very angry, that the flying of the Confederate Flag and songs like "Dixie" and "My Ole Kentucky Home" keeps this white slave owner mentality alive in the "DEEP SOUTH". It gives white people who live in States that fly the Confederate Flag in public, the right to think they can treat African Americans like second-class citizens. When you listen some of the rhetoric from white Southern politicians or the white leaders of racist organizations like the KKK, you would think that the Confederate States of America won the Civil War. Wake up people, the Civil War ended nearly 150 years ago, and whether you want to believe it or not, the South lost. Just as the last black people that were actually owned by a white person are dead, the same can be said about the last white people to own black slaves are also dead. The enslavement of African Americans in this Country is part of our social, cultural and economic history. Slavery as part of American should never be forgotten. The horrific physical cruelty, mental anguish and the long-suffering endured by my ancestors should be remembered, but only as an example of man's inhumanity to other men.

When my ancestors were first brought to this Country as slaves they did whatever they had to in order to survive in white America. After the Civil War, my freed black ancestors had to do whatever they could in order to survive the "JIM CROW" laws that governed white America. As African Americans today, we should rejoice in the fact that "JIM CROW" is dead and we no longer have to do whatever it takes just to survive in America. When it comes to race, there may not be a totally level playing field in the United States, but we now all get to play in the same game. We now have the white supporters of Apartheid on the run. However, as African Americans we still have to face the question, when will the last generation of blacks, who continue to exhibit this slave like behavior in America, cease to exist? For some black people who suffer from the disease of low self-esteem, continuing to live the life of a servant of a white master may never end. In my book, *"No Land No Mule No Freedom"*, I made the point that racism is a disease. In addition, I made the point that the disease of racism affects blacks and whites equally. Finally, I made the point that the disease of racism can and will be cured. As a proud African American male, I fully support the need to pass on the history of slavery in America to our children so that they may in time, pass it on to theirs. However, the demeaning behavior that comes along with having a slave's mentality must die.

Moving back to Dixie

"Oh, I wish I was in the land of cotton, Old times there are not forgotten, look away, look away, look away Dixie Land." Reportedly, "Dixie Land" was the theme song of the Confederate Army, and believe it or not, at his request "Dixie Land", was played at the "Great Emancipator", Abraham Lincoln's Presidential inauguration. The problem with "Dixie Land" is just as the song states, "Old times there are not forgotten". Not only are they not forgotten, many black and white Southerners refuse to abandon the lifestyle that supported white supremacy and black inferiority. Fortunately for us, the National TV and print media has opened a window and allowed the world to look at the "Dixie Land" that time forgot. The media now reports in detail the conflicts between blacks and whites in the struggle for racial equality in the "DEEP SOUTH". Now, the rest of America and the U.S. Government refuse to "look way" when it comes to "Dixie Land". No longer are the overt acts of racism ignored. Whenever there are crimes committed that have the slightest implication that race, religion or sexual orientation were involved, the media covers it, and the FBI investigates as a potential hate crime.

African American families that once migrated to the North and West to find a better life are now returning to the "DEEP SOUTH".

African Americans are better educated and they refuse to return to the days when their ancestors wished they could stay "in the land of cotton". No longer satisfied with just picking cotton, the new generation of black Americans is demanding their rightful place in the social, economic, cultural and political structure today in the "DEEP SOUTH". A perfect example of change is the City of Atlanta, Georgia. Once known as the heart of Dixie, it has been transformed into a racial diverse metropolis. It has been called the "New York City" of the "DEEP SOUTH". In Atlanta, African Americans have taken a prominent role in the social, economic, cultural and political growth of this city. The City of Atlanta has elected at least four African American to the office of Mayor. As we enter the year 2014, many other major cities in the "DEEP SOUTH" are following in Atlanta's footstep. An NBA team, the Charlotte Bobcats, located in Charlotte, North Carolina is owned by a group of African Americans headed by Michael Jordan.

Why not fly the "Union Jack" and the Swastika?

Some white historians will argue the fact that white Southerners have the right to preserve their heritage, and that the Confederate Flag is a representation of that history. White Southerners will argue that their ancestors fought and died in the Civil War in an Army that carried the stars and bars of the Confederate Flag into battle. If we bury the flag, we bury the memory of both the white and black soldiers that fought in the Confederate Army. The point that white historians and white Southerners fail to accept is that America does not honor the losers of any wars. The ancestors of millions of white Americans in this Country came from England. Think about it, the British lost the Revolutionary War and none of the 13 States that made up the original colonies flies the "Union Jack" or Flag of Britain over their State Capital Buildings. We still have a region in the Country that we refer to as the "New England". We even have a NFL team named the New England Patriots. I have never seen the Patriots or any other team from that area run onto the field waving the Union Jack.

The States of Texas, New Mexico and California were part of Mexico, and there is still a large Hispanic population in these States. Can you imagine how upset white Texans would be if Mexican Flags were flown over their State's Capital or at the site of the Alamo in memory of all the ancestors of Mexican Americans? Many of these States have cities and sports teams that have names that have Mexican or Hispanic roots, such as Lobos, Aztecs, Los Angeles, Padres, San Diego, San Antonio, El Paso, and San Francisco. Again, I have never seen the Mexican Flag being waved at a Dodgers' game. I have never heard the Mexican National Anthem ever played as a team from one of these Cities or States took the field. Many white Americans have German ancestors. There are communities in Maryland and Pennsylvania called "Germantown". There are probably some German Americans whose ancestors fought in the Nazi army. The commander of that Army, Adolph Hitler, was the world's most notorious bigot and racist.

As hard as it would be for you to imagine the Mexican Flag being honored in Texas, it would be mind-boggling if the Jews allowed a swastika to be flown in Germantown or for that matter anywhere in this Country. In fact, just as painting the "N" word on a public building or home is a hate crime, painting a swastika on a public building or home is also considered a hate crime. Why is that Jews do not have to be constantly confronted with flags bearing a swastika and reminded of the horrors associated with the Holocaust, and African Americans are supposed to accept the Confederate Flag which is a symbol of the horrors of slavery without any protest? Neo-Nazi groups are required to have a permit and usually require police protection to display flags with swastika in public. Anti-Semitism is frequently being compared to racism as an ugly scar on the social conscience of America. Yet, on any given day, you will see the Confederate Flag openly displayed on bumper stickers, on public buildings, at sporting events, and flown on flagpoles in your neighbors' yard. Regardless of the demographic, I never seen or heard of a swastika displayed flying from a flagpole in any neighborhood in these Unites States or on the license plates of any car.

An Apology from President William "Bill" Clinton

I remember in June 1997, when President William "Bill" Clinton called for a National dialogue on race relations as part of a Commencement address at the University of California, during this same period, he also raised the issue of apologizing to African Americans for slavery in the Congress of the United States. According to Jesse Jackson, a leader in the black community, "an apology for slavery is a meaningless gesture with no meaningful commitment to deal with the impact of something so serious as slavery". The far right-winged conservative white Republican Congressmen from Georgia, House Speaker Newt Gingrich, stated that any attempt at an apology for slavery as a resolution was "backward-oriented". In addition, Gingrich stated, "it's only emotional symbolism that will not help poor black children." "Any American, I hope, feels badly about slavery," Gingrich said, and then added, "I also feel badly about a lot of things." Senate Majority Leader Trent Lott, a white Republican from Mississippi, said he would likely oppose such a bill because the nation should look to the future, not the past. The nerve of Trent Lott or any other white politician from the "DEEP SOUTH", to say the Country needs to look to the future and not the past.

I need you to take a closer look at Chester Trent Lott Sr. because for close to 15 years he was one of the most powerful politicians in the Country. A former United States Senator from Mississippi, who served in numerous leadership positions in both the U.S. House of Representatives and the Senate, which included the Senate Majority Leader in 2001. Throughout Trent Lott's political career, he embraced of all things Confederate. In 1978, after his election to the U.S. House, Lott led a campaign to restore the U.S. citizenship of the President of the Confederate States of America, Jefferson Davis. In 1981, as a member of the U.S. Congress he supported the effort to preserve the tax-exempt status of Bob Jones University, the notorious South Carolina College that was under fire for prohibiting interracial dating. Lott insisted that, "Racial discrimination does not always violate public policy."

Despite the fact that he represented the State with the largest percentage of African American citizens in the U.S., Lott has throughout his career been an active supporter of the Sons of the Confederacy, a group that celebrates the soldiers who fought to defend the "right" of Mississippians to own African Americans as slaves." Lott even appears in recruitment videos for the group. Lott gave the keynote address at a 1992 National Executive Board meeting of the Council of Conservative Citizens (C of CC), a successor organization to the old white Citizens Councils. Lott was photographed meeting with National Leaders of the C of CC in his Washington office. When the Washington Post began to detail Lott's ties to the C of CC, his office announced that he had "no firsthand knowledge of the group's views." Yet, a column written by Lott appeared on a regular basis in the Citizens Informer, the group's publication. The same publication that printed the statement; "Western Civilization, with all its might and glory, would never have achieved its greatness without the directing hand of God and the creative genius of the white race. Any effort to destroy the race by a mixture of black blood is an effort to destroy Western Civilization itself." It is easy to see why the Confederate Flag still so popular in the State of Mississippi. As an African American, I would like to say to Trent Lott, I am sure glad that I do not live in Mississippi.

President Clinton was sincere about the apology for slavery and he was sincere in his efforts to bring about racial healing in America. Unfortunately, his term as President ended before he could make this dream a reality. Unfortunately, for African Americans, George Bush, whose administration placed racial healing for America on the back burner, succeeded Mr. Clinton, one of the most popular Presidents in history. To apologize to African Americans that do not have the slightest idea of what it meant to be slaves in this Country for a State's or for that matter a Nation's participation in slavery; is just like throwing a bucket of water in the Atlantic Ocean. The black men and women, and the sons and daughters of the slaves who actually deserved an apology, are dead. If the States that issued these apologies for slavery really want to make an impact on the black communities, let them pass legislation that makes it mandatory to teach African American history from a black perspective rather than the watered down version of Black History that is taught during the month of February. An even greater impact would be to pass legislation that would make it illegal to display the Confederate Flag in public or at public events, and ban the unsolicited public singing of any songs that contain racially sensitive lyrics.

The New Massar

The black players in the NFL have it somewhat better than the African Americans that play in the NBA. In my opinion, the reason for the difference is the plantation overseer for the NBA, also known as the commissioner, David Stern. Based on years of observation, it is my opinion that David Stern, has actually taken on the mentality of a white overseer of black slaves on a big plantation. According to published reports, David Stern saved the NBA and is now the most powerful man in sports. Lord Acton, a British Historian, originally wrote, "Power tends to corrupt, and absolute power corrupts absolutely. Great men are almost always bad man." In my opinion, the quote by Lord Action is an accurate description of David Stern. All the major sports in this Country have gone through a down period. The resurgence of a sport is usually attributed to a player or players. Very seldom does a League Executive garner as much credit as David Stern has for his role with the NBA. In 1919, baseball was nearly ruined by the Black Sox Scandal, when it was alleged that players such as "Shoeless" Joe Jackson took money from gamblers to lose the World Series. Along came "Babe" Ruth and the world forgot about the Black Sox Scandal and turned its attention to the greatest player to ever play the game. During that same period, there is very little mention of the role played by Judge Kennesaw "Mountain" Landis, the first Commissioner of Baseball, as to what he did to help restore baseball to prominence. However, it was said that for 24 years, Judge Landis ruled baseball with an "iron hand".

In 1994, there was a work stoppage or strike in MLB and it lost a majority of its fan base. It was Mark McGuire and Sammy Sosa's battle to break Roger Maris' single season homerun record and Cal

Ripken's attempt to break Lou Gehrig's consecutive game streak that saved baseball, not the commissioner. The only Executives that had an impact on saving the game of football and basketball were the men who brokered the deals that merged the NFL and AFL in football in 1970 and the NBA and ABA in basketball in 1976. The NBA has had its ups and downs, but the star power of black players in the 1980s like Earvin "Magic" Johnson, Charles Barkley, Patrick Ewing and Michael Jordan took the NBA to a new level. Today, players like, Kobe Bryant, Dwayne Wade and Lebron James have taken the NBA to the highest level that it has ever been. Since the 1980s, as a result of its popularity, the NBA has expanded to 30 teams, with one of the newest teams located in Vancouver, Canada.

In the 1980s, basketball replaced baseball and football as the means by which a poor black kid from nowhere could become a millionaire. Inner city kids started playing basketball year round and Michael Jordan and the Nike Shoe Company made basketball an addiction. Like "Hip Hop" and "Rap", white kids were just as addicted to it as inner city black kids were. White kids were just as addicted to basketball as black kids. Just as it is with "Hip Hop" and "Rap" music, the most skilled and most popular players in the NBA are African American. Subsequently, the role models for black and white kids that are into "Hip Hop", "Rap" and basketball are black. Imitation is the sincerest form of flattery. The problem is that white America does not approve of their white children wanting nothing more out of life than to be like black men such as Michael, Magic, Charles, Kobe or Lebron. I remember watching games on TV when Dennis Rodman, a NBA "bad boy", played for the Chicago Bulls. Whenever the TV camera would focus on the fans in the stands, you would literally see dozens of white kids with a number 91 Chicago Bulls jersey on with their hair dyed red, green or orange to imitate their favorite NBA player, Dennis Rodman.

It was ok for white kids to want to be like Mike, but something had to be done to discourage these same white kids from wanting to emulate the negative behavior of a black player like Dennis Rodman. The other problem with white kids choosing an African American NBA player with a negative image as his or her role model is that their parents might stop coming to games. You see the other thing that you would notice if you were watching an NBA game on TV, when the TV camera shows the fans in the stands, you would see that 90% of them are white. For the most part, African Americans have taken over the Executive Management along with every other aspect of the "Hip Hop" and "Rap" music industry. Although black players dominate the basketball court at a NBA game, white America has taken over the stands. The white owners of NBA teams have increased the price of a ticket to a game. The higher ticket it prices means only the upper middle class, which is mostly white, can afford to attend games. Since he became commissioner in 1984, David Stern has done exactly what the white owners of the NBA teams hired him to do; control the on-court passion and the off-court behavior of the African American players that dominate the game. It is my opinion, that in the minds of these white owners, this control will insure that the white people that fill the stands and buy the paraphernalia marketed by the NBA, will keep coming to games, keep bringing their kids and keep spending their money.

The resurgence of the NBA can be directly attributed to the fact that the new wave of young stars; Kobe Bryant, Allen Iverson, Lebron James, Carmello Anthony and Dwayne Wade, have become immensely popular in the "Hip Hop" culture. The argument for the dress code was that the NBA players were starting to dress like their fan base of black "Hip Hop" and "Rap" enthusiasts. The problem is that the "Hip Hop" and "Rap" fans may buy their favorite players jersey or basketball shoe, but they do not buy tickets to games. However, the bigger problem is that the black "Hip Hop" and "Rap" enthusiasts do not spend millions of dollar on for products advertised on during TV commercials. "Any venue in which our ads appear that is offensive to our target audience is not acceptable to us"; I used this quote when Procter & Gamble pulled its ads from the Don Imus National radio talk show because it was a positive response to a negative situation. David Stern implemented a dress code in the NBA because white Corporate America and the white team owners felt that "Hip Hop" and "Rap" style of dress was offensive and unacceptable to the target audience of the NBA, which is the white upper middle class. David Stern, white

Corporate America and the white NBA team owners know nothing about the "Hip Hop" culture. White America is frightened of tall black men with "doo-rags", lots of jewelry, and throwback jerseys. When they see a black man dressed like that, they automatically think thug and gangster.

I will be the first to admit that I am not a fan of the "Hip Hop" or "Rap". The lyrics to the music demean the African American culture in which I grew up. Children, mothers and old people were off limits when it came to the use of profanity. I am totally opposed to the violent lyrics of today's "Hip Hop" and "Rap" music, which supports drive by shooting, promotes drug use, the verbal and physical abuse of women and the use of language that is inappropriate for public conversations. I will also admit that I have some concerns when I see young black or white men and women, with "doo-rags", lots of jewelry, and throwback jerseys, driving expensive cars and living in luxurious houses and they appear to have no visible means of how they acquired these assets. I am old school. It is hard for me to remember when our parents and grandparents looked at my generation with the same questions that I have about young people of today. Yet, having said all that, I can easily differentiate a black or white kid that likes to listen to "Hip Hop" and "Rap" music and dress in the style of that culture, from a thug or hoodlum whose intent is to support his or her lifestyle by any means necessary, which includes committing violent criminal acts.

In 2014, David Stern is a 72-year-old white Jew. He was born in New Jersey during the "JIM CROW ERA", and started public school when they were still segregated. In the America that David Stern grew up, the expectations for black people was to be seen and never heard. David Stern is old enough to be the father of NBA stars like Dwayne Wade and Carmello Anthony. He is old enough to be Lebron James' grandfather. Why would anyone in his or her right mind believe David Stern understands anything about the African American cultural or the environment of today's black NBA players? Lets' compare; David Stern is white. The majority of the players in the NBA are black. David Stern is Jewish. Most of the players in the NBA are either Christian or Muslim. David Stern is over 70 years-old and most of the players in the NBA are around 30-years-old. I am sure David Stern's response to my assessment of his qualifications to manage a league dominated by African Americans would be that he prepared himself. Stern would say the he conducted extensive studies on the black culture, by consulting with some of the leagues greatest black players of the past. In addition, he seeks advice and council from the highly paid and well-educated black members of his Executive Staff that he personally selected. Why is that white people think they can become experts on the black way of life by studying books that were probably written by another white person?

I worked at a job that required me to wear a shirt and tie. As an ex-United States Marine and an ex-police officer, I was accustomed to wearing a uniform. There was a specific dress code for wearing the uniform and you were not allowed to deviate from that dress code, especially in the Marine Corps. As an Ex-Marine, when I see young men, white or black walking around in public with their pants hanging down over their butts, I want to scream. After I scream, I want to stop them and say "pull your pants up" that does not look good". Again that is just part of who I am and the way I was raised. I have played team sports in high school and college and I will have to admit that the coaches required us to wear a shirt and tie for road games. However, I never had a coach or a commander that dictated how I dress when I was off duty. An NBA player's job is playing basketball and that job begins when he steps foot onto any part of the arena. Once in the arena or on the basketball court, the NBA has every right to tell players what they can or cannot wear. When the game is over, and the players leave the court and the arena, the job is over and you should have the right to wear whatever you like. If a player is required to attend a press conference after the game, have the player wear their team uniforms or warm up suits. If a player is injured and cannot play and the team still requires that player to be on the bench, have the player wear a warm up suit or have the player remain in the locker room out of view of the paying customers.

An NBA player's job and ultimate goal is to win games on the court. They should not be required to be role models, fashion models or an example of what the perfect image of a black man should be in America. According to a published report, Phil Jackson, former coach of the Chicago Bulls and L.A. Lakers, called what they players are wearing "prison garb". The same Phil Jackson, that as an NBA player in the 1970s, was a bearded hippie, who reportedly smoked "wacky tobacco". The same Phil Jackson, that as a coach, supported different rules for black superstar players like Michael Jordan, Shaquille O' Neal and Kobe Bryant. The same Phil Jackson, the so-called "Zen Master" who enjoys mediating while on his ranch located in the Midwest. Jackson would not know what the latest trends are in African American men's clothing if they fell on him. Personally, I do not have a problem with Phil Jackson. The problem I have is that his comment about what the players were wearing as looking like "prison garb" is racist. What Phil did was feed into the racial stereotype, tall black men with "doo-rags", lots of jewelry, and throwback jerseys are thugs and gangsters. When white America hears the word prison, they immediately think of black men. What Phil happened? Did you have a brain cramp when you made that "prison garb" comment?

Why am I so upset about a dress code? Just as the white Southern plantation owners, featured in the song "My Ole Kentucky Home", could never understand what it felt like to be black. Could never understand how it feels to be owned by another human being, and to be denied your freedom. Men like David Stern will never understand what it feels like to be a black man whose livelihood is controlled by a white man. You see the dress code is just the tip of the iceberg. Just as a line from the song "My Ole Kentucky Home" states, by implementing the dress code David Stern was insuring that "The head must bow and the back will have to bend, wherever the darkey may go". The white plantation owner has chained, whipped, raped, and physically and mentally abused my black slave ancestors just because they had the power. According to a published report, Stern has a severe case of the "Napoleon complex". A "Napoleon complex", or "short man syndrome", is an uncomplimentary slang term describing a type of psychological phenomenon which is said to exist in people, usually men, of short stature. It is characterized by overly aggressive or domineering social behavior. In addition, the "Napoleon complex" carries the implication that such behavior is compensatory for the subjects' stature. In my opinion, Stern is power hungry and a bully. He has threatened both players and coaches telling them that if they do not do it his way, they can find their way out of the NBA. In 2011, in an article writer by the world famous reporter, Bryant Gumbel, I found it very interesting that another black writer would make the "slave master" mentality comparison when talking about NBA Commissioner David Stern. Of course, the white media criticized Mr. Gumbel for making what they considered an insulting statement about Stern. White men upset over an outspoken black man. What else is new!

The White List for Black People

In my opinion, Stern used his power to black list Mahmoud Abdul-Rauf, formerly known as Chris Jackson, from playing in the NBA. Mahmoud Abdul-Rauf was the best pure shooter ever to play in the NBA. He has Tourette's syndrome, an inherited neurological disorder, characterized by the presence of multiple physical (motor) tics and at least one vocal (phonic) tic. Yet, in spite of this physically debilitating disease, Mahmoud Abdul-Rauf managed to play college and professional basketball at the highest levels. Mahmoud Abdul-Rauf was born Chris Jackson, in Gulfport, Mississippi, the son of a white man and a black hospital cafeteria worker. Young Chris, who never knew his father, graduated from Gulfport High where he was honored two consecutive times as Mississippi's Player of the Year. Mahmoud Abdul-Rauf excelled as a point guard and shooting guard at Louisiana State University (LSU). Mahmoud Abdul-Rauf set a NCAA freshman record of 55 points in his fifth game against Florida. In an effort to overcome the effect of Tourette's syndrome, Mahmoud developed a ritual of repeating daily routine tasks until he perfected them, which included making a specific number of shots; go through the nets perfectly before leaving the basketball court. After his record-setting college career at LSU, the Denver Nuggets selected him with the third pick in the 1990 NBA draft.

Mahmoud Abdul-Rauf changed his name in 1991 upon his conversion to Islam. He played with Denver until 1995, winning the Most Improved Player award in 1993, and he led the NBA in percentage of free throw made in 1994 and 1996. Yet, in spite of all he accomplished in the NBA, Mahmoud Abdul-Rauf is best known by the white media for the controversy created when he refused to stand for "Star Spangled Banner" before a game, stating that the flag was a "symbol of oppression" and that the United States had a long "history of tyranny". According to published reports, Mahmoud Abdul-Rauf said that standing to the National Anthem would therefore conflict with his Islamic beliefs. On March 12, 1996, David Stern suspended Mahmoud Abdul-Rauf for his refusal to stand, but the suspension lasted only one game. Two days after the incident, David Stern and Mahmoud were able to work out a compromise, whereby Mahmoud would stand during the playing of the National Anthem but could close his eyes and look downward. Reportedly, he usually silently recited a Muslim prayer during the time the Anthem was playing. I remember this incident, because the uninformed white media labeled Mahmoud Abdul-Rauf as being unpatriotic for not honoring the Flag and his Country. Just as was compulsive about routine tasks, Mahmoud Abdul-Rauf was even more dedicated to the practice of Islam.

Although the white NBA team owners may not fully support the African American players that have converted to Islam or were born Muslim; they have never voiced any public displeasure. In my opinion, it was the lack of support by Commissioner Stern and the white media's portrayal of Mahmoud Abdul-Rauf unpatriotic, along with the fact that he is a Muslim that prematurely ended his career in the NBA. White Corporate America, combined with the white NBA team owners, along with David Stern, used the excuse that not anything that appears to be offensive to our target audience was acceptable to them. If you remember, Mahmoud Abdul-Rauf's protest during the playing of the National Anthem was not the first time an African American had used that spotlight to make a statement. At the 1968 Summer Olympic Games in Mexico City, Mexico, the most memorable medal ceremony of all time occurred. Two black American sprinters stood on the medal podium with heads bowed, wearing black gloves; they raised their fist in the air during the playing "Star Spangled Banner" after receiving their medals. It not only represented one of the most inspiring moments in Olympic history but a milestone in America's Civil Rights Movement. Tommie Smith and John Carlos, teammates at San Jose State University, secretly planned a non-violent protest in the manner of Dr. Martin Luther King.

At the 1968 Summer Olympic Games, Tommie Smith won the Gold Medal and John Carlos won the Bronze Medal in the 200-meter race. As part of the Olympic Games medal ceremony, the American Flag was raised in the stadium to honor the Country of the winner of the event and the National Anthem of the winner's Country was played on the loud speakers. As the "Star Spangled Banner" was being played, the two black men closed their eyes, bowed their heads, and began their protest. I was just 19 years old when I watched this incident live on TV. I was watching because I loved the Summer Olympics. The African American athletes from the United States dominated the short distance running events, the broad jump, and the decathlon; and the African countries dominated the long distance running events. The Summer Olympic were an opportunity for young black American men and women to showcase their talent and their natural speed. Tommie Smith was favored to win the 200-meter race and it came as no surprise when he won. However, like the rest of the world, I was shocked when Tommie Smith and John Carlos bowed their heads and raised the black fists in the air on the medal stand.

In the fall of 1967, amateur black athletes formed Olympic Project for Human Rights (OPHR) to organize a boycott of the 1968 Olympics in Mexico City. Reportedly, the OPHR had three central demands: 1. "Restore Muhammad Ali's title." In 1967, Ali's heavyweight title had been stripped for his resistance to the Vietnam draft. By expressing solidarity with Ali, the OPHR were also expressing their opposition to the war. 2. "Remove Avery Brundage as President of the International Olympic Committee (IOC)." Reportedly, Brandage's "racism and anti-Semitism are well documented". Brundage was a notorious white supremacist, who is best remembered for sealing the deal that allowed

Hitler and Nazi Germany to host the 1936 Olympics in Berlin. 3. "Disinvite South Africa and Rhodesia." This was a conscious effort to express solidarity with the black freedom struggles occurring in these two apartheid states. The IOC buckled on the third demand, banning Rhodesia and South Africa. This took the wind out of the sails of a broader boycott. However, many athletes were still determined to make a stand.

While the world prepared for the 1968 Summer Olympics in Mexico City, African American were fighting and dying for their Country in record number in Vietnam. The assassination of Martin Luther King resulted in violent riots in major cities throughout America. This was followed by the growth of the Black Panther Party in the United States. There was supposed to be a boycott of the 1968 Summer Olympics by the black athletes on the American team. However, Mr. Smith and Mr. Carlos did the only noteworthy action. It was the black power salute, which had become the symbol of black pride during the Civil Rights Movement in the 1960s and 70s in America. My first response to this black power salute was "WOW" and then I followed it with "Right On My Brothers". It never dawned on me that Tommie and John were doing the salute as a protest; I just thought they were giving the black power salute as a demonstration of pride in their African American heritage. It was not until later, when I heard Tommie Smith tell the media that he raised his right, black-glove-covered fist in the air to represent black power in America while John Carlos' left, black-glove-covered fist represented unity in black America. Together they formed an arch of unity and power; the black scarf around Tommie Smith's neck stood for black pride and their black socks, with no shoes, represented black poverty in racist America. John Carlos wore a string of beads, to commemorate black people who had been lynched in this Country.

A very interesting point, but a little known fact about the protest, is that the 200 meter Silver Medalist in 1968, Peter Norman of Australia, who was white, also participated in the protest on the medal podium that evening by wearing a the Olympic Project for Human Rights (OPHR) badge. In every picture of this famous Olympic moment from the 1968 games in Mexico City, you see the three men together on the medal stand. Another little known fact is that John Carlos forgot his black gloves and it was Peter Norman who suggested that Tommie Smith give John one of his gloves to wear on his left hand. Reportedly, the Olympic Crew Team, all white and entirely from Harvard, issued a statement: "We as individuals have been concerned about the place of the black man in American society in their struggle for equal rights. As members of the U.S. Olympic team, each of us has come to feel a moral commitment to support our black teammates in their efforts to dramatize the injustices and inequities which permeate out society." In addition, to show their support of the protest, the anchor of the women's Gold Medal winning 4×100 relay team, Wyomia Tyus said, "I'd like to say that we dedicate our relay win to John Carlos and Tommy Smith."

As a result of their protest, Tommie Smith and John Carlos were stripped of their medals, suspended from their National Team and banned from the Olympic Village, where the U.S. Olympic Team was housed during the games. The white officials that accompanied the U.S. Olympic Team to Mexico were reportedly outraged by what Tommie and John had done and said. These white officials, like the majority of white America, thought that political statements had no place in the supposedly apolitical Olympic Games. They cried out that the actions of Tommie Smith and John Carlos were militant and disgraced America. During the 1960s and 70s, African Americans had conducted demonstrations, marched, boycotted and protested as part of the Civil Rights Movement in every major city in America. Yet, this was the first time that a black person had protested the racial injustice that existed in America on an international stage that was promoted by the white media and sponsored by white Corporate America. Just as they did to Mahmoud Abdul-Rauf, the white media attacked Tommie Smith and John Carlos. They compared their black power salute on the medal stand at the Olympics to the one used by the Nazi army to salute Hitler during WWII. Reportedly, the famous white sportscaster, Brent Musburger referred to Tommie Smith and John Carlos as "black-skinned storm trooper". Another white media report, printed the Olympic logo, but instead of the motto "Faster, Higher, Stronger", it had "Angrier, Nastier, Uglier." This was another case of white Corporate America being driven by whatever appears to be offensive to their target audience being unacceptable to them.

Like me, the supporters of Tommie and John were moved by their protest and praise them for their bravery. I touched on the bravery of Tommie Smith and John Carlos in my second book, "No Land No Mule No Freedom", by comparing their bravery with that of Rosa Parks. The protest had lingering effects for both men, the most serious of which were death threats against them and their families. In the United States, winning an Olympic Gold medals usually translates into making millions of dollar in commercial endorsements and a lucrative sports contract. In the past, African American sprinters such as Jesse Owens, Wilma Rudolph, Bob Hayes and Carl Lewis, turned their triumphs in the Olympic into big bucks. Tommie Smith was one of the fastest men in the world to compete in the 200 meters; and during the Olympic trials in 1968, John Carlos defeated Tommie Smith while setting a world record for 200 meters. Yet, in 2014, over 46 years after their protest in Mexico City; since 1978, Tommie Smith has been a social science and health teacher and track and field coach at Santa Monica College, in California, and John Carlos, is a high school track at Palm Springs High School in California.

Tommie Smith and John Carlos were both multisport stars in High School, who ultimately wound up at San Jose State in California. People often assume the pair were great friends but, in truth, they were never close. They never competed at the same time at San Jose State. According to published reports, John Carlos' first wife committed suicide because she could not deal with the pressure from the results of the harassment and threats from the people who would let them forget about Mexico City. Reportedly, the two men are still receiving death threats from white people that remain angry and full of hatred. According to Mr. Smith, "One rock came through our front window into our living room, where we had the crib". After graduating from college, Tommie Smith was given an exemption from serving in the army services for what was classified as participating in "un-American activities". Tommie was reported as saying that probably did him a huge favor, since the Vietnam War was raging and the body count growing. John Carlos had two brothers serving in the military, but after his protest in Mexico City in 1968, both were immediately discharged. In October 2003, San Jose State held a ceremony to honor their protest. In 2005, San Jose State University honored former students Smith and Carlos with a 22-foot high statue of their protest. According to Tommie Smith, what was surprising about the tribute at San Jose State, it was the "brainchild" of a 23-year-old white student.

From the song "My Ole Kentucky Home", "The head must bow and the back will have to bend, wherever the darkey may go". All Tommie Smith and John Carlos did was bow their heads and bend their back[s] like the "darkey[s]" of the past. The only thing they did differently was to raise black-glove-covered fists. It never upset white America in the past to see black people bend their backs and bow their heads in fear of being lynched for looking directly into the face of a white person in this Country. Why was there so much hate from white America for two black men who just added a little wrinkle to the old custom of bending their back wherever the "darkey[s]" may go? Tommie Smith and John Carlos did not run for an African Country, they ran for the United States of America; according to the constitution, and like any other U.S. Citizen, they were merely exercising their freedom of speech. I like to think that I am a patriot. I am protective of the Flag and the American way of life. However, I was not insulted when Mahmoud Abdul-Rauf did not stand for the National Anthem at the beginning of a NBA game, and I certainly was not offended when Tommie Smith and John Carlos conducted a protest at the 9168 Summer Olympics. The only people that were offended by the actions of Mahmoud Abdul-Rauf, Tommie Smith and John Carlos are the same ones that were offended when Jackie Robinson stepped on the field with the Brooklyn Dodgers. The same people that were upset when Rosa Parks dared to remain seated when a white man demanded that she give him her seat on a bus and when Hank Aaron broke Babe Ruth's homerun record. As long as they have Olympic Games, the world will always remember Tommie Smith and John Carlos. However, unless we as

African Americans make a point to remember Mahmoud Abdul-Rauf, his act of courage and dedication to his faith will be forgotten.

Have you ever taken the time to examine the fight that got NBA basketball player, Ron Artist suspended for 73 games in 2004? It is the longest suspension in the history of the NBA. I do not usually watch NBA basketball until the playoffs start because the season is too long and too many teams make the playoffs, which makes the regular season games somewhat anti-climactic. However, on November 19, 2004, I decided to watch the game because Detroit and Indiana have a heated rivalry and I knew it would be a very competitive contest. The incident started on the basketball court when two black players, Ron Artest of the Indiana Pacers, and Ben Wallace of the Detroit Pistons, got into a physical confrontation. Rather than becoming part of ugly fracas on the court, Ron Artest calmly went and stretched out on his back on the scorer's table. At this point, if there had been no other action, the referees would have been able to restore order and the game would have continued, and it would have ended in about two minutes. In the white media reports of the "Auburn Hills Brawl", no one mentioned the fact that the minor scuffle between Ben Wallace and Ron Artest was over. The major disturbance began when a white fan threw a cup, of what was reported to be ice, at Ron Artest was he was peacefully lying on the scorer's table. When the cup hit Ron Artest, he went into the stands and punched the white man who he thought threw it. Several other white fans, who were sitting in this area, attempted to help the white man by either hitting Ron Artest or pulling at him.

Enter Stephen Jackson, another black player and teammate of Ron Artest, who started hitting a white fan that was either hitting or pulling on Ron Artest. Once Stephen Jackson entered the stands, the riot started. A crowd of predominately-white fans started throwing objects onto the court at the black players from the Indiana Pacers. Soon after, this white mob, whose actions were fueled by too much beer, actually came on to the basketball court and started attacking the black players from the Indiana Pacers. While Jermaine O'Neal was trying to leave the court, a young white male fan started throwing punches at him. This white fan had to be at least a foot and a half shorter.

207

Yet he started swinging up at Jermaine. In my opinion, this white fan had to be drunk. Of course, the black players defended themselves and finally, the arena security force was able to escort the players from the court into the locker room. All the time they were being escorted from the court, the fans were pelting them with all sorts of debris. The players were very fortune not to have sustained any injuries. I am fully aware of the rule that forbids professional athletes from any sport from going into the stands. However, in this case, Ron Artest was an innocent bystander who was assaulted and in this Country, citizens have the right to defend themselves.

Unfortunately, with the help of the white media that were on hand to report this incident, all David Stern, the white overseer could see was the two black NBA players who went into the stands and started assaulting white fans. In the aftermath, other black players were also caught on tape punching the white fans that stormed the basketball court. The immediate blame for this riot at Auburn Hills was placed squarely on the shoulders of Ron Artest, who had a reputation as being the league's number one "bad boy". A reputation that was supported by Michael Wilbon, a black reporter with the Washington Post, and an ESPN TV broadcasters who regularly appears on the popular ESPN TV show, Pardon the Interruption (PTI). Reportedly, Wilbon said for years that Artest's much talked about on court "antics" and flagrant fouls were not funny and someone in Pacers management needs to step in and get him professional help before "something terrible happens." Ron Artest may have some issues, however, on more than one occasion, I have heard Wilbon state on PTI, that if a fan threw something at him or called him the "N" word, he would go up into the stands and personally have it out with that fan. Problems aside, Ron Artest did exactly what Wilbon stated on National TV that he would do in a similar situation.

We have so very few black professional in the National media. Wilbon, in my opinion, you need to decide if you are black reporter or merely a puppet that changes his ethnic perspectives based on the views of white Corporate America. Ron Artest was already worked up because of the physical altercation with Ben Wallace. However, before he could recover from being upset about his encounter with Ben Wallace, a spectator assaulted him. Most men, black or white, in a similar situation, assaulted for no reason, would have reacted the same way Ron Artest did. Any true teammate, especially the ones that I have played with, like Stephen Jackson, would have come to my assistance if they saw me being attacked. How do African American NBA players compare to black slaves? For years in this Country, my black slave ancestors had to endure, without even the slightest opposition, whatever physical and mental abuse their white masters felt necessary. If you need to be reminded of these abuses, they included but were not limited to, beating, rape, castration, and lynching. Today, the NBA's white overseer, the white NBA owners, and white Corporate America, want the black NBA players to mimic the behavior of their ancestors; bow their heads and take whatever abuse white fans have to give and take no offense and whatever you do, as an African American you must never fight back.

I thought that the never fight back attitude for black athletes no matter what they do to you, died with Jackie Robinson and Branch Rickey. Remember, not fighting back was one of the conditions that Branch Rickey gave to Jackie Robinson in order for him to play in all white Major League Baseball. No matter what the white players or white fans did to him, Jackie Robinson was banned from fighting back with words or with his fists. The overseer, David Stern is returning the Branch Rickey rule to the NBA. No matter what a white fan does or says to the African American players, if the react, they will be suspended. David Stern saved the white owners of the Indiana Pacers approximately 20 million dollars when he suspended Ron Artest 73 games, Stephen Jackson 30 games, and Jermaine O'Neal 25 games. Anyone that thinks if this would have been black on black rather than black on white, the penalties for this fight would have been far less; I will sell you my stock in the Brooklyn Bridge.

A perfect example is the National Hockey League, where there is a majority of white players. Fighting with players from the other team is not only accepted, it is encouraged. If a fan throws a drink on a NHL player in the penalty box, I have seen that white NHL player go into the stands and get into a physical confrontation with that fan. Before long, other players have joined in and you a small riot on your hands. I have even seen NHL coaches get into it with fans. The NHL fights, no matter how violent, make the news on ESPN. However, unless a player or fan is seriously hurt, the fights are limited to local sports news. The "Brawl at Auburn Hills" was shown on every National and TV network in America and was replayed over and over for at least three weeks.

David Stern never broached the racial aspect of the "Brawl at Auburn Hills" incident. His only point was that with the fines and suspensions, he would send a message to the other black players in the NBA, not to go into the stands. It upsets me when the white media praised Stern for how he is able to control the wealthy athletes that dominate the NBA. It should come as no surprise that a little white man could control a league made up of large black men. Remember his ancestors had hundreds of years of experience controlling our African American ancestors during slavery and the "JIM CROW ERA". David Stern does such a good job as an overseer; the NFL commissioner, Roger Goodell, has announced that he wants to uses Stern as his role model. I hope both Goodell and Stern read my books. In Addition, if they read my books, I hope they change the attitudes regarding their management styles.

To borrow a quote from the infamous boxing promoter, Don King who said "only in America". Only in America can a white man change the rules to punish a black man and call it justice. We, as African Americans, still point to black success in college and professional sports as a sign of progress. Yet, the NFL and NBA deny young African American men access to millions of dollars and justify it by stating that they are not old enough to handle the physical and emotional stress of the professional game. The NBA and NFL both agree that the age restriction is in the best interest of the young men. In the sports dominated by white males, such as baseball, tennis, golf, and soccer, white kids can play as young as 18-years old. The NFL and NBA have concluded that men under 18 cannot handle the physical contact. I will be the first to agree that an 18 year-old right out of high school is not ready for the NFL. However, 18 year-old white males can sign multi-million dollar contracts to play in the NHL in a sport that is jam-packed with contact. Did you hear any disdain when golfing phenom Michelle Wie, 16-years old, turned professional and signed several million-dollar endorsements? I have never heard any negative complaints from white Corporate America about pro tennis players Jennifer Capriati, Anna Kournikova, or Andre Agassi. All turned pro and became millionaires in their teens. Why teenage basketball players, who are African American, cannot have the same choices, and the same chance to support their families, who may need it just as much or even more than those typically upper middle class white teen-age hockey players, tennis players and golfers?

According to published reports, this rule should be called "I do not want young black men in the NBA". Statistics show that over the past 10 years, the best players in the NBA are all high school entries; Jermaine O'Neal, Kobe Bryant, Lebron James, Kevin Garnett, Tracy McGrady and Amare Stoudemire, etc. How is this helping the league in anyway except to keep young black men who are even closer to the hip-hop generation out of the NBA? If you have an opportunity to make millions of dollars, have no desire to go to college and a NBA team is willing to draft you, why should you be restricted? The high school players that I mentioned performed at an all-star level either as soon as they step out on the floor or within the first couple of years of their development. The theory that some do not make it does not fly because the majority of the college graduates drafted do not make it either. Jermaine O'Neal, an African American All Star NBA player, made a statement that black kids are being denied the right to play in the NBA right out of high school is a clear-cut case of racial discrimination. The white media printed Jermaine O'Neal's comments, but once the NBA's white overseer, David Stern made a statement in opposition of what Jermaine had to say; Stern's statement became the voice of reason and trumped any comment that had come from Jermaine O'Neal, who Stern considered to be uninformed regarding the issue.

Unfortunately, the entire black community is uninformed as to the driving force that denies young black men from becoming millionaires. The same white Corporate America that controls the NBA, control the white male Executives that control NCAA and the white Presidents of the major colleges and universities in this Country. The NBA's age limit rule allows the major NCAA colleges and universities to make millions of dollars by showcasing the best black athletes in America on their basketball teams. Can you imagine what would happen to college basketball if the best high school players in the Country all decided to become pros? What is now known as "March Madness" would soon be known as "March Sadness". More people watch and wager on the NCAA men's basketball tournament than any other sporting event in the world. The white NBA owners need the colleges just as much as the colleges needed the age limit rule. The college and university basketball teams provide the NBA a free, tax-funded farm and developmental systems. In addition, the fact that the NBA Players Association, mostly black veterans, support the age limit rule because it keeps these kids from taking their jobs. Therefore, it is hard for America to see the NBA's and David Stern as being racist, when the player union, which is predominately black, concurs with the age limit. The old house slaves verses the field hands. Will it ever change? Things will never change as long as we keep calling the David Stern's of the world "massa".

Let me make it perfectly clear. I do not condone the inappropriate off duty behavior of some of today's multi-millionaire black athletes. It is almost a daily occurrence for us to pick up a newspaper or to turn on your TV and find a black athlete accused of domestic violence, illegal weapons charges, dog fighting, illegal drug use, disorderly conduct and other deliberate violations of the law. It is an embarrassment to the black community. Whether they realize it or not, these young African American athletes owe their success to the thousands of black men and women who fought the battles to gain freedom and equality in the world of sports. Each of the major professional sport in America had its own version of Jackie Robinson. The African American athletes of today have to realize that their behavior on and off the field of play has a direct impact on white societies perception of black people. Therefore, I am not asking that these young black athletes be role models, I am asking them to be responsible citizens and show some respect for the African America athletes that paved the road for their success.

In the midst of all the complaints about Don Imus, MSNBC TV canceled his show and CBS radio fired him. As I close this chapter, I cannot understand why Don Imus can be fired for referring to African American women as "nappy headed hos". Yet, the State of Kentucky gets to use the word "darkey" in their state's song. In addition, the states of South Carolina and Mississippi get to fly the racist Confederate Flag, which is a tribute to a time when my ancestors were brutally enslaved by white Americans. The bottom line is simple; in the big picture, we as African Americans do not matter. These quotes are attributed to Rev. Jesse Jackson and Rev. Al Sharpton. "Any venue in which our [white Corporate America] ads appear that is offensive to our target audience [white America] is not acceptable to us [white Corporate America]". If you listen to Al Sharpton and Jesse Jackson, they take credit for having Imus fired. Black America; please do not believe that same old tired rhetoric from Jesse and Al. The only reason Imus was fired after 30 years of making the same kinds of insensitive remarks his radio show, was money. If Al and Jesse had that kind of power and influence, they could change some other equally offensive racial issues in America.

I voted for Jesse in 1984 and 1988 when attempted to become the Democratic Party's Presidential Candidate. I applaud him because his election campaign single handedly registered more black voters than any other political candidate in modern history. However, over the past 25 year, having been involved in some personal family issues, Jesse has lost power as a force in the black community. I think Al Sharpton is a strong voice for in the African American community. However, it is hard to separate his in front of the media persona from the Al Sharpton who needs to be a leader of the black community when the media in not watching. The song "My Ole Kentucky Home", and the Confederate Flag are both offensive to African Americans. I would be impressed if Jesse or Al can have them removed from public display. I would be impressed with Jesse and Al if they prevented the NCAA from slapping the black community of Durham, North Carolina in the face when they reinstated a year of eligibility for the Duke Lacrosse Team that includes three rich white boys that allegedly sexually assaulted two black women, and used vulgar racial slurs at team party. If the same target audience that Imus offended, and if it cost white Corporate America millions of dollars in potential revenue, just like Don Imus was fired, the song "My Ole Kentucky Home" would not be played in public; the Confederate Flag will disappear for public view and the 2006 Duke Lacrosse would be remembered as racists and bigots.

As a final note and some food for thought, in 2007, the University of South Carolina (USC) football coach, Steve Spurrier said, "The Confederate Flag shouldn't fly at the Statehouse". He continued by saying, "we don't need the Confederate Flag at our Capitol," "I don't really know anybody that wants it there, but I guess there are a lot of South Carolinians that do want it there." In 2000, the former football coach at USC, Lou Holtz, joined the Clemson University's football coach Tommy Bowden and both schools' basketball coaches in calling for the Flag to be removed from the Capitol. The Flag was removed from the dome in 2000, but placed at the Confederate Soldier Monument on Statehouse grounds. The State Chapter of the National Association for the Advancement of Colored People said that was not good enough and continued its boycott. The initial boycott drew wide support from inside and outside the State, but encouragement for the ongoing effort has waned in recent years. The NCAA has prohibited the State from holding predetermined championships like basketball regionals since 2001 because of the Confederate Flag. I would suggest that African American athletes decide not to perform for these States and white rebels that revere the Confederate Flag and that would bring down that racist rag quick, fast and in a hurry.

Finally, in 2007 Don Imus was fired by CBS after 30 years on the radio for his "nappy head hos" comment when referring to African American women on the Rutgers University basketball team. Yet, another white TV broadcaster, Brent Musburger, who in 1968 called two African American heroes, Tommie Smith and John Carlos, "black skinned storm troopers", which is a reference used for Nazi soldiers in War II. He also referred to the actions by Smith and Carlos at the 1968 Summer Olympics as "ignoble," "juvenile," and "unimaginative. In 1968, Musburger worked for CBS, the same company that fired Don Imus.

Chapter 5
THE FUTURE

When you read my books, I do not want you to come away with the impression that I am a racist or a bigot; that I do not get along with white people; that I think that there are not any good white people in the world; or that I do not have any white friends. Before I go too far, I need to mention that the white people that I am about to talk in this chapter are far from all of the white people that have had a major impact on my life. This book primarily deals with the sport of horseracing and the white people that are named in this chapter have had an impact on that part of my life. It was not my intent to offend anyone by not mentioning his or her name. I had to add this little disclaimer because in my first book, I forget to mention certain members of my family. As a result of that little faux pas, I got a four page handwritten letter from one of my aunts who reminded me that I forgot to mention her mother and father, who were my mother's parent's, and that I had forgot to include details about this specific aunt and the experiences she had as a child. Although I do include many of my own personal encounters and many of my own opinions, this is not an autobiography. Therefore, I cannot include everyone by name in my books, by I have mentioned more than once that my family and friends have been supportive and I thank them all.

I am a proud black man, and there is nothing wrong in being proud of your heritage. The motive for writing my books is to share my personal opinions of the history of my American Heritage. America is a melting pot. All you have to do is keep looking around you and eventually you will come to realize that we live in the new culture of the Rainbow Coalition. As we journey further and further into the new millennium, the traditions, cultures and even the religious beliefs that this Country was built on will fade from our memories. Yes, we have books, movies, and other types of recordings to preserve our memories of the past, but most of the documented history of African Americans is biased, inaccurate and incomplete. If the history of my African American ancestors is not preserved for the future from the perspective of proud black writers, film makers and others who tell the stories of our past, our children and our children's children will never know the truth about their forefathers and mothers.

In addition, before we go too far, I need to make another point perfectly clear. I do write from the perspective and opinions of a proud black American. Yet, if you have read my other books, I have stated time and time again that there are as many ignorant black people in America that are racists and that hate people for no other reason than the color of their skin, as there are ignorant red, yellow, brown and white people that suffer from the same disease. Unfortunately, in the black community, rather than identify our black neighbors as racists, we give them the more palatable label of "militant". However, a racist buy any other name and no matter what the color, is just as ugly and just as ignorant. In this Country, why is it that the black racists feels the "white man" has never done anything for them. When the truth of the matter is that, I do not know any African American that does not owe their success in part to at least one white person.

In America, the only way anyone could avoid contact with someone of a different race color, creed or National origin is to be totally self-sufficient. Fortunately, no matter what the black, red, yellow, brown or white man thinks, in America today no one race of people in this Country can be very successful without having diversity in their lives. Just look around and you will see that the Butcher, the Baker, and the Candlestick Maker are not the same color anymore. Sure, we still have the "die hard" racists and bigots that think they can live separate and apart from anyone that does not look, think or worship the same way they do. However, the ideal separatist lifestyle, that racists and bigots in America seem to think they have. During the "JIM CROW ERA" this lifestyle that was in full bloom in this Country. However, modern day bigots and racists get a strong dose of the new reality whenever they enter a McDonalds, a bank, or a hospital and they encounter a person of another race as their server, or primary care giver and they have no choice in allowing them to render service or do without.

Time Heals All Wounds

The expression that America is a melting pot has been used for decades. Yet, based on the state of race relations in this Country, I do not believe that all Americans understand what being a melting pot really means. The reason we do not fully understand how being a melting pot society has affected the development of this Country is because the early white historians as well as the white print media failed to provide us with the intricate details necessary to stress the very important points of racial bonding that had an impact on growth of America. The reason we did not receive the intricate details about the successful bonding of the races to complete a task; whether it be winning a war or settling the frontier, was money. Much the same as it is now it was then; the so-called facts related to an event were presented to the public based on the whims of the wealthy. The Founding Fathers of this Country were wealthy landowners who used their money as a mean to gain power and influence people.

I have been blessed to live for 6 decades. In that time I have found that the saying "time heals all wounds" is nothing but the truth. The problem is that the deeper the wound, the longer it takes to heal. The wounds left by the enslavement of African Americans in the Country are extremely deep and as we enter 2014 and the healing process is still not complete. The sores created by these wounds of slavery were infected by hatred, racism and bigotry. The healing process required many antibiotics; love, patience, understanding, and education are just a few of the ones that have been most effective. Unfortunately, gangrene ate away at some of the wounds that were created by hatred, racism and bigotry in this Country and the only way to save the healthy

217

portion of the bound was for the Doctor, better known as the "Grim Reaper", to cut out the rotten portion some of these wounds.

Most of history is filed with the heroic accounts of close encounters between black, white and red men that reach epic proportions. We have all heard tales, read the books and watched the made for TV movies about White, Black and Red Americans who fought together in war; who demonstrated against social injustice and who together, won battles, World Series, Super Bowls and Olympic Gold. Have you ever asked yourself why black celebrities, such as famous athletes or entertainers, are accepted in white communities that refuse to allow an ordinary person of color access to their neighborhood? The same can be said of famous white people being allow access to black communities that reject the average white person. It could be because we never get to know the average man. Very seldom do we chronicle the routine day-to-day encounters between the diverse cultures that make up what is the heart of this Country, the average American. These routine encounters are the basis for the future of racial equality in America and the eventual end of racism. It is important that we understand that the slightest kindness shown to a member of another race of people could be the spark that starts the eternal fire of peace and understanding.

In the 1860s the primary reason the Civil War was fought was to determine if America would be divided into the two countries, the Confederates States of American and the United States of America. The historical facts support my statement regarding the primary reason we fought the "War Between the States" in this Country. In fact, in some remote areas of the South some white people are still fighting the Civil War. They believe that the Confederacy still exists. As evidence, we have States that continue to proudly display the Confederate Flag. Many liberal white Historians would have us believe that the Civil War was fought to end slavery. However, the truth is that the abolition of the enslavement of Africans in Confederate States and the economic change in power from the farms in the South to the factories in the North were secondary reasons for the Civil War. The so-called "Great Emancipator", Abraham Lincoln, made it quite clear that if he could have saved the Union without ending slavery, he would have done so. The main reason President Lincoln enacted the Emancipation Proclamation, which made slavery illegal in Confederate States only, was to remove the source of free labor that would bring to a standstill the agriculture industry that was the economic foundation of the South.

I bring up the Civil War is because there were hundreds of thousands of white Americans fought and died as soldiers in the Union Army for the sole purpose of ending slavery. Many of these white Americans had no political, economic or social agenda other than the fact they believed it was morally wrong for one human being to own and treat as property any other human being regardless of their race, color, creed or National origin. After the Civil War, we moved into the 20th century and began the Civil Rights Movement, which continued into the next millennium, and millions of white Americans are still fighting and sacrificing the lives for freedom and equality for African Americans in this Country. I called this chapter the "Future" because it will be through the combined efforts of white, black, brown, red and yellow Americans that will eventually end racism in this Country. To the survivors and families of all the brave Americans that fought in the Union Army during the Civil War and marched and protested along with Dr. King during the Civil Rights Movement in America; regardless of their race, color, creed or National origin, I personally thank you from the bottom of my heart for my freedom.

It started with the Underground Railroad

I named this chapter "The Future". However, before I talk about the future, I need to mention historical partnerships of African Americans and white Americans, working together for the freedom of black slaves in this Country. The reason I included so much information about the past in this chapter is that without the white people that I talk about in this chapter many African Americans that received the help of these Abolitionists, Freedom Fighters and soldiers, may not have had a future.

I have written about the "Underground Railroad" in both *"American Apartheid"* and *"No Land No Mule No Freedom"*. The most important fact about the "Underground Railroad" and the abolitionists that ran it was that it facilitated the freedom of black slaves. One of the most important components of the "Underground Railroad" was its most famous Conductor, Harriet Tubman. Reportedly, during a ten-year span, Ms. Tubman made 19 trips into the South and escorted over 300 slaves to freedom. It was said that she once proudly pointed out to black Abolitionist Frederick Douglass that in all of her journeys on the Underground Railroad, she "never lost a single passenger."

I was born and raised in Maryland, which make me so very proud to be able to write about another native Marylander, Harriet Tubman. First, I need to make it perfectly clear that long before I put these words on paper, many writers and Historians of all races had already immortalized the great Harriet Tubman. I just need to use a few facts about her life as a point of reference for the partnership between the black and white people that had such a great impact on how many of my ancestors escaped the oppression of slavery and found freedom in Canada. Araminta Ross, who later changed her name to Harriet, to honor her mother, was born a slave sometime between 1820 and 1822 in Cambridge, which is located on the Eastern Shore of Maryland in Dorchester County. She was the fifth of 11 children, 5 boys and 6 girls, born to Ben and Harriet Greene Ross. As an African American, along with your ability to read and write, your education and the freedom to vote in public elections, do not ever take your birthday for granted. As I have stated in my other books, in most cases, the date of birth for black born into slavery, can only be estimated. The only specific dates of birth for my slave ancestors had to be recovered from records kept by their white owners.

Reportedly, when she was about 12 or 13-years old, Harriet suffered an injury that would follow her for the rest of her life. Several different accounts of the incident involve a blow to the head, inflicted by a white overseer. Some reports state that she was struck in the head by an angry white overseer for refusing to assist in tying up a black man who had attempted to escape. Other reports state the blow to her head was from a dry goods store weight, thrown by a white overseer who was attempting to capture a runaway slave and Harriet stepped in the way to protect a fellow slave. No matter how the report is written, it supports the fact that at a very early age, Harriet Ross realized that her purpose in life was to protect her fellow man from the cruelties associated with being a slave. As a result of this severe blow to the head, Harriet Tubman reportedly suffered from narcolepsy for the rest of her life. The condition caused her to suffer intermittent epileptic seizures, which subjected her to spells in which she would fall into a deep sleep without any warning.

Reportedly, it was in 1849, with the assistance of a white woman from Cambridge, Maryland, that Harriet Tubman escaped for the first time. She set out one night on foot; traveling only at night, she followed the North Star by night, making her way to Philadelphia, where she found work. Harriet saved her money, and the following year she returned to Maryland and escorted her sister and her sister's two children to freedom. She made the dangerous trip back to Cambridge, Maryland to rescue her brother and two other men. Assisted by members of the Abolitionist movement, both black and white, who were instrumental in maintaining the "Underground Railroad", Ms. Tubman returned to the South again and again. Harriet Tubman's name will always be linked to the historical references to the "Underground Railroad", and her name will be associated with one of the most celebrated champions of all times, "Moses". For as Moses led the slaves out of Egypt into the "Promised Land", Harriet Tubman, and the "Black Moses" led African American slaves out of bondage in the South to freedom in the promise land of the North.

For over 50 years, as if it was a rite of passage, I have watched the movie *The Ten Commandments* on TV. I was eight years old in 1956 when I first saw the movie on the big screen. *The Ten Commandments* was the unforgettable story of Moses and his struggles to free his people from slavery. For me, it is by far the greatest movie about an even greater story ever told. There have been a few attempts to capture the life of Harriet Tubman in made for TV movie. They were good, but like most other historical depictions of slaves and former slaves, the made for

TV movies were written and portrayed from a white perspective. As Cecil B. DeMille created *The Ten Commandments* and Charlton Heston so brilliantly performed the role of Moses, It would be a monumental undertaking if any one of the great African American filmmakers of this generation would create a movie on the life and times of Harriet Ross Tubman from a black perspective. As we now have a holiday to honor the birthday of great Presidents, maybe someday we can also celebrate the Birthday of "Black Moses".

During the Civil War Harriet Tubman worked for the Union Army as a cook, a nurse, and even a spy. Reportedly, in 1863, Harriet Tubman was the first American woman, white or black, to plan and lead a military operation, the raid by the Union Army against the Confederate Army at Combahee Ferry, South Carolina, which freed over 750 slaves. After the war, she settled in Auburn, New York, where she would spend the rest of her long life. She died in 1913. Reportedly, a short time before the Civil War, Harriet Tubman worked closely with John Brown, the famous white abolitionist to plan his famous raid on Harper's Ferry, Virginia. Ms. Tubman missed the raid on Harper's Ferry because of illness.

There have been many descriptive terms used to distinguish the great Harriet Ross Tubman. Writers talk about her courage and shrewdness. John Brown, who called her "General Tubman" once described her as "one of the bravest persons on this continent." Yet, few writers used the word intelligent when describing Ms. Tubman. Without the benefit of a formal education, Ms. Tubman devised all sorts of clever techniques to keep from being captured while leading slaves to freedom. When planning her escapes, Ms. Tubman was smart enough to leave on Saturday night because runaway slave notices could not be placed in newspapers until Monday morning. Reportedly, Ms. Tubman would turn and head toward the nearest Plantation if she encountered slave hunters, explaining that they were just heading home from working at a neighboring farm. She was a master of disguise, who often dressed as a man to hide her identity and to protect her virtue. Ms. Tubman carried a drug to use on babies to keep them from crying and giving away their position. Traveling at night, she was able to remember the trails that lead to every safe house along the route of the "Underground Railroad". I hope that this brief summary about Harriet Tubman will help you to remember her as being very courage and as well as being very intelligent.

The Legendary "John Brown"

John Brown was not like most of the abolitionists wrote newspaper articles that made public speeches and covertly worked on the "Underground Railroad" to assist with the escape of runaway slaves. Instead, Mr. Brown devised a plan to take a more direct approach at ending slavery in America. On October 16, 1859, John Brown set out for Harpers Ferry with 21 men, 5 black slaves or ex-slaves, and 16 white men, two of which were Brown's sons. In a heavy rain, John Brown and his men crossed the Potomac; then walked all night in heavy rain before reaching the town of Harper's Ferry early the next morning. Mr. Brown and his troops captured the Federal Armory in Harper's Ferry, their arsenal and a local supplier of weapons to the Government. Mr. Brown and his men rounded up 60 prominent citizens of the town and held them as hostages. Due to a shortage of troops, Mr. Brown hoped that the slaves from Harper's Ferry would join the fight.

Reportedly, no slaves came forth, and in my opinion, that was a shame. You need to understand that in the days prior and during the Civil War, most black slaves were so confused and brainwashed by their white masters, they had no idea what John Brown was trying to do. Maybe if Harriet Tubman would have the black slaves there, who were familiar with the reputation of "Black Moses", they would have joined John Brown's army. On the other hand, if Ms. Tubman had been a part of the raid on Harper's Ferry, she would have been killed. While holding a white flag, one of Mr. Brown's sons was killed as he was attempting to negotiate terms for surrender. In the end, 10 of the 22 men in Mr. Brown's army were killed, including two black men and both of Brown's sons. It should be noted that Colonel Robert E. Lee led the U.S. Marines that helped defeat Mr. Brown at Harper's Ferry.

This same General Robert E. Lee commanded the Confederate Army during the Civil War

John Brown, along with his loyal soldiers, both black and white, were quickly tried, sentenced, and executed. In my opinion, John Brown was the first white American to lead an attack against the Government of the United States to end the enslavement of African Americans. In my other books, I have compared his attack on Harper's Ferry to the raids conducted by the former slave, Nat Turner, who burned Southern Plantations. If it were possible, I would tell Mr. Brown that he should not be discouraged by the fact that no black slaves in the Harper's Ferry area joined his army during the raid. Nat Turner was black man and a former slave, his army made up of runaway slaves and when he lead his raids throughout the South to free slaves, very few of the black slaves from the Plantation that were being attacked would join in the fight. The raids on the South by John Brown and Nat Turner so enraged white supporters of the Confederacy, that both men were hung by the neck until dead and then they were both set on fire. It was indeed an honor and a privilege for me to link my hero Nat Turner, an African American, to a white American Hero John Brown. It is an equal privilege to link National Heroes like John Brown and Harriet Tubman together in the fight for freedom

Quakers and other GOD Fearing Freedom Fighters

The interaction between white American that opposed slavery and black Americans, such as Harriet Tubman and Frederick Douglas, is probably the first recorded accounts of peaceful demonstration to end racial injustice in this Country. As early as the 1700s in America, the Society of Friends, also known as the Quakers, spoke out against the enslavement of black people. According to their religious beliefs, a piece of God, the Inner Light, exists in all human beings. Therefore, since God exists in all people, the Quakers oppose violence, war and the ownership of one human being by another. Other white Americans, better known as Abolitionists, began to oppose slavery during the late 1700s in the United States and unlike the Quakers; most of these people did not oppose slavery on just the moral grounds. I found it very refreshing to learn that in 1776, there were some white American Abolitionists believed slave owners violated the values that were established by the Founding Fathers and the Declaration of Independence. These white American citizens believed that the white owners of black slaves were hypocrites for fighting for their own freedom from England during the American Revolution while keeping African Americans enslaved. What gives this an even greater impact is the fact that black slaves fought alongside white Americans to gain independence from England. In essence, white Americans were not creating a Country where all people had the right to "life, liberty, and the pursuit of happiness." As I have stated so many times before, at the end of the Revolutionary War, what most of white America thought they had created was a Country where only white people had the right to "life, liberty, and the pursuit of happiness."

According to published reports, in 1817, Quaker Charles Osborn, a resident of Mt. Pleasant, Ohio, published the first anti-slavery newspaper in the United States, "The Philanthropist". In 1821, Benjamin Lundy, also known as the "Father of Abolitionism," began to publish his newspaper, the "Genius of Universal Emancipation", in Mt. Pleasant. Ohio Quakers were active participants in the Underground Railroad. Growing up in Maryland, my only associations with Quakers were quiet farmers that lived in Pennsylvania. Quakers or Friends hid runaway slaves until they reached safety in Northern states, or Canada. While slavery was illegal in Ohio, the United States Constitution and the Fugitive Slave Law of 1850 permitted slave owners to reclaim their runaway slaves, even if the African Americans now resided in a free state. Prior to the end of the Civil War, in order to gain their freedom, African Americans would have to leave the United States. As a result of this law, the Underground Railroad safe houses that existed throughout Free states could only provide temporary shelter for runaway slaves on their way to Canada.

According to published reports, one of the most famous participants on the Underground Railroad was white man named John Rankin, a Presbyterian minister from Ripley, Ohio. Mr. Rankin's home stood on a three hundred-foot high hill that overlooked the Ohio River and he would signal runaway slaves in Kentucky with a lantern, letting them know when it was safe for them to cross the Ohio River. Reportedly, Mr. Rankin provided shelter and food to as many as two thousand runaway slaves during his career with the Underground Railroad. Harriet Beecher Stowe, another famous Ohio abolitionist, immortalized Mr. Rankin's efforts to help African Americans in her book, "Uncle Tom's Cabin". Mr. Rankin's home was the first stop in Ohio for Eliza, one of the book's main characters, as she sought freedom in the North. Ms. Stowe wrote Uncle Tom's Cabin to educate Northern whites of slavery's brutality. In 1852 alone, Northerners purchased more than 300,000 copies of the book.

What I found to be even more refreshing; the inspiration for hope for future generations, during the 1830s, was a new type of white abolitionist called for the immediate end to slavery. The most prominent of these "radical" abolitionists was William Lloyd Garrison, from Newburyport, Massachusetts, who called for slavery's immediate end as well as equal rights for African Americans. The key ingredient here is that Mr. Garrison defined equal rights as black people having the same rights as white people. The reason this gives me hope is that 180 years ago there were white Americans that actually spoke in public about equality for my black ancestors. In 1831, Mr. Garrison began to publish an anti-slavery newspaper in Massachusetts, known as "The Liberator"; reportedly, this paper's purpose was to educate white Northerners about slavery's cruelty by educating and informing them about the injustice of slavery. Mr. Garrison used his paper to recruit members to the abolition movement and in 1833; he helped establish the American Anti-Slavery Society. This organization sent lecturers across the North to convince whites of slavery's brutality.

In my books, I talk about the United States Constitutions and how if it had simply been enforced, there would never have been a need for the 13th and 14th amendments or the Civil Rights Bill. The Constitutions was created to safeguard the freedoms of all Americans citizens. William Lloyd Garrison was far ahead of his time by contending that the United States Constitution was an illegal document for denying

African Americans their freedom. Why is it most of the American History taught in this Country does not include information about Mr. Garrison? Long before the formation of the Confederate States of America, Mr. Garrison proposed that if the South would not agree to create a new nation that outlawed slavery, the North should secede from the United States and form its own Country. Unfortunately, for my ancestors, many members of the American Anti-Slavery Society did not support the radical views of Mr. Garrison. Most of the American Anti-Slavery Society agreed that slavery was wrong but they felt that the United States Constitution had created a legitimate form of Government under which the people had the right to end oppression. Reportedly, these abolitionists hoped to elect people that supported their beliefs to political offices so that they could make laws outlawing slavery. As a result, the American Anti-Slavery Society formed its own political party, the Liberty Party. Over time, the Liberty Party evolved into the Free-Soil Party and then the Republican Party.

Hazel Brannon Smith

As we move forward in history, it is quite possible that Harriet Beecher Stowe, the author of "Uncle Tom's Cabin" will have inspired Hazel Brannon Smith, from Cleveland, Tennessee, a Pulitzer Prize winning writer, and a next generation white female abolitionists. The next goal for the modern abolitionists is the monumental task of ending the practice of "JIM CROW", defeating racists and racism and fighting for racial equality in America. Hazel Brannon Smith endured more than 20 years of violence, ostracism and economic stifling. During this period, her newspaper was boycotted and later bombed. Her husband was fired from his job as an administrator at the county hospital. She received death threats and suffered through cross-burnings courtesy of the KKK. In return for "telling the people the truth and defending their freedom" and her suffering, she won the Pulitzer Prize for editorial writing in 1964, the first woman ever to be so honored.

What makes Hazel Brannon Smith special and part of this chapter about the future? Mrs. Smith did not start out as an abolitionist that opposed "JIM CROW". Ms. Smith actually wrote articles in her newspaper supporting segregation. Just look at some of the quotes attributed to Ms. Smith.

- "Segregated schools are not equal and can't be made equal"
- "We know that it is to the best interest of both races that segregation be maintained in theory and in fact, and that where it isn't maintained trouble results"
- "Try as we may we cannot legislate human desires, appetites or emotions, prejudices and fears"
- "We believe that intermarriage of the races is a sin and that God did not intend for us to mix in marriage. If he had he would not have created separate races, only one."

After reading these quotes, there was no way that, I wanted to include Ms. Smith in my book. However, as you are about to find out, she changed. On the Fourth of July weekend in Holmes County, Mississippi, in 1954 the same year, that Ms. Smith opposed the U.S. Supreme Courts' ruling to end segregation in public schools, the local Sheriff approached a group of black men and told them to start running. The sheriff opened fire, and he shot a 27-year-old black man, wounding him in the leg as he ran. This incident changed Hazel Brannon Smith's life. She immediately started a campaign to have this local Sheriff removed from office by placing articles on the front page of her newspaper calling for his resignation. In spite of her own segregationist beliefs, Ms. Smith felt that most the white people in her community would not support the mistreatment of any citizen based on their skin color. Ms. Smith was wrong about the white citizens in Mississippi, as an all-white jury ruled in favor of the Sheriff when he sued her newspaper for libel. Fortunately, an Appellate Court reversed the jury's lower court verdict that found her guilty. What Ms. Smith discovered by voicing her anger about black being mistreated in Holmes County, was that she was now on the wrong side of the racial fence in her own hometown.

Unlike most of the white Northerners who joined the fight for racial equality in the "DEEP SOUTH" during the 1960s, many of whom took an active part in marches and demonstrations as Civil Rights Workers,

Ms. Smith was actually born and raised in the "DEEP SOUTH". Hazel Brannon Smith was born in 1914 in Gadsden, Alabama, and lived in several small towns in Mississippi and she never left the South as she died in 1994 in Cleveland, Tennessee. Did her passion and her sacrifice make a difference? That is not an easy question to answer. Over and over again, she asserted that most white people in Mississippi were decent and could be changed from their tolerance of hatred and bigotry if she could help them overcome their fear. "Surely one day, some of my former friends will come to understand it is their personal freedom for which I have been fighting as well as my own," she wrote plaintively in 1966. If they did, they kept quiet about it.

Ms. Smith purchased several newspapers throughout the State of Mississippi: In 1943, she acquired the "Durant News" and the "Lexington Advertiser". In 1956, she purchased the "Banner County Outlook" in Flora, Mississippi and the "Northside Reporter" in Jackson, Mississippi. Early on, Ms. Smith's newspapers support of the Civil Rights Movement was from her strong belief in the rights guaranteed under the First Amendment. Ms. Smith, the one-time segregationist, stated, "I don't approve of enforced integration any more than enforced segregation, but there ought to be a middle ground". In the early 1960s, Hazel Brannon Smith changed her moderate views and became a wholehearted supporter of integration and of black political power. According to published reports, she detested the corrupt system of the Government in the "DEEP SOUTH" that allowed the Citizens' Council or KKK to promote American apartheid. By the way, I did not invent the term "American Apartheid"; I just made it the title of my first book. Reportedly, Ms. Smith in some of her editorials compared the Citizens' Council to the Gestapo.

As a supporter of the Civil Rights Movement Ms. Smith featured stories in her newspapers about the Student Nonviolent Coordinating Committee's (SNCC) as they organized voter registrations campaigns to enlist blacks throughout Mississippi and increase the number of registered black voters in the state. Both Hazel Brannon Smith and her husband attended NAACP meetings and spoke on several occasions with Medgar Evers, the leader of the NAACP in Mississippi. As a result of association with such groups as SNCC and the NAACP, the Citizens' Council boycotted Ms. Smith newspapers and the KKK threatened her white advertisers who then became afraid to give her any business. Money was collected in the black communities in Mississippi and donated to Ms. Smith in order to keep her newspaper running. In response to her support from the African American communities, Mrs. Smith told Jet magazine, "If every businessman in Holmes County doing business with Negroes should be deprived of that business, it would be only a short time until they were all broke".

Hazel Brannon Smith proved to America that even a white segregationist born in the "DEEP SOUTH" could change and accept racial equality as the wave of the future. In the end, the sympathy and support from the supporter of the Civil Rights Movement in Mississippi could not save the life work of Hazel Brannon Smith. The roof literally fell in on her printing press and in 1985; she closed the second oldest newspaper in the state. Ms. Smith was bankrupt and beginning to show signs of Alzheimer's disease. After closing her last newspaper, she moved in with her sister's family in Gadsden, Alabama where she grew up. According to published reports, she died in 1994, nearly destitute, in a nursing home in Cleveland, Tennessee. In the same year, that she died there was a made for TV movie titled, "Passion for Justice: The Hazel Brannon Smith Story". Jane Seymour starred as the Ms. Smith. I have never seen the movie. Now that I have studied the life of Ms. Smith, I will make a concentrate effort to find the movie and watch it and hopeful enjoy her life story.

Viola Liuzzo: Died Fighting for Freedom

From Harriet Beecher Stowe to Hazel Brannon Smith the history of white women whose names are synonymous with the battle to achieve racial equality in America continues with Viola Liuzzo. Viola Fauver was born in Pennsylvania on April 11, 1925. Viola, as a child, lived in Tennessee and Georgia. After an unsuccessful marriage and the birth of two children, Viola married Anthony J. Liuzzo, a Teamster Union official from Detroit. Ms. Liuzzo had three more children and at the age of 36, she resumed her education at Wayne State University. After graduating with top honors, Viola Liuzzo became a medical lab technician. As a member of the NAACP, Viola Liuzzo decided to take part in the Selma to Montgomery March on 25th March, 1965, where Martin Luther King led 25,000 people to the Alabama State Capitol and handed a petition to Governor George Wallace, demanding voting rights for African Americans.

According to published reports, after the demonstration had finished, Ms. Liuzzo volunteered to help drive marchers back to Montgomery Airport. Leroy Moton, a young African American, offered to accompany her to assist with the driving. On the way back from one of these trips to the airport, a car carrying four members of the Birmingham KKK passed Ms. Liuzzo and Mr. Moton. When these white men saw a white woman and black man in the car together, they immediately knew that they had both been taking part in the Civil Rights Demonstration at Montgomery. The men decided to kill them. After driving alongside Ms. Liuzzo's car, one of the men put his arm out of the window, and fired his gun. Viola Liuzzo was hit in the head twice and died instantly. Leroy Moton was uninjured and was able to get the car under control before it crashed.

Reportedly, after Mr. Moton recovered, he left the car and began running down the highway toward Montgomery until he spotted a truck he recognized as belonging to fellow marchers. Mr. Moton climbed into the truck and told them what happened and that Ms. Liuzzo was dead from two shots in the head. Reportedly, within 24 hours after Ms. Liuzzo was killed, President Lyndon B. Johnson was on television, personally announcing the arrest of the four assailants and vowing to exterminate the KKK. Viola Liuzzo's body was returned home to Detroit on March 27, 1965, where her husband Anthony, daughter Penny, 18 and son Thomas, 13 were trying to cope. Ms. Liuzzo's sister was caring for the youngest children, Sally, 6 and Anthony Jr., 10. Another daughter, Mrs. Mary Johnson, 17 was on her way to Detroit from Georgia.

The immediate arrest of these murderers was attributed to an FBI undercover agent that just happened to be one of the men in the car when Ms. Liuzzo was shot. During the trial of her murderer, ugly lies started to circulate about Mrs. Liuzzo's character. In an attempt to prejudice the case, rumors began to circulate that Viola was a member of the Communist Party, a drug addict, and had abandoned her five children in order to have sexual relationships with African Americans involved in the Civil Rights Movement. Rumors supported the attitude among some white Southerners that Mrs. Liuzzo was out of "her place" in Selma, Alabama, and that she should have stayed home with her children. According to published reports, the "Ladies Home Journal" conducted a survey that showed only 26 percent of its readers approved of Ms. Liuzzo's participation in the Civil Rights Movement in Alabama. It was later discovered that these highly damaging stories and rumors that appeared in the press had come from the FBI.

As a boy, I believed the FBI was the greatest law enforcement agency in the world. I actually dreamed of someday being like "Elliot Ness" the fictional FBI agent that always defeated the bad guy on his weekly TV show. I fully realize that there is corruption, bigotry and racial injustice in Local, State and Federal Government. However, it was my belief that in the eyes of the U.S. Military and Federal Law Enforcement Agencies, freedom and justice for all were their top priority. Throughout the "JIM CROW ERA" in America, the FBI has labeled outspoken African American or any outspoken group of African Americans as being either Communist or being under the influence of the Communist Party. The same Communist Party affiliation was given to any white person or white group that supported the Civil Rights Movement. The U.S. Congress has spent millions of dollars investigation the use of steroids in baseball. Over 50 years after the assassination of JFK, the U.S. Government is still issuing reports on alternate theories of the crime.

In spite of the fact that an undercover FBI agent testified as an eyewitness to the crime, an Alabama jury acquitted the three members of the KKK of Ms. Liuzzo's murder. The irony was that the three KKK members claimed that the FBI's undercover agent, who was known by the FBI to be a violent racist, had actually pulled the trigger. The three KKK members passed lie detector tests, which the FBI's undercover agent failed. In October 1977, the Liuzzo family filed a civil claim against the FBI, charging that an FBI employee had failed to prevent Mrs. Liuzzo's death and may have participated in her slaying. In May of 1983, a judge rejected the Liuzzo suit, saying there was "no evidence the FBI was in any type of joint venture with the undercover agent in question nor were they involved in any conspiracy against Mrs. Liuzzo". Shortly after their first trial, President Lyndon Johnson, instructed his officials to arrange for the men to be charged under an 1870 Federal Law of conspiring to deprive Viola Liuzzo of her Civil Rights. The three white KKK members were found guilty and sentenced to 10 years in prison. The undercover FBI was placed in the Federal Witness Protection Program.

When is the Federal Government going to conduct an investigation and issue a report to explain the unscrupulous behavior of the FBI under the infamous Director J. Edgar Hoover? Why did the FBI find it necessary to degrade such a beautiful person like Viola Liuzzo? Why is the man that allegedly shot her living the good life on our Federal Tax dollars? Reportedly, the evening the KKK members were arrested, President Johnson told Anthony Liuzzo, "I don't think she died in vain because this is going to be a battle, all out as far as I'm concerned". Anthony Liuzzo thanked Mr. Johnson and said, "My wife died for a sacred battle, the rights of humanity. She had one concern and only one in mind. She took a quote from Abraham Lincoln that all men are created equal and that's the way she believed." Viola Liuzzo's name is on a Civil Rights Memorial in Montgomery, three blocks from the State Capitol. Memorials are also maintained near her home in Detroit and at the place in the highway where she was killed. Viola Liuzzo's dreams were finally made a reality when Congress passed the Voting Rights Act, which guaranteed that every American could exercise the right to register and vote.

Beginning with the war in Vietnam in the late 1960s and continuing with every military action that has involved troops from the United States, we received televised reports as breaking news. The reason I do not particularly want to see American Troops engaged in battle and being shot and killed on National TV is that it reminds me of the media's coverage of the Civil Rights Movement in the "DEEP

SOUTH". In the "DEEP SOUTH", in the 1960s, when segregation was king, racism the status quo, and bigotry the law, the white news media cameras captured the inhuman treatment of Civil Rights Workers as they were beaten with clubs and attacked by vicious dogs. In an effort to have the laws guaranteed in the Civil Rights Act of 1964 and the Voting Rights Act of 1965 enacted throughout the South, many marched, demonstrated, suffered brutal beatings, and some died. I literally watched with tears in my ears and these horrible sights were broadcast on the TV evening news reports. In the televised reports of the war, we could see that both sides were armed and fighting was from both sides. However, in the war for Civil Rights, the leader of the movement, Dr. Martin Luther King, vowed that his soldiers would be unarmed and they would conduct themselves peacefully, which made the brutal assault on these black people even harder to stomach.

They Also Fought and Died For Freedom

In spite of the violent attacks, young people rose to the challenged and black youth from the "DEEP SOUTH" and both black and white volunteers from the North led the fight for freedom and justice. Three young men that answered the call to fight for racial equality in the "DEEP SOUTH" were Michael Schwerner, James Chaney, and Andrew Goodman. They all died in the war. According to published reports, these Civil Rights Workers disappeared at approximately 10:00 p.m., Sunday, June 21, 1964. The next day their burned-out station wagon was found in the Bogue Chitto swamp, Mississippi, and the bodies of the three men were found forty-four days later, buried fifteen feet in an earthen dam. I write about black history because I strongly believe that African American history needs to be written and passed on to the next generation from a black perspective. As a result of my research and interviews, I have been better able to understand the problems encountered by the white and black volunteers who became Civil Rights Workers during the 1960s in the "DEEP SOUTH". It is my very strong opinion that because two of the three men were white, the murders of Schwerner, Chaney, and Goodman was thoroughly investigated by the FBI and the incident was well documented and while studying events of the Civil Rights Movements, their names have become legendary. In there have been several movies, TV documentaries and books written about the murders of the three Civil Rights Workers. Yet, I have yet to find any detailed information about whom and/or why these two white men gave their lives to win justice, freedom and racial equality for black citizens in the "DEEP SOUTH".

You dare not for even a millisecond make the assumption that I am in any way shape or form attempting to trivialize the death of James Earl Chaney because he was black. The death of James Earl Chaney ranks right along with the deaths of African American Civil Rights Leaders such as Dr. Martin Luther King and Medgar Evers, as the greatest tragedies associated with the Civil Rights Movement. It is my dream, as an ex-U.S. Marine and ex-police officer, that they have a memorial someday be to honor all the men, women and children that lost their lives in the war for racial equality in American during the Civil Rights Movement. The same kind of memorials they have for soldiers, police and firefighters that have lost their lives in the line of duty. As a black man, I can fully understand why African Americans joined the NAACP, Congress of Racial Equality (CORE), Student Nonviolent Coordinating Committee (SNCC), and followed MLK and Medgar as they lead the war to end racism in the "DEEP SOUTH". The reason I can understand it so well is that as soon as I was old enough, I too joined the NAACP and started taking an active role in the Civil Rights Movement.

As proud as I am of my association with the NAACP, and I still make monetary contributions to the organization. I am no longer an active member. I do not know if it was all the internal bickering that has took place over the past 35 years or I could have been influenced by the stories published about R.L. Bolden, an officer in the Mississippi State Chapter of the NAACP, who was identified as the person who spied on Michael Schwerner. According to published reports, R.L. Bolden, a black Mississippian, gave information to local white law enforcement officers in Meridian and Philadelphia, Mississippi that were known Klansmen, the exact route, including arrival information, license plate number and destination, prior to the murders of Michael Schwerner, James Chaney, and Andrew Goodman. With so many black people fighting against us in the battle for racial equality, that it why it is fascinating to me that the majority of white people do not see the color of a person skin as a reason to like or dislike that person or to treat that person differently from any other human being.

On the other hand, I am just as confused by the people who do see the color of a person skin as a reason to like or dislike that person or to treat that person differently. Why did a black man commit an act of treason, which resulted in two white men losing their lives? Was it fear or his lack of trust of white people? In my opinion, the same slave mentality has plagued my ancestors for over 400 years. I wonder if R.L. Bolden even considered the fact that the information he provided to the KKK would also result in the death of a black man, James Chaney. There are books and movies that chronicle the life stories of some of the famous white abolitionist such as John Brown and Harriet Beecher Stowe. The movies and books about three slain Civil Rights Workers only talk about their deaths and provide very little information about their lives. My fascination for an answer to why so many white Americans joined the Civil Rights Movement in the face of danger and why they would risk their lives and leave their families behind is why I went looking for personal information about Michael Schwerner and Andrew Goodman.

Andrew Goodman

Andrew "Andy" Goodman was only 20 years old when he was killed on Rock Cut Road on June 21, 1964, near the end of his first full day in Mississippi. Mr. Goodman had arrived in Mississippi early the previous morning after attending a three-day training session in Ohio for volunteers for the Mississippi Summer Project. The Freedom Ballot set the stage for the Mississippi Summer Project. SNCC worked hard in the winter and spring of 1963-64 preparing for the project, which was an urgent call to action for students in Mississippi to challenge and overcome the white racism in the State of Mississippi.

The Mississippi Summer Project had three goals: registering voters, operating Freedom Schools, and organizing the Mississippi Freedom Democratic Party (MFDP) precincts. One strategy of the project was to hold Freedom Days every two or three weeks. On Freedom Day, SNCC gathered black people together to collectively try to register to vote. However, SNCC faced the challenge of overcoming intimidation by whites, as several people had been killed on Freedom Days across the state. The Freedom Schools helped the Freedom Days succeed. These schools taught children, many of who could not read or write, to stand up and demand their freedom. The children returned home, told their parents about the Freedom Days, and convinced them to register for freedom.

Not only did Andrew Goodman volunteer to help register black voters in Mississippi, he attended a three-day training session to prepare himself so that he could be the most effective volunteer possible. As a result of his training, Mr. Goodman arrived in Mississippi excited and anxious to get to work. One of the reasons the Civil Rights Movement in America today has slowed to a crawl is that our young people have become disinterested in fight for racial equality. They know very little about their African American history and the only time they become concerned about racial discrimination is when it has a direct impact on them. Most young African Americans are familiar with the NAACP, but few of today's youth are familiar with the SNCC. I admit that before conducting this research, I had never heard of the Freedom Ballet and the Mississippi Summer Project, which makes it me even more impressed that Andrew Goodman took the time to find out about the Mississippi Summer Project.

I never met Andrew Goodman, but according to published reports, he was intelligent, unassuming, happy, and outgoing. He grew up as the second of three sons in a liberal household on the Upper West Side of Manhattan, New York. Visitors to the Goodman home included Alger Hiss, blacklisted actor Zero Mostel, and the Attorney who represented the Hollywood 10, Martin Popper. The houseguest that I just mentioned, indicate that Mr. Goodman's family was wealthy, which allowed him to enjoy his summer vacations at the lake near their summer home in the Adirondacks. Prior to going to Mississippi in 1964 to work as a volunteer in the Civil Rights Movement, a 14 year old Andy Goodman participated in the "Youth March for Integrated Schools", which was held on October 25, 1958 in Washington D.C. In 1958, I was 10 years old and I will have to admit that there was no way that I had the guts to put myself on the front line of the war for Civil Rights.

However, once again we have Andrew Goodman, front and center, attending a monumental event in the Civil Rights. Bayard Rustin, A. Philip Randolph, Dr. King, Daisy Bates, Ralph Bunche, Jackie Robinson, and Roy Wilkins, the most distinguished names in the Civil Rights ERA, organized the "Youth March for Integrated Schools" to show that students from across the nation support for integrated schools. More than 10,000 people attended the march in Washington D.C., paraded down Constitution Avenue, and rallied at the Lincoln Memorial. The march includes delegations from most of the main universities and colleges, church, labor, and civic organizations, and from as far away as California. I study black history and I think I do a better than average job of re-writing African American history in a different color. Yet, I will have to admit that I envy this white man, Andrew Goodman, who was an active player in fight for racial equality in America. I would envy anyone that worked alongside Bayard Rustin, A. Philip Randolph, Dr. King, Daisy Bates, Ralph Bunche, Jackie Robinson, and Roy Wilkins as they fought for equality. As a black historian, I should have been so lucky.

After graduating from Walden, a top-notch Prep School in upstate New York, Andrew Goodman enrolled at Queens College, because of its strong drama department. Queens College in Flushing, Queens, which is in New York City, opened its doors in 1937 with the goal of offering a first-rate education to talented people of all backgrounds and financial means. Queens College enjoys a National reputation for its liberal arts and sciences and pre-professional programs. Andrew Goodman's longing for commitment led him away from his interest in drama and back to politics. In April 1964, Andrew Goodman was in New York where he listened to a speech given by Allard Lowenstein was well known for his ability to attract energetic young volunteers for his political causes. In the mid-1960s, many young Jews listened to speeches by Allard Lowenstein as he outlined a bold strategy for bringing Civil Rights to Mississippi. Mr. Lowenstein described Mississippi as "the most totalitarian state in America," a feudal backwater where racism was woven into the fabric of society. If the battle for Civil Rights could be won in the heart of the resistance, it could be won anywhere.

In the early 1960s, Allard Lowenstein taught social science at North Carolina State University in Raleigh, where he was very active in Civil Rights Movement, participating in protest and demonstration both on and off campus. Mr. Lowenstein was credited with assisting another Jew, Robert Moses, in planning the Freedom Ballet and the Mississippi Summer Project. Mr. Lowenstein and Mr. Moses were just two of many Jews that actually recruited other Jews to join the Civil Right Movement in the "DEEP SOUTH". In answer to my question, how and why Andrew Goodman wound up in Mississippi. Allard Lowenstein recruited him, and he applied for and the position and was accepted into the Mississippi Summer Project.

Michael Schwerner

Michael Schwerner, was known as "Goatee" to the KKK members of Neshoba and Lauderdale counties, and was the most despised Civil Rights Worker in Mississippi. Reportedly, the Klan's Imperial Wizard ordered Schwerner's "elimination" in May 1964. Just 24 years old, Michael Schwerner had come to Mississippi in January of 1964 with his wife Rita, reportedly after having been hired by the Congress of Racial Equality (CORE).

Just as I provided some history about SNCC, I will provide some facts about the history of CORE. It was founded in Chicago, in 1942 by three students at the University of Chicago, James L. Farmer, George Houser and Bernice Fisher. CORE sought to apply the principles of nonviolence as a tactic against segregation. Reportedly, the group's inspiration was Krishnalal Shridharani's book *War Without Violence*, which outlined Gandhi's step-by-step procedures for organizing people and mounting a nonviolent campaign. Shridharani, a popular writer and journalist as well as a vibrant and theatrical speaker, had been a Disciple of Gandhi and had been jailed in the Salt March. Reportedly, Gandhi had been influenced by the writings of Henry David Thoreau. Mohandas Gandhi engaged in non-violent resistance against British rule in India. The group that created CORE believed that nonviolent civil disobedience could be used by African Americans to challenge racial segregation in the South and eventually other parts of the United States.

Michael Schwerner was the second of two sons; his father operated a wig manufacturing plant and his mother taught high school biology. Michael "Mickey" Schwerner lived in New York City until he was age eight after which, the family moved to Westchester County in the Southeastern part of New York State. Family and friends as friendly described Michael Schwerner, good-natured, gentle, mischievous, and "full of life and ideas." At an early age, Schwerner believed all people were essentially good. He named his cocker spaniel "Gandhi". I wonder if the non-violent teachings of Gandhi had an influence on Mr. Schwerner. Reported, he loved sports, animals, poker, W. C. Fields, and rock music. Mr. Schwerner enrolled at Michigan State; transferred after a year to Cornell, where he majored in rural sociology. While at Cornell, Mr. Schwerner campaigned successfully to have a black student accepted as a Pledge at his fraternity. Following his graduation from Cornell, he enrolled in Columbia's graduate program in sociology, but dropped out to take a job as a social worker in a housing project on New York's Lower East Side.

Mr. Schwerner was a gifted social worker with a special rapport with teenagers. Michael Schwerner married Rita Levant, then an education student at Queen's College. In his application for the CORE position, Mr. Schwerner, a native of New York City wrote, "I have an emotional need to offer my services in the South." Mr. Schwerner added that he hoped to spend "the rest of his life" working for an integrated society. On January 15, 1964, Michael and Rita left New York in their VW Beetle for Mississippi. After talking with Civil Rights Leader Bob Moses in Jackson, Mississippi, Michael Schwerner was sent to Meridian to organize the community center and other programs in the largest city in Eastern Mississippi. Mr. Schwerner became the first white Civil Rights Worker to be permanently based outside of the Capitol of Jackson, Mississippi and he received $9.80 a week for his work for CORE. Once in Meridian, Schwerner quickly earned the hatred of local KKK by organizing a boycott of a variety store until the store, which sold mostly to blacks, hired its first African American. Mr. Schwerner also came under heavy attack for his determined efforts to register blacks to vote.

After just a few months in Meridian, despite hate mail and threatening phone calls and police harassment, Mr. Schwerner believed he made the right decision in coming to Mississippi. He said that Mississippi "is the decisive battleground for America. Nowhere in the world is the idea of white supremacy more firmly entrenched, or more cancerous, than in Mississippi." On Memorial Day, 1964, Schwerner and Chaney went to Longdale in Neshoba County, where Schwerner asked permission of a black congregation at Mount Zion Church to use their church building as the site for a new "freedom school." On June 16, while Mr. Schwerner was in Oxford, Ohio attending a training session for Freedom Summer volunteers, Mount Zion was burned to the ground by local Klansmen. It is not surprising that the first thing Schwerner wanted to do when he returned from Ohio with James Chaney and Andrew Goodman on June 21 was to return to Longdale and meet with those who had been beaten and lost their church as a result of his efforts on their behalf. It was after that return visit to Longdale, during the drive back to Meridian that the blue CORE station wagon was pulled over by Deputy Sheriff and the three Civil Rights Workers fell into the KKK's fatal trap.

The beauty of the future is that books like mine and the white people that I have already written about and the one I am about to tell you about, have helped to improve some of the horrible conditions that existed in the past on the "Back Side". New ideas and fresh perspectives along with the cooperative effort of the white and black people that labor together will bring about a much-needed transformation of the old stable area. It will eventually replace the old-fashioned slave owner mentality that has been part of the traditional behavior for whites and blacks for years on the "Back Side". The intellectual renaissance combined with the antibiotics of education, love and understanding will kill the infection of ignorance, hatred and bigotry, heal the wounds of racism on the "Back Side", and cure the disease of racism that has flourished for over 200 years. However, if the antibiotics do not heal the wounds, we can always count on the Grim Reaper who will eventually take his toll and the disease of racism will die along with its couriers.

Jerry and Clark

I met the first of many white people on the "Back Side" at the racetrack in Bowie, Maryland that would have a lasting impact on my overall opinion about the sport of thoroughbred horseracing. Two young white men, Jerald "Jerry" Ferris and Clark Cassidy, made a lasting impression on me because of the way they treated me when I first met them in the stable area at Bowie racetrack. I was not only impressed with the way they treated me but the way they treated and showed respect for everyone else they came in contact with in the stable area. They worked hard to take care of their horses, but would always be available to help the other guy if he or she needed help. It surprised me that these two young white men made it a practice to call everyone that was older as Mr. or Mrs. before they called them by their first or last name. My grandfather and grandmother taught me the same thing. Unfortunately, over the years, I was to find that these two young white men were the exception and not the rule for the majority of the white men and women I would encounter on the "Back Side".

This further explains why I was so very impressed with Jerry and Clark. Jerry and Clark's parents taught them to follow the golden rule, which simple means that you treat all people they way you want them to treat you and they taught them to respect all men. I was amazed at the fact that these young men seemed to enjoy the hard work involved in taking care of their horses. During the six months that I spent around the barn, I never heard them say a discouraging word. I was to learn that both of these young white men came from families that had established themselves as being very successful on the Maryland Thoroughbred Racing Circuit as owners and trainers of some very good horses. It is now obvious to me that Jerry and Clark's family did not subscribe to the same principles as the white farmer.

I actually remember coming to Bowie Racetrack as a bettor in the late 1970s and opening the program to find the name Richard Ferris, Jerry's father, as one of the leading trainers. In fact, the horses that Clark and Jerry were taking care of when I met them, belonged to Clark's family, and were being trained by Jerry's father. Over the years, I have lost contact with Jerry, who is now a full time trainer, but on the few occasions that I have seen him at the track, he still has that smile on his face. Clark Cassidy, who I call "Murph" because he is married to trainer James "Jimmie" Murphy's daughter, is a member of the legendary Christmas Family. One of the reasons I will always feel a connection with Clark is that he gave my son Alan, who was four years old at the time, his first ride on a horse. Clark, who is strong as a bull, lifted my son on to his horse as if he was a light as feather and let him ride with him around the shed row. I know people that tried to lift my son when he was four years old that hurt their backs.

I now run into Clark whenever I come to the "Back Side" or to the races. Clark became an Outrider, which can be compared to being a traffic cop on the racetrack. His job is to make sure all the Exercise Rider have control of their horses and that the stay in the assigned lanes and travel in the proper direction during the morning work-outs. In the afternoon, the Outriders also control the activity on the track before and after races. The most exciting job for an Outrider in the morning or afternoon is catching "loose horses". They are called "loose horse" because they have lost their riders and will run around the track aimlessly out of control until they are caught. The Outriders job is to catch the "loose horse" before they hurt themselves or before they run into another horse and rider, which could lead to a very serious injury.

In 1990, after my first horse, *Miss Casey Jane* broke her leg in a training accident at Charles Town Racetrack, and had to be euthanized, I kind of lost some of my interest in horseracing. I would still come to the track to watch and bet on the races, but I did not have enough money to buy another racehorse. Later that year, out of the blue, my uncle Charlie asked me if I wanted to go partners on a couple of 3-year-old thoroughbreds that had never run, but had a lot of "potential". My uncle knew that after my first experience as a racehorse owner, I was "chomping at the bit" to get back in the game. If you know anything about sports or business deals in general, whenever the word "potential" is used, you need to run away from that deal as fast as your legs can carry you. Needless to say, the partnership between my uncle and me along with some other parties that will remain nameless was doomed from the start and turned out to be a disaster. I lost a lot of money and both the horses that I invested in died maidens. After being trained for nearly a year, neither horse actually started in a race. However, as it has been the case with all my experience in the business of thoroughbred horseracing, I learned a valuable and very expensive lesson.

My Cousin Danny Wright

I referred to this negative experience with my uncle Charlie as a lesson. As painful as it was, I write about it now as a positive episode on the "Back Side" because it resulted in my being introduced to a truly great American named Danny Wright. After I got to know Danny Wright, I jokingly called him "Cousin Danny" and although we shared the same last name, you probably already knew that we were not related. When I first met him, he was a jockey who routinely rode races in the afternoon and exercised horses in the morning for trainer James P. Simpson. He had more energy than any two people that I had ever met. Danny was so upbeat and cheerful that even at 5 o'clock in the morning, he could lift the spirits of everyone around him, brighten up their day no matter what the weather, wake you up, and share his energy no matter how sleepy or tired they were.

It made no difference who you were or what your position was on the racetrack, be it a Groom, Hotwalker, Trainer or Steward; Danny would always greet you with a firm handshake, a big smile and a kind word. At the time I met Danny, he was just about at the end of his career as a jockey and spent most of his time on the "Back Side" as an Exercise Rider. As jockey and even more important as a man, Danny earned the reputation of being the most honest rider to ever mount a horse for a race at Maryland Racetrack. In a sport that is known for winning by whatever means necessary. Some of the tactics used to win races have been questionable when it comes to whether or not it involved bending or even breaking the rules. Danny Wright never broke the rules. It was said that if Danny Wright was walking in the dessert with a full canteen of water and he saw a sign that read "DO NOT DRINK WATER FOR 1000 MILES". He would not take a sip of water until he reached the 1000-mile marker.

I remember watching the late news on TV one night, as I was about to go to sleep. The news reporter started taking about a heroic rescue of a man in a wheel chair, who had rolled off the pier and into the water at the Inner Harbor in Baltimore City. The hero in this story was none other than Danny Wright. Without any hesitation or reservations regarding his own safety, this 5 ft. 105 lb. dynamo, jumped in the murky water and saved the man in the wheel chair from drowning. When asked about his heroic actions, Danny merely shrugged it off as just being in the right place at the right time. Just like everything else about this man, he felt that risking his life to save another human being was the right thing to do and it was no big deal. It may not have been a big deal for Danny Wright, but I will always remember it and I have never again watched a news story about someone being rescued as just routine news story.

Charlie J and Kevin

The next two white men that I talk about are perfect examples of the "you can lead a horse to water, but you can make him drink" theory of raising children. Charles Hadry and Kevin Mitchell are both the products of fathers and/or grandfathers that learned their skills as horsemen during the "JIM CROW ERA". Yet, I can say without a shadow of a doubt that neither of these two white men has ever shown any signs of ever being the slight bit conscious of another person's race. I frequently talk about the "JIM CROW ERA" and the impact that it had on race relations in America from the late 1860s through the late 1950s. We all remember that during this time blacks and whites were not allowed to participate in any social, educational, recreational or religious activity together. It most States, the mixing of the races in public was against the law. Therefore, when white horsemen like Charles H. Hadry, Charles J. Hadry's father and Stewart H. Mitchell, Kevin Mitchell's grandfather, started their careers in thoroughbred horseracing, they did not have any social contact with the African Americans that worked on the racetrack.

Whites ate in the track dining hall, while blacks ate from the back of the track kitchen. Whites rode in the front of the bus, while blacks rode in the back. During the "JIM CROW ERA" black were not even allow to bet on races in the grandstand. There were segregated sections of the grandstands for blacks to watch and wager on the races. Rather than go over to the grandstand, most of the black men that worked on the "Back Side" would get a white person to place their bets while they stood by the rail and watched the races from the stable area. During the "JIM CROW ERA" on the "Back Side", every white man that a black worker came in contact with had to be called "Sir" or "Boss"; if you remember, this was part of the lyrics in "My Old Kentucky Home"; "The head must bow and the back will have to bend, Wherever the darkey may go". During this period, it was safe to say that the sport of horseracing mirrored American Society and the song "My Old Kentucky Home", in its ignorant racist attitudes.

The late Charles H. Hadry and the late Stewart H. Mitchell were two of the best and most successful trainers in the history of the sport of thoroughbred horseracing. All I knew about the personal side of Stewart H. Mitchell and Charles H. Hadry is what I heard from the "Ole Timers" at the racetrack, and from Mr. Mitchell grandson, Kevin and Mr. Hadry son Charlie. Of course one of the first questions I asked Kevin when I first met him was if he was related to the Stewart H. Mitchell that owned the largest asphalt business in the State of Maryland and his answer was that he had the exact same name as his grandfather, but they were not related. Stewart Mitchell owned a big horse farm that was located less than a mile from Bowie racetrack and I used to drive by it on my way to the track. Sometimes I would stop to just gaze and admire the horses as they grazed in the field. I remember that on race day, horses trained by Mr. Mitchell wore bright Kelly green bridles. Mr. Mitchell a very special person. His loyalty to jockeys, like Danny Wright and Lynn Cline, and to his workers, like a black groom, John Bowman who was his constant companion whenever he came to the races, that made Stewart H. Mitchell special.

Junior

In my lifetime, I have come to realize that some white professionals, no matter what their personal feeling were about very sensitive issues like racial equality, went along to get a long. When segregation was the accepted norm on the "Back Side", it would have possibly ended the career of a white trainer or a black groom to buck that trend. However, through their grandson and son respectively, Mr. Mitchell and Mr. Hadry have left a legacy of offspring that support the future of racial equality on the "Back Side". I have talked quite a bit about my uncle, Charlie Hall throughout this book. It was through my uncle that I met Charles H. and Charles J. Hadry. Better known as "Junior", "Little Charlie" or "Charlie J", Charles J. Hadry is the son of Charles H. Hadry, one of the most respected trainers in the history of Maryland Horseracing. My uncle Charlie Hall worked for Mr. Hadry when Junior was a young teenager. I found out later that one of Junior's best friends was my cousin Kelsy, who lived with my Aunt Zeedie in Jessup, Maryland. The Hadry family lived on Montevideo Court in Jessup, just a few houses away from my aunt Zeedie. My Aunt Zeedie and Junior's mother were also friends. Junior would often be a dinner quest at my aunt's house and sleepover so that he could hang out with Kelsy. According to my aunt, when they were in High School, Kelsy and Junior were inseparable. To this day, the two of them still maintain a special relationship.

Although my uncle introduced me to Charles J. Hadry, we did not establish our relationship until a few years later when we started playing softball together at the racetrack. My cousin Kelsy recruited me to play softball with his friend Charlie Hadry and the team manager Victor Espinosa, who was also the son of a trainer. I was in my early 40s and Charlie Hadry was in his late 20s when I started playing softball at the racetrack. We quickly learned that we both were very competitive and neither of us liked losing. I think the first four years or five years we played softball together we won the league championship and Charlie and I became close friends in a relationship that can best be described brothers; of course he becoming my little brother. Through my close relationship with Charlie Hadry, I met Donnie Krone, the brother of Hall of Fame Jockey, Julie Krone. Donnie is a superb exercise rider, a trainer, a GOD fearing Christian, and a white man from the Midwest that helped enforce my belief that as long there are people like Donnie Krone, the future of race relations on the "Back Side" is in good hands. You would think that because his sister, Julie Krone is a multi-millionaire Hall of Fame Jockey, Donnie Krone would show signs of being arrogant. Yet, since the first day I met him, his work ethic is second to none. Donnie Krone is actual the last of a dying breed; he works hard, loves his work and takes pride in a job well done.

Donnie was the exercise rider for my first winning horse *Kegler*, and he trained a horse for me called *Snipes Tornado* that won a race. He worked on my car, listened to my personal problems and let me hangout with him at his part-time job in the press box at Laurel and Pimlico. I loved to talk about horseracing with Donnie. While hanging around with Donnie in the press box; I ate food that was delivered by a caterer; met Jockeys, professional sportswriters, and of course Julie Krone. With his commitment to two jobs, his teenage son, and a new girlfriend, it was hard for Donnie to find time to hang out with me, an old married guy with an insatiable appetite for talking about horseracing. Which makes the story of how I met Kevin Mitchell very simple; one day while I was having a discussion with a group of people at the racetrack, this young white man walked up, joined the discussion and Kevin and I have been friends ever since. Of course, the bond that ties us together is the love of talking about the sport of thoroughbred horseracing. As the grandson of a Hall of Fame trainer like Stewart Mitchell, Kevin loves horses and the sport of horseracing probably can be traced back to the first time his mother, father or grandfather took him to the racetrack.

As I recall, I met Kevin in 1999 and unlike the other white people that I have met at the racetrack, he has been to my house, met my wife and family and I have met his family. Two years after we met, we became partners in claiming a horse named *Irish Crossing*. Lack of funds had been the cause of me being in and out of the horseracing business for close to 15 years and I had promised myself that I would not get back into the business until I could find a partner to share the financial burden. It takes a lot of money to make it in the sport of horseracing. Money is why horseracing is so aptly referred to as the "Sport of King". It takes a King's ransom to be even moderately successful. Yet, in spite of my moderate resources, every chance I get, I try and try again to be a player in this "Sport of Kings". Although we both invested the same amount of money, Kevin trusted me to call the shots and based on my trust in a young black trainer, we claimed a horse that never lived up to the potential that the trainer insisted she had when we claimed her. Kevin and I wound up losing our original investment and again I was out of business.

I was very disappointed. This young man had trusted me to make the right decision on selecting a horse and I let him down. The reason I took all the blame was because I knew better than to claim a horse from Dale Capuano. I studied the past performance records of horses and trainers, and I knew that no one had ever claimed a horse from Dale Capuano and gone on to be successful with that horse. Most importantly, years prior to claiming *Irish Crossing* from Dale, I had purchased a horse named *Silverano* from him. Dale knew the horse was a "bleeder" and he sold him to me anyway. A "bleeder" is a horse that whenever it ran, their lungs fill up with blood and they cannot breathe. In talking with Dale about this horse later, he told me that horseracing is a business and his selling me a defective horse was nothing personal, it was just business. Rather than use the knowledge and the lesson

I learned with *Silverano*, I trusted this young black trainer, who had recently worked for Dale and felt he had some inside information on *Irish Crossing*. What the young black trainer did not know was that *Irish Crossing*, like *Silverano*, was a serious "bleeder". This was information that Dale had purposely failed to share with is former employee while he was working for him. After he found out that I had claimed *Irish Crossing* another "bleeder", Dale reminded me that it is nothing personal, it just a business.

After sharing this information with Kevin, I thought he would be angry. However, he took it in stride and said that we would have better luck next time. The operative word here being "we" would have better luck next time. After what happened, I thought that I had not only lost a partner, I thought that I had lost a friend. I had heard all my life that the best way to loss a friend was to either lend them money or go into business together. Kevin and I maintained our friendship and in February 2005, we purchased a horse named *Legendinthemakin*. Although, we did not win a lot of money, we had a lot of fun and the *"Legend"* as we fondly called him, gave us many exciting moments. If you need to determine the true character of a person, get to know their children. I met Kevin's, mother, stepfather, sister and his 2 nieces at the Maryland State Fair's Racetrack in Timonium. They had all come to watch the *"Legend"* run.

After being introduced to his family, Kevin's youngest niece, who might have been about 4 years old, took me by the hand, squeezed it real tight, held on to me the entire time I was with her family and talked to me as if she had known me forever. Yes. I was impressed that this little white girl was not the least bit afraid of a black man that she had just met and I was even more impressed that her mother was not concerned that her daughter had attached herself to a black man that the mother had just met. The future and the eventual end to racism in America are families like Kevin's. The reason it was easy for Kevin to trust me in making the decision to purchase *Legendinthemakin* was that I was buying this horse from another friend. This friend's name is Rodney Jenkins, and as strange as is it may sound, he was a white trainer who put friendship and family ahead of business. The other strange thing was that I met Rodney Jenkins in much the same way that I met Kevin Mitchell. The fact that I love to talk about the sport of horseracing at any time with anyone has resulted in two good friends.

Rodney Jenkins

I am not sure, but I think I met Rodney in the spring of 2001 at Pimlico Racetrack. He was smoking a pipe and the smell of his brand of tobacco reminded me of the familiar smell of my Grandfather's pipe. Although, I have never smoked, I grew to love the smell of pipe tobacco. The fact that I loved my Grandfather and Rodney's pipe smoking reminded me of him, could be the reason I felt so comfortable talking with a man I had never met. First and foremost, I consider Rodney Jenkins to be my friend. However, just as I needed to know more about the personal lives of Civil Rights Hall of Fame Members, Viola Liuzzo, Andrew Goodman and Michael Schwerner, I needed to learn more about Rodney Jenkins, the winningest rider in the history of U.S. Show Jumping. Rodney Jenkins dominated the American show ring in the 1960s, 1970s and through most of the 1980s before retiring as the most successful rider in its history. Rodney was a member of 16 Nations' Cup teams from 1973-1987, and helped Team USA wins ten world championships.

Born in Virginia, Rodney Jenkins grew up in the saddle and soon earned recognition as a "natural horseman" who could ride just about any horse and get it to perform at its best. In 1999, Rodney was inducted into the Show Jumping Hall of Fame. I have never seen him ride, but I have seen him train horses. Watching Rodney around horses, I can only surmise that the natural ability he had to make horses perform at their best when he rode has carried over as he has shown the same natural ability to make the horses that he trains perform at their best. After nearly 60 years, Rodney has the unique ability to look at a horse walking in the shed row or in a post parade and tell if that horse his sound or sore. I have witnessed him tell a groom that one of his horses seemed a little off, make a diagnosis as to what was wrong with the horse, and have that diagnosis proven to be right on after the horse is examined by a veterinarian. In 1989, Rodney used his natural ability, as a horseman, to "pin hook", a term used for buying a horse for the purpose of reselling, a "weanling", a horse between the age of 6 months to a year old, named Mane Minister. Rodney picked this horse out of a field of horses on a farm in Kentucky. As proof of his eye for horse, in 1991 *Mane Minister* became the first horse to run third in all three Triple Crown Races.

For those of you that do not follow the sport of horseracing, the Triple Crown Races are the Kentucky Derby, Preakness and Belmont Stakes. In the more than 125 years in the history of the Triple Crown races, only 11 horses have ever won the Triple Crown; none since 1978 when *Affirmed* did it. Only one horse in 125 years has ever finished second in all three races and that was *Alydar* in 1978, which adds to the significance of what *Mane Minister* accomplished in 1991. Since 1991, when he made the switch to training thoroughbreds fulltime, Rodney Jenkins has been one of the most successful trainers in the Mid-Atlantic, winning with 19% of his starters and saddling over 40 stakes winners. Whenever we are together, Rodney and I talk about horses; horseracing; past experiences with love marriage and our children; and how we grew up in rural America in the late 1940s. I have literally talked for hours at a time with Rodney, yet I knew very little about his riding career. Of course, I knew he was a Hall of Fame Show Jump Rider, but I did not have any idea how successful he had been. Rodney won 70 of this Country's most prestigious Grand Prix classes, including the American Gold Cup five times, Presidents Cup three times and the National Horse Show Grand Prix three times.

In 1987, Rodney rode for the United States Equestrian Team (USET) on the Pan Am team and won two Silver Medals. Rodney was quoted as saying, "All the money I've won with horses, these two pieces of silver mean as much as all the money". In the short time that I have known him, I can attest to the fact that when it comes to horses, and the sport of horseracing, it true that the money really does not matter to Rodney Jenkins. Throughout the years that I have known him, Rodney has never taken credit for all he has accomplished as a horseman. If you ask him what he thinks are his greatest accomplishments, Rodney will be quick to name his wife and their two children. In conducting my research on Rodney Jenkins, I read quotes articles printed in popular horseracing magazines, "My philosophy is people don't make the horse. They manage the horse and direct the horse, but the horse makes the people", and "The horse makes the rider, I don't care how good you are". As I was reading it in the magazine, I could recall all the times that I have actually heard him say the same things during one of our many conversations.

In dealings with my Uncle Charlie Hall and trainer Dale Capuano, I had been convinced that the sport of thoroughbred horseracing was a cutthroat business and there was no room in it for friendship. That is why I thank GOD for allowing me to meet a man like Rodney Jenkins. As I stated early, if you need to determine the true character of a person, get to know their children. Rodney would often bring his wife and sons to the racetrack. His sons were just little fellows when I first met them. When I would see the boys at the racetrack I would always talk to them and Rodney would tell told his sons to call me "Uncle Mike". Just in case I had not mentioned it, my friends and family called me "Michael" or "Mike". One day after a race, Rodney was saying goodbye to one of the owners of one of his many horses. As they were leaving, the owners tried to say goodbye to Rodney's oldest son. The little guy was tired and sleepy so he did not seem to want to be bothered and he ducked in behind his mother. All of sudden as he saw me coming toward them, he ran and jumped into my arms and hugged me around my neck. I almost cried; children are the best judges of character in the world.

After years of listening to me talk about my love for the game of thoroughbred horseracing and after learning of the many times that I would be victimized by the cutthroats that are associated with the business of horseracing, Rodney made me a promise. If I trusted him, he would find me a horse that would not only make me a winner, but it would also allow me to have some fun. Another one of Rodney's philosophies was that life is too short not to have some fun doing the things you love. In February 2005, he kept his promise by not only brokering the sale of *Legendinthemakin*, he also trained him to the best record of any horse I ever had. After the *Legend* suffered a careering ending injury, Rodney found him a good home and sold him to a young lady who retired him to a farm in South Carolina. The sudden end to the Legend's career left Kevin and I without the means to pay the expense incurred by the owners of a thoroughbred racehorse. Rodney never said a thing about the money we owed him, he just wanted to make sure we used the money from the sale of the *Legend* to pay the veterinarian bills and we could pay him whenever we got the money.

Ms. Katie

As I am writing this book, I do not own any horses. However, I am looking forward to the day that I can get back in business with my friends Rodney Jenkins and Kevin Mitchell. Although we never developed a close relationship, Katherine "Katie" Voss is another white female trainer that I need to mention before I end this chapter. I met Ms. Voss in passing, and I do not really know her. I do know that she is a member of the Merryman family, who have a long a distinguished history is the sport of thoroughbred horseracing in the State of Maryland horsemen. When I purchased a bad "bleeder" from Dale Capuano, I called Ms. Voss because I was told that she had a cure. She did not know me from Adam, yet she took the time out of her busy training schedule to offer me whatever information she had on the subject. If that was not enough to include her in this chapter of my book, reportedly, Ms. Voss, who is a prominent member of the Maryland Horsemen's Association, had a Racetrack Security Guard fired after she overheard him using the "N" word when referring to African American workers on the "Back Side". Just a little respect "R-E-S-P-E-C-T", as black men and women, that all we want and that why I am proud to know people who understand what the word means.

Now do not get me wrong, the "Back Side of the Sport of Kings" is still full of racists and bigots. For the most part, the sport of thoroughbred horseracing is still controlled by rich white men and women whose mommies and daddies earned their money from the blood, sweat and tears of my black ancestors. The Mecca of the sport of thoroughbred horseracing is the State of Kentucky. If you have ever listened to the racist lyrics of the Kentucky State Anthem, "My Ole Kentucky Home", which is played during the post parade of the Kentucky Derby, you can understand why the racist attitude is still alive and well in the sport of horseracing. If you need a better understanding of what makes the lyrics to "My Ole Kentucky Home" racist, read the chapter one.

The reason the white people that I wrote about in this chapter are so special and so refreshing to talk about is because they are the sons and daughters, grandson and granddaughters of parents and grandparents that were born in the "JIM CROW ERA". These offspring of white fathers and mothers attended segregated schools. That lived in all white communities and for the most part, the only African Americans they came in contact with were the servants that cleaned their houses and took care of their horses. This only helps to prove my point that racism and bigotry is not an inherited disease. In order for racism to continue to infect our offspring, we must take the time and effort to teach them how to be bigots. No matter how hard racists try to teach children to hate people of a different race, color and creed. No matter how hard they try to infect them with the disease of racism; the children become immune to the disease because they realize how wrong it is and just refuse to the learn the lesson of hatred and bigotry that the parents and others try to teach.

MARK!!!!!

As we look to the future, I end this chapter by thanking someone else from my past. A special thanks to my friend Mark McClelland. Without Mark's special skills, this book would still be a manuscript. I use the word "special" to describe Mark because in my 65 years I never met anyone like him. My son calls him Mr. Mark. He was so comfortable around my family that Mark calls my aunts "Aunt Zeedie" and Aunt Tootsie" as if he has known them all his life. If I were to give more details about Mark, or provide any personal information about this "special" person, it would only make him uncomfortable when he reads this part. Again, I say to my good friend. Thank you MARK! Enough said!

Chapter 6

HISTORY DOES REPEAT ITS' SELF

I need to make it clear that conducting the research used to write my books has been an enlightening experience as well as educational. I have never read "Uncle Tom's Cabin", but I have seen the movie adaptation and it made me angry. You see, I will have to admit that the movie did portray the brutality and cruelty endured by black slaves at the hands of a monstrous white Overseer and that was disgusting and it did make me angry. However, what angered me even more was that the movie featured an old black man who actually loved the very white people that took away his freedom and it portrayed him as wanting to remain a slave rather than be free. This famous book/movie is the source from which African Americans derived the derogatory label of "Uncle Tom", which is given to black people who bow their heads and grin, as they are being insulted and disrespected by white people. The same derogatory term, "Uncle Tom" is given to black people who choose to be in the company of white people and turn away or even try to deny their African American heritage.

Uncle Tom and The Crab Syndrome

Before conducting the research for this book, I had been very critical of this white author Harriet Beecher Stowe. My criticism of Ms. Stowe was based her interpretation of the character "Uncle Tom". I was opposed to any white person that characterized any black slave as accepting the conditions of slavery. However, like it or not, Ms. Stowe's

257

depiction of "Uncle Tom" was accurate; they were then and they still are now, black people that accept the restrictions that white bigots and racists impose upon them. During the era when slavery was legal in America, the cause and effect of being an "Uncle Tom" could be attributed to my ancestors needing to do whatever it took to survive and to being brain washed by their captors. Today, I attribute the scars of having a slave's mentality to blacks that continue to be "Uncle Toms". Harriet Beecher Stowe was an outspoken white female Abolitionist in a time when it was very unpopular for women to be political involved in any legal or moral issues. I applaud Ms. Stowe for her contribution to the cause to abolish slavery, "Uncle Tom's Cabin" and from this point on, I will view this book in a positive light.

Ask Americans to donate money to support the families of those who died on 9 -11 and you would collect millions of dollars. The U.S. Congress passed emergency legislation that allocated Federal monies to provide special funding for the family members of victims of 9 - 11. We still honor the anniversary of the tragic events of 9 - 11. Americans are still upset and they are still donating money to any cause that has a 9 - 11 theme. Yet, white America turned a deaf ear to black Americans who gathered in Washington D.C. to support legislation that would fund reparations for the ancestors of black slaves. Wake up America! As long as there is one black face in America, the fact that African Americans were brought and sold in this Country is never going to be forgotten. Just like the Jews, we were the victims of a Holocaust, and like the Jews, we deserve compensation.

In 2007, Baltimore, Maryland, where the population has been 60% to 75% blacks for close to 40 years, is about to elect only their second African American mayor in the past 40 years. I can talk about Baltimore because I grew up in Anne Arundel County, just 10 miles South of the Baltimore City line and I currently live in Gwynn Oak, which is less than a mile West of the city limits. Baltimore is a city that has an eight to one ratio of Democrats to Republicans. Therefore, it is a foregone conclusion that whoever wins Baltimore's Democratic primary election is the next mayor elect of Baltimore City. This was the case 40 years ago and the tradition is still alive and well. With such a strong political party bias, along with the fact that the majority of the African Americans in Baltimore are Democrats, you have to ask the question, "Why one African American elected to the office of mayor?" The answer to that question and the reason Baltimore has only elected one black mayor can be directly attributed to a problem that I detailed in my book "No Land No Mule No Freedom" and that is the "Crab Syndrome".

The "Crab Syndrome" is simple. If you put one crab in a bushel basket, he will claw his way to the top and succeed in gaining his freedom. However, if you put more than one crab in a bushel basket, whenever one of them reaches the top, the others, who are also attempting to reach the top, will band together to pull the crab at the top down and keep him from achieving his goal. In 1971, I remember when the first African American candidates, George Russell and Clarence Mitchell III, ran for mayor in Baltimore City. A white candidate, William Donald Schaefer, defeated them because the black vote was split between the two black candidates. In this situation, all that was needed to insure the election of Baltimore City's first African American mayor was for one of the black candidates to drop out of the race. Neither of the black candidates would back down. George Russell the first African American elected to the office of City Solicitor in Baltimore, and Baltimore City State Senator Clarence Mitchell III, were at the time both equally popular in the African American communities. The result of this "Crab Syndrome" behavior was a white man, City Council President William Donald Schaefer, became mayor of Baltimore for close to 12 years, before becoming the Governor of Maryland and later the Comptroller of Maryland.

You would have thought that the black political leaders in Baltimore City would have learned their lesson from what happened in 1971 when Russell and Mitchell split the black vote. Apparently, these black leaders are not familiar enough with their African American History to understand the impact of the "Crab Syndrome". The result of this lack of knowledge became evident in 1999 when two black candidates, Baltimore City Council President Lawrence Bell and Baltimore City Councilman Carl Stokes, again split the black vote, and a white candidate, Baltimore City Councilman Martin O'Malley won the election and became mayor of Baltimore. The "Crab Syndrome" dates back to a time in America when black people were the property of white slave owners. In order to gain special favor from their white masters, slaves would compete against each other. The competition ranged from physical feats of strength, speed and endurance to fighting. To please their masters, slaves would compete to entertain by trying to be the best dancing, singing and or comedian, which meant doing anything they could to make white people laugh or applaud. In 1999, in spite of the pleas and meetings held to persuade one or the other of the black candidates to get out of the race, Martin O'Malley captured more votes than the two black candidates combined. If in 1971 and 28 years later in 1999, the two black candidates had been familiar with their African American history, the "Crab Syndrome" may not have had an impact on the election of the mayor of Baltimore City.

I make a point of the history of the office of mayor of Baltimore City because in 2007 the confirmation that history will continue to repeat its' self is being played out again. In 2007, at least five African Americans ran for the office of mayor of Baltimore City. Unfortunately, at this same time in history, a more disturbing phenomenon is having a statistical impact in the African American communities in Baltimore City. The fact that on January 20, 2007, twenty black people had been murdered in Baltimore City in the first twenty days of the New Year. This devastating phenomenon, is called" genocide", also known as, us killing us, which I talk about in detail in my book "No Land No Mule No Freedom". Would a black mayor have made a difference in the number of murders in the black community? I do not know. The sad part is that while the black political leaders are allowing the "Crab Syndrome" again to have an impact on an election for mayor of Baltimore City.

The social, economic and political imbalance and the disparity in our criminal justice system as it relates to minorities in America has replaced most of the blatant acts of racial discrimination of the past. Note that I said most of the blatant violent acts of racial discrimination in America, because black people are still being physical, mentally and emotionally abused and killed in this Country just for just being black. The problem is many black Americans would rather turn a deaf ear or remain blind to any information regarding racial discrimination and racial injustice, for fear that if they acknowledge the existence of racism they might offend their white friends and neighbors. As African Americans, how long will we continue to go along just to get along when there are States in America where it is still against the law for a black person to marry a white person? There are high schools throughout rural America that have integrated their classrooms, but have separate school dances for white and black students. Native Americans still live on reservations in the Midwest and we help put them there.

The problem with history repeating its' self is that so very few of us know the truth about the history of African Americans in this Country that when these racist actions and behaviors from the past resurface, we do not have the knowledge base to recognize this disgusting behavior as being a repeat performance. The only way we can truly recognize when history repeats its' self is to know our history. The American Apartheid Series gives you a snapshot of Black/African American History. Unfortunately, to capture the entirety of our American History, I would need to publish an encyclopedia of African American History with volumes from 1400 to today. I challenge any of our Historical Black Colleges or Universities to accept this project. I would be more than glad to donate part of the proceeds from the American Series to this project. In 2006, a black Historian, Louis Diggs, published his eighth book on the history of the African Americans communities throughout Baltimore County, Maryland. In order to preserve our history we need Historians like Mr. Diggs to chronicle the history of the black communities throughout America. I urge you to read Mr. Diggs' books.

Native Americans Still on the Reservation

After their battles for equality, the Native Americans were forced to live on reservations in the swamps of Florida or in the Southwest. Once the dominant race in this Country, the Native Americans are now a minority that have never integrated into American society. At the end of the Civil War, African Americans were given very few choices to earn a living as free men and women. We could remain in the South and work on the old plantations as sharecroppers; take low paying jobs as laborers in Northern factories; go West and help build the railroad or join the army. Although the choice to join the army offered the best career choice, it helped to create an obstacle between the African American and the Native American that has never between repaired. If freed black slaves had joined the Native Americans in their fight for justice and equality in this Country, America would now be truly the home of the brave and the land of the free. Issues of racism in America started with the Native American and continued with other people of color that included African Americans. Battle to end racial discrimination should be about race.

Are Women Really A Minority?

A very sticky situation that historians fail to associate with the study of racism and the battle to end racial discrimination in America are the other causes that have nothing to do with race. These causes have always attached themselves to the plight of Native Americans and African Americans like parasites. In the early 1800s when white and black men started the movements to abolish slavery in America, white women were inspired by this movement and started their own protest for the right to vote. The "Women Suffrage" movement was a long hard struggle that lasted for close to 100 years and ended with the 19th Amendment to the Constitution that stated that no person could be denied the right to vote based on that person's sex. As early as the 1840s or 1850s, white women joined white men in the cause to abolish slavery with the self-servicing long-term goals of gaining equal rights for women. It seemed to be a forgone conclusion, that if black slaves were free to vote and own property, white men would have to grant the same rights to white women. It was sound strategy and eventually it worked. However, the results did not come as fast as the women thought it might.

In 1868, the 13th and 14th Amendments to the Constitution ended the enslavement of my ancestors in America. In 1870, the 15th Amendment to the Constitution insured African Americans the right to vote. However, it was 50 years later, in 1920, before the Congress ratified the 19th Amendment to the Constitution that gave women the right to vote. I appreciate the fact that white women supported the cause to abolish slavery. I am all for women's rights. Just as it should have been for African Americans, the rights for female citizens should have come with the Declaration of Independence. From the very beginning of this Country when our forefathers wrote, "All men are created equal and shall have equal rights". The word man means mankind. The term mankind includes all human being regardless of race, color, creed or sex. As much as I am for equal rights under the law for all human beings, I am strongly against women being classified as a "minority". According to the latest census, there are approximately 5 million more women in American than there are men.

Yes, it did take women 144 years after we gained independence from England to win the right to vote. However, over the past 50 years women have become one of the most powerful social, economic and political forces in America. Perfect examples of this is the fact that in 2006 we had a white woman, Nancy Pelosi, become the first female Speaker of the United States House of Representatives; and in 2008 a white woman, Hilary Clinton, became the first serious female candidate for President of the United States. If women want to attribute their lack of progress in this Country to the sexist mentality of the white men who controlled this control, I totally agree. Discrimination based on your sex does not make you a minority. Therefore, women should not qualify or be compensated by receiving any benefits that have been set aside based on race. The closest the Federal Government has come to reparations for the ancestors of black slaves is Affirmative Action and minority set-asides. However, the white men who control this Country have been allowed to circumvent the purpose of Affirmative Action and minority set-asides by allowing women to qualify as a minority.

It is very simple. White men would much rather hire or provide funding for a white woman than a black man. In most cases, behind every successful white woman is a white man. In order to maintain racial dominance in America, white men need a strong ally. The strongest group for white men to align with is white women. As African Americans, we are still fighting for racial equality in America. If white women were, a true minority and they all joined in the fight to gain equal rights for all human beings in America, the battle for Civil Rights, the War against racism would be over, and equality would be the law of the land. Unfortunately, once white women used their minority status to gain the power they hold today, they distanced themselves from the true minority population in this Country and made it clear that "people of color" cannot play in the same social, political, and economical game as "soccer moms". How dare Martha Burk, former Chair of the National Council of Women's Organizations, equate the struggle for women rights with the fight for equal rights by African Americans! She honestly felt that a black professional golfer, Tiger Woods, should boycott Augusta National and the Masters Golf Tournament until they allow women members. In 2002, the Augusta National Golf Club did not allow women to become members.

Are Jews and Gays Minorities?

Not only are women being considered a minority, America has found other new groups to divert attention away from the primary issue of discrimination, which is racism. The new groups that are associating with all the old stereotypes that were directed at African Americans are gay men and lesbian women and Jews. I detest anti-Semitism and homophobia. Religious freedom and sexual orientation are choices that we as human being should be able to make without any negative reactions. In spite of all the studies that have been conducted, being Jewish is not part of one's hereditary. In addition, people are born gay or lesbian. I have made it clear in both of my first two books, that in my opinion, being Jewish or a homosexual is an individual's choice and being born a person of color is a birthright. The problem I have is when Jews or homosexuals are treated differently; or when they are discriminated against; or suffer acts of violence, these acts are compared to black people that experiences these same acts of disparate treatment or violence. People, nothing compares to being the disparate treatment received because of the color of your skin.

The indifferences or extreme dislike directed toward Jews and homosexuals are based on morals. If you are a devout Christian, it is very difficult for you to accept Judaism or homosexuality because it is in direct conflict with your beliefs. Gay men and lesbian women are protesting the fact that they cannot be legally married in many of these United States, and the Jews are protesting the treatment of their fellow Jews in Israel. When they are interviewed on TV, the first thing they say out of the mouths is "they wouldn't do this to us if we were black". Wake up gays and lesbians, there are still States in America that do not allow black and white couples to marry; why would you think that they would make an exception for homosexuals? Jews, did you see Spike Lee's movie "When the Levee Broke". The movie details the horrendous neglect by the United States Government of the black people in Louisiana who were victims of Hurricane Katrina. We respond to disasters in foreign countries in less than 24 hours. We respond to hurricanes that hit predominately-white areas in Florida in less than 24 hours. Why did it take so long to respond to the black victims of hurricane Katrina?

Homosexual and Jews, get off the racial discrimination ban wagon, there is no room. In 2007, a black professional basketball player, John Amaechi, "came out of the closet" announcing that he was gay after he had officially retired. After hearing this announcement, another black retired NBA star issued a statement that he hated gay people. This upset the NBA Commissioner, who barred the former NBA player that said he hated gays from ever being associated with any NBA sponsored activities. Other black current and former NBA players and professional entertainers, were very critical of the retired NBA player that made the "hate gay people" statement. My grandmother taught me never use the word hate. The term mankind includes all human beings regardless of race, color, creed, religion, sex or sexual preferences. Much of the criticism directed at the retired NBA player was because he was black. Based on how blacks have being treated in this Country, as black people we should not discriminate against any other human beings for any reason. As much as I am for equal rights under the law for all human beings, I am strongly against non-minorities being classified as such.

A Mix of White, Brown & Black Power

In the new millennium the shouts of "Brown Power" by Hispanic Americans has replaced our cry in the late 20th century for "Black Power". How long will African Americans continue to turn their backs on the racial discrimination and bigotry that face other people of color in this Country rather than unit to defeat our common enemy? Unfortunately, black people still refuse to believe that history can and will continue to repeat its' self in America. Therefore, I feel it is my duty, to refresh the memory of African Americans, that feel the past transgressions of white America against their black ancestors, should remain in the past. As we were about to enter the new millennium, for no other reason than being black, an African American man from Jasper, Texas, who merely wanted a ride, was attacked by two white men; had a chain tied around his neck. The chain was hooked to the back of a pickup truck and the black man was dragged to death. How many more blacks have to be lynched; how many more published cases of racial profiling by law enforcement agencies; how many more cases of blatant acts of racial discrimination will we have to endure before we realize that as far as racism in America is concerned history does repeat its' self? I ask these questions today in hope that tomorrow there might be an answer.

Even during the dreaded "JIM CROW ERA", major media outlets in Northern States reported the violent crimes committed by white men against black people who lived in the "DEEP SOUTH" during. Violent crimes, such as murder, arson and rape, are often investigated by the FBI, as what would be classified as hate crimes. Although the reports may not have been complete and/or accurate, the media coverage of these violent incidents helped to preserve the history of these events. During the early 1960s, America tuned in and watched the televised attacks by State Troopers on the peaceful marchers at the Edmund Pettis Bridge. The marchers were on their way to Selma, Alabama to add their voices to the cry for justice. Although I am not a big fan of the late J. Edgar Hoover, the former Director of the FBI, to their credit, the FBI would locate suspects and make arrest in the more publicized cases of white on black crimes. However, the corrupt and bigoted white criminal justice system along with the equally corrupt and bigoted with political structure in the "DEEP SOUTH" made it next to impossible to convict a white man of committing a crime against a black person.

According to published reports, on June 21, 1964, three Civil Rights Worker, Michael Schwerner, James Chaney, and Andrew Goodman drove to the site of burned church in Neshoba County, Mississippi. On their way back to Meridian, Mississippi, they were arrested by the Deputy Sheriff and taken to the county jail in Philadelphia, Mississippi. In a conspiracy with local members of the Ku Klux Klan, the Deputy Sheriff released the three Civil Rights Workers from jail. Shortly after leaving the jail, the Civil Rights Workers' station wagon was overtaken on a rural road, and the three were beaten and shot and their bodies buried in an earthen dam. Almost a year later, a white female member of the NAACP, Viola Liuzzo decided to take part in the Selma to Montgomery March 25, 1965. After the demonstration had finished, Ms. Liuzzo volunteered to help drive marchers back to the Montgomery Airport. Leroy Moton, a young African American, offered to work as her co-driver. On the way back, from one of many trips to the airport, a car carrying four members of the Ku Klux Klan from Birmingham, Alabama, passed Ms. Liuzzo and Mr. Moton. Reportedly, when these KKK members saw a white woman and black man in the car together, they immediately concluded that they had both been taking part in the Civil Rights Demonstration at Montgomery. According to published reports, these white men decided to kill the white woman and black man. After driving alongside Ms. Liuzzo's car, one of the men put his arm out of the window, and fired his gun. Viola Liuzzo was hit in the head twice and died instantly. Leroy Moton was not injured but was unable to get the car under control from the passenger seat before it crashed. The four white men were quickly arrested. However, in a feeble attempt to prejudice the case, rumors began to circulate that Ms. Liuzzo was a member of the Communist Party and had abandoned her five children in order to have sexual relationships with African Americans involved in the Civil Rights Movement.

According to published reports, it was later discovered that some highly damaging stories that appeared in the press had come from the FBI. The fourth KKK member in the car received a deal from the State Prosecution for testifying against the other three. It came as no surprise that an Alabama jury acquitted three KKK members of the murder. However, to his credit, President Lyndon Johnson, instructed his officials of the U.S. Government to arrange for these three white men to be charged under an 1870 Federal Law of conspiring to deprive Viola Liuzzo of her Civil Rights. The three members of the KKK were found guilty and sentenced to 10 years in prison. The FBI finally arrested, almost three years after the murders of Schwerner, Chaney and Goodman, twenty-one Klansmen. On February 27, 1967, a Federal Grand Jury for the Southern District of Mississippi indicted nineteen members of the KKK under Title 18, section 241, for conspiracy. A two-week Federal trial in Meridian, Mississippi, resulted in seven guilty verdicts and sentences ranging from three to ten years.

How is it possible for members of a white racist organization, like the KKK, to kill American citizens that were merely exercising their rights that are guaranteed under the first and fourth amendments of the Constitution of the United States, and only be sentenced to 3-10 years in jail? When the FBI conducted the investigations of these brutal crimes, it came as no surprise to me that the murder suspects were members of the KKK. Not only were they members of this racist organization, some of the murder suspects that were identified were law enforcement officers. I know some of you find it hard to believe. State Troopers, local police officers and members of the Sheriffs' Department, who all sworn an oath to protect and serve and enforce the law as well as the Constitution of the United States, either took an active part in committing these heinous crimes or they were part of a conspiracy to plan and/or cover up the murders.

History reports the fact that these were not the first support- ers of the Civil Rights Movement to be killed by white racists in the "DEEP SOUTH". However, one distinction made these murder cases very different from the others. Two of the three Civil Rights Workers killed in Mississippi, Michael Schwerner and Andrew Goodman were white men, and a white woman, Viola Liuzzo, was killed in Alabama. According to published reports, the media assumed that the KKK was responsibility for the deaths of the three Civil Rights Workers and the fact that for the first time during the modern Civil Rights Movement, white men had been murdered for the cause. The death of these three Civil Rights Workers gained National attention and started a major investigation by the FBI. Over 100 years ago in this Country, white abolitionist protested against the enslavement of my African American ancestors. The basis of their protest was that it was morally wrong for any human being to own another person regardless of the color of their skin.

Strange Fruit: The Next Generation

History does repeat its' self, as it did in the incident involving the lynching of a black man in Jasper, Texas. The man was merely looking for a ride on a hot day and he was beat up, tied to the back of a pickup, and dragged until he was dead. In spite of all the public attention, in spite of all the FBI investigations, in spite of all the HBO made for TV movies, black people continue to be murdered by white men simply because of the color of their skin. I watched the interview of the law enforcement officers that investigated the case and the local District Attorney that presented to case to the Grand Jury once the white sus- pects had been arrested. I listened as they tried to be politically correct as the attempted to explain the motive for this sickening hate crime and they could never come up with any rationale answer other than the fact that the victim was black.

According to published reports, in 1999, four white New York City police officers, working in plain clothes, fired 41 shots at an unarmed West African immigrant, Amadou Diallo. The man never had a criminal record and was shot and killed in the doorway of his Bronx apartment building. Other than the four white police officers, there were no civilian witnesses. To this day, it is still unclear why these police officers opened fire on Amadou Diallo, who was a 22-year-old street peddler in Manhattan, New York when he was killed. His relatives, friends and neighbors described Mr. Diallo as a shy, hard-working man and devout Muslim. On the other hand, three of the four white police officers involved in the shooting of Amadou Diallo, had been involved in other shootings. Reportedly, the four officers shot at Mr. Diallo, who was standing in the entrance to his apartment building, a total of 41 times, striking him 21 times, because all four of the white officers thought Mr. Diallo was reaching for a cell phone.

I was not there and the only people that actual know what happened on that late night or early morning in the Bronx, are the four white police officers and Amadou Diallo, and unfortunately Mr. Diallo is dead. However, as an ex-police officer who spent 14 years in uniform, it's hard to believe that any sane and rationale thinking person, white or black, when confronted by four men that had identified themselves as police officers, and had their guns drawn, would do anything that could lead to that person being shot at 41 times. What was the probable cause; the reasonable suspicion; or motivating factor for the confrontation between Mr. Diallo and the four white police officers? It was later determined that at the request of the police to provide identification, Mr. Diallo reached in his pants for his wallet. Reportedly, the police told Mr. Diallo not to make any sudden moves and they could not understand him because Amadou Diallo was from West Africa and he spoke broken English.

As a result of this incident, the New York City District Attorney's office conducted an independent investigation. Like the majority of African Americans, I was encouraged when the New York District Attorney presented this case to the Grand Jury, and the four white police officers were indicted for the murder of Amadou Diallo. You see the strange thing about this case was not only did not the four white police answer any of the DA's questions; these white police officer did not even try to cover up the fact that they shot an unarmed man. In some cases, the police have allegedly planted a gun or a knife on the victim to justify their claim that they were being attacked and in fear of their lives and had to use deadly force. In my opinion, just as it was in the "DEEP SOUTH" when the Civil Rights Workers were killed, it was obvious that the only reason Amadou Diallo was shot and killed was he was black. It is also my opinion that it was just as obvious that Amadou Diallo was shot 21 times, as was the Civil Rights Workers shot multiple times, to insure the victim was dead and of course dead people cannot testify.

The connection with historical injustices regarding violent crimes committed by whites against blacks in America and the murder of Amadou Diallo became evident at the trial of the four white police officers. The theory of the crime that was presented to the jury was that these white police officers had been conditioned to believe that all black males were dangerous and hate the police. Their conditioning made them react to any movement made by Amadou Diallo as a threat to their lives. A jury of their peers, or people who felt they could relate to what it must have been like for these white police officers in a black neighborhood, found the four white police officers not guilty of murder. The question that I asked myself when I heard the verdict was who in that courtroom or on that jury tried to put themselves in the shoes of Amadou Diallo as he faced four white police officers with guns drawn.

Did the verdict in the Amadou Diallo case give police in New York the right to shoot black men and ask questions after the fact? Seven years later in November 2006, according to published reports, the New York City authorities were scrambling to contain an angry backlash after police shot a group of three unarmed black men, killing one of them on his wedding day. The shooting took place after a stag party at a strip club in Queens, a few hours before Sean Bell, who was 23 years old, was due to marry the mother of his two small daughters. Mr. Bell was struck in the neck and arm and was dead on arrival at hospital. One of the other passengers, and a friend, Joseph Guzman, was in a critical condition after being hit 11 times, and yet another, Trent Benefield, was in a stable condition with wounds to his leg and buttocks. The

African American community was not only outraged over the shooting of three unarmed black men; they were also infuriated at the fact that Mr. Guzman and Mr. Benefield were shackled to their hospital beds like common criminals.

Reportedly, everyone who witnessed this incident was surprised at the apparent wildness of the pattern of shots that had been fired. The police officers claimed to have overheard one of three men mention a gun, but no weapon was ever found. The police officers on the scene fired a total of 50 bullets, and despite being fired at close range; fewer than half the shots hit the intended target, which was the car carrying the three black men. The rest of the wildly sprayed shots hit nearby cars and buildings. Reportedly, local residents jumped out of bed and huddled on the floor. One of the stray bullets shattered a window at a train station in the neighborhood. The flying glass injured two New York City Transit Department Police Officers. The shooting quickly became political with the appearance of community leaders, such as the Reverend Al Sharpton, the black Civil Rights Leader who has led previous protests against police brutality. Reportedly, Reverend Sharpton directed his assistant to the families of the three black men that had been shot. According to published reports, New York's mayor, Michael Bloomberg, urged patience, saying it was too early to draw conclusions. "We know that the officers on the scene had reason to believe an altercation involving a firearm was about to happen and were trying to stop it, and just as they did in the Amadou Diallo case, the District Attorney promised to conduct a complete investigation.

Scottsboro Boys Vs. Duke's Lacrosse Team

In 2006, the Southern town of Durham, North Carolina, home to the prestigious Duke University, was the site of trip down memory lane when three rich white boys, who were all members of the Duke University Lacrosse Team, were accused of raping a young black female college student. The young black lady, a resident of the town of Durham, at the time of the incident, was an exotic dancer that was hired by the Duke Lacrosse Team to be the entertainment for a party held at an off campus "Frat" house. After leaving the party, the young lady accused three members of the Duke Lacrosse Team of rape. After receiving the complaint from the young black female, the local Prosecutor filed rape, sexual assault and false imprisonment charges against these three rich white Duke students. When the National news media released the details of this incident to the public, all hell broke loose on both the Duke University Campus and in the black community of Durham, North Carolina.

Other Duke University students were upset because they viewed this as another case of inappropriate behavior by pampered college athletes. Duke students, both male and female, held demonstrations on campus to protest the preferential treatment of male athletes who commit violent acts against women and receive little or no punishment for their crimes. The black community, whose concerns were voiced through the local NAACP, was upset that a group of rich white boys from Duke University felt that they had the right to take advantage of a female member of their community just because she was black. The black community was not only upset with the rape and sexual assault charges, but the racial insults and threats of perverted sex acts that attacked the dignity of the victim. This indeed was a nightmarish trip down memory lane for many of the older African Americans in Durham, North Carolina that recall a time when white men could rape and sexual abuse black women and suffer little or no consequences for their actions.

White men raping black women in the "DEEP SOUTH"

History does continue to repeat its' self. Let us not forget the fact that prior to 1865 in this Country; it was a common practice for white slave owners to rape black female slaves. Young female slaves were forced to have sex with their white masters or face the possibility of being viciously assaulted or having their parents sold away or killed if they did not submit willingly. Sadly, some slave parents offered sex with their young female child to the masters in exchange for special favors. Unfortunately, this slave mentality is still affecting some ignorant black parents today as they are still offering sex with their female children for monetary favors or for illegal drugs. The even sadder issue about these acts of rape is the fact that white historians often failed to describe the violent acts as "rape" and will used the term "sexual encounters" to conceal the inhuman brutality of this disgusting behavior on the part of white slave owners.

There are white writers that have created bestselling novels based on their ability to romanticize the disgusting behavior of white slave owners, like our third President Thomas Jefferson, and change the practice of habitual rape to an ongoing relationship by adoring white lover with the female slaves who were the mothers of their bi-racial children. According to those white writers, the black slaves loved Jefferson and these white slave owners and were willing participants in what was described as passionate lovemaking. Of course in this a romance novel, and in this novel, not only did the black female slaves love "Massar" Jefferson, the children that resulted from these encounters also loved their white slave owner father and were treated like his children and not like other black slaves. However, the truth is that Jefferson may have loved his black slave mistress, but he treated his bi-racial children the same as any other black slave and sold them whenever he stood to make a profit.

In this Country, first-degree rape is determined by the fact that the perpetrator put the victim in fear of their life. The fear could result from the use of a weapon, a threat of bodily harm, mental stress or restricting the victim's freedom. Even the current sexual harassment laws in America are based on whether or not the person committing the act of inappropriate sexual behavior had the power or authority to affect the victim's life. I hope that this convinces you that the white slave owners raped my ancestors. Since this is the last book in the American Apartheid Trilogy, let me make this clear for the last time to all of you that have read my books. My African American ancestors did not enjoy being slaves and white men raped my female slave ancestors. There were never any pleasurable experiences for my black ancestors that resulted from being brought, sold and treated like an animal. Black slaves in America did whatever they needed to do to survive what can only be described as a horrific ordeal. I do not care how many times you read the books or see the movies "Gone With The Wind" and "Uncle Tom's Cabin", or you watch reruns of Shirley Temple [Black] dancing with Bill "Bojangles" Robinson, African Americans were the victims of slavery.

Duke Lacrosse Team Rape Case

When I first heard about the facts surrounding the allegations of what was labeled by the media as the "Duke Lacrosse Team Rape Case". This alleged crime involved a young black woman accusing three young white men of rape. I immediately thought about another famous rape case that involved nine black men being that were accused of allegedly "gang" raping two white women and the media called this the "Scottsboro Rape Case". Accordingly, no crime in American history produced as many trials, convictions, reversals, and retrials as did an alleged gang rape of two white women by nine black men in Scottsboro, Alabama in March 1931. For more than 20 years, the case of the "Scottsboro Boys," the name the given to the nine black men by the predominately white media that covered this event, made news in every major city in America, drawing much needed attention to the racial discrimination and unfairness in the criminal justice system in the "DEEP SOUTH".

Reportedly, the "Scottsboro Rape Case" came about as the result of two white women from Huntsville, Alabama hitching a free ride on the same train as nine young black men. Some white men that had been forced off the train by what they called a "gang" of black men went to the stationmaster in Stevenson, Alabama to report the incident. The white stationmaster wired ahead and a posse in Paint Rock, Alabama made up of dozens of angry white men with guns, rushed the train as it came to a stop and arrested every black man they could find. One of the white women, either in response to a question or on her own initiative, told one of the posse members that a gang of twelve blacks with pistols and knives had raped them. Now before I go too far with my analogy of the "Duke Lacrosse Team Rape Case" and the "Scottsboro

Rape Case", you need to understand that when I speak of the events that took place in Alabama in 1931, I am being very politically correct when I use the words "black" or "African American" when talk about the "Scottsboro Boys". I doubt very seriously if any of the local white residence living in Scottsboro, Alabama in 1931 used a term other than "colored", "Negro" or the distasteful "N" word when discussing black people. I doubt very seriously if any of the local white residence living in Scottsboro, Alabama in 1931 used a term other than "colored", "Negro" or the distasteful "N" word when discussing black people.

According to a published report, after being arrested, "The Scottsboro Boys," were tied together with plow lines, loaded on a flatbed truck, and taken from Paint Rock to a jail in Scottsboro, Alabama. While in the Scottsboro jail, the two white women who hitched a free ride identified the nine black men as being the ones that raped them on the train. A lynch mob, made up of several hundred white men, gathered outside the Scottsboro jail the night the nine black men were arrested. However, the plan to lynch the "Scottsboro Boys" was spoiled when the Governor of Alabama, Benjamin M. Miller, ordered the National Guard to protect the suspects. The trials of the "Scottsboro Boys" began twelve days after their arrest. Fearing that a single trial might support an appeal base on reversible error and overturn what was already predicated to be guilty verdicts, the State Prosecutor decided to try the defendants in groups of two or three rather that hold one trial for all nine defendants.

Reportedly, in the first trial of what was to be many trials for the "Scottsboro Boys", the Court Ordered Defense Attorney or Public Defender, only took a few minutes to cross-examine the white female rape victims who were the Prosecution's star witnesses. Some might have considered the fact that the Defense Attorney did not subject these white female to an abrasive cross-examination as being a prudent strategy. What if they broke down on the witness stand and started to cry as they recalled this alleged rape by a gang of black men? However, it was later determined that it was not brilliant strategy of the part of the Defense Attorney, it was inadequate representation. You see, not only was the Defense Attorney lax in his cross-examinations of the white female victims; he did not even bother to cross-examine the white doctors that examined the alleged rape victims. The only evidence offered by the defense was the testimony of the defendants. Further evidence of an inadequate defense was the fact the Defense Attorney did not even bother to make a closing argument. A guilty verdict in the first trial was announced while the second trial was still underway. The large crowd outside the courthouse let out a roar of approval that was clearly heard by the second jury inside.

I remember how I cheered when I heard the not guilty verdict in the O.J. Simpson murder case. The white people who worked with me were appalled that I would actual cheer out loud, because O.J. was found not guilty. The decision in the O.J. Simpson murder case divided this Country along racial lines; 77% of white America thought he was guilty and 77% of black America thought he was innocent. I remember watching the HBO Special called "Black and White"; they interviewed this white woman, who at first glance appeared to be very intelligent, sophisticated and classy about her opinion of the O.J. verdict. This white woman said she was upset at O.J. because she thought he was one of the "good ones", and she had accepted him as being part of white America. To be perfectly honest with you, in the black community it did not really matter whether O.J. was guilty or innocent. What really mattered to me, as an African American, was that in a high profiled case that involved a black man accused of murdering a white woman and a white male Jew, the black man had not been dragged from the local jail by a mob of white men and lynched. Remember, this was the tradition during the "JIM CROW ERA" in this Country. Secondly, based on the case presented by the Prosecutor, there was not enough evidence to find this black man guilty beyond a reasonable doubt, which is the standard that during this same "JIM CROW ERA" was limited only to white citizens.

The reason I, along with millions of other African Americans cheered when the jury foremen in the O.J. murder case read the not guilty verdict, was because we can still remember the "Scottsboro Boy's Rape Case". We remember what happened when two white women in Alabama falsely accused nine black men of rape and based on that accusation and their testimony in court, the nine men were found guilty. The story of the "Scottsboro Boys" is one of the most shameful examples of injustice in our nation's history. It makes clear that in the "DEEP SOUTH" of the 1930s, jurors were not willing to afford a black man charged with raping a white woman the usual presumption of innocence. According to published reports, the jurors in April 1933 that had just voted to sentence one of the "Scottsboro Boys" to death were seen laughing as they emerged from the jury room. Maybe this will help some of my white readers understand why I cheered after the O.J. verdict.

Roundup the Usual Suspects

You could say that what happened in 1931 to the "Scottsboro Boys" was just a sign of the times. I understand that things have changed and the racial mentality of America has made a tremendous amount of progress. Yet, it was less than 25 years ago in South Carolina that a white woman, Susan Smith, accused a black man of forcing her from her car and taking her two children. During this same time, almost the same situation happened in Boston, Massachusetts when a white man, Charles "Chuck" Stuart, accused a black man of carjacking. Stuart told the police that during a carjacking, a black man killed his pregnant wife when he shot her in the head and shot him in the stomach. Without any hesitation, the hatred associated with racism reared its ugly head in both cases. The police in South Carolina setup roadblocks and arrested every black male old enough to drive a car.

The police in Boston searched every black neighborhood in the vicinity of the crime and locked up every black man that fit the general description given by the murdered victim's husband. Police found a young man, Willie Bennett, who fit Stuart's description. Stuart identified Bennett as his attacker in a lineup. However, the case against Bennett abruptly collapsed, when Charles Stuart's brother Matthew identified Charles as Carol's killer. Matthew admitted that he had driven to meet Stuart that night to help him commit what he had been told was to be an insurance fraud. Upon arrival, Matthew said that he had seen that Carol had been shot, and that his brother had shot himself to make it appear as a carjacking. Matthew took the gun and a bag of valuables, including the couple's wedding rings, and threw them off the Pines River Bridge in Revere. Some of the items, including the gun, were later recovered. In both cases, the white media jumped to the conclusion that a black man committed these crimes and it was all over the TV and newspapers. It was later determined that Susan Smith killed her children. She is now in prison serving a life sentence. Charles Stuart committed suicide before he could be charged with is wife's death.

Over 50 years after the "Scottsboro Case", these two white citizens never gave it a second that when they accused a black man of committing these crimes and the media never hesitated in reporting these allegations as being nothing but the truth. Fifty years after the "Scottsboro Rape Case", white America reaction to the news that a black man committed a crime against a white woman has not changed. Most of white America took it for granted the black men accused of these crimes were guilty and the white community was enraged over the media reports that black men had committed these disgusting crimes against white women. The sad part is that the law enforcement agencies that received these accusations from white citizens did not stop for a second to consider the possibility that the white citizens reporting these incidents may not be telling the truth. As fate would have it, after the police, with malice aforethought, erroneously arrested unsuspecting black men for the crimes reported by these two white citizens; the police would later find that the two white citizens did in fact kill the victims themselves. What happened to the black men that were arrested for these crimes and how did the law enforcement agencies un-ring the bell police harassment in the black community? After a bullet strikes a target, the damage is done.

In 1996, a situation developed in my office when a white female co-worker burst out my office crying. First, my white female supervisor, who saw my co-worker leave my office, came running into my office and started angrily shouting at me, "what did you do to make her cry?" Before I could respond, the white male Assistant Director, who had also seen my co-worker crying, stormed into my office demanding to know why I had made my white female co-worker cry. When I recall this incident, I guess it was a good thing that I was not in the "DEEP SOUTH" in the early 1900s, because I might have been taken out and lynched or at least tied down and whipped. However, before I started to defend myself, my white female co-worker came to my rescue. She explained that it was her fault. She stated that she was frustrated with something the Director had said to her and took her frustration out on me. When I told her that I had not done anything and that she needed to stop yelling at me and leave my office, she started crying and immediately left my office.

Again, we witness evidence of the mindset of white America; white woman screaming; black man in the area; therefore the black man must be guilty of doing something harmful to the white women. How could an incident like this happen in an office environment that can best be described as being "normal" and the intelligence level of the people in this office rated as being above average? Unlike the black men who were falsely accused in the "Scottsboro Rape Case", I was not a stranger to my accusers. The white female supervisor and the white Assistant Director had known me for over four years. In fact, my white female co-worker and I started to work in this office at the same time. Just as the police had done in South Carolina and Detroit, my white female supervisor and the white Assistant Director, made a feeble attempts at an apology. After jumping to the wrong conclusion; after a lame attempt at an apology; my white co-workers added insult to injury by suggesting that I look at how things appeared from their perspective. Do white people still think that the white way is always the right way?

Son-of-a -Rabbi

In 2005, Moshe Khaver, the19 year old son of a Jewish Rabbi from Baltimore, Maryland was sentenced to 5 years in prison for an assault charge. In 2003, the Rabbi's son assaulted another young man because he failed to pay him for a $20 bag of marijuana. Moshe used his father's car to run over this young man. The victim of this assault suffered injuries to his head, lower back, arms and a leg, resulting in partial paralysis and obstructed vision in one of his eyes. The historical impact of this incident is that after being sentenced to 5 years in prison, the Rabbi's son was placed in protective custody in the Baltimore City Jail rather than being sent to a Maryland Division of Correction's facility. Prior to his trial, the Rabbi's son was detained at the Baltimore City Jail. However, in the State of Maryland, anyone convicted of a crime that receives a sentence of longer than 18 months is to be sent to a prison rather than being detained in a local jail or detention center. I worked for the Maryland Department of Public Safety and Correctional Services for over 30 years and I know for a fact that in Maryland offenders that receive a sentence of longer than 18 months are placed under the jurisdiction of the Division of Correction and are assigned to one of the State's prisons.

In a State, were the correctional system has a prison population that is 70% African American; the question is why did this white Jew receive preferential treatment? The answer is simple. He was white and he was Jewish. However, based on an article that appeared in the Baltimore Sun Newspaper, Mary Ann Saar, former Secretary, Maryland Department of Public Safety and Correctional Services attempted provide a different answer to question regarding the special treatment received by this white Jewish inmate. Ms. Saar wrote that the teen's first request for parole was recently denied as being the reason he was not moved from jail to a prison. A public safety spokesman said that Moshe Khaver was initially granted parole in December 2005, less than 4 months after his August 15, 2005. The next question is why the Parole Commission would grant parole to an inmate after just 4 months of a 5-year sentence. Again, the answer is very simple. The man is white and Jewish.

The decision to grant parole for Khaver was reversed on September 22, 2005, a week before that reversal the Sun reported that Khaver appeared to be being treated differently than most other inmates. According to Mark Vernarelli, a spokesman for the Department of Public Safety, "the decision to keep Mr. Khaver at Central Booking was a sound and absolutely proper one." In a letter to the Sun Paper dated September 29, 2005, Ms. Saar responded, "I can state categorically there is nothing different about Mr. Khaver, and he is not being treated differently than other inmates." Ms. Saar wrote that Khaver's stay at Central Booking was approved only because of the "projected short time of his incarceration," and she criticized The Sun Paper for characterizing his case as "special treatment." Ms. Saar stated that there were other "unique circumstances resulting from his sentencing" that played into Khaver's extended stay at the pretrial facility, but did not elaborate.

It came as no surprise to me when local black lawyers and others familiar with the criminal justice system stated that several of Secretary Saar's assertions made no sense. Bridget Duffy Shepherd, the Circuit Court Chief of Baltimore's Public Defenders, said that even offenders with sentences as short as a few months are not held at Central Booking (the local detention center). Reports about Khaver's treatment angered Maryland Circuit Judge Evelyn O. Cannon, who wrote to Secretary Saar in September 2005 demanding answers. Judge Cannon wrote that the Khaver situation "plays directly into the very deep perception in this city that race is a major factor in the operation of our criminal justice system." From the other side of this issue, Howard L. Cardin, Khaver's Attorney, said that the moving of his client to a prison on a Jewish holiday sounded "strange and clandestine" and that he would look into the situation. In addition, one of the visiting clergy for Khaver was Sander Goldberg, a rabbi who gave the benediction at former Governor Robert L. Ehrlich Jr.'s swearing-in ceremony, and who Gov. Ehrlich named a State Tax Judge. In 2004, on Rabbi Goldberg's recommendation, Ehrlich appointed Khaver to a State Juvenile Justice Advisory Council. This appointment was made after Khaver had pleaded guilty in June 2003 of assault. In addition, Khaver violated his Court-Ordered Pretrial Home Detention to attend his first Council Meeting.

I will be the first to admit that the criminal justice system in the State of Maryland is far too lenient on criminals. The same criminals that have recently been released from jail commit far too many offenses. Having said that, there is no way a black inmate would have been treated like Moshe Khaver. Reportedly, because he required a strict kosher diet, his mother was allowed to bring his meals to the jail every day. In addition, Khaver was housed in protective custody and kept away from any contact with the general jail population because his family was afraid that the black inmates would attack him because he was a young white Jew. Many of the African Americans that are incarcerated are Muslim or convert to the Muslim religion after being incarcerated. The Muslim inmates receive no special treatment or protection from the general inmate population. The American Civil Liberties Union had to go to court on behalf of the "Black" Muslims in order for them to be granted permission to receive special meals while incarcerated. Having worked in the correctional system, I know that the special diet for these Muslims consists of meals of vegetables, fruits, milk and white bread. If the Muslims refuse to eat this "special diet", they have no other option but to eat the food served to the non-Muslim prison population.

Khaver's lawyer complained that his client was moved from jail to prison on a Jewish holiday. Again, the Muslims receive no special consideration from the correctional system for any of their Holy Days. As a former law enforcement officer and employee of the DPSCS, you can understand my frustration when I say that crime never takes a day off. However, under normal circumstances, if the traffic officers at the jail were made aware of the fact that Khaver was a Jew and that he requested not to be moved on a Jewish holiday, his request may have been granted. However, with all the negative publicity surrounding the "special treatment" of Moshe Khaver, he was going to be transported on the next bus leaving from the jail to the Division of Corrections (DOC). Due to the overcrowding in the prison system, the Parole Commission has been forced to grant early paroles to inmates. However, most inmates serve at least of third of their sentence before they submit a request for a parole hearing. Moshe Khaver was granted parole in record time. The only reason he remained in jail is because a news reporter got wind of his early release and notified the judge in Khaver case and the request for parole was immediately revoked.

Khaver's release was the direct result of having friends in high places. Rabbi Khaver is a friend of Rabbi Goldberg who is a friend of Governor Erhlich. That is how the justice system works if you are white and you have the ear of a powerful politician.

My Cousin Louie

If you have read my other books, you know that in order to make my point, I like to add some of my own personal experiences. If you have not read them, I strong recommend that you read *"American Apartheid"* and *"No Land No Mule No Freedom, American Apartheid the saga continues"*. In the late 1980s, my cousin was involved in fatal car accident. As a result of a collision with another car, he was critically injured and the two people in the other car were killed. My cousin was flown to the shock trauma unit at Maryland University Hospital and remained in intensive care for weeks. After several weeks in the intensive care unit, his condition had improved enough for him to have visitors other than his immediate family members. I went to visit my cousin in the hospital. I am an ex-police office and that prompted me to ask him what happened. He looked at me with tears in his eyes and said that he honestly could not remember and I believed him. Although he is my cousin and I love him like a brother, as an experienced law enforcement officer, I have interviewed enough drivers after accidents to know when their lying or telling the truth.

Before I go too far, let me make it clear that my cousin was no saint. At the time of this incident, he was a young black man in his prime with a hardy appetite for life. As a result of this hardy appetite he was known to indulge himself with fast cars, even faster women and he had been known to experiment with several kinds of controlled dangerous substances (CDS) and mixed them alcohol. It is a strong possibility that at the time of this accident, my cousin could have been driving faster than the posted speed limit. In addition, his ability to operate a motor vehicle could have been impaired by alcohol and/or drugs and he could have been exhausted from a night on the town fallen asleep behind the wheel of his car. We can speculate. We can "what if" from now until the next millennium, but no one on this earth knows exactly what happened to cause this tragic accident. Yet, as a result of the accident the State's Attorney charged my cousin with vehicular homicide.

Dead Men Tell No Tales

The accident happened earlier in the morning on a deserted stretch of highway and there were no witnesses. My cousin could not remember what happened and the only other witnesses were dead. Due to the fact that he spent several weeks in intensive care fighting for his life, the police who were conducting the accident investigation were not allowed to talk to my cousin. The police were not allowed to ask questions about the accident or gather any physical evidence, such as a blood test to determine whether my cousin was under the influence of drugs or alcohol at the time of the accident. There were no witnesses and no evidence that my cousin's ability to operate his vehicle was impaired. This was a very tragic incident. Two people died, another was nearly killed, and my cousin will be both physically and mentally scarred for life. The injuries he suffered as a result of this accident have healed. Although my cousin still cannot remember exactly what happened, the fact that two people died in an accident he was involved in is a memory that will never go away.

It is my very strong opinion, as a former police officer, that this case should have been dismissed. If anything based on the evidence, my cousin could have been charged with negligent driving or at the most reckless driving. Negligent driving because he failed to control his vehicle resulting in an accident. Reckless driving if the police were able to determine if there were other circumstances such as excessive speed or disobeying a traffic signal that caused the accident. There was no way that the State's Attorney had enough evidence to support of charge of vehicular homicide. If they had no evidence, why did they charge him? Again, there is a very simple answer. The two people that were killed were both white. O.J. Simpson may have gotten away with killing two white people in California, but in the State of Maryland, a black man involved in the death of a white person is going to jail. That is not an opinion; that is a fact. If you do not believe me there has been some extensive research conducted on the African American inmates that have been executed or are currently on death row in Maryland. The research determined that the majority of these men have been found guilty of committing a violent crime against a white person.

A different set of rules for Jews

Khaver, the white drug-dealing son of a Jewish Rabbi used a car to run over a man because he owed him $20 dollars for a bag of marijuana. Rather than being charged with attempted murder, this white man confessed to the crime, made a deal with the States Attorney, and was charged with the lesser charge of aggravated assault. There were no witnesses against my cousin, but the victim was available to testify against Mr. Khaver and the judge and jury would have been able to see the mangled body of the victim. They would have been able to listen to the victim portray Mr. Khaver, the son of a Jewish Rabbi, as a common drug dealer. Let us see, the States Attorney offered Mr. Khaver 5 years for a plea of guilty to aggravated assault verses 10 to 15 years for attempted murder. Of course, Mr. Khaver was delighted and he took the plea bargain. When it comes to drug dealing and white drug dealers, the white community is in denial. To most upper and middle class white people in America, the use of illegal drugs and drug dealers is a social disorder that is associated with the black inner city neighborhoods.

I still remember the line from the movie the "Godfather" when the late Marlon Brando's character, Don Corleone, said he would only sell drugs in the "colored" neighborhood because they were animals. Even today, these same upper and middle class white people believe that the only way their children are exposed to CDS is by their association with African Americans. Khaver was labeled a drug dealer, which made him an embarrassment to his white Jewish community. The legal system would have to send a message to other white drug dealers and that made Khaver's guilty plea a "bargain" for him. If he had not pleaded guilty, Khaver would have been convicted of attempted murder and his sentence would have been at least 10 years in prison. The State's Attorney also gave my cousin a choice. Going to trial and being found guilty of 2 counts of vehicular homicide and receiving a mandatory sentence of 25 years without the possibility of parole years or he could plead guilty to 2 counts of vehicular manslaughter and receive a sentence of 10 to 15 years with the possibility of parole.

There was no "bargain" when the States Attorney presented the choices to my cousin. If the States Attorney's Office had a solid case against my cousin, they would never have bothered to offer him the opportunity to plead guilty to a lesser charge. If there had been just one witness or one piece of physical evidence or if my cousin had made a statement that would have indicated he was at fault in this accident, the State's Attorney would been him hauled into court he would have been and found guilty of two counts of vehicular homicide. The only reason my cousin was offered a plea was that the States Attorney was afraid to take even the slightest of chance that some liberal minded judge or jury might find my cousin innocent. For the State's Attorney this plea bargain was a win-win situation. As we often say in the black neighborhood, in this plea bargain from the States Attorney, my cousin had two chances of winning, and they were "slim and none" and "slim had just left town". Although, we did not want to accept it, my cousin pleaded guilty to the lesser charge of vehicular manslaughter and served 8 years in prison. He knew that there was less than a 10% chance in this State that a predominantly white jury or a white judge would find him innocent in the death of two white people.

You might be asking the question, based on the lack of evidence in this case, why did not my cousin take his chances in a trial. How could any judge or any jury find him guilty beyond a reasonable doubt of vehicular homicide, which is just a kinder term for murder, when there was no conclusive evidence? With a good lawyer in a fair justice system, it should be easy to establish reasonable doubt. My cousin had to decide if he wanted to spend the next 25 years in jail, which would have meant he would be close to 50 years old when got out or take plea and be out jail in his mid-30s. We had all watched the O.J. Simpson trial. We all watched as the Prosecution presented tons of circumstantial evidence against O.J. Yet, and in the end the jury could not find him guilty beyond a reasonable doubt. The O.J. Simpson trial cost the citizens of the State of California millions of dollars. Anne Arundel County would have spent a million dollars in an attempt to convict my cousin of killing two white people. Unlike O.J. Simpson, my cousin did not have a legal team lead by Johnnie Cochran.

White Justice Vs. Black Justice

We grew up in Anne Arundel County, which is a rural area of Maryland where conservative white males dominate the political system. Just as the court had to send a message to Mr. Khaver, a white drug dealer, we fully realized that the white political forces in Anne Arundel County definitely had to send a message to the black community. The message would have been loud and clear that Anne Arundel County will never allow an African American that is directly involved in the death of a white person to get away "Scott Free". For those of you that are not familiar with the term "Scott Free", in 1846, slaves Dred Scott and his wife Harriet filed suit for their freedom in the St. Louis Circuit Court. This suit began an eleven-year legal fight that ended in the U.S. Supreme Court, which issued a landmark decision declaring that Dred Scott and his wife had to remain slaves. Reportedly, this Supreme Court decision contributed to rising tensions between the free and slave States just before the American Civil War.

In 2005, there was an incident in Anne Arundel County. A young white beating a young beat a young black man to death and the white man was charged with manslaughter. The young white man was found not guilty in an Anne Arundel County Court by a white judge and an all-white jury. Again, this is another case of black America history repeating its' self. How can we still manage to have a white judge and an all-white jury in a trial involving the death of a black man who was killed by a white man? When the case was originally presented to the State's Attorney they refused to indict the white man citing insufficient evidence as the reason. It was only after pressure from the NAACP and the possibility that this case might be turned over to the FBI and investigated as a hate crime, that the Anne Arundel County State's Attorney made the decision to indict the young white man for manslaughter. Yet again, a message was sent to the black community. The same message that had been sent many years ago when a white farmer struck and killed an African American waitress with is cane. No white juries in this State will punish a white person for killing a black person, no matter what the circumstances.

During this same time in Maryland, a young white soldier carjacks a young black man's car and drives off with the man's son. The black man forces the door open and attempts to pull the white man from his car. After being dragged along the pavement, the black man finally had to let go and the white man drove away with the black man's car and with his son fastened in a car seat in the rear. The police eventually caught the young white solider and the child was found in the car unharmed. However, the black man was severely injured and it was reported that he could possibly lose his legs. Carjacking has become an epidemic. In an attempt to control this violent crime, the Federal Government made carjacking a Federal offense. In the carjacking cases that involved a black suspect, the focus of the media attention was on the heinous act committed by a heartless criminal. In this case, the focus shifts from the criminal act committed by the young white boy, to the fact that the black man left his car running with his son in the back seat while he went into a convenience store.

The white media made it seem as if this black man had intentionally invited this white boy to steal his car and take his child who had been abandoned in the rear of the car. The media even suggested that the black man be charged with leaving his vehicle unattended and reported to child welfare for leaving his son alone while he went into a convenience store. To add insult to the trauma of a black man who thought he was about to have his son kidnapped. A black man who faced the possibility of losing his legs, the media portrayed this white carjacker as a depressed young solider, recently home from the war, who was having problem coping with his return to society and his eventual return to the war in Iraq. I remember how angry I was when this young black thug carjacked this young Asian woman's car with her child inside. This monster dragged this woman to her death because she hung on to the seat beat in an attempt to save her child. My sympathy went to the mother and all my rage to the black man that killed her. Why is there a difference in the direction of sympathy and rage when the carjacker changes from black to white?

In Ohio in 2005, a small black community's protest of KKK or Neo-Nazi group's racist demonstration in a local neighborhood park erupted into violence. Reportedly, the white Chief of Police who issued the permit to this group of white racists pledged the Department's protection and he was quick to point the finger at "Black Gang" activity as the source of the violent protest. Yet, when the media showed the films of the protest, you could clearly see African American men, women, boys and girls displaying their anger as a result of being provoked by these white racists were not members of any gang. Not only were these black citizens outraged by the group of white racists that dared to invade an African American community, they were also displaying their frustration with their local Government for supporting and allowing this group of bigots to conduct this demonstration in their neighborhood.

Why would any metropolitan police department issue a permit to a white neo-Nazi or Klan organization in America to conduct a so-called "white power" march through a black community under the guise of a peaceful demonstration? Why is it in America that we never see the Klan or Neo-Nazi groups march through the streets of a Jewish neighborhood? How dare anyone associate a gathering sponsored by the KKK or Neo-Nazi with the term "peaceful demonstration"! The police in the "DEEP SOUTH", to deter the peaceful demonstration of the Civil Rights Workers used attack dogs, nightsticks and fire hoses. Now, how dare the Chief of this Ohio Police Department or any other law enforcement agency pledge their protection for a group of white racists?

Why is it when white people act in ways that degrades and demeans the character of African Americans in general, they want us to examine the rationale for their nauseating behavior from their perspective. Yet, for years, white America has failed to look at the historical events that helped shape this Country from a black perspective. Major historical events such as the Revolutionary War, slavery and the Civil War and all the other Wars that American have fought and died in, have rarely been totally inclusive of the role of African American perspective. I was 45 years old when I started conducting the research for my books and I have discovered more about black history in America in the last 15 years than I learned in the first 45 years. I wrote the American Apartheid trilogy to change attitudes and to encourage both white and black Americans to look at history in more than one color and more than one perspective.

Back to Scottsboro Vs. Duke Lacrosse

Back to the "Scottsboro Boys", reportedly, when four trials were over, eight of the nine black men had been convicted and sentenced to death. A mistrial was declared in the case of one of the black men, a twelve-year old whose last name was Wright; I do not think we are related. The judge declared a mistrial in Wright's case when eleven of the jurors held out for the death penalty for the twelve year old. According to published reports, it was the Communist Party and not the NAACP that provided a much-needed legal defense in the "Scottsboro Rape Case". Unfortunately, it was reported that because the rape of a white women by a "gang" of black men was highly sensitive and could have explosive racial implications, NAACP thought it was in its best interest, not to get involved in the "Scottsboro Rape Case". All I can say is that if this is true, shame on you NAACP.

According to published reports, the Communist Party, through its legal team, the International Labor Defense (ILD), pronounced the case against the "Scottsboro Boys" a "murderous frame-up", petitioned the court in Alabama and eventually named the Attorneys of record for the "Scottsboro Rape Boys". In addition, the NAACP finally came to the realization that the "Scottsboro Boys" were most likely innocent and that the NAACP's leadership in the case would have large public relations benefit in the African American community. However, the "Scottsboro Boys" decided to allow the white ILD Attorneys from the Communist Party represent them rather than the white Attorneys that the NAACP hired to represent them. The ILD Attorneys appealed the convictions in the "Scottsboro Rape Cases" to the U.S. Supreme Court, and as a result of the appeals, eight of the nine men were granted retrials.

Just as in the "Duke Lacrosse Team Rape Case", the defense lawyers and the Prosecutor in the "Scottsboro Rape Case" also gained a lot of positive and negative attention form the media. According to published reports, the Prosecutor in the "Scottsboro Rape Case" retrials was Alabama's newly elected Attorney General Thomas Knight Jr. What made this noteworthy is that Knight's father, Thomas Knight, Sr., had authored the Alabama Supreme Court decision upholding the original convictions. The ILD selected two Attorneys to represent the Scottsboro Boys in the retrials. Samuel Liebowitzto, a New York Criminal Attorney who had secured a record of 75 acquittals and one hung jury in seventy-eight murder trials, was the lead Defense Attorney, and Joseph Brodsky, the ILD's Chief Attorney, was selected to assist Liebowitz.

According to published reports, in the second trial of one of the "Scottsboro Boys", the defense pointed out a flaw in the justice system that had plagued African Americans since the end of slavery. The Defense Attorney, Mr. Liebowitz, moved to overturn all the indictments against the "Scottsboro Boys" on the ground that "Negroes", had been systematically excluded from juries. Throughout the "JIM CROW ERA" in the "DEEP SOUTH", it was impossible for an African American to face a jury of his or her peers or to be tried by a black judge. An African American could not serve on a jury because the rules required that a juror be a registered voter and blacks were not allowed to register to vote. In a few Southern States where African Americans were allowed to register to the voter's registration test was so difficult that it required a college law degree to pass it. Therefore, the number of registered black voters was few and far between.

A jury of their peers

Unfortunately, the local Jury Commissioner, whose position it is to select qualified jurors, failed to include the few blacks that did pass the test to become registered voters, in the pool of eligible jurors. Reportedly, Mr. Liebowitz raised some eyebrows by questioning the veracity of local Jury Commissioners. He created even more of a stir when he insisted that the Prosecutor tried to stop him from calling black witnesses, who Mr. Liebowitz had called to show that they had never served on juries. Reportedly, the local white citizens took Mr. Liebowitz tactics as a personal insult. It was one thing for this white man to defend these black rapists, but it was another, unforgivable thing for this white Attorney to come to Alabama and attack their social order and way of life. It came as no surprise that the judge denied Mr. Liebowitz's motion to quash the indictments. Just by the fact that these black men were receiving a trial, the judicial branch of the Government in Alabama felt it was being more than fair to the "Scottsboro Boys".

Just as in the "Scottsboro Rape Case", the Defense Attorneys in the "Duke Lacrosse Rape Case" attacked the character of the alleged rape victim. The young black female in the "Duke Lacrosse Rape Case" was an "Exotic Dancer". I was not there on the night the alleged rape or sexual assault took place. I never like to make assumptions, but the black female "Exotic Dancer" or stripper, that hired out to entertain an all-male audience at a private party, may have sent signals that lead to some of the inappropriate behavior on the part of the members of the all-white Duke Lacrosse Team. In addition to the black female being called a stripper by the media, the white police officer, who was first on the scene of this alleged rape, made a public statement noting the fact that the alleged victim was intoxicated. The black female was cast in the media as a drunken stripper, who had charged these clean cut All American white boys from Duke University with rape. On the other, in the "Scottsboro Rape Case", according to published reports, the Defense Attorney provided evidence that one of the white females that accused the nine black men of gang rape, Victoria "Big Leg" Price, was an adulterous prostitute and liar.

DNA

Another similar twist in these two rape cases was the fact that DNA from the sperm taken from the black female victim in the "Duke Lacrosse Team Rape Case" was proven to have come from a black male. The DNA from the sperm found on the white female victim in the "Scottsboro Rape Case" was proven to have come from a white male. In the "Scottsboro Rape Case", according to published reports, the white female victim, Victoria Price, inflamed the all-white jury when she added to her original account of the rape that while she was being penetrated, her attacker told her that when he pulled his "thing" out, "you will have a black baby." Reportedly, after she made that statement it was hard for the judge to maintain order in the courtroom full of angry white men. In the 1930s in America, this ignorant white woman, who was alleged to be a prostitute and adulteress, had played on the white man's greatest fear that a white woman might have a black baby after being raped by a black man. It is no wonder the "Scottsboro Boys" were not dragged from the courthouse and lynched.

After the allegation, it was determined that the black female victim in the "Duke Lacrosse Team Rape" was in fact pregnant. The judge in the "Duke Lacrosse Team Rape" case ordered the black female victim to submit to a paternity test to determine if any of the three white Duke Lacrosse Team members was the father. The judge in the case was not trying to gather the DNA to support the victim; the evidence was gathered to support the white boy's claims of innocent. According to published reports, the black female rape victim could not name the father of her baby. The only thing that was established from the DNA test was the father was black and not white. The defense in the "Scottsboro Rape Case" had established the fact that one of the white victims was a prostitute and that the DNA found on her could have come from any number of white men. All the judges and all the juries in the all the "Scottsboro Boys" trials never gave any consideration to the fact that Victoria "Big Leg" Price, was an adulterous prostitute and liar.

What happened to Reasonable Doubt?

According to published reports, in 1933, two years after the first trial, and the Defense Attorneys for the "Scottsboro Boys" called their final and most dramatic witness, Ruby Bates. In the months before the trial, Bates' whereabouts was a mystery. Mr. Liebowitz announced that he was resting his case, then approached the bench and asked for a short recess. Minutes later National Guardsmen open the back doors of the courtroom, and to the surprise of all the spectators and the Prosecutor, in walked Ruby Bates. Reportedly, under direct examination, Ruby Bates said that a troubled conscience and the advice of famous New York minister Harry Emerson Fosdick prompted her to return to Alabama to tell the truth about what happened on March 25, 1931. Ms. Bates said that there was no rape, that none of the defendants touched her or even spoke to her, and that the accusations of rape were made after Victoria Price told her "to frame up a story" to avoid morals charges. Finally, the truth was told under oath in a courtroom. One of the white women that had allegedly been raped had changed her story. In a fair and equal justice system where reasonable doubt is the standard for determining quilt or innocence, you would think that Ms. Bates' statement would have been enough to free all the "Scottsboro Boys".

According to published reports, on cross-examination, the Prosecutor, Knight, ripped into Bates, confronting her both with her conflicting testimony in the first trials and accusations that her new versions of events had been bought with new clothes and other Communist Party gifts. He demanded to know whether he had not told her months before in his office that he would "punish anyone who made her swear falsely" and that he "did not want to burn any person that was not guilty." "I think you did," Bates answered. Why was it so easy for these white Southerners to believe Ms. Bates when she said that she had been gang raped by nine black men? Yet, these same white Southerners were quick to brand Ms. Bates to be a liar and a sellout to her race when she told the truth. The inexcusable reaction to Ms. Bates testimony in the 1933 trial was the fact that based on the character of Victoria "Big Legs" Price; everyone knew that Ms. Bates was telling the truth. The problem was that it had been the tradition in the "DEEP SOUTH" during the "JIM CROW ERA" that white men had to protect the honor of white women who had been violated by a black person. It did not matter if the white women were right or wrong or if she was telling the truth.

It is almost unbelievable how two rape cases can have such similarities. There were two white female victims in the "Scottsboro Rape Case" and although only one black female was allegedly raped, there was a second black female "Exotic Dancer" at this private party who original stated that she heard the victim screaming as she was being raped and/or sexually assaulted by the three white boys. The first time I saw the other "Exotic Dancer", Kim Roberts, interviewed on TV after rape charges had been filed against the three members of the all-white Duke Lacrosse Team, she advised the media that she was not sure that her girlfriend had been the victim of rape and/or sexual assault. According to the team of Defense Attorneys for the Lacrosse Team, Ms. Roberts told them that she did not believe the accuser's allegations. The Duke Lacrosse Team Defense Attorneys said that Ms. Roberts changed her story to gain favorable treatment in a criminal case against her. In addition, according to the defense lawyer, Ms. Robert e-mailed a New York public relations firm, asking in her letter for advice on "how to spin this to my advantage."

According to published reports, Ms. Roberts stated that she could not remember all the faces of the white boys that were indicated for rape and sexual assault, but said she did positively identify one of them, whom she described as the "little skinny one." Reportedly, she said, "I was looking him right in the eyes." Although she would not talk extensively about the party, she confirmed some of what the victim told police, including that the women initially left the party after one of the players threatened to sodomize the women with a broomstick. Ms. Roberts went on to state that the white boys at the party had called them all sorts of names, threatened bodily harm and hurled racial insults at them as they were leaving the house were the party was held. Just as in the first trial of the "Scottsboro Boys", Ruby Bates, the other white female victim, agreed with everything Victoria Price, the other white female victim, testified too. Ms. Bates changed her story and it did not really help the "Scottsboro Boys". Kim Roberts changed her story and it did not hurt the white boys in the "Duke Lacrosse Team Rape Case".

Another comparison in these two cases is the fact that any local white judge that made a ruling that was favorable to the "Scottsboro Boys" was voted out of office. On June 22, 1933 after Ruby Bates changed, her story on the witness stand, Judge James Horton, convened court in his hometown of Athens, Alabama to hear a defense motion for a new trial. Reportedly, Judge Horton was convinced that Victoria Price was lying and not only was her story full of inconsistencies, other witnesses as well as the medical evidence did not corroborate her story. Reportedly, a white doctor who examined the victims, but refused to testify for fear of losing practice in Scottsboro, advised Judge Horton that he was sure the victims had not been raped. According to published reports, Judge Horton believed one should "let justice be done, though the heavens may fall", and he shocked the courtroom when he announced that he was setting aside the verdict and death sentence, and ordering a new trial for one of the "Scottsboro Boys". Judge Horton, who was unopposed the previous time he ran, lost his judgeship in the next election.

Mike Nifong, the Durham, North Carolina District Attorney, who was very aggressive in charging three white members of the Duke Lacrosse Team with rape and sexual assault, was replaced. A judge in Durham ruled that some of the tactics used by Mr. Nifong during his pursuit of a rape indictment against the three white Duke Lacrosse Players were unethical. Reportedly, the North Caroline Bar Association had filed sanctions against Mr. Nifong for his behavior in this case. You need to understand that during the investigation of the "Duke Lacrosse Team Rape Case", Mr. Nifong was campaigning for re-election. Based on the racial impact of this incident, Mr. Nifong promised his constituents in the black community of Durham, that just because the suspects in this case were rich white students from Duke University, this case would not be swept under the rug. Unfortunately, Mr. Nifong forgot just how powerful; just how much political clout; and just how much money the predominately white Alumni of Duke University could muster in defense of these rich white boys that were members of the lacrosse team. Mr. Nifong also forgot that Duke University was the largest employer in the Durham area. Aside from the local NAACP and the few blacks that supported the victim's family, the remainder of the black and white communities in Durham was not going to go against the people that sign their paychecks.

On February 15, 1935, the United States Supreme Court heard arguments in the two of the "Scottsboro Boys" cases. Mr. Liebowitz argued that the convictions should be overturned because Alabama excluded blacks from its jury rolls, which is a violation of the equal protection clause of the Constitution. Six weeks later the U.S. Supreme Court announced their decision in the two cases; they unanimously held that the Alabama system of jury selection was unconstitutional and they reversed the convictions of the two "Scottsboro Boys". The similarities in these two cases continues; the U.S. Supreme Court reversed the convictions of two of the "Scottsboro Boys", and the Durham District Attorney that replaced Mike Nifong dropped the rape charges against the three white members of the Duke Lacrosse Team. Through either paroles or escapes, all of the Scottsboro Boys eventually found their way out of Alabama. Two of the original nine went on to participate in the writing of books about their lives. "Scottsboro Boy", was published in 1950 while Mr. Patterson was still a fugitive. Shortly after its publication, the FBI arrested Mr. Patterson, but the Governor of Michigan refused Alabama's extradition request. Mr. Norris published his book, "The Last of the Scottsboro Boys", in 1979, and ten years later, on January 23, 1989, the last of the Scottsboro Boys was dead. The story of the Scottsboro Boys lives on through the efforts of such writer as

Douglas O. Linder who was responsible for most of the descriptive facts and information contained in this chapter.

Navy Midshipman or Scottsboro Boy

In 2006, Lamar S. Owens Jr., a black Naval Academy Senior Midshipman, who was the star quarterback on the football team, was accused of raping; whom we can only assume was a white female cadet. The law does not allow the media to publish any information about the alleged victim of a rape. That is strange. In the Duke Lacrosse Team rape case, the media printed as much about the alleged black victim as they did the alleged white suspects. There was a long military trial, which was followed very closely by the National media. At the conclusion of the trial, the verdict was that the black Midshipman was not guilty of rape. However, he was found guilty of the lesser charges of conduct unbecoming an officer for having consensual sexual intercourse with a female cadet and failure to obey a lawful order, and the military jury recommended a sentence of no punishment. However, any conviction at a general court-martial amounts to a felony. Reportedly, the black Midshipman and the white female cadet had been out drinking; after a night of partying, the two woke up in bed together in the white female cadet's dorm room. Embarrassed by the fact that she had sexual intercourse and had woke up in bed with this black man, the white female cadet's called her white fiancée and advised him that she had been raped by a black Midshipmen.

The academy superintendent recommended that black Midshipman be expelled from the Naval Academy and not be allowed to graduate with his class. In addition, he would have to pay the United States Government over $136,000 for classes he attended while attending the Naval Academy. According to his contract, the Midshipman was required to graduate and serve four years in the Navy in return for his four years of college. Now do not get me wrong, this black Midshipman violated the strict honor code of the United States Naval Academy. As one who served in the U.S. Marine Corp, I am fully aware of the high regard given to the honor code. This black Midshipman knowingly violated the honor code and in my opinion, he should forfeit his right to be a leader in any branch of the Armed Services. Ironically, in the "Duke Lacrosse Team Rape Case", the one white male suspect who was a senior was allowed to graduate with his class. The alleged rape occurred during the 2006 NCAA Lacrosse Season and due to all the negative publicity surrounding this incident, the managing officials for Duke University decided to suspend the Lacrosse Team for the remainder of the season. However, after the rape charges were dismissed, the Duke University officials reinstated the Lacrosse Team and the other two white suspects were invited to return to the team.

The fact the black Midshipman was the quarterback on the Naval Academy Football Team, did not help his case at all. This young man's character was never doubt. The fact the he was an outstanding leader and Captain of the football worked against him because as a leader he should have known better than to break Naval Academy rules. The fact that this Midshipman was black should not have mattered in this case. However, we all know that when it is a black man and a white woman, race always matters. This Midshipman violated a code of honor and as a potential leader of soldiers into battle, his actions are inexcusable, and in my opinion, he can no longer be trusted to command. However, is the punishment far greater than the crime? To be denied his commission as an officer in the United States Armed Forces after four years of dedicated service at the Naval Academy is a major penalty. To deny his college degree and return the money for his education is too severe a punishment for one night of making foolish decisions. Although it was too little and too late, realizing his mistake, this black Midshipman called the young white female cadet and apologized for his behavior. The white members of the Duke Lacrosse Team have yet to apologize for the racial slur directed at the two black females that danced at their party.

Kobe - No longer one of the "Good Negroes"

How quickly did white America turn on Kobe Bryant, a black professional basketball player, when he was accused of allegedly raping a white girl in Colorado. At the time of the incident, Kobe was well on his way to replacing Michael Jordan as the face of the NBA. Kobe had been seen on major soft drink company and McDonald's TV commercials. He had an eight-figure endorsement contract with either Nike or Reebok Shoe Company. His NBA jersey was the number one selling jersey in the world. Yet, in less than a week after the rape allegations were made public, Kobe Bryant became persona non grata. His TV commercials were pulled and the shoe companies put his endorsement contact on hold. The sale of his NBA jersey slipped from first to third, with sales rapidly declining. According to Kobe, he did have sex with this white woman, but insisted that the sex was consensual. Kobe stated publicly that he was by his own admission, guilty of adultery; but he would never rape a woman. President Clinton is a perfect example of the fact that America will forgive a sexual indiscretion. What white America has yet to forgive is any black man accused of raping a white woman, no matter how rich or famous.

They Used the "N" and the "B" Word

During the investigation, it was determined that the members of the Duke Lacrosse Team, who were angry because the black "Exotic" Dancers had "ripped" them off by leaving the party early, threatened to two black women and hurled all sorts of racial insult at them as they were leaving. Reportedly, an email message found on the computer of one of the white men that attended the party, confirmed that they threatened to use a broomstick to sodomize the black women and he referred to them as "black bitches". As I watched some of the media coverage, a few black Duke University students expressed their anger over the racist language reportedly used by members of the all-white Duke Lacrosse Team. As the 2007 Duke Lacrosse Team took the field to begin the season, there was still no mention of an apology to the black female dancers or to the African American student body for their behavior at this party. As a further insult to both the black students that attend Duke University and the black community of Durham, North Carolina, in honor of the three white rape suspects, the lacrosse team has embroidered their numbers on their Duke University Lacrosse uniforms.

Forget the fact that these three white men were charged with rape and sexual assault. They held a party at which two black females from the Durham community were held against their will and were physically threatened and abused with racially explicit language when they left the party. When Chris Webber, a member of the "Fab Five" confessed to accepting money from a booster, the University of Michigan removed all the championship banners and trophies for the basketball team that Chris Webber had helped to win. Why would such a prestigious school like Duke University allow one of its major sports programs to honor three suspected sexual predators and bigots? I hope that the black student body and/or the black alumni of Duke University will at least protest this insult to the African American community. In the midst of all the confusion as to whether the District Attorney had enough evidence to charge the three white Lacrosse players in the first place, when Mr. Nifong was removed as Prosecutor, as I expected when the case first made headlines, in April 2007, all charges were dropped.

Tears of Joy - Support from NCAA & ESPN

In my home State, the University of Maryland's Lacrosse Team, when interviewed for their reaction to the charges being dropped, actually cried tears of joy in support of the Duke Lacrosse players. I was watching ESPN's "Around the Horn", when a white female sports reporter, Jackie MacMullen of the Boston Globe, who is a regular on the show, made personal comments in support of the NCAA returning a year of eligibility to the Duke Lacrosse Team because their 2006 season was canceled because of the false rape allegation. Again, will anyone remember that these pristine white rich boys from the Duke Lacrosse Team sexually assaulted and used vulgar racial slurs during the time these black women were held against their will at this party? I wonder if this same white female sports reporter would support the NCAA restoring eligibility for members of an all-black, basketball team from a college in North Carolina that sexually assaulted and verbally abused a white female exotic dancer at a party and as a result, false allegations of rape, the college canceled their season? The next step will be to have the alleged victim apologize to the Duke Lacrosse Team for soiling their good names. What upsets me is that years from now, the only thing that will be remembered about this case is that these upper class rich white boys, members of the prestigious Duke University Lacrosse Team, were falsely accused of rape by a black woman. In 2007, the NCAA did return a year of eligibility to all the non-seniors on the 2006 Duke Lacrosse Team.

The last bit of salt in this wound came after all the charges were dropped against the Duke Lacrosse players. Michael Nifong, the District Attorney that charged three white male Duke Lacrosse players with the rape of an African American female, resigned his position and was disbarred after a hearing conducted by the North Carolina Bar Association. In the 1930s, the white District Attorneys that prosecuted the nine black "Scottsboro" rape suspects became heroes in the white community. Some went on to become judges and hold other powerful political offices. There is no doubt in anyone's mind that the three white Duke Lacrosse players were not guilty of rape. However, it was just a clear to anyone with common sense that several white members of the Duke Lacrosse Team made racist remarks and directed very inappropriate sexually explicit remarks at the two black women that were hired to dance at their party; therefore, the Duke Lacrosse Team was not completely innocent. On the other hand, the black "Scottsboro Boys" were completely innocent because they had absolutely no contact with the two white women that they were accused of raping.

Never Forget

The fact that many African Americans refuse to forget the past has given the black families and friends of some victims that were murdered many years ago, a chance to bring the public's attention back to those unresolved crimes of the past. In Mississippi a white man who was a member of the KKK, Byron de la Beckwith was convicted in 1994 for the 1963 sniper killing of NAACP leader Medgar Evers. A white man, Bobby Frank Cherry, was convicted in 2002 in Alabama of killing four black girls in the bombing of a Birmingham church in 1963. In 2001, another white man, Thomas Blanton was convicted in the Birmingham church bombing. In June 2005, a white man, Edgar Ray Killen, an 80-year-old former Klansman, was convicted of manslaughter in the deaths of James Chaney, Andrew Goodman and Michael Schwerner, the three Civil Rights Workers who were killed in Mississippi in 1964.

In 2004, the FBI reopened the 1955 murder case of Emmett Till, a black teenager who was beaten and shot after whistling at a white woman in the Mississippi Delta, but decided not to press charges. The FBI turned the case over to local Prosecutors in Jackson, Mississippi, with the suggestion that they take a closer look at Carolyn Bryant Donham. Reportedly, some witnesses said a woman's voice could be heard at the scene of Till's abduction. The District Attorney in rural Leflore County had sought a manslaughter charge against the white woman, Carolyn Bryant Donham. She was suspected of pointing out Emmett Till to her husband to punish him for whistling at her, which was a grave offense for a black man in the segregated South in 1955. The Jackson, Mississippi grand jury refused to bring any new charges in the 1955 slaying of Emmett Till. We must keep hope alive that someday there will be justice for the senseless murder of a 14-year old child.

Just as we get little discouraged about justice for past crimes, James Ford Seale, of Roxie, Mississippi, a former sheriff's deputy, was arrested in 2007, for the 1964 slayings of Henry Dee and Charles Moore, two black teenagers who were long believed to have been kidnapped and killed by the Ku Klux Klan. The former Mississippi sheriff, James Ford Seale, was named in a Federal Indictment charging him in connection with the teens' disappearance and deaths while they were hitchhiking in a rural area of the State, East of Natchez. James Seale was thought to be dead, and the investigation into the two deaths had long been abandoned. In 1964, two months after Henry Dee and Charles Moore disappeared, their bodies were pulled from the Mississippi River as part of an FBI led search for James Chaney, Andrew Goodman and Michael Schwerner, and the three Civil Rights Workers reported missing about 160 miles away near Philadelphia, Mississippi

The FBI, who was focusing their attention on the more famous "Mississippi Burning" killings, turned the Dee and Moore case over to local authorities. A short time later, a justice of the peace called an end to the inquiry without presenting evidence to a grand jury. In 2000, the Justice Department's Civil Rights Unit reopened the case, the most recent in a string of Civil Rights Era killings that have been revived by State and Federal Authorities in the South. James Seale and Charles Marcus Edwards were first arrested in this case in November 1964, four months after the bodies were found. At the time, Seale was asked if he knew why he had been arrested. The FBI said he responded: "Yes, but I'm not going to admit it. You are going to have to prove it." Reportedly, both men were reputed members of the KKK, which at the time was cracking down on a rumored gunrunning operation by black Muslims in rural Franklin County, Mississippi.

On May 2, 1964, according to Federal Documents, Seale offered the two black hitchhikers a ride then drove them to a wooded area where he and others whipped them with beanpoles. An informant later told the FBI that the Klansmen took the unconscious men to the river, lashed their bodies to a Jeep engine block and old railroad rails and dumped them, still breathing, into the muddy water. Edwards initially told Federal Investigators the two black men were alive when he left them and he had nothing to do with any murders, according to FBI documents. This case is just the latest long-dormant Civil Rights Era killing to be reopened decades after the crimes were committed. If Germans can be prosecuted 70 plus years after the Holocaust, there should be no statute of limitations for the white racists that slaughtered the peaceful demonstrators during the Civil Rights Movement.

Paul Robeson: Outstanding and Outspoken

The problem with outspoken African Americans during the "JIM CROW ERA" in America is that they were like dogs that chased cars. Both dogs that continued to chase cars and black people, who continue to speak out against racism and racial injustice, do not live long. In order to survive and be accepted, many of the African Americans that have made the greatest impact on achieving racial equality in America had to tactfully address the issue in what was called "peaceful demonstrations".

Just as I have done with Nat Turner, I have made it a point to mention Paul Robeson in my other books. It is most imperative that we, as African Americans, never forget one of the most gifted men in the history of the world. While a student at Rutgers University in New Jersey, Mr. Robeson earned fifteen varsity letters in sports that included football, baseball, basketball, and track and field. He was twice named a first-team All American football player in 1917 and 1918. The legendary football coach Walter Camp described Paul Robeson as "the greatest to ever trot the gridiron." Mr. Robeson was an actor, author, attorney, a scholar and concert singer. Born April 9, 1898, Paul LeRoy Bustill Robeson was a man of many talents. He gave 296 performances as Othello on Broadway and was recognized as an internationally famous singer and performed on concert stages throughout the world. Mr. Robeson spoke and performed in over twenty languages and dialects, and became a spokesman throughout the world against exploitation, injustice, and racism. His attacks on injustice and racism in the United States became a severe international embarrassment to the United States Government.

In 1950, the U.S. State Department revoked Mr. Robeson's passport, and President Truman signed an Executive Order forbidding Mr. Robeson to leave the United States under penalty of five years in prison and a $500 fine. In 1958, Mr. Robeson left the United States for England and did not return until 1963. Throughout his lifetime, Mr. Robeson fought against all forms of racism and oppression perpetuated on blacks in the United States. He died in Philadelphia, Pennsylvania on January 23, 1976. If not for the facts that he was so very outspoken against racism; so very intimidating to white America at 6'3" tall, over 220 lbs., with the perfect athletic body, and one of the deepest bass voices every recorded, Paul Robeson would still be a household name and the world's model for all that any man would want to be. It has been my dream that an African American movie producer and director would make a film about the life and times of Paul

Robeson. The late Burt Lancaster was a brilliant selection to portray Jim Thorpe, the greatest athlete of all time, in a movie about his life. Unfortunately, I cannot think of any actor that could do justice to the role of Paul Robeson, in my opinion is the most all around talented man in the history of this Country.

Barry Bonds – Better Than Babe Ruth

In 1973, with the impending fall of Babe Ruth's homerun record, baseball's great white hope being passed by a black man brought out a steady stream of death threats and ugly racial insults directed at Hank Aaron. The treats and insults directed at Hank Aaron caught everyone by surprise because Hank was an all-around good person who until this time was loved by black and white, fans, teammates and fellow professional baseball players. The treatment of Hank Aaron was an example of that old slave owner and plantation mentality of white America that establish a rule that the good Negroes were OK as long as they stayed in their place, but as soon as one of these "field hand" stepped out of line, we will find a rope and a tree. In 1974, in spite of the insults and death threats, the talent, mental and physical strength, along with the courage of Hank Aaron never wavered as he pursued and finally broke Babe Ruth's record. The one thing that was never questioned during his pursuit of Babe's record was Hank's integrity. Unfortunately, the white media has not only questioned Barry Bond's integrity; they flat out called him a cheater. Based on a book written by two white reporters, Barry was accused, tried and conflict of using steroids, which according to these reporters, was the only reason Barry was able to break the home run record.

According to a book, written by two white sports reporters, who allegedly were able to obtain "confidential" information from a transcript of Barry Bonds' Federal Grand Jury testimony, alleged that Bonds used illegal performance enhancing drugs and/or steroids. No matter when and/or if he used the drugs/steroids as indicated in that book, I must emphasize that the book was written by two white men who obtained confidential Federal Grand Jury information. In

2004, Lance Williams and Mark Fainaru-Wada, obtained Barry Bonds Federal Grand Jury testimony from a white lawyer. Troy Ellerman, the white lawyer, pleaded guilty on Feb. 14, 2007, to leaking the Federal Grand Jury information, lying to Prosecutors, obstructing justice and disobeying a Court Order not to disclose grand jury information. Ellerman ended up serving 16 months of a 30-month sentence in a Federal Prison, and forfeiting his license to practice law. In 2014, the Federal Prosecutor has yet to charge the two white reporters for obtaining confidential information from a Federal Grand Jury. After Ellerman confessed to the crime, why did the Federal Prosecutor not charge the two white reporters with being an accessory after the fact or conspiracy in this criminal act?

In 2004, rather than being jailed for their crime, Williams and Fainaru-Wada received a journalism award for their report on Bonds. One of the two white sports writers remarked that Bonds makes more money in three innings that he makes in a year. Would that be a motive to violate the rules governing confidential Federal Grand Jury testimony? By the way, Barry Bonds has never tested positive for any illegal substances. In 2006, MLB Commissioner Bud Selig formed a special committee to investigate the use of performance enhancing drugs in professional baseball. The most prominent name mentioned in this investigation was Barry Bonds. On the eve of Bonds' hitting his 715th homerun and passing Babe Ruth in the record books, certain members of the print media demanded that the Commissioner suspend Bonds in the best interest of the game. If the Commissioner bans Barry Bonds for committing an illegal act that was not specifically against the rules of baseball, then he will open up a can of worms that could result in the suspension of many active players and coaches.

Civil Rights Violation

In America today, although it was not the case during the "JIM CROW ERA", it is a Civil Rights Violation to single out one person or group for punishment for a crime. When the media first reported that Barry Bonds was in contention to break Hank Aaron's homerun record, Hank was supportive of Barry. They even made a TV commercial together. As Barry Bonds rapidly approached the MLB's home run record, Hank Aaron stopped encouraging Barry. Unfortunately, Hank has fallen for the white media's propaganda that Barry Bonds is not deserving of breaking this haloed record. If nothing else, Barry Bonds is a student of the game of baseball. His father, Bobby Bonds played the game at its highest levels. Bobby Bonds loved and respected the game of baseball and he passed that love and respect along to his son. Although, he is dead, Barry has his Godfather, the legendary Willie Mays to mentor and encourage him as he attempts to break the homerun record. My hope is that Hank Aaron will join Willie and add his support to Barry Bonds because he has been in Barry's shoes. You see, just as Hank Aaron received racially motivated death threats as he approached breaking a record that was held by a white player, Barry Bonds is now receiving racially motivated death threats because white people think the record still belongs to Babe Ruth and that no black man that ever lived is good enough to hold Babe's record.

I played amateur football until I was 35, basketball until I was 52 and at 65, I still play softball. Personally, I think this is quite an accomplishment for a man with chronic arthritis. I have studied the game from both a player's and a fan's perspective. I also know enough about what goes on in a locker room to have some credibility when I speak about sports. Back in my day, without asking what it contained, if a trusted teammate brought in a concoction that would help you heal a sore arm, shoulder or legs and would get me back in the game, I would try it. Some of these home remedies smelled so bad they would turn your stomach or were so hot they would raise a blister. If you love playing as much as I do, you endure the smells or the heat just to play. Fortunately for me, there was not anyone on my teams sophisticated enough to inject anything, but if it were a cream we would rub it on, if it were liquid we would drink some and if it were a pill we would swallow it. Some players used energy busters to help them make it through the grind of back-to-back games. As long as no one got sick and there were no signs of any negative effects, nobody complained. In my opinion the only thing steroids or growth hormones do is expedite an athlete physical development and help an athlete to recover from injuries faster. The downside to the use of any chemicals or drugs, the legal or illegal kind, is that if you take too much or use them too often, chemicals or drugs can destroy your body.

Do you honestly think "Iron Man" Cal Ripken Jr. would have broken Lou Gehrig's MLB record for most consecutive games played if it had not been for cortisone, which is a steroid or some other type of painkillers? I remember there was one game in particular during the streak when Cal was injured during the pre-game warm-ups. At first report, the severity of the injury was reported as bad enough that Cal would not only miss this game; but he might have to go on the disabled list. After reportedly receiving a shot of cortisone, Cal not only played through the pain to finish that game, he never missed another game and went on to shatter Lou Gehrig's MLB consecutive games played record. The bottom line was that Barry Bonds, a very arrogant African American, was about to become the second black man to pass Babe Ruth, the great white American Hero. Bonds' was the victim of the same threats and racial insults that plagued Hank Aaron faced, as he was about to break Babe Ruth's homerun record. The only difference in Aaron and Bonds is that every major sports media personality in America loved Hank Aaron and most of this same group despised Barry Bonds. During his professional career, Hank Aaron was very low key. All he did was play the game of baseball the way it was supposed to be played. Hank Aaron was a five-tooled player. He could hit, run, hit for power, catch and throw and he did it all without drawing any negative attention off the field.

The Federal Government has offered deals to Bonds' former teammates, his personal trainer, and Victor Conte, the man that confessed to providing illegal drugs to several big name athletes. As of this date, has testified against Barry Bonds. Talk show hosts have tried to coax his former mistress into making a public statement that while she lived with Barry she witnessed him use steroids. They offered her money and promised they would put her story of alleged abuse at the hands of Bonds on National TV. However, just as the story was about to break, the woman changed her mind and her story. If we are to condemn a baseball player based on the information contained in a book, we should have started with the book, which was made into an HBO movie, about Ty Cobb. The Book/Movie portrayed TY COBB as a violent racist. It was not against the rules of MLB at the time to be a bigot and a racist during Cobb's era ("JIM CROW ERA"). If Cobb were playing today, much like the former relief pitcher for the Atlanta Braves, John Rocker, he would have been suspended for his racist actions. The question is, based on the Book/Movie, should Ty Cobb be removed from the Baseball Hall of Fame? Many baseball writers have stated that Barry Bonds should not be allowed in the Baseball Hall of Fame. I wonder how many of these same writers would vote to kick the Ty Cobb out of the Hall of Fame?

In 1970, when Muhammad Ali returned to the ring, most of white America chose to root for an African American named Joe Frazier, rather than cheer for Ali, a Muslim who refused to fight for his Country. However, after he regained the heavyweight championship by defeating Joe Frazier, he regained his status as an American Hero and as the most recognized athlete of the 20th Century. The same thing happened again with Barry Bonds verses Hank Aaron. Many white Americans hated Hank for breaking Babe Ruth's record. Now white America loves Hank because they would rather hate Barry Bonds. Yet, until white America made Barry Bonds a villain, Hank Aaron never received the National attention or acclaim for breaking a record that has always belonged to Babe Ruth. What many of the media fail to realize and report to the American public is that whatever they think Barry is using now, he probably was not using when he won at least four or five of his seven National League MVP awards. It is ironic that most of the same people that sent racist hate mail to Hank Aaron when he was about to break MLB's homerun record sent the same racist hate mail to Barry Bonds. You see, in the eyes of many white Americans, the homerun record does not belong to Major League Baseball; the homerun record will always belong to Babe Ruth.

Just like Joe Frazier, during Barry Bonds' chase of the homerun record, Hank Aaron became the more acceptable black athlete for white America to cheer for. It is hard to believe that the same sports reporters, the majority of whom are white males, voted for Barry Bonds for MVP of the league seven (7) times, now refuse to acknowledge Barry's accomplishments because these reporters believe Barry used steroids. Most of the media and the Commissioner of Baseball changed their opinion of Barry based on statements made in a book written by two white male reporters that work for the San Francisco Chronicle. Because these reporters work for the San Francisco Chronicle, one of the local newspapers that cover the San Francisco Giants, the team that Barry played for most of his career, in all likelihood they voted for Barry for MVP at least once during the same period they accused him of using steroids.

The question has been asked; if information in the book written by two white reporters from the San Francisco Chronicle was not true, why did Barry Bonds not file a Civil Lawsuit for defamation of character? Just ask yourself how many times you have actually heard of a newspaper, TV station or a writer, sue for a statement they made about an entertainer, athlete or politician. There is a very simple answer to why public figures do not sue reporters; it is called "absence of malice". In other words, the public figure has to prove that the reporter intentionally set out to disseminate false information.

A white Federal Prosecutor illegally gave most of the so-called damning information in the book that reportedly supports the fact that Barry Bonds used steroids to the two white reporters. The Federal Government is conducting an investigation into the illegal use of steroids. Barry Bonds, along with several other players and non-players, testified before a Federal Grand Jury. A trusted white male Federal Prosecutor, that had access to the transcripts from that Grand Jury hearing, violated the confidentiality statutes of the Federal Government, by providing a copy of the transcripts to the two white reporters from the San Francisco Chronicle. How sad a commentary on race relations is it that these white men entered into a conspiracy to diminish the accomplishments of Barry Bonds. Even sadder is the fact that as our young men and women were dying in the war in Iraq, the United States Government is spending millions of dollars on an investigation to determine whether Barry Bonds used steroids.

312

Even more ironic is the fact that most of white America and both African American and white representatives of the media in this Country, have chosen Hank Aaron over Barry Bond as the more suitable black player to be mentioned along with Babe Ruth as the Home Run Kings of Major League Baseball. Yet, statistics will support the fact that Barry Bonds is the greatest pure hitter to ever play Major League Baseball; not Babe Ruth, not Ted Williams, not Joe DiMaggio, not Mickey Mantle, not Hank Aaron, not Alex Rodriquez, and not even Willie Mays; the greatest all around baseball player in the history of the game. Barry is the only player in the past 50 years that has been intentionally walked each time he has come to the plate in a game and intentionally walked with the bases loaded. Most of his peers have the ultimate respect for him. It is the media that is trying to ruin his reputation as a player. What many baseball fans failed to notice, if not for the hundreds of intentional walks, Barry Bonds would have been on the verge of hitting 800 home runs.

Barry Bonds: Role Model?

However, what concerns me the most is how the negative image portrayed in the media will affect his children and all the other the black youth of today and in the future. Today, we have far too many young African American athletes making headlines for all the wrong reasons: shootings, domestic violence, infidelity, and drug use. On the eve of Barry Bonds' eclipse of the most recognized record in sports, we need to applaud Barry and we need to portray him as an African American who is worthy of our praise and admiration. Also, black writers and media personalities, such as Mike Wilbon of the Washington Post and ESPN, who has publicly taken the stance that Barry is guilty until he proves himself innocent, should consider that fact that white America has condemned blacks for centuries without due process.

Remember when America was searching for a "Great White Hope" to end the dominance of African American heavyweight champions. Now that Barry Bonds has been crowned the new Home Run King, white America is hopeful that a "Great White Hope", Alex Rodriguez, aka "AROD", will soon pass Barry and take his crown. The funny thing is that AROD is not white; he is Hispanic and very proud of his heritage. I am a sports fan. I loved to play baseball, basketball and football. Now that I am too old to play, I enjoying watching. Having played baseball and football at the little league, high school and college levels, I know how difficult the game becomes as you move from one level to the next. I know how difficult the game becomes, as you get older. I know that one of the most difficult things to do in any sport is hitting a round ball with a round bat when the ball traveling at speeds in excess of 90 mph.

More White Experts

If you do not know anything about the game, you do not have the right to publicly criticize and demean the accomplishments of the people who play the game for a living. White ex-professional athletes like Tim McCarver, Mark Grace and Buck Martinez, have become on-air TV commentators after long careers in Major League Baseball. They express their opinions, good or bad, about Barry Bonds' accomplishment as a baseball player on National broadcasts, such as FOX SPORTS or ESPN. I may not always agree with their opinions. However, based on their experience in the game, I do feel they have earned the right to make comments about Barry Bonds. However, white sports reporters, such as Mike Lupica, Mitch Albom and Bob Costas, who probably never made it out of little league, do not have the right to make negative remarks about any of our great African American athletes. These white writers especially do not have the right to criticize Barry Bonds, who has proven that he is one of the best ever at hitting a round ball, traveling in excess of 90 miles per hour (mph), with a round wooden bat.

Let us take a closer look at just what makes these three white reporters experts on sports. Mike Lupica is a newspaper columnist for the New York Daily News and is a regular on the EPSN TV show, "The Sports Reporters". He has written several books on topic of sports. Bob Costas is a TV sports reporter for NBC, who according to published reports, is 5ft 61/2 inches tall and weighs 150 lbs. Mitch David Albom is a novelist and newspaper columnist for the Detroit Free Press and he is a regular on the EPSN TV show, "The Sports Reporters". These "Sports Reporters" are considered by many Americans to be authorities on all things related to professional sports in this Country. Conducting research is an excellent quality for a reporter preparing to interview an athlete on TV or for writing books. However, conducting research is not how Kobe Bryant and Barry Bonds learned to play their particular sport. I searched "high and wide", but I was unable to find any mention of Lupika, Costas or Albom ever having played sports in High School, College or even Little League. However, having listened to them, it sounded like Lupika, Costas and Albom would have liked to have been professional athletes.

I was unable to find any evidence in the published biographies of these three white men that would actually qualify them to be authorities on any sport. In my opinion, what I did see in the published reports that I read were three white men, Lupika, Costas and Albom, all rather small in physical stature, who probably feel that any chance they may have had in sports was denied because of their race and size. Rather than work hard to develop their own talents, these three white men became sports reporters. As they gained a National following, they used that forum to attack the very black athletes that were taller, faster, stronger and more talented than they could ever imagine, the very athletes that denied them the right to live out their fantasies of becoming professional base-ball, basketball or boxers. Listen to how bitter these men sound when-ever they talk about Barry Bonds or when they talk about a black athlete that has run afoul of the law. Under the guise of being impartial white reporters, Mike Lupica, Mitch Albom and Bob Costas have come very close to using some of the racist rhetoric that was very popular in describ-ing the behavior of African Americans during the "JIM CROW ERA". The problem I have is that black sports reporters like John Saunders and Mike Wilbon have sat next to these white men and failed to rebuke them for their reporting style when making statements about African American athletes. The only African American reporter that I have seen defend the black athlete when they are attacked by these white reporters on the ESPN broadcast is William Rhoden, who is a regular on the show and a columnist for the New York Times.

Chapter 7

THE END OF MY TRILOGY – A NEVER

ENDING SAGA

Over 23 years ago, when I started writing the American Apartheid Series, it was my intent to end the series after my third book. Just in case you did not know, a trilogy is defined as being a set of three works of art, usually literature or film, that develop a single theme even though they are generally created at different times. They may tell an extended story, or involve the same characters or the same setting; or have only the most tenuous of connections. My books tell an extended story and involve some of the same characters and same settings. However, the characters in my books have a strong connection, rather than the "tenuous" of connections as defined by a trilogy. With this book, I have completed the American Apartheid Series and the end of a trilogy. In 1990, I started writing my first book *"American Apartheid"* and it was completed and published in 1997. In 1998, I started the second book, my personal favorite, *"No Land No Mule No Freedom, American Apartheid the Saga Continues"*, and it was published in 2002. In 2004, I started writing my latest book, *"The Back Side of the Sport of Kings, American Apartheid the never Ending Saga"*, and I finished the book in 2014. If you have not read my other books, you can find them online by using the author's name and titles.

Always remember that history is a very valuable part of what may possibly happen in the future. Therefore, we need to know our history in order to recognize any repeat of past events. For those of you that have not read my other books; the term "America Apartheid" is based on the primus that the much publicized and criticized concept of racial apartheid did not originate in the deepest "Dark Continent" of Africa and more specifically, South Africa. We have all read the stories and watched the televised news reports about the struggles of the native Africans under the oppressive white Government in South Africa. We know about Bishop Desmond Tutu and his peaceful battle to end apartheid. Nelson Mandela scarified his freedom to end apartheid in South Africa. Yet, believe it or not, "Apartheid" is as American as "Mom, Apple Pie and Chevrolet". However, it is hard for white America to use the word Apartheid in their history books. Rather than call it apartheid or racial injustice, the more accurate descriptions of what it really happened, white historians have used words like "discovery", "pioneering" and "conquered" to describe the brutal takeover of this Country from the Native Americans.

The basic definition of apartheid, which is a Dutch word, is to separate by race. Europeans who settled in South Africa in 1948 established apartheid. Apartheid ended in 1989, when the Native Africans defeated the European's apartheid based Government. Unfortunately, in1492, apartheid started in America and is still going strong. Why is it that over 500 years after Christopher Columbus "discovered America" and over 360 years after the Pilgrims landed at Plymouth Rock, we continue to be separated by race and skin color? Why is that over 360 years since we celebrated the first "Thanksgiving Day" with the Native Americans; tribes of red men still live on reservations in this Country? The answer is "American Apartheid".

I was born in October 1948, one year and six months after April 15, 1947, when Jackie Robinson became the first African American to play professional baseball in the Major Leagues for the Brooklyn Dodgers. In my lifetime, this is one of the single most courage acts and one of the greatest accomplishments in the fight for equal rights for blacks in America. Why would a black man being allowed to play a game on the same field as a white man, have such an impact on the racial balance of America? The world of sports is a reflection of society. If African Americans could be accepted on the playing field as equals, they could be accepted in other social arenas as equals. Just think about it. There may have never been a Rosa Parks, Martin Luther King or Tommie Smith and John Carlos, if not for the courage of Jackie Robinson. The integration of professional baseball in America was so very special that MLB and the world continues to celebrate April 15, 1947 as a monumental day in history.

Nat Turner – An African American Hero

When Jackie Robinson broke the color barrier in a sport that had been dominated by white men, it was like the shot heard around the world. After the game on April 15, 1947, the name and/or picture of Jackie Robinson in his Brooklyn Dodgers uniform appeared in every major newspaper and magazine in the free world. Throughout the early history of this Country, there have been some other very outspoken African Americans. In the 1800s, the words and actions of a former black slave, Nat Turner, made him a militant leader who denounced slavery. Nat Turner was born on October 2, 1800, in Southampton County, Virginia. While still a young child, Nat was overheard describing events that had happened before he was born. This, along with his keen intelligence, and other signs marked him in the eyes of his people as a prophet destined for great things. In February 1831, there was an eclipse of the sun. Nat Turner took this to be the sign he had been promised and confided his plan to attack white slave owners to the four men he trusted the most. They decided to hold the insurrection on the 4th of July and began planning a strategy. However, they had to postpone action because Turner became ill. On August 13, 1831, the sun appeared bluish-green in an atmospheric disturbance. This was the final sign, and a week later, on August 21, 1831 Nat Turner and six of his men met in the woods to eat dinner and make their plans. At 2:00 pm that morning, they set out to the Travis household, where they killed the entire family as they lay sleeping.

They continued on, from house to house, killing all of the white people they encountered. Nat Turner's force eventually consisted of more than 40 slaves. Before Nat Turner's army was defeated, they killed at least 55 white people. Nat Turner was an African American patriot and one of the main reasons our history needs to be taught in more than one color and from more than one perspective. Nat Turner was a black slave who led a rebellion to end slavery in America. If he had led this revolt 30 years later during the Civil War, he may have won a Congressional Medal of Honor. However, because he killed white people during a time when black people were considered animals, white historians will never honor him as an American hero. On November 5, 1831, Nat Turner was tried in the Southampton County Court in Virginia. He was found guilty and sentenced to be executed. On November 11, 1831 he was hanged, and then skinned, and finally he was burned, which were the ultimate insults and the white man's way of signaling how much they hated Nat Turner and what he had done. My books were written to provide information to those who have never looked at history from the perspective of an African American. They were written to give proper recognition to the accomplishments of black men such as Nat Turner.

Frederick Douglass

Former slave, Frederick Douglass, also was a black abolitionist who spoke out against slavery. Frederick A. Douglass was born in 1817 on a Maryland plantation. His given name was Frederick Augustus Washington Bailey. Frederick Douglass constantly fought against his slave conditions and was constantly in trouble with the white overseer. He escaped on September 3, 1838, and settled in New Bedford, Massachusetts. He changed his name to Frederick Douglass. In 1845, against the advice of his friends, Mr. Douglass decided to write an account of his life, fully aware of the possibility that this would mark him as the Bailey runaway slave. The autobiography was called "The Narrative of the Life and Times of Frederick Douglass".

Besides writing his autobiography, in 1845, Mr. Douglass founded and edited the North Star newspaper. It should be noted that Frederick Douglass is one of the very few African American that were able to write an accurate account of what it actual felt like to be owned by a white man as a black slave. When the Civil War broke out, Frederick Douglass urged President Lincoln to free and arm the slaves. In the movie "Glory", you see Frederick Douglass on a balcony watching a company of former slaves that are now soldiers in the Union Army march off to war. Mr. Douglass was also a great spokesman for universal suffrage, women's rights, and world peace. In 1848, Mr. Douglass participated in the first women's rights convention in Seneca Falls, New York. In 1872, he ran for vice President on the Equal Rights Party ticket. In 1889, he was appointed minister to Haiti. Frederick Douglass died on February 20, 1895.

Marcus Garvey

I have also talked about Marcus Mosiah Garvey, born August 17, 1887 in St. Ann's Bay, Jamaica, as being an outspoken African American. Mr. Garvey's program for the return of African people to their motherland shook the black cultural foundations of both America and Africa. All subsequent "Black Power" movements have owed a debt to this example. In 1914, Mr. Garvey founded the Universal Negro Improvement Association (UNIA). In just five years, the UNIA had over six million members. Mr. Garvey started black newspapers, schools, churches, printing operations, and food and clothing stores. In 1919, he launched the "Black Star Shipping Lines". Mr. Garvey's program was one of black self-determination and independence and they set the theme for all black development today. Marcus Garvey died in London, England on June 10, 1940.

Dr. William Edward Burghardt "W.E.B." DuBois

Next, there is Dr. W.E.B. DuBois, born on February 23, 1868 in Great Barrington, Massachusetts. Mr. DuBois is one of the founders of the NAACP and the first Black to receive a doctoral degree from

Harvard University. On behalf of the NAACP at the United Nations, he tried to get a firm anti-colonial commitment from the United States in 1945 and in 1947 to abolish the "JIM CROW" laws. His theme in his later years was always economic democracy and the channeling of "Black Power" through a unified Black society. Dr. W.E.B. DuBois died on October 27, 1963 in Accra, Ghana where he had established his new home.

Asa Philip Randolph

You can add the late A. Philip Randolph to the list of outspoken African Americans. His accomplishments had a personal impact on my life. Mr. Randolph was born April 15, 1889. He was a champion of equal rights. In 1917, Mr. Randolph co-founded "The Messenger", a weekly magazine of African American protests. For his outspoken leadership, Mr. Randolph was characterized by white Corporate America as "the most dangerous Negro in America" because of his proven power to create change. Mr. Randolph came to National prominence in 1937 by organizing the labor union for African American railroad workers, the "Brotherhood of Sleeping Car Porters". Mr. Randolph achieved the first union contract signed by a white employer and an African American Labor Leader for African American workers. The reason this had such a personal impact on my life was that my grandfathers were both original members of this union. One of the proudest days of my grandfather, Wilbur Wright's life came in 1987 when he received a gold plated union card from the BSCP. The gold plated union card was to celebrate the union's 50th birthday and to honor of my grandfather's 50 years as a loyal member.

In 1941, Mr. Randolph conceived a March on Washington D.C., to protest exclusion of African American workers from defense jobs. Faced with the public relations threat of 100,000 marchers, President Franklin Roosevelt established the Wartime Fair Employment Practice Committee. Mr. Randolph founded the League for Nonviolent Civil Disobedience against Military Segregation. In 1948, Mr. Randolph and the League for Nonviolent Civil Disobedience pressured President Harry Truman into ending segregation in the armed forces. In 1963, Mr. Randolph, along with many other notable black leaders, helped organize the historic, 250,000 strong March on Washington.

James Cleveland "Jesse" Owens

One of the men who helped pave the way for Jackie Robinson in this more tactful mode of peaceful demonstration was the legendary James Cleveland "Jesse" Owens. Born in 1913, the grandson of black slaves opened the eyes of the world in the 1936 Olympic games in Germany, when he won four Gold Medals while Adolph Hitler, who proclaimed that Germans were the master race, looked on in disbelief. Like Jackie Robinson, the exploits of Jesse Owens at the 1936 Olympics have been well documented. Jesse Owens let his actions on the running track speak for his opinions on racial equality. Jesse Owens used his international track-star reputation to land jobs helping his people, such as National Director of Physical Education for African Americans with the Office of Civilian Defense, which reportedly, he called "the most gratifying work I've ever done."

Joseph "Joe Louis" Barrow

The second blow to Hitler's master race theory came in 1938 when an African American Joseph "Joe Louis" Barrow, who in my opinion is the greatest boxer in history, defeated the Heavyweight Champion, a German named Max Schmeling, to regain the Championship. According to Rachel Robinson, Jackie's wife, Joe Louis was one of Jackie Robinson's heroes. In the early 1940s, Joe Louis, the world championship boxer, just happened to be in the same unit as Jack Robinson at Fort Riley, Kansas. In the 1940s, the U.S. Army, which was still segregated, refused to accept Jackie Robinson's application for officer candidate school. Joe Louis wrote Washington D.C., protesting discrimination in the army, and succeeded in getting the army to allow Jackie Robinson and other black soldiers to go for officer training. Jackie Robinson did become a lieutenant in the Army.

Bob Gibson

It is my hope that my books will inspire African American historians and/or writers to conduct the research and invest the time necessary to write about great black Americans such as Robert "Bob" Gibson, who was born November 9, 1935 in Omaha, Nebraska. Mr. Gibson is a former right-handed pitcher for the St. Louis Cardinals baseball team. He played in the Major Leagues for the Cardinals from 1959 to 1975. In 1981, his record-setting career led to his election to the Major League Baseball Hall of Fame. Some of the inspiration for my writing started with men like Bob Gibson. The reason I feel it necessary to talk about Mr. Gibson in this book; if there were a totally level playing fields in America, the name Robert "Bob" Gibson would be mentioned as often as we hear the names Don Drysdale, Tom Seaver and Nolan Ryan. The most dominate right-handed pitchers in the modern era of Major League Baseball. Let me make it perfectly clear, the only reason the white media does not mention Bob Gibson when they refer to the best pitchers to play the game is because he is black and he did not tolerate any foolishness when it came to the game of baseball. He was a fierce competitor on the field; he did not have much to say to reporters before and after games and he did not socialize with other players.

According to published reports, Bob Gibson was such a fierce competitor that he rarely smiled. He was known to have intentionally hit batters to let them know he was in charge. Known by many as the best pitcher in Cardinals history, Mr. Gibson dominated with his fastball, sharp slider, and a slow looping curveball. Named "Pack" to honor his father who died 3 months before the hall of fame pitcher was born, at 18 years old Pack Gibson changed his name to Robert. Reportedly, the Gibson family could not afford a camera; therefore, no photographs of Bob Gibson's father exist. In 1957, Mr. Gibson received a $4,000.00 bonus to sign with the Cardinals. He delayed his start with the organization for a year to play basketball with the

Harlem Globetrotters, earning the nickname "Bullet" Bob Gibson. His nickname in baseball was "Hoot", after Hoot Gibson, the cowboy and silent movie star. One of the star players on the Basketball team, Mr. Gibson was famous for backhanded dunks. He resigned from the Globetrotters to play baseball because he could not stand the clowning. Very few people remember that the Globetrotters were not always a team that played just to entertain with trick shots and clowning. The Globetrotters were initially a serious competitive team, and despite a flair for entertainment, they would only clown for the audience after establishing a safe lead in the game. In 1958, Mr. Gibson spent a year with the Cardinal's Triple – A Minor League Baseball team in Omaha, Nebraska. He was called up to the Cardinals' Major League team in 1959.

Before I continue with Mr. Gibson here are a few more facts about the Globetrotters. According to published reports, in 1937, the Globetrotters accepted an invitation to participate in the World Professional Basketball Tournament where they met the New York Rens in the semi-finals in the first big clash of the two greatest all-black professional basketball teams. The Rens defeated the Globetrotters and went on to win the Tournament. In 1940, the Globetrotters avenged their loss by defeating the Rens in the quarterfinals and winning the championship beating the Chicago Bruins. The Globetrotters beat the premier professional team, the Minneapolis Lakers, led by George Mikan, for two consecutive years in 1948 and 1949. The February 1948 win was a hallmark in professional basketball history. The all-black Globetrotters proved they were on an equal footing with the all-white Lakers. This victory was momentum for ending the National Basketball Association's color line grew. In 1950, Chuck Cooper became the first black player drafted by a NBA team. The information about the Harlem Globetrotters has great historical value as well as the fact it highlights Bob Gibson as a great athlete all-around athlete, who could have been a NBA Hall a Fame basketball player. In 1962, Bob Gibson had the first of nine 200-strikeout seasons. The Cardinals retired his number "45" in 1981. A statue of Bob Gibson stands outside Busch Stadium in St. Louis, Missouri.

In 1999, Bob Gibson ranked 31st on The Sporting News' list of the 100 Greatest Baseball Players, and was elected to the MLB All-Century Team. Bob Gibson has a star on the St. Louis Walk of Fame. In 2004, he was named as the most intimidating pitcher of all time from the Fox Sport Net series "The Sports List". The street on the North Side of Rosenblatt Stadium, home of the College World Series in his hometown of Omaha, named Bob Gibson Boulevard. In the 1967 World Series, Mr. Gibson allowed only three earned runs over three complete game victories, and hit a vital home run in game seven. Mr. Gibson had come back late in 1967 season from having his leg broken earlier in the season from a line drive by Roberto Clemente. The next time he faced Clemente, he threw a pitch over Clemente's head, which forced Clemente to take a dive into the dirt. Roberto Clemente never had another hit off Gibson during the remainder of Clemente's career. Mr. Gibson's 1.12 ERA (earned run average) in 1968 is a live-ball era record. Also in 1968, he threw 13 shutouts, and allowed only two earned runs in 92 straight innings of pitching. Mr. Gibson also pitched 47 consecutive scoreless innings, at the time the second longest scoreless streak in Major League history behind only Don Drysdale's 58 2/3 consecutive scoreless innings, which had been set earlier that very season. He also won the National League MVP in 1968 and in the World Series Bob Gibson struck out 17 Detroit Tigers to set a World Series record for strikeouts in one game, a record that stands to this day.

On May 12, 1969, Mr. Gibson struck out three batters on nine pitches in the seventh inning of a 6-2 win over the Los Angeles Dodgers. Mr. Gibson became the ninth National League pitcher and the 15th pitcher in Major League history to accomplish the nine-strike/three-strikeout half-inning. On August 14, 1971, at Pittsburgh's Three Rivers Stadium, he pitched his only career no-hitter in an 11-0 victory over the Pirates. He was the second pitcher in MLB history to strike out over 3,000 batters, and the first to do so in the National League. Mr. Gibson was also one of the best-hitting pitchers of all time. In 1970, he hit .303 for the season. Sometimes the Cardinals used him as a pinch-hitter. For his career, he batted .206 with 24 home runs and 144 RBIs. Mr. Gibson is one of only two pitchers since World War II with a career batting average of .200 or higher and with at least 20 home runs and 100 RBIs. Mr. Gibson was above average as a base runner and occasionally the Cardinals used him as a pinch runner, despite the managers' general reluctance to risk injury to pitchers in this way. Dusty Baker, who played for the Atlanta Braves received the following advice from his teammate Hank Aaron about hitting against Bob Gibson; "Don't dig in against Bob Gibson; he'll knock you down. He'd knock down his own grandmother if she dared to challenge him. Do not stare at him, do not smile at him, and do not talk to him. He does not like it. If you happen to hit a home run; do not run too slow; do not run too fast. If you happen to want to celebrate, get in the tunnel first. And if he hits you, do not charge the mound, because he's a Gold Glove boxer". Dusty said "like what about my 17-game hitting streak?" Hank said, "That was the night it ended."

The lack of information and conversation by the media about the great Bob Gibson is one of several reasons why I decided to write this book that chronicles a variety of different aspects of life on the "Back Side" of the sport of thoroughbred horseracing. The first reason is that I love thoroughbred horses and I am addicted to the sport of horseracing. Secondly, I truly admire the men and women that have dedicated their lives to the sport of thoroughbred racing. Finally, I could not find documentation that provided an up close and personal look at life on the "Back Side". I would like to be able to say that life on the "Back Side" of the sport of thoroughbred racing is a mirror image of American society. The sport of thoroughbred racing is very competitive. In the 40 plus years that I have been around the sport of horseracing, I have met some amazing characters; some of them were nice and some were not. Unfortunately, many of the characters practice old racist traditions and stereotypes that existed nearly 100 years ago, which are still part of the culture and societal norms of life on the "Back Side". You need to understand that tradition represents the voices of our past and I will be the first to admit that without the voices of our past we would have no direction for our future. Just as there are some very good traditions in the sport of horseracing, such as courtesy and politeness, that need to be preserved. There are some very bad traditions in the sport, such as hatred and bigotry that we must replace.

Jackie Robinson and the Color Barrier

I made this same point about white historian that attempted to express the personal views of blacks about being slaves. I have watched the movie, "The Jackie Robinson Story" on TV at least 10 times. It starred the late Jackie Robinson (as himself) and a young black actress, Ruby Dee as Jackie's wife Rachel. Ruby Dee married Ossie Davis and they are the standard-bearers for African American performers on stage, TV and motion pictures. The first time I watched the movie, the only thing I was interested in was seeing Jackie Robinson play baseball. As a child, maybe 6 or 7 years old, I heard stories about him, but I had never really seen Jackie Robinson play. I can remember that every time they showed a scene with Jackie playing football and later baseball, I was glued to the front of the TV. The movie featured some films from his actual playing days. I could see from those films that Jackie Robinson was a good overall athlete and a great baseball player. When I first watched the movie, I did not understand the racial issues that were the motivation and the major factor for The Jackie Robinson Story. The more times I watched the movie; it became clear to me that the black characters did not really act like black people. The black characters in the original Jackie Robinson Story dressed, talked and acted like white people in black face. With the exception of Ruby Dee, none of the other black characters, including Jackie Robinson, exhibited any emotion in their speech or facial expressions. The movie was written from the perspective of white people and for white characters that just happened to be African Americans. The Jackie Robinson Story was written by two white men, Lawrence Taylor and Arthur Mann, directed by a white man, Alfred E. Green, and produced by yet another white man, Mort Briskin.

No white writer, director or producer could paint a picture of the anger, pain and frustration of a black man who was only trying to play the game he loved in a Country that was hailed to be the land of the free. The movie never showed how Jackie vented his frustrations. Did Jackie punch holes in the walls when he got home? Did he kick the dog, or beat his wife and kids? To cope with all the racial attacks, did Jackie seek out the help of a clergyman or therapist? From the perspective of these white filmmakers, the racial insults, physical and mental abused endured by Jackie Robinson were portrayed as not being that cruel or severe. Not only did the white writers and director fail to accurate portray the feeling of the black characters in the Jackie Robinson story, they failed to depict the ignorance, bigotry and hatred of the white characters that disliked Jackie because of the color of his skin.

What made the accomplishments of Jackie Robinson in baseball so important is that it not only changed the face of sports, it changed the face of America. By breaking Major League Baseball's color barrier, Jackie inspired African Americans to break the social and economic color barriers that existed in America during the late 1940s and early 1950s. Although he may not have received the proper recognition for this accomplishment, Jackie Robinson was the father of the modern "Civil Rights Movement". Jackie Robinson even practiced non-violence as his way of demonstrating African Americans have a right to be treated as equals. Dr. Martin Luther King was the leader of the Civil Rights Movement and Engineered the "Freedom Train" built by Jackie Robinson. Like the movies on Malcolm X and MLK, it is my hope that someone like "Spike Lee" will see the need to remake the "Jackie Robinson Story" from a black perspective. A "Spike Lee" or another black director's version of the Jackie Robinson Story would give America a more realistic look at what Jackie went through to play baseball in the Major Leagues.

Jackie Robinson removed a few of the color barriers in America, yet, many racial hurdles remain in professional sports. A few years ago, Jesse Jackson, and his supporters, held a peaceful demonstration on the opening day of the professional baseball season to protest that lack of African Americans in the front offices of Major League Baseball. The good thing is that as we enter the new millennium, there has been some progress in the hiring of blacks in management positions throughout the popular sports, such as, baseball basketball and football. Unlike the days when the white media swept issues involving racism in sports under the carpet, today in America, issues involving racial discrimination or disparity in the popular sports make headlines. The issues or incidents of racism are dissected and discussed from all angles in newspapers and on TV by reporters on broadcasts from Good Morning America to ESPN.

More about Number 42

In 1930s and 40s, there were many African Americans still alive that were the sons and daughters of black men and women that were actually slaves; the property of a white person. I remember my grandmother, who was born in 1909, telling stories about her grandmother, who was a slave. To these sons and daughters of slaves, the impact of Jackie Robinson playing on the same field as white men could be compared to how the rest of America felt when man landed on the moon. The Jackie Robinson story is well documented. Unfortunately, due to the fact that white America would not readily accept the truth about racial discrimination in this Country written by an African American, the majority of the books, white men wrote newspaper and magazine articles, about Jackie Robinson, including his biography and his baseball career. I have read many of these books and articles. I have seen the movies "The Jackie Robinson Story", "The Court Martial of Jackie Robinson" and the latest movie "42".

The latest remake, "42" does portray a more realistic view of what Jackie Robinson had to endure when he broke the color barrier in professional baseball over 65 years ago. The original movie, in black and white, was a watered down version of the events; it showed some ugly white characters shouting insults and making threats directed toward Jackie. However, what any of the movies fail to do is accurately depict the white characters, as the vile and disgusting low-life bigots, we in the African American community know were part of the white social structure of this Country during the "JIM CROW ERA" in late 1940s. Finally, over 40 years after his death, black America may finally get to look at a more accurate and factual account of the life and times of Jackie Robinson, from the perspective of the person who knew him best of all, Rachel Robinson. According to the interview with Ms. Robinson, she never called him "Jackie". The name did not have the intimacy that calling him by his given name, "Jack". According to Ms. Robinson, racial discrimination in Northern California was very subtle; African Americans were being segregated almost without knowing it. However, when I went South for the first time in 1947, I was shocked by the legal discrimination where I had to use a drinking fountain labeled "for Negroes only", or where I had to use a Negro women's bathroom in the airport. These are just a few of the details that Rachel Robinson being involved in the production may have added to the movie "42".

In my opinion, not one of the books, articles or the movies captured the whole truth about the hatred and bigotry endured by Jackie Robinson when he was the only black player in Major League Baseball. It is impossible for a white man to understand the hatred being directed at Jackie Robinson by the white fans, white players from the opposing teams and even his own teammates, just because the color of his skin was different. I compare a white man's ability to accurately depict the mental and physical abuse endured by African Americans in this Country to any man being able to accurate describe what it feels like to have labor pains. It is impossible!

Rachel Robinson

I had the privilege of watching and listening to Rachel Robinson, the widow of Jackie Robinson, as she was being interviewed on TV. At the time, Ms. Robinson is 85-years old and does not look anywhere close to her age. She was very sharp and articulate in her responses. In my opinion, Ms. Robinson is the perfect model of a proud black woman, who is still in love with a man that has been dead for over 40 years. Rachel Robinson is no stranger to me or to the rest of the world; like the late Eleanor Roosevelt, the late Coretta Scott King, and Hillary Clinton, she was the wife of an American Icon and for most of us, while Jackie Robinson was alive; Rachel Robinson had no identity outside of that of her famous husband. Like the famous wives of FDR, MLK, and

President Clinton, Rachel Robinson stood by her man. I have compared Ms. Robinson to Eleanor, Coretta and Hilary, each of whom are my personal heroines. Each has also been on the National stage to receive worldwide acclaim for their contributions to society, above and beyond the recognition they received from their association with their famous husbands. Unfortunately, we rarely get to see Rachel Robinson on a National stage unless it is to celebrate the accomplishments of her late husband, Jackie Robinson.

Ms. Rachel Robinson was born Rachel Annetta Isum July 19, 1922, and raised in Northern California. Rachel Isum attended UCLA, where she met Jackie Robinson in 1941, and in 1946, she married him. Jackie Robinson, Jr. was born in November 1946 and the Robinson's would later have a daughter, Sharon, and another son, David. In 1971, after he was able to overcome an addiction to heroin, her oldest child, Jack Jr., was killed in a car in accident. After Jackie Robinson's retirement from baseball, Rachel Robinson went back to school after many years as a homemaker. She got her Master's Degree in Psychiatric Nursing at New York University, and pursued her nursing career, eventually becoming an Assistant Professor of Nursing at Yale University and later, the Director of Nursing at the Connecticut Mental Health Center. Some of the awards, which have acknowledged her many significant contributions, are the Florence Nightingale Award, the Distinguished Humanitarian Award, and Equitable Life's Black Achievers Award. She has also received Honorary Degrees from St. John's College, as well as Springfield and McAllister Colleges. In 2007, MLB Commissioner Bud Selig awarded her the Commissioner's Historic Achievement Award. Mrs. Robinson is an active participant in the works of others, including the Phelps-Stokes Foundation, the New York Historical Society and the American Society for Training and Development.

I truly admire Eleanor Roosevelt for her forthright stand on ending racial discrimination in America, and Hilary Clinton, who has not only talked the talk, but also walked the walk in the battle to end racism in this Country. However, Coretta Scott King shares a common and unique bond with Rachel Robinson. More accurately, just as Jackie Robinson set the tone for Dr. King's philosophy of peaceful demonstrations, Rachel Robinson provided an example for Coretta Scott King as to how to endure the death threats, the taunts, the provocations, and the stinging insinuation, directed at the father of your children and the man you love. During a TV interview, Don Newcombe, a former pitcher and black teammate of Jackie Robinson, who joined the Dodgers in 1949, stated that Rachel Robinson was just as courageous as her pioneering husband, and that she silently was the most important supporting player in "The Jackie Robinson Story". Mr. Newcombe continued by saying, "Who's shoulder do you think Jackie cried on, when he came home after taken all that abuse at the ball park?" I was pleased that Mr. Newcombe shared that with a National TV audience. Remember, it was Roy Campanella, another one of Jackie's black teammates, joined the Dodgers in 1948, along with Mr. Newcombe and their wives that were probably the only African Americans that got a chance to take and up close and personal look at what Jackie and Rachel Robinson had to go through.

Birth of the Civil Rights Movement

The name Jackie Robinson and the date April 15, 1947, will be forever linked to the breaking of Major League Baseball's for white's restriction by becoming the first African to play for the Brooklyn Dodgers. What needs to also be associated with that date and event is that it was the start of the modern Civil Rights Movement in America. Just as important, the names of Jackie and Rachel Robinson should be mentioned as prominently as the names of Dr. Martin Luther and Coretta Scott King when we review the history of African American men and women that made a tremendous personal sacrifice and an outstanding contribution to realizing the dream of racial equality in America. According to Ms. Robinson, Jackie met Dr. Martin Luther King, Jr. in the 1950s, when the Reverend King began organizing for the Civil Rights Movement in the South. What Jackie admired most about Dr. King was his nonviolent protest, and his use of organization and strategies that drew on the human spirit, and his sense of being entitled to all that America promised. Jackie had a very strong sense of responsibility. Even in the post-baseball period, he worked very hard to get into the Civil Rights Movement, and to work on behalf of others. In her interviews, Ms. Robinson never mentioned if she met or spent any time with Coretta Scott King, or if she had the opportunity to share any of her experiences as being the wife of a man who also risk his life to change the world.

Over the years, I have seen several different movies that revealed a number of different accounts of the life and times of Dr. Martin Luther King. The early versions were done from the more acceptable viewpoint of white Corporate America. Later versions were done strictly from an African American perspective. All the movies about Dr. King's life allowed us to view facts about the man and his mission that may not have been common knowledge. It was not until the black director; Spike Lee made a movie about the life of Malcolm X that the world was able to see this great African American leader for who and what he really meant to the world.

Just months after his premature death from cancer, Rachel would start the Jackie Robinson Development Corporation, an organization that provides housing for low and middle-income families in New York. A year later, she would found the Jackie Robinson Foundation, the New York-based organization that provides mentoring and dozens of annual scholarships to outstanding African American and Hispanic students. Ms. Robinson stated during her interview, "If you have an overriding goal," she would say, "there are times when you must transcend the obstacles that are being put in your way. Rise above them." I think the lesson for us is, if you have an overriding goal, a big goal that you are trying to achieve, there are times when you must transcend the obstacles that are being put in your way. Jack wanted to integrate athletics. He could not afford to create an incident on the field that would interfere with reaching this goal. There had been predictions that if you integrated sports, there would be riots in the stands and on the field, and that the races could not play together. Jack had to demonstrate that this was incorrect. Jack did so at considerable personal sacrifice. He was a personality who would usually fight back in an instant if he sensed that he was being mistreated. However, he knew that he had to turn the other cheek for a short period of time, two years. That was a very clear part of the pact. This offer came as a total surprise to both of us. We were very excited, but we did not know what it really meant in the larger sense. At the time, Jack needed a job. He had just gotten out of the army and we wanted to get married. So initially, we were just pleased that we could carry out our plans. Our families were extremely happy for us, and somehow knew that if Jack were given an opportunity, he could make the most of it.

Rachel Robinson is still committed to the virtues Jackie Robinson has come to symbolize. She had learned, the hard way perhaps, about the value of struggling toward a higher aim. According to Ms. Robinson, Jack had an interesting statement to make about what life meant to him, which the Jackie Robinson Foundation now uses. It was that a life is not important, except in its impact on the lives of others. Now, 66 years after Robinson's historic debut, Rachel Robinson remains the keeper of the flame. She is a medium of sorts, constantly summoning up her husband's spirit for new generations of Americans to behold. Her goal for the 40 plus years she has lived without Jackie has been to honor his legacy, to preach, practice and encourage its message of fortitude, character and opportunity. In 2014, as I am writing this book, she is 92 years old, yet hardly a day goes by when she is not doing just that, invoking or promoting the memory of her late husband, who in becoming the first black Major Leaguer in the 20th century became so much more. Now, 66 years after Robinson's historic debut, Rachel Robinson remains the keeper of the flame.

In my other books, I have made it perfectly clear that in my opinion, the greatest all around baseball player ever, was Willie Mays. I remember when Mickey Mantle, the great New York Yankee Centerfielder, was dying of cancer; in one of his last televised interviews, he was asked who he thought was the best ballplayer he had ever seen. Mickey did not hesitate. He said without a doubt, it was Willie Mays. We need to be reminded that if not for the two years in the Armed Forces during the prime of his baseball career, Willie Mays would have shattered Babe Ruth record. All things being equal, it should be Willie's all-time homerun record that Barry Bonds broke. In spite of the fact that he has never failed a drug test, sportswriters and most of white America, have convicted Bonds of using steroids. What ever happened to being innocent until proven guilty in this Country? I guess I forgot that innocent until proven guilty still only applies to white Americans. In addition, I know most white reporters did not want an arrogant African American like Barry Bonds to break a record that will be forever linked to Babe Ruth, the "Great White Hope" of baseball. The majority of white America did not want Hank Aaron to break Babe's record and now there is even more of united campaign to discredit Barry Bonds, who has passed both Babe Ruth and Hank Aaron.

Like me, many of you are old enough to remember when America had this love hate relationship with Muhammad Ali, possibly the greatest Heavy Weight Champion of all time. They loved him in the early 1960s when he was young Cassius Clay, winning a Gold Medal for the USA as the light heavyweight champion in the 1960 Olympic in Rome, Italy. They love Mr. Clay when he defeated the brutish villain Sonny Liston. Yet, they hated Cassius Clay, when he converted to the Muslim religion, changed his name to Muhammad Ali and refused to be inducted into the United States Military during the war in Vietnam. After a hearing, he was stripped of his championship and was not allowed to box professionally.

African American Soldier

As far back as the Civil War, when the Union Army was segregated, white officers were assigned to command the battalions that were made up of former black slaves. In 1864, near the end of the Civil War, the rare exception to the rule was Lieutenant Stephen Atkins Swails. Lt. Swails was a black soldier in Union Army, who was a member of the 54th Massachusetts, the first official African American unit in the United States Armed Forces. Lt. Swails started as an enlisted man and worked his way up through the rank until he received a commission and became the first African American officer in the history of United

States Military. Black men were not able to assume command of white troops in the military until after World War II. Although Benjamin O. Davis, Sr., one of only two black combat officers in the U.S. Army in World War I, became the first African American General, his military career was seriously limited by the fact that this Country's Armed Forces were segregated.

General Benjamin O. Davis Jr. and Sr.

General Benjamin O. Davis Sr. never had the opportunity to command white troops. However, it was not his military record or the fact that he was the first black General in the U.S. Army that made Benjamin O. Davis, Sr. one of the most famous African Americans in history. His fame rests in the fact that he was the father of Benjamin O. Davis Jr., the Jackie Robinson of the United States Armed Forces. Benjamin Jr. grew up the son of a soldier and like his father; he despised segregation and was determined to destroy it. Benjamin Davis Jr. wanted to be a fighter pilot. In an effort to fulfill that ambition, he set his sights on the U.S. Military Academy at West Point. After briefly attending the University of Chicago, in 1932 Benjamin Davis Jr. earned an appointment to West Point from the Republican Congressman from Illinois, Oscar S. De Priest, who was the only black Congressman in the United States at that time. Benjamin O. Davis Jr. was the only black cadet in his class and his white would only speak to him for official reasons. He had no roommate and took his meals in silence. His white classmates hoped their indifference would drive Cadet Davis from the Academy, but their actions only made him more determined to succeed and he graduated thirty-fifth out of 276 in the Class of 1936.

Benjamin O. Davis Jr. had several different assignments after he graduated from West Point, including an assignment with the "Buffalo Soldiers" of the 10th Calvary. Reportedly, in 1940 President Franklin Roosevelt worried about keeping a strong hold on the black vote in this Country. President Roosevelt promoted the elder Benjamin Davis to brigadier general and ordered the Army Air Corps to create a black flying unit. The Army Air Corps wanted a black Academy graduate to command the first unit. Captain Benjamin Davis Jr. was the only living black West Point graduate and was ordered to begin training at Tuskegee's Army Air Field in Alabama. On March 7, 1942, Captain Davis pinned on the Silver Wings of Army Air Forces pilots along with four other black officers. In time, almost 1,000 Tuskegee Airmen joined them. In the spring of 1943, Major Davis and the 99th Fighter Squadron departed for North Africa to join the fight against the Germany in WWII. Reportedly, about 90 days after the squadron had flown many combat missions, Colonel William W. Momyer, the white commander of the 33rd Fighter Group, accused the Tuskegee Airmen of not having the same desire to fight as white pilots. Colonel Momyer, a high-ranking white officer, recommended removing the Tuskegee Airmen from combat. The general who reviewed the report endorsed it and commented, "The Negro type has not the proper reflexes to make a first-class fighter pilot."

General George C. Marshall, the Chief of Staff of the Army, decided to study the issue, assigning review of the 99th to the War Department's permanent Advisory Committee on Negro Troop Policies. Mr. Davis testified before the committee. He advised them that on June 9, 1943, during one of its first missions, the 99th formation disintegrated when it was struck by a German fighter force twice its size. The Germans surprised the Americans by attacking from above and out of the sun. Nobody could cite another example of a Tuskegee Airmen formation crumbling. In this single case, his men did not flee the battle but fought it out man-to-man against superior German aircraft. Mr. Davis maintained that his men were as eager for combat as white pilots. They were flying more often because his squadron was undermanned and replacements were short. He stated that his men flew six combat missions per day, far more than white pilots. Mr. Davis' testimony convinced the Advisory Committee, who along with General Marshall agreed that the 99th should not be pulled from combat and the new group of black fighter pilots, the 33rd Fighter Group, should move overseas when they completed training.

Tuskegee Airmen

The most spectacular mission flown by the 332nd was its' mission on March 24, 1945, when Lt. Colonel Davis led the 332nd on a 1,600-mile round trip escort mission to Berlin, Germany. On that day, the Tuskegee Airmen met least 30 of the new German jet aircraft. The Tuskegee Airmen shot down three of the jets and damaged another six fighters. Only one of the Tuskegee Airmen was killed on this mission, but none of the bombers was shot down, despite the fact that the Germans threw their latest and fastest fighters at the Americans. How good were the Tuskegee Airmen? Colonel Davis' squadron shot down 111 enemy aircraft; destroying 150 aircraft on the ground; disabled more than 600 boxcars and other rolling stock; sunk one German Navy destroyer, and more than 40 other enemy boats and barges. Equally impressive was the fact that the Tuskegee Airmen did not lose a bomber to an enemy fighter during 200 escort missions. After the Tuskegee Airmen returned to the United States they were assigned to Lockbourne Air Force Base just outside of Ohio. It should be noted that most all of the Civil Servants working at Lockbourne Base were white and all of their supervisors were black. There is nowhere else in America that one could find this situation. For centuries people said whites would never work for blacks, but at Lockbourne several hundred whites worked professionally and well for Colonel Davis and the Tuskegee Airmen.

Based on their performance, the Tuskegee Airmen under the command of Colonel Davis, overseas and at Lockbourne AAB, the U.S. Air Force, in 1949, became the first of the U.S. Armed Services to integrate its troops. In the summer of 1949, Colonel Davis attended the Air War College, a key assignment because promotion beyond colonel depended upon attending War College. Before Colonel Benjamin O. Davis, no black officer in any service had ever attended War College. Segregation had barred such attendance. Colonel Davis excelled, despite the fact that the Air War College was located on a base in Montgomery, Alabama, an area hostile to any African Americans who aspired to rise economically or professionally. The best restaurants, hotels, and housing in the city were closed to Colonel Davis and his wife, Aggie. Colonel Davis detested the treatment he received in Montgomery Alabama, but tolerated it to graduate from the Air War College. In 1953, during the Korean War, the Air Force assigned Colonel Davis to take command of the 51ˢᵗ Fighter-Interceptor Wing, Suwon AB, South Korea. Colonel Davis supervised a wing of thousands of airmen, almost all white. As a result of this assignment, the Air Force learned that white airmen and officers would work loyally for a black commander, and the wing was as effective as any other Air Force unit in Asia.

Having again demonstrated his skills as a commander, Colonel Davis was transferred to Japan, where he was appointed director of operations and training in Far East Air Forces. Three months later, he was promoted to Brigadier General, the first black officer in the Air Force to achieve that rank. General Davis was soon reassigned to what proved to be his most significant postwar position, vice commander of 13th Air Force and commander of Air Task Force 13 at Taipei, Taiwan. He was to build a defensive air force from scratch, to deter Communist forces on Mainland China from launching an air or sea attack on Taiwan. In two years, General Davis built a formidable defensive air force. General Davis next moved to 12th Air Force in Germany and in 1957, he became the Deputy Chief of Staff for operations for U.S. Air Forces in Europe. He returned to the U.S. in 1961 as a Major General and as USAF Director of Manpower and Organization. He served in the Pentagon for four years, earning a third star, and moved in April 1965 to Korea to become chief of staff of the United Nations Command and U.S. Forces Korea. General Davis became commander of 13th Air Force in August 1967, taking command of more than 55,000 people all over Asia, including many thousands who were flying and fighting in the Vietnam War.

In 1968, General Davis was moved back to the U.S., where he was assigned as Deputy Commander In Chief of U.S. Strike Command. No other assignment for General Davis had such worldwide implications as this assignment. He traveled widely to see for himself the conditions under which his men and women might have to fight. In 1970, after two years as the Deputy Commander In Chief, General Davis retired from the Air Force. He served more than 33 years on active duty, had been all around the world, and had excelled in every position. He left the Air Force and the military service a much better institution than he found it. In1998, almost 30 years after he had retired, President Clinton promoted Lt. General Benjamin Davis to full General. After retiring from the Air Force, Benjamin O. Davis Jr. became the director of public safety for Cleveland, Ohio, overseeing the city's fire and police departments. He later became director of Civil Aviation Security and an Assistant Secretary at the U.S. Department of Transportation. When Benjamin O. Davis Jr. joined the Army Air Forces, he was the only black officer. When the service integrated in 1949, there were only 375 black officers in the service, about 0.6 percent of the total number of officers. Today, there are over 4,000 black officers in the Air Force, almost six percent of the total. General Davis can claim the largest portion of the credit for opening the doors to black men and women to become officers and to bringing about the integration of the U.S. Air Force.

Why is it that white team owners have no problem hiring a white man to lead teams dominated by black men, but they resist the hiring of a black man to lead a team period? For years, African Americans were stereotyped as lacking the intelligence needed for positions that required the ability to make quick decisions. Did white team owners every study the history of the Tuskegee Airmen? The U.S. Armed Forces questioned the ability of African American to fly planes. The Tuskegee Airman dispelled that myth. It also took a span of 100 years for the U.S. Armed Forces to realize that white soldiers would follow the leadership of African American officers.

Colin Powell

General Benjamin O. Davis, Jr. opened the door for black officers and General Colin Powell parlayed that opening with his career in the U.S. Army to become the first African American Secretary of State. As a Four Star General, Colin Powell broke the color barrier by becoming the first African American Commander-in-Chief, and he achieved the highest rank in the military when he became Chairman of the Joint

Chiefs of Staff. How long will it take white Corporate America to come to the same conclusion as the U.S. Armed Forces? White Americans have no problem with African Americans leading their sons and daughters into battle, but they will not hire an African American to lead their sons into victory in the world of sports.

After he retired from the military, in 1996 the Republic Party made a legitimate effort to persuade Colin Powell to be their candidate and run against the incumbent Democrat, President "Bill' Clinton, in the coming Presidential election. This was another groundbreaking precedent for African Americans. In 1960, the first African American U.S. Presidential candidate was Rev. Clennon King, on the Independent Afro American party. In 1972, Shirley Chisholm, a democrat, was the first African American Presidential candidate from a major party. In 1969, Ms. Chisholm made history by becoming the first African American female to be elected to U.S. Congress. In 1984, Jesse Jackson became the third and most successful African American to run in the Presidential primary election as a Democrat. With very little chance that he would win the Party's nomination, Jesse ran an exceptional campaign and was single handedly responsible for the largest recorded registration of African American voters in the history of this Country. Like Ms. Chisholm, Jesse never received any support from the National Democratic Party, and just as Ms. Chisholm before him, Jesse lost the nomination. However, in 1996 an African American, Colin Powell, did have the support of the National Republican Party. The historical event was that the right –winged conservative, predominately affluent white males, Republican Party considered an African American to be their Presidential candidate. Reportedly, after much consideration and his thanks, Colin Powell declined the nomination. In 2001, a Republican President, George W. Bush, appointed Colin Powell to his cabinet as the 65th Secretary of State. Mr. Powell was the first African American to serve in that position.

Led Us Not

Does it make sense that the leaders of white leaders of our Country and the white leaders of Corporate America would trust the lives of their offspring to African Americans in war, but not trust these same African Americans to make sound business decisions when it comes to managing a business in this Country during peace? It does not surprise me because it is the same white Southern plantation mentality in affect. Since the beginning of slavery in America, white slave owners have entrusted the care and well-being of the children to black slaves. It makes sense that the white ancestors of these black slave owners would have no problem entrusting the lives of their sons and daughters to the ancestors of black slaves. Just as it is today, during the time when slavery was legal, a few white plantation owners used a black slave to be the overseer of the other black slaves. A few white professional sports team owners hire African Americans to manage their teams. Unlike their slave ancestors who never had a choice, the black professional athletes of today hired African Americans as the leaders of the player's union for professional football and basketball. In addition, to their credit, the players in both basketball and football do not allow any blatant acts of disparate treatment against African Americans.

Smith & Carlos: The Shot Heard Around the World

Tommie Smith and John Carlos, teammates at San Jose State University, secretly planned a non-violent protest to be conducted at the1968 Olympic Games in Mexico City in full view of the entire free world. After Tommie Smith finished first and John Carlos finished third in the finals of the 200 meters, they stood on the medal stand bowed their heads and thrust their black-glove-covered hands in the air, the world took notice and understood the nature of their protest. Over the past 40 years, I have watched the video replay of this protest at least 100 times. Each time I watched this historic event, I was further impressed with the courage it must have taken for these two young black men to stand up before the world and protest racism. However, I will have to admit that the more I watched; I would pay far less attention to the white person on the medal stand. When I first saw this event live on TV, I remember that there was another person standing at attention on the medal stand that day and that other person was a white man. Being familiar with the Olympic medal ceremony, I knew that the first, second and third place finishers in an event always received medals. Like millions of other viewers around the world, my focus on this day was on the actions of Tommie Smith and John Carlos. I hate to admit that I really did not care to know who the other person on the stand was on this day. For close to 40 years, I just thought the other person on the medal stand, who just happened to be white, was an innocent bystander.

As important as the actions of Tommie Smith and John Carlos are to African American history and the battle to end racial discrimination in this Country, the role of the Australian runner and the 1968 Silver Medalist in the 200 meters, Peter Norman, is just as important. The actions of Peter Norman on this day are a great history lesson as well as an even greater life lesson. I have watched the protest by Tommie Smith and John Carlos at least 100 times. I have watched documentaries on the planning of the protest, interviews with Mr. Smith and Mr. Carlos and listened to commentary on the impact of the protest. Mr. Norman is hardly ever mentioned in discussions or presentations of this major event. Yet, it was not until I conducted the research for this book, that I took a close look at the other man on the medal stand on October 17, 1968 in Mexico City, Mexico. If I would have looked closer at the protest and paid more attention to details, I would have noticed the black scarf around Tommie Smith's neck, which stood for black pride. I would have noticed their black socks, with no shoes, which represented black poverty in racist America. I would have noticed that John Carlos wore a string of beads, to commemorate black people who had been lynched in this Country. I would have noticed that the white man was wearing an Olympic Project for Human Rights (OPHR) badge in support of the black American athletes, was standing at attention throughout and never bothered to look at either Mr. Smith or Mr. Carlos during this protest.

I was in the Marine Corps. I was trained to stand at attention without moving for long periods of time. Yet, in spite of my training, I would turn my head just slightly to catch a glimpse of someone or something that surprised me. If you watch any video replays or see any pictures of this event, you will notice that Peter Norman never moved. I was not in Mexico City on October 17, 1968, but I can only imagine the reaction from the crowd as they looked on in disbelief, when Tommie Smith and John Carlos raised their black fists. The screaming and shouting from the spectators in the stands drew attention to what was happening during this medal ceremony. Yet, in the midst of all this confusion, this young white man, never turned to see what was going on behind him. Norman never registers surprise or alarm. During the shock of this historic protest, his back was as straight as any proud Marine's would be standing with his brothers. Like most people, I made the mistake of assuming Mr. Norman to be just another of those unwitting witnesses to history who always end up as a face in the crowd. What I did not know was that the Silver Medalist with the white skin stood with Mr. Smith and Mr. Carlos as part of this protest. They agreed before the race, that if the three, as expected, were the ones on this National stage, they would stand together: Norman may not have raised his fist, but the three young anti-racists stood together in struggle. It was Mr. Norman who suggested that Tommie Smith and John Carlos share the black gloves used in their salute, after Mr. Carlos had left his gloves in the Olympic Village. This is the reason for Tommie Smith raising his right fist, while John Carlos raised his left.

Although he was allowed to keep his Silver Medal and he did not receive any sanctions from the Olympic Committee in Mexico City, the Australian Olympic authorities reprimanded Mr. Norman and the Australian media ostracized him. Despite qualifying fifteen times for the 100 meters and 5 times for the 200 meters, the Australian Olympic track team did not pick Norman for the 1972 Summer Olympics. In fact, 1972 was the first time ever that no Australian sprint team went to the Olympics. Black historians, including this writer, have documented the backlash endured by Tommie Smith and John Carlos as a result of their protest at the 1968 Summer Olympics. Very few of us in the black community known what happened to Mr. Norman as a result of his involvement with these two black men and their protest against racism. According to published reports, he was a pariah in the Australian Olympic world, and despite being a five-time National Champion in the 200 meters, Mr. Norman was blacklisted and was unable to get a job as a track, in spite of the that he worked as a Physical Education teacher. Reportedly, John Carlos said of Mr. Norman, "At least me and Tommie had each other when we came home. When Peter went home, he had to deal with a nation by himself. Yet, Peter Norman never wavered, never denied that he was up there with us for a purpose and he never said 'I am sorry' for his involvement. That is indicative of whom the man was; Norman earned the love and respect of his peers".

When the 2000 Olympics came to Sydney, Australia, Mr. Norman was deliberately outcast from the festivities because of his association with Tommie Smith and John Carlos. In a conversation at that time with sportswriter Mike Wise, Mr. Norman was absent of bitterness and wore his ostracism as proudly as that solidarity button from 1968. "I did the only thing I believed was right," he said to Wise. "I asked what they wanted me to do to help. I could not see why a black man was not allowed to drink out of the same water fountain, sit in the same bus, or go to the same schools as a white person. That was just social injustice that I could not do anything about from where I was, but I certainly abhorred it." Norman was eventually part of the 2000 Olympics in Sydney after being invited by the United States when they heard that his own Country had failed include him in their plans. Norman kept running, but contracted gangrene in 1985 after tearing his Achilles tendon during a training session, which nearly led to his leg being amputated. Mr. Norman died of a heart attack on October 3, 2006 in Melbourne, Australia at the age of 64. His death followed a recent triple bypass operation. USA Track and Field Federation proclaimed October 9 2006, the date of his funeral, as Peter Norman Day. Reportedly, John Carlos said in a statement about the sudden passing, "Peter was a piece of my life. When I got the call, it knocked the wind out of me. I was his brother. He was my brother. That is all you have to know." Two people who knew the depth and conviction of Peter Norman's solidarity were the two who acted as lead pallbearers at his funeral: Tommie Smith and John Carlos.

Colored Blind - OREO

In 2006, Devon Sherwood was the only African American member of 47 men on the lacrosse team at Duke University in Durham, North Carolina. Like Peter Norman, Devon Sherwood will be remembered as the forgotten man in an incident that gained National attention. However, Sherwood did not further the cause of racial solidarity, as Peter Norman did with his relationship with Tommie Smith and John Carlos. Instead, Devon Sherwood's relationship with the 46 white boys on the Duke Lacrosse Team revisits the bond between the black and white characters in "Uncle Tom's Cabin" and "Gone with the Wind". Sherwood acted as the stereotypical African Americans during the "JIM CROW ERA" in America that was portrayed as "helpless ignorant niggers" that could not survive without the help of the white man. In televised interviews, Sherwood said that his three white teammates who have been accused of sexually assaulting a black woman had been "stereotyped" by class and skin color. "It's almost a reversal," Sherwood said, "I've even been stereotyped for being rich, being on full scholarship, [being] not in touch with my own black community at Duke. It's terrible to find yourself being stereotyped". Sherwood said he found it "impossible" to believe that the rape allegations are true. "I'm 100 percent confident," he said. "I know nothing indeed happened that night at all". Asked how he could be so sure if he was not present when the alleged attack took place, Sherwood said he knew the defendants well enough. "I don't hesitate," he said. "I believe in the character of my teammates. I believe in the character of specifically [the three defendants]. I would never ever doubt them or think they were lying?' I would never do that, because I believe in them."

Why is that after over 400 years of disparate treatment in this Country, we still have a 19-year old African American male running around with a severe case of racial identity. Did Devon Sherwood and his parents stick their heads in a hole in the ground and refuse to hear or see what and who Devon's bigoted white teammates really are? Yes, his parents, who both graduated from Duke University, and who are probably right wing conservative Republicans, have to assume some of the responsible for their son's negative attitude toward his own race. The Sherwood's represent a growing number of African Americans; educated at a prestigious white college or university and have achieved upper class social and economic status; who now feel they are white. The Sherwood's likely live in a predominately-rich white neighborhood, which has little or no contact with the "down to earth" black community. The Sherwood family fit the description of "Oreos", black on the outside but white on the inside. Devon Sherwood's rich white upbringing is the only excuse for some of the comments made in support of his white teammates. How could anyone, black or white, believe that a group of teenage boys, black or white, could have a party that involved alcohol and exotic female dancers, and be totally void of some form of immature, irrational and just plain stupid behavior that could have been borderline criminal in nature.

If Devon Sherwood read the police report, he knew that witnesses confirmed and the white lacrosse players never denied directing racial slurs at the black female dancers as they left the party. Both dancers told the police that they were called racial epithets and that one of the young men yelled, "Thank your grandfather for my white cotton shirt," as the pair departed. A neighbor confirmed to police that he heard the comment about the shirt. According to published reports, Devon Sherwood seemed to struggle a bit as he grappled with the notion that his teammates could have made these remarks. "If it is in fact true, it's disgusting," Sherwood said.

The fact that Devon Sherwood used the term "if" indicates that he is in denial. Devon, the reason your white teammates never called you a "nigger" is because you have always acted like just another white boy. Devon, just ask yourself, why did 46 white lacrosse players decide to have a party, knowing that alcohol was going to be served to under age boys, hire two black female "strippers" to perform at this party. At Duke University, in Durham, North Carolina, the majority of the college age females are white. Did your teammates usually date black women? If the answer to the question is no, then you would have to assume the only reason your white teammates invited black, rather than white female dancers, is because they have no respect for African

American women. During the investigation of this incident, reporters criticized the States' Attorney, stating he had a political agenda for charging the three white Lacrosse Team members. The media portrayed the three white rape and sexual assault suspects as victims of a false allegation. Yet, during the ordeal that dragged on for months, I do not remember anyone asking; "Why were only black women invited to this party?"

Devon Sherwood, before you come to the defense of white people or feel that reverse discrimination or stereotyping is being used against white people, you and your parents need to read my books and study African American history, specially the Dred Scott Decision. In 1857, it was the majority opinion of the Supreme Court of the United States and Chief Justice Roger B. Taney that Dred Scott, a Missouri slave who had traveled with his white master into free territory and wanted his freedom made permanent, should remain enslaved. The language used by Chief Justice Taney in his decision, is still a source of shame and a black eye on the Supreme Court. Chief Justice Taney, who was born on a slave holding tobacco farm in Maryland, wrote that the Founding Fathers regarded blacks as "beings of an inferior order, and altogether unfit to associate with the white race, either in social or political relations, and so far inferior that they had no rights which the white man was bound to respect."

What Devon Sherwood needs to realize is that his white teammates at Duke University, had the same attitude toward blacks as Chief Justice Taney. These young white boys, using the false courage acquired from the alcoholic beverages consumed at the party, felt it was well within their rights to engage themselves in whatever form of lewd and lascivious conduct they desired, using these young black women as their pawns. Remember, Sherwood family, history does repeat its' self. One day your daughter or granddaughter may attend Duke, and she might be invited to one of these lacrosse team parties.

In my trilogy, I used the term "nigger" very sparingly in my first book, *"American Apartheid"*. The term "nigger" was used more frequently in my second book, *"No Land No Mule No Freedom"*. It is in this book that the term "nigger" is used the most. Let me once again make it perfectly clear that I detest the term and what it stands for. However, I am a realist and a writer, and I use the term "nigger" to make a point. In 2012, I watched a movie titled "Django Unchained". An American Western film written and directed by Quentin Tarantino, who made the film as a very stylized variation of the "spaghetti Western", which takes place in the "Old West ", primarily taking place in America's pre-Civil War South. In the movie, Samuel L. Jackson played the role of "Stephen", the white plantation owner's "staunchly loyal house slave". The character "Stephen" is best described as the "head house nigger". If you have seen the movie, you have a better understanding of my description of "Stephen". According to the history of slavery and slaves that has been passed down for generations by my African American ancestors, the character "Stephen" is the perfect example of a "house nigger".

I write about history because, as I have stated throughout this book, I believe history will and does repeat its' self. While conducting the research for my books, I have watched the news on TV, read a lot of books, magazines and newspaper articles to keep abreast of current events. Most of the reports that address racial issues in America are usually buffered in order to pass mutter and not offend the white male Corporate Structure that that owns and controls the print media and TV media in this Country. Earlier, I compared the Duke Lacrosse Team rape case with the infamous "Scottsboro Boys" rape case that occurred during 1930s, which was the height of the "JIM CROW ERA" in America. There is another incident that can be compared to the "Scottsboro Boys"; it took place in a small town called Jena, Louisiana. Usually, I do not like to reference specific articles in my books; however, for the first time in my writing career, I read an article written by a white female reporter, Alice Woodward, that gave an in-depth description of a racial incident that was worthy of a Pulitzer Prize. It was the first document written by a white person that featured a totally unbiased perspective of the events that occurred during this racial incident. This exceptional article was titled "The Jena 6". In order to understand what occurred in Jena, Louisiana, you need to read this article in the July 10, 2007 "Revolution Newspaper".

349

"Jena Six"

The "Jena 6" incident is another perfect example of how history will continue to repeat its' self until those of us that truly care about the future of America, end the practice of racism in this Country. After Hurricane Katrina, the eyes of the world were on the City of New Orleans and State of Louisiana. Why would the little town of Jena think that they could continue to live in the "JIM CROW ERA" and go unnoticed? Why did the white people, of this small town located about 230 miles from New Orleans think that the statement "equal justice under the law" was merely words? Let us look at the disparity; a group of white male students assaulted a black male student on school property, this incident is handled by the principle and the white boys receive some form of administrative discipline. Basically, they were suspended from school; ironically, that was the same punishment given to the white students that hung ropes with "nooses" in a shade tree after black students sat under the tree; which violated the tradition of the shade tree only being reserved for use by whites students only. After the noose incident, during a fight on school property, a white male student was injured, six black male students, between the ages of 15 to 17, were arrested, and the local District Attorney charges them with attempted second-degree murder. The white boy did not sustain any life threatening injuries and the DA reduced the charges against the six black students, now known as the "Jena 6", to aggravated assault. The first of the six black students was tried and convicted by an all-white jury without having any witnesses testify on his behalf.

The first of the "Jena 6" to be convicted could be sentenced to 22 years in prison. Are the people in Jena, Louisiana living in a time capsule from the 1930s or in a land that time has forgotten? Did anyone in the La Salle Parish District Attorney's Office ever read the United States Constitution? Did they ever hear of the term "due process" or being tried by a jury of your peers? If not for all the attention directed at the City of New Orleans and the State of Louisiana as a result of hurricane Katrina, the La Salle Parish DA may have continued to get away with this "JIM CROW" brand of justice. Maybe for the first time after years of disparate treatment, the African American community of Jena finally stood up and said that enough is enough. The families and friends of the Jena 6 organized a protest to overcome the "JIM CROW" brand of justice being applied to their sons. Along with their local protest, they asked for outside help to show the town's white power structure that they will not sit idly by as their loved ones are railroaded into a life behind bars. One of the outside sources was the Reverend Al Sharpton, and although I may not always agree with his tactics, Rev. Sharpton does draw National attention to a situation. The National attention given to the incident got a response from the Governor Blanco and had an impact on the La Salle Parrish DA, who decided to the delay the sentencing of the first member of the "Jena 6" and the trials for the remaining members. One thing that has not changed; when you shine the light on roaches they will always run for cover. Hurricane Katrina was the light that brought attention to the racial disparity in areas throughout the City of New Orleans and the State of Louisiana.

Once More and Again

For those of you that think that this was just an isolated incident, in 2005, in Douglas County, Georgia, an above average student and promising high school athlete, 17-year-old Genarlow Wilson was convicted of molestation and sentenced to 10 years for engaging in consensual oral sex with a 15-year-old girl. Genarlow Wilson was convicted of aggravated child molestation because, he had engaged in oral sex with a consenting fifteen-year-old at a New Year's Eve party. Both Wilson and the girl are African American. However, the age of consent in Georgia is sixteen. The conviction was based on an amateur video tape showing Mr. Wilson engaging in sex with a 15-year-old girl during a private party, and later being offered and receiving oral sex from that same girl. The video shows the 17-year-old girl on the bathroom floor, then later having sex with Mr. Wilson. She appeared sleepy or intoxicated during the sex act; but did not ask Mr. Wilson to stop. Waking up naked and disoriented the next morning, she claimed to have been raped. Investigating the alleged rape, police later found condoms and evidence of drinking, as well as the video camera, in the motel room used for the party. A jury acquitted Mr. Wilson of raping the older girl, but convicted him of aggravated child molestation against the 15-year-old. The "aggravated" nature of the charge refers to fellatio (oral sex) rather than a mere "immoral or indecent act." Had the two teenagers had intercourse without oral sex, Mr. Wilson would have been charged with a misdemeanor, punishable up to 12-months, with no sex offender status, instead of the mandatory 10-year minimum term that the judge gave him.

Reportedly, the 15-year-old girl, who has remained unnamed in the press as a "victim of a sex offense", has repeatedly stated that the act of oral sex was consensual, though she legally could not consent. The jury acquitted Wilson of the rape charge, but as the age of consent in Georgia is 16, they voted to convict him of aggravated child molestation for the oral sex incident, with the forewoman tearfully reading the verdict. Some jury members later complained they had not understood the verdict would result in a 10-year minimum sentence, plus one year on probation. Mr. Wilson received the 10-year sentence following a refusal to enter into a proposed plea bargain, stating of his adamant belief that "It's all about doing what's right; and what's right is right, and what's wrong is wrong; and I am just standing up for what I believe in." His decision to reject the plea agreement, as well as his continued fight to overturn his conviction, takes into account that sex offenders in Georgia must register and for life. As the law stands, Mr. Wilson would not even be able to return to his own family after an early release, as he has an 8-year-old sister and would be forbidden contact. The other young black males involved accepted plea bargains. They are required to register as convicted sex offenders. Mr. Wilson had been offered, and rejected, a plea bargain for a five-year sentence with the possibility of parole before the trial. After the jury had returned the guilty verdict, the Prosecutor offered the same 5-year plea bargain again, and Wilson refused again. Another young man involved in the case had accepted a similar 5-year plea bargain and was paroled after two years.

In part because of the publicity surrounding this case, the law under which Mr. Wilson was convicted was changed after his conviction. The act would now be treated as a misdemeanor with a maximum sentence of one year in prison, and no sex offender registration. While Mr. Wilson's Attorneys argued that such a change in the law should reverse his conviction, the Legislature specifically prohibited the law from being applied retroactively. A bipartisan group of legislators introduced a bill in the 2007 Georgia legislative session that would allow Mr. Wilson's sentence to be reduced by the courts. Reacting to District Attorney David McDade's releasing the videotape to legislators, media and the public upon request, Georgia State Senator Emanuel Jones said he would introduce legislation to block District Attorneys from handing over photographic images in sex cases. Since the participants shown having sex in the video were under 18, the videotape constitutes child pornography under Federal Law. The Adam Walsh Child Protection and Safety Act prohibit Prosecutors from allowing defendants in criminal proceedings to possess a copy of any evidence that constitutes child pornography, even if the purpose is to mount a defense against the charge. Under this law, Mr. Wilson and his defense team are prohibited from having a copy of the videotape that Prosecutor has distributed to everyone else. In 2007, after serving more than two years in prison, the Georgia Supreme Court earlier Friday ordered that Mr. Wilson be released, ruling 4-3 that his sentence was cruel and unusual punishment.

Take the Genarlow Wilson case, travel forward in time 10 months; move from one rural community, Douglas County, to another rural area Rome County, Georgia; make the 15-year old girl white rather than black, and you have the Marcus Dixon rape case. According to published reports, which included a feature on EPSN TV Series "Real Sports", Marcus Dixon went from a top student athlete to an accused rapist. It is a classic case of "he said/she said" with two teenagers at the center of controversy. Marcus Dixon had it all. He was an honor roll student, a talented high school football star with a full scholarship to Vanderbilt University. Kristie Brown was a happy sophomore at the same school, who loved fishing, the outdoors and had dreams of becoming a nurse. On February 10, 2003, both of their lives would change forever. Marcus Dixon went from a top student athlete to an accused rapist after having sex with Kristie in a classroom after school. He says it was consensual; she says it was rape. The case sparked a whirlwind of controversy nationwide. Marcus is black, and Kristie is white. Ironically, Marcus Dixon was adopted and raised by white parents. It took a jury only 20 minutes to acquit Marcus of the rape, battery, assault and false imprisonment charges. However, just like Genarlow Wilson, Marcus Dixon was found guilty of statutory rape and aggravated child molestation because Kristie was under the legal age of 16 by just three months. The jury had no choice but to find him guilty of these charges. Under Georgia law, the punishment for aggravated child molestation is a 10-year mandatory sentence. Some say the case is not about sex between two teenagers, but really about the racial prejudices that still exist in Georgia. Similar to what happened in the Genarlow Wilson case, in 2004, the Georgia Supreme Court ordered that Marcus Dixon be released. In 2012, Marcus Dixon is played in the NFL with the Kansas City Chiefs.

No Chains Still Slaves

As I have come to the finally chapter of this book, I like to revisit or update some of events that I covered earlier. Let me update some information on "Massa" David Stern, Commissioner of the NBA, and his newly installed clone, Roger Goodell, Commissioner of the NFL. It seems while Commissioner Stern was using his absolute power to control the African American players that dominate the NBA; he allowed a "lily" white fox, under the guise of a referee, to sneak into the hen house and steal the preverbal eggs and annihilate the integrity of professional basketball in America. David Stern, renowned as the most powerful Commissioner in the history of organized sports, allowed a gambling scandal that has rocked the very core of the integrity of the NBA, take place under his watch.

Whenever Commissioner Stern addresses the media about the unprofessional conduct of an NBA player, (75% of the players are

African Americans) he makes it clear that if the inappropriate behavior is not controlled, it could become an epidemic that could destroy the NBA. Yet, when he addressed the media regarding the NBA referee involved in the gambling scandal (69% of the NBA referees are white), he assured the media that this was an isolated incident, by one rogue official, and this incident will in no way have a lasting impact on the NBA. Commissioner Stern is responsible for the NBA referees. Why did he not scrutinize the off court conduct of the referees as closely as he watched the NBA players? In the absence of a rational or reasonable response to this question, we can apply the principle of disparate treatment. It was based on race, the referees are white and the players are black, it is just that simple.

The "Massa" of the "Ole Plantation" was so busy monitoring the activity of his black slaves that he could not see his white overseer stealing the family jewels right under his nose. Does that sound familiar? I would be willing to wager every dollar that I earn from the sales of this book, that if basketball players, Michael Jordan or Charles Barkley, who have a reputation of being excessive gamblers, were involved with the so-called "Mafia" or "Underworld", Commissioner Stern would have known about it in a "New York" minute. It does not really matter to me whether Tim Donaghy, the white referee involved in this scandal, acted alone or in concert with other NBA referees or NBA players.

My concern is that the media failed to recognize and report the racially disparate treatment of this incident by Commissioner Stern. It is my opinion that Commissioner Stern treats black different from whites. The media has made tongue in cheek types of insinuations about whether or not Jordan and Barkley wager far too much money at the tables in Las Vegas and on the golf course during their amateur matches. Reportedly, they lose millions of dollars gambling. Would this have an impact on their professional basketball playing careers? They are both multi-millionaires. Who cares how much money they lose? According to published reports, in August 1993 when it was discovered that James Jordan, the father of Michael Jordan had been murdered near his home in North Carolina, the news media impiously attributed his death to the gambling debts of his son. The media even went as far as to suggest that Jordan was the victim of a mob hit in retribution for Michael Jordan throwing games.

After these ridiculous allegations surfaced about the death of Michael Jordan's father, why did Commissioner Stern not immediately address the media on Michael's behalf? He had no problem scheduling a press conference to address the scandal involving this white referee. Why did the Commissioner not make it perfectly clear that there was no way possible that Michael Jordan would be involved with any activity that would dishonor his family, his teammates, the Chicago Bulls organization, the NBA and the game he loves? The Commissioner took an immediate stand and made it perfectly clear that this was an isolated incident when he addressed the press about the white referee involved in gambling. Why did he not make a positive statement about Michael? The murder of James Jordan gained National attention; yet with all the statements being made, I do not remember any statement from Commissioner Stern. The most powerful and influential Commissioner in all of sports, David Stern fails to protect the most popular NBA player in the history of the league. As fate would have it, after he was indicted in Federal Court, Tim Donaghy, the white referee involved in this gambling scandal, contradicted "Massa" Stern statement that he acted alone, by providing information about approximately 20 other NBA referees that bet on NBA. If there were 20 other referees involved, like Tim Donaghy, the majority of them would have to be white men.

Guilty Until Proven Innocent

What do O.J. Simpson, Adam "Pacman" Jones and Michael Vick have in common? They are all very successful African American NFL players that were convicted in the court of public opinion long before they had their day in a court of law. Personally, it upsets me that these African American males have set such a poor example for future generations of black children. O.J is old news and I have already expressed my feeling about Pacman Jones. It is my opinion that Michael Vick deserved to go to jail for being stupid. He was stupid enough to get involved with criminals who were operating an illegal dog fighting operation. Michael was stupid enough to trust convicted criminals to keep his involvement in illegal activity confidential. However, America needs to realize is that "dog fighting" and hunting deer with an assault rifle with a scope are both cruel to the animals. The problem is one is legal and the other is not.

If you check, the State and Federal Correctional Facilities, I would be willing to bet a year's salary that only one out of every 400,000 inmates is incarcerated for dog fighting. As a matter of fact, in some States in the Mid-West, dog fighting is a misdemeanor. Michael Vick deserved to be punished. What he did not deserve was to be publicly lynched by the media as an example of what white America will not tolerate from an affluent black man. Whatever happened to innocent until proven guilty? Whatever happened to due process? Whatever happened to truth, justice and the American way? Are we returning the "JIM CROW ERA", when no matter the guilt or innocence, a black person could not receive equal treatment under the law in America?

What about the statement made by "Massa" Roger Goodell, Commissioner of the NFL, after Michael Vick pleaded guilty to the Federal charges associated with dog fighting? Goodell seemed to be more upset over the fact that Michael Vick lied to him and his "owner", Arthur Blank, the owner of the Atlanta Falcons, than he was over the fact that Michael had plead guilty to a crime that involved gambling and cruelty to animals. Goodell kept repeating the fact that Michael Vick lied to his face. If we go back a few years, it may be understandable why lying to the white man was such a crime.

Remember, some of my slave ancestors were actually lynched for lying to their white "massa". I have talked about black people that function as if they were still slaves. I call it a "slave's mentality". Unfortunately, there are white people that have a "plantation mentality" because they act as if African Americans are still slaves. In 2006 the NFL owners, with close to 78% of the players in the league being African American, replaced a white man, Paul Tagliabue, as Commissioner, with another white man Roger Goodell. In 2014 the NBA owners, with close to 78% of the players being black, used the same "plantation mentality", to replace a white man David Stern, as Commissioner, with another white man Adam Silver. White "Massa" got to have a white overseer to keep them "darkies" in place. History continues to repeat its' self.

Just Another "Massa"!

I talked a lot about former NBA Commissioner David Stern and NFL Commissioner Roger Goodell. In 2014, I end with Commissioner Rodger Goodell. Just when you think the plantation, mentality of white team owners has gone as far South as they can go, these white team owners do something that is more egregious anything they have ever done before. The word "nigger" or "nigga" is offensive. The words are even more offensive when white people use them. I have made it clear throughout my books, that the use of the "N" word, for any reason, by anybody, is an insult to the history of African Americans. In 2013, two white NFL players used the "N" word when referring to an African American.

During a concert, Riley Cooper, a white football player for the Philadelphia Eagles, was seen and heard on video saying, "I will jump that fence and fight every nigger here, bro." A white player for the Miami Dolphins, Richie Incognito, used the "N" word in the company of his African American teammates on a regular basis. The irony of his use of the "N" word is that his black teammates have stated that Richie Incognito is an honorary black man. No matter how much time Richie Incognito spends with black people, he will never know the pain endured by my black ancestors as a result of the "N" word. As a result, the 32 white NFL owners decided to make it a 15-yard penalty for a player to use the "N" word on the field during a game. Players can be subject to a fine if they use the "N" word in the locker room or other place that belongs to the team. These are the same white own-ers whose ancestors owned slaves. These are the same white owners whose ancestors created the word "nigger" and gave it all its' power and ugliness. How dare they decide to create more attention for the word by making the use of it a penalty during a football game. These same owners support the use of the word "Redskins" as a team name.

The First of Their Kind

In writing my books, I always like to provide my readers with some statistical data that may be of some assistance in conducting future research projects. There are literally thousands of African Americans in the history of this Country that have made a positive impact and a lasting influence on who we have become as black people in America. I would like to think that I have mentioned many of these individuals in my books. However, based on the number of African Americans that had a lasting impact on the history of this Country, my books barely scratch the surface. History has recorded many firsts by African Americans in this Country, such as the first black professional athletes to play in all the major sports, the first black officer and general in the U.S. Armed Forces, the first African American to be elected to U.S. Congress, the first African Secretary of State and many others. As always, I recommend that you visit your local library and/or the Internet when researching historical events. Information on the following African Americans should be found in your local library. However, if you cannot find the information, I have given you enough basic information to conduct the research on these famous individuals and the events associated with them and request assist from the librarian. In addition, you can "google" or use ask.com on the Internet.

The following is a list of many of these first by African Americans in this Country:

- Religion: Richard Allen was the founder of the African Methodist Episcopal Church (AME), the first independent black denomination in the United States. He opened the first AME Church in 1794 in Philadelphia, Pennsylvania. He organized a denomination where free blacks could worship without racial oppression and where slaves could find a measure of dignity.
- Government: Local elected official, John Mercer Langston, 1855, Town Clerk of Brownhelm Township, Ohio.
- State elected official: Alexander Lucius Twilight, 1836, the Vermont Legislature.

- Mayor of a major city: Carl Stokes Cleveland, Ohio, 1967-1971.
- The first black woman Mayor of a major city was Sharon Pratt Dixon Kelly, Washington D.C., 1991-1995.
- Governor (appointed): P.B.S. Pinchback served as Governor of Louisiana from December 12, 1872– January 13, 1873.
- Governor (elected): L. Douglas Wilder, Virginia, 1990–1994.
- Nobel Peace Prize winner: Ralph J. Bunche received the prize in 1950 for mediating the Arab-Israeli truce.
- Military: Combat pilot: Eugene Jacques Bullard, 1917, denied entry into the U.S. Army Air Corps because of his race, served throughout World War I in the French Flying Corps. He received the Legion of Honor, France's highest honor, among many other decorations.
- First Congressional Medal of Honor winner: Sgt. William H. Carney for bravery during the Civil War. He received his Congressional Medal of Honor in 1900.
- General Benjamin O. Davis Sr. 1940 –1948; Chairman of the Joint Chiefs of Staff: Colin Powell, 1989–1993.
- First astronaut: Robert H. Lawrence, Jr., 1967, was the first black astronaut, but he died in a plane crash during a training flight and never made it into space.
- Guion Bluford, 1983, became the first black astronaut to travel in space.
- Mae Jemison, 1992, became the first black female astronaut.
- Frederick D. Gregory, 1998, was the first African American shuttle commander.
- College graduate (B.A.): Alexander Lucius Twilight, 1823, Middlebury College.
- First black woman to receive a B.A. degree: Mary Jane Patterson, 1862, Oberlin College.
- Ph.D.: Edward A. Bouchet, 1876, received a Ph.D. from Yale University.
- In 1921, three individuals became the first U.S. black women to earn Ph.Ds: Georgiana Simpson, University of Chicago; Sadie

Tanner Mossell Alexander, University of Pennsylvania; and Eva Beatrice Dykes, Radcliffe College.

- Rhodes Scholar: Alain L. Locke, 1907.
- College President: Daniel A. Payne, 1856, Wilberforce University, Ohio.
- Ivy League President: Ruth Simmons, 2001, Brown University.
- Pulitzer Prize winner in Drama: Charles Gordone, 1970, for his play, No Place to Be Somebody.
- Nobel Prize for Literature winner: Toni Morrison, 1993.
- Poet Laureate: Robert Hayden, 1976–1978.
- First black woman Poet Laureate: Rita Dove, 1993–1995.
- Music and Dance Member of the New York City Opera: Todd Duncan, 1945.
- Member of the Metropolitan Opera Company: Marian Anderson, 1955.
- Principal dancer in a major dance company: Arthur Mitchell, 1959, New York City Ballet.
- Film: First Oscar: Hattie McDaniel, 1939, Best Supporting Actress, Gone with the Wind. Oscar.
- Best Actor/Actress: Sidney Poitier, 1963, Lilies of the Field.
- Halle Berry, 2001, Monster's Ball.
- Oscar, Film director: Oscar Micheaux, 1919, wrote, directed, and produced The Homesteader, a feature film.
- Hollywood Director: Gordon Parks directed and wrote The Learning Tree for Warner Brothers in 1969.
- Television Network television show host: Nat King Cole, 1956, "The Nat King Cole Show".
- Oprah Winfrey became the first black woman television host in 1986, "The Oprah Winfrey Show."
- Star of a network television show: Bill Cosby, 1965, "I Spy".
- Firsts Millionaire: Madame C.J. Walker.
- Billionaire: Robert Johnson, 2001, owner of Black Entertainment Television.
- Portrayal on a postage stamp: Booker T. Washington, 1940.

- Miss America: Vanessa Williams, 1984, representing New York.
- Explorer, North Pole: Matthew A. Henson, 1909, accompanied Robert E. Peary on the first successful U.S. expedition to the North Pole.
- Explorer, South Pole: George Gibbs, 1939–1941 accompanied Richard Byrd.
- Sports: Major League Baseball player: Jackie Robinson, 1947, Brooklyn Dodgers.
- Baseball Hall of Fame: Jackie Robinson, 1962.
- NFL quarterbacks: Willie Thrower, 1953.
- NFL football coach: Fritz Pollard, 1922–1937.
- Golf champion: Tiger Woods, 1997, won the Masters Golf Tournament.
- NHL hockey player: Willie O'Ree, 1958, Boston Bruins.
- Tennis Champion: Althea Gibson became the first black person to play in and win Wimbledon and the United States National Tennis Championship. She won both tournaments twice, in 1957 and 1958.
- The first black male champion was Arthur Ashe who won the 1968 U.S. Open, the 1970 Australian Open, and the 1975 Wimbledon Championship.
- Heavyweight Boxing Champion: Jack Johnson, 1908.
- Olympic medalist (Summer Games): George Poage, 1904, won two Bronze Medals in the 200 meter hurdles and 400 meter hurdles.
- Olympic Gold Medalist (Summer Games): John Baxter "Doc" Taylor, 1908, won a Gold Medal as part of the 4 x 400 meter relay team.
- Olympic Gold Medalist (Summer Games; individual): DeHart Hubbard, 1924, for the long jump
- The first woman was Alice Coachman, who won Gold Medal in the high jump in 1948.
- Olympic medalist (Winter Games): Debi Thomas, 1988, won the Bronze Medal in figure skating.

- Olympic Gold Medalist (Winter Games): Vonetta Flowers, 2002, bobsled.
- Olympic Gold Medalist (Winter Games; individual): Shani Davis, 2006, 1,000 meters speed skating.

The greatest pleasure I have received from writing these books has been my interaction with you the readers. The greatest reward in writing these books has been the wealth of knowledge that I obtained about the history of my African American ancestors. There was no way when I started this project almost 20 years ago that I thought it would be so enjoyable. I have always loved to write, but I never imagined that writing about black American history would give me such an emotional high. In my three books, we traveled back in time to reconstruct the history of African Americans from the past; and we returned to the present to discuss current events from the opinionated perspective of the author. If given the opportunity, it is my firm belief that my black ancestors would have described the events that shaped our history a lot differently from the way it was written by white historians. It is my hope that my style of writing has given my readers a glimpse of what might have been written by black men and women during slavery and the "JIM CROW ERA".

For the most part, the fight to end racism in America has been replaced by the more general topic of equality. Rather than dealing with the specific issues of racial discrimination, Americans are more concerned with equal rights issues. Under the leadership of the great Dr. Martin Luther King, the historical fight for racial equality in America was an epic battle. However, the national attention that was once held by the Civil Rights Movements has been watered down by other causes to achieve equality in America. The media attention given to the Civil Rights Movement helped change the way black people throughout America were treated. The right to vote; attend better schools; better jobs and access to better health care, were all the benefits that we, as African Americans, received as a result of the modern Civil Rights Movement. As we entered the 1990s and on into the new millennium; causes such as women rights; the rights of the disabled;

and gay rights have diluted the original foundation for the formation of the Civil Rights Movement, and that was racial equality.

Fortunately, I am not the only one that will not let any Americans, and for that matter the entire free world, forget about the horrific acts of violence committed by white America against the black people in this Country. Throughout this chapter as well as throughout this book, you will see the phrases, "according to published reports" or "reportedly" without identifying a specific reference or source. I do this to let my readers know that someone else published this information and that I discovered it while conducting my research. It is public information that you can find on the Internet, in the library or in a newspaper article. In the event you might have already read the same articles, I do not want you to think that I am guilty of plagiarism. Remember, anyone that writes about history is using information that was in fact written and published by someone from the past. From time to time, I may change the prospective of how history is retold, but I cannot change the facts of what actually happened.

The American Apartheid Series, they are not just books, they are an experience.

Made in the USA
Middletown, DE
07 November 2023

42100970R00229